Global Democracy for Sustaining Global Capitalism

The Authors

Jose Miguel Andreu is Professor of Economics at the University of Sevilla (Spain) and currently works at the UNED (Open University of Spain). He has also taught Economics at the University of the Basque Country and at the University of Alcalá de Henares. For more than 30 years he has lectured on introduction to economics, intermediate and superior macroeconomics, theory of economic growth, money and banking etc. In addition, he has published several textbooks for students as well as reports for governments and written more than a hundred articles on Spanish and international economic matters. For two years (1981-82) he was economic advisor to the Prime Minister of Spain. From 2000 to 2003, he served as a diplomat to India, heading the Economic and Commercial Office of Spain. A forthcoming publication (2009) of Jose Miguel Andreu deals with the theory and politics of economic globalisation.

Rita Dulci Rahman has more than 30 years of experience in international economics and politics. She has intensively worked in the fields of development co-operation, trade and investment, migration, conflict resolution, good governance and global environment, and was committee-member or chair in several European and Dutch governmental and non-governmental bodies. Born in the Dutch Antilles, she currently works as a diplomat for the Netherlands Government. She is Master in Development Studies at the University of Leiden (Netherlands) and Bachelor in Mathematics, University of Surinam. She has published many articles on international economic and political relations and two novels.

Together, Rita Dulci Rahman and Jose Miguel Andreu have published several books on global economic and political matters. Among them, "China and India: Towards Global Economic Supremacy?"(2006), "Overcoming the EU Crisis" (2005), "Responsible Global Governance" (2004) and "Financing Economic Development and Human Security" (2002).

Global Democracy for Sustaining Global Capitalism

The Way to Solve Current Global Problems

JOSE MIGUEL ANDREU
RITA DULCI RAHMAN

ACADEMIC FOUNDATION
NEW DELHI

First published in 2009
by

ACADEMIC FOUNDATION
4772-73 / 23 Bharat Ram Road, (23 Ansari Road),
Darya Ganj, New Delhi - 110 002 (India).
Phones : 23245001 / 02 / 03 / 04.
Fax : +91-11-23245005.
E-mail : academic@vsnl.com
www. academicfoundation.com

Cataloging in Publication Data--DK
Courtesy: D.K. Agencies (P) Ltd. <docinfo@dkagencies.com>

Andreu, Jose Miguel.
Global democracy for sustaining global capitalism : the way to solve current global problems / Jose Miguel Andreu, Rita Dulci Rahman.
p. cm.
Includes bibliographical references (p.).
Includes index.
ISBN 13: 9788171887309
ISBN 10: 8171887309

1. Globalization. 2. Democracy. 3. Capitalism. 4. International economic integration. 5. World politics. 6. Sustainable development. I. Rahman, Rita, 1952-, joint author. II. Title.

DDC 330.122 22

Typeset by Italics India, New Delhi.
Printed and bound in India.

Contents

Note from the Authors

Writing a book on global capitalism and democracy at a time in which "masters" of democratisation and globalisation are so abundant, could be seen as a useless exercise. Nevertheless, readers should note that current approach of capitalism seems to be failing while "well-known" masters-in-the-democratisation-of-other-nations seem to have no clear ideas on how to achieve sustainable democracies in certain countries (Afghanistan, Iraq), while most of them have not ever thought in terms of 'global democracy' for the legitimate provision of global public goods and the correction of global externalities.

Indeed, we have arrived to a time in which most of the relevant problems of mankind (peace, security, global environment protection, space and sea exploration, global natural resources management, global economic regulation, etc.) are of a collective nature. Therefore, any essayed "national solution" to correct these global problems will prove to be ineffective, as likely will be ad hoc "multilateral treaties", always difficult to set up (by general consent) and to enforce, due to political breaching or economic "free riding".

In this context of indispensable global solutions, confusing the priorities of the global community with those of the West (16 per cent of the global population)—whose leadership has for centuries defined the good and the evil in its manifold expressions—cannot longer be considered as "democratic behaviour". Indeed, future definition of means and ends on global issues, will only reach legitimacy when decision-making is done in a global democratic framework.

Besides, current trends of capitalism based on radical individualism, inexistence of global democracy to control global capitalism, and a wrong approach to globalisation, are inducing global environmental degradation and extended worsening of the personal income distribution that, altogether, may jeopardise sustainability of capitalism and democracy.

Against this background, the creation of a new democratic UN with executive powers on mentioned global issues will be the sole solution to manage common problems of mankind. But the construction of a new democratic UN will only take place when global problems become acknowledged as nationally unmanageable, and a new breed of democratic leaders, capable of getting rid of the current non-operative international power structure, appears.

Hoping to positively contribute to this necessary change of attitude, we have to finally underline that the views presented in this book, are strictly personal and do not reflect any official line of thought of the institutions to which we belong.

—José Miguel Andreu and Rita Dulci Rahman

Preface

The French Revolution, initiated in 1789, has for long been considered as a paradigmatic process of political and economic claims and change that, founded on the principles of democracy, economic liberty and equity, would enable to fulfil the political aspirations of common citizens and to improve their lives.

However, since the French Revolution the combination of democracy with rapid economic progress has not been easy. This is due to the existence of a difficult equilibrium between efficient economic growth—always in need of individual inequality to provide stimuli for the adoption of risky economic initiatives—and democracy, a political system which is intrinsically prone to more egalitarian solutions. As a consequence, many nascent democracies along the last two centuries—including the French one born in 1789—failed little time after their birth.

Along the 19th century and a great part of the 20th, the way of combining dictatorships or "purported" democracies with traditional forms of "capitalism"—which many a times induced unacceptable personal income distribution—was often the core-trigger of internal uprisings and external conflicts among nations. In fact, once the Industrial Revolution in Europe had entered in frank progress, it became clear that the fruits of industrialisation and urbanisation had only favoured some few, reason why some social observers started criticising contemporary economic and political systems.

As a result of the Marxian analysis of capitalism and its assumed trends, and the progressive spreading of such conceptions, unionists, socialists and communists appeared (mainly in Europe) in the last decades of the 19th century and started their political action in order to improve wages and working conditions of labourers; and also to change the economic and political order. However, their initiatives were systematically repressed by the so-called "liberal states", which did not hesitate to send the police, or even the army, to stifle economically based political uprisings, or simple demonstrations.

After several attempts in different scenarios, the revolution of proletariat, as foreseen by Marx, succeeded in 1917 in Russia, resulting in the establishment of the Soviet Union. For decades, this Federation of Socialist Republics behaved as the leader and promoter of socialism and communism in the world, until it proved its failure at the end of the 1980s.

In front of the "socialist threat", already perceivable by the upper class in the last decades of the 19th century, international-colonial European capitalism, combined with dictatorships or limited democracies, tried to basically keep untouched the traditional economic structures and the political institutions that had given little say to the masses in common political issues and economic claims.

Although mentioned traditional capitalism, sometimes combined with limited democracy, had already showed its difficult tenability in the West, in the 30s of the 20th Century a new phenomenon of massive and persistent unemployment, apparently without signals of automatic correction, appeared. This was a development that was considered by many as a prelude of the end of capitalism. Indeed, at that time, capitalism and (the then recently born) real socialism had started a mutual competition in economic and political terms that only would end six decades later with the crumbling of the Soviet Union, in the beginning of the 90s.

Even though many thought that socialism was emerging in the 30s while capitalism was in a straightforward decline, a way of rescuing the then sick capitalist economies by means of a new understanding of macroeconomics appeared: Keynesianism.

Despite its uninterrupted use in different forms and manners by most Western governments in the post-Second World War period (1945-2007), Keynesian macroeconomic theory and policy has been widely criticised over the past 30 years (1977-2007). This criticism has ranged from its lack of internal micro-macro consistency to its "alleged" bet in favour of inefficient socialism.

Indeed, the confusion of Keynesianism—an economic doctrine that mainly defends the use of fiscal and monetary actions for achieving full employment—with Socialism, has its roots in the writings of conservative economists such as Von Hayeck, Knight and Schumpeter; a line of thought that was continued by Friedman, Stigler, and Lucas in the 60s and 70s. Since the reliability of an economic theory ultimately lays in its success or failure when applied as policy, reckless application of some Keynesian recipes—resulting in exaggerated growth of public sector, public deficit, and global inflation in the late 60s and 70s—were used by conservative economists to support their critiques on the dysfunction of public sector actions.

Particularly interesting but somewhat different was the perspective of Joseph A. Schumpeter (1883-1950) concerning public sector actions and efficiency. In his book, titled *Capitalism, Socialism and Democracy* (1942), he tried to explore from a conservative perspective the most relevant economic and political problems of those years: the disputable future of capitalism in a democratic context, and the feasibility of some sort of socialism as a workable economic system.

Contrary to the Marxian analyses of the decadence of capitalism—which would arrive as a consequence of growing exploitation of labour, growing unemployment, progressively growing economic cycles, etc.—in the rhetoric of Schumpeter (traditional) capitalism would finally enter into decadence due to its "own success".

Under the perspective of Schumpeter, emergence of "socialism" (comparable to modern social-democracy) would not only be a consequence of the worsening of the personal income distribution, many times induced by (traditional) capitalism, but also the result of the growing influence of intellectuals, who were progressively defending different forms of public intervention to mainly solve problems of economic stability, externalities, income distribution and social protection. Note that traditional conservative economists had mostly discarded the application of these public interventions, due to their alleged "counterproductive" results.

After the Great Depression of the 30s and the application of the ("socialist") New Deal Policy in the US, Schumpeter wondered on the possibility of substitution of capitalism by some sort of socialism, and on its consistency with (national) democracy. The Schumpeterian answers for these two questions were positive and to some extent, continue being valid today, on the condition that "socialism" adopts the market-system for the economic allocation of most resources.

Despite valuable contributions of Schumpeter in relation to the consistency between capitalism and democracy, experience in past decades suggests that mutual dependence between capitalism and democracy is not as linear as suggested many a times by western conservative scholars. It is true that democracy requires—for its tenability—free markets for the economic allocation of most resources; but it is also true that an economy with extended free-markets can for long coexist without democratic governance (indeed the world works today with many global and free markets while it politically works without a global democracy).

Letting aside former considerations, we have to highlight that new variables have complicated the Schumpeterian analysis on capitalism and democracy. Firstly, we have to underline that capitalism has become global while remaining combined with inefficient (national) power structures, thus creating meaningful dysfunction in relation to economic policy, always developed in a national and fragmentary way. And secondly, the appearance of new problems of a global nature are time ago calling for democratic global governance. These new problems concern the common provision of global public goods (peace and security with respect to human rights, global environment protection, space and sea exploration, global economic regulation, etc.) and the correction of global externalities (in the fields of common natural resources, etc.).

Indeed, in the last 60 years (1946-2006) the world has significantly changed in all aspects—sociologically (family life, women emancipation), technologically (IT revolution), politically (de-colonisation, collapse of the Soviet Union, advent of an "apparent" hegemonic power, obsolescence of the UN, etc.), and economically (globalisation, acknowledgement of the existence of global public goods and externalities, rapid structural change favouring some developing countries as China and India, problems in the West with the economic adjustment to the new situation, etc.).

Concerning politics, we have to underline that along the last decades, democracy has become the last reference for the governance of nations. Extrapolating this democratisation trend to the global sphere, we will suggest all along this book that only the setting up of a global democracy (a new democratic UN) will endow with legitimacy the necessary political actions to be undertaken for solving the new common problems of the global society. But one cannot be naïve; given the current international political interests, a new democratic UN will only appear when it becomes patent that national or treaties-based solutions for common problems are not operative.

Note as well that the concept of global democracy and the way of its implementation has practically remained absent in the "multilateral" political debate (although not in the academia). This has mainly occurred because the current UN—an embryo of the global democracy that will necessary emerge in the first half the 21st century—was initially conceived as a non-democratic organisation, in which the five permanent members of the UN Security Council, the victors of the Second World War, gave themselves a veto-privilege on all discussed international issues.

Facing the new global problems—which demand global solutions endowed with global democratic legitimacy—we consider that overlooking them, or denying their existence, will only result in an economic and political impasse or even in wars. We do also believe that a "re-legitimisation" of traditional pure capitalism (neo-liberal movement), which hardly admits the existence of global economic problems while it systematically rejects collective solutions, should be discarded what so ever, because such a "re-legitimisation" would indeed be a political time bomb, even for "consolidated" democracies in the West.

Finally, and as result of our long reflections, we have concluded that mankind has only one way out of the difficult time we are living in: abandonment of any aspiration of hegemony by current potential candidates for undemocratic global leadership, and instead of that collaborating with the rest of countries on a global democratic basis under the aegis of a new UN. Indeed, given the highly demographic fragmentation of nations, the current definition of human rights and the present process towards democratisation at national and (also) global levels, hegemony is already an impossible illusion, contrary to the logic of global democracy. As a consequence, we do firmly believe that the times of hegemonies or empires have already passed away, this implying that any country interested in reaching hegemonic power will just behave as an undemocratic contender doomed to gather growing frustrations at high economic, political and social costs.

1

A World in Accelerated Change in Need of Democratic Global Governance

Acceleration of History and Non-tenability of the Current Capitalism-Democracy Combination

The world we live in has recently undergone huge and accelerated mutations. Observe that although the invention of agriculture took place around 400 generations back, "only 10 generations ago, hereditary monarchs and aristocracies still ruled much of the world. Only six generations ago, millions of Americans lived in slavery (...). Four generations ago, women had yet to win the right to vote in most countries in the world, including the US, (and) two generations ago, environmental protection agencies had not been established."[1]

One could add to this rapid overview of changes in politics and governance, that only two generations ago the decolonisation process of Asia and Africa started, and that only one generation ago the need for democratisation of societies progressively became common wisdom in almost all corners of the planet. Closer to our memories, we find in the past 15 years the development of a massive structural economic change based on an additional step (freer movements of capital) towards globalisation[2] that, unexpected by many, is shifting the economic gravity centre of the world towards Asia.

In the last three decades of the 20th century and the beginning years of 2000, the world as a whole—although unevenly—has registered a continuation in the positive evolution of its political indicators, in particular the increase in the number of countries

---

1. Boyce, J.K. (2002). *The Political Economy of the Environment*. UK: EE Publishing. p.135.
2. "Globalisation" is a phenomenon that, letting aside previous historical manifestations, basically started after the Second World War; although, when it started, it did not receive that name. Indeed, the word "globalisation" became popular only when, in **1990s**, international movements of capital were liberalised.

ruled under democratic regimes. This has occurred in parallel with relevant economic progress, that by itself has reduced (although mildly) the absolute volume of poor, as conventionally measured.[3] Contrary to expectations, mentioned economic progress has induced additional per capita GDP divergence at international level[4] and an almost generalised worsening of personal income distribution within nations.[5, 6] Even middle classes in the rich world have economically slimmed,[7] a phenomenon that in the long run could jeopardise western democracies.

Economic Growth, Environmental Degradation and Democratic Governance

Note that in the last decades the positive (growth) and negative (income distribution) phenomena have occurred in parallel with a fast and severe degradation of the environment of the planet, that, if correctly measured, would have significantly trimmed down the registered growth rate of the economic activity of mankind.

As a consequence of the current acceleration of history and the new and overwhelming global problems appearing, or just unveiling, the collective solutions have to come urgently if the international community wants to avoid violent global conflicts induced by access

---

3. The WB and other multilateral institutions define the volume of poverty as the number of people whose daily per capita income (or per capita GDP) is less than one US-dollar per person (the so-called "poverty line"). Apart from other critiques to this poverty measure, one should not forget the severe inflationary erosion of the US dollar since mentioned poverty line was defined.
4. Mentioned per capita GDP divergence refers to the quotient between that of the nation or region with the highest per capita GDP and that of the lowest one. Vide Maddison, A. (2001). *The World Economy: A Millennium Perspective*. OECD Paris. p.126. Vide also UN Development Programme (2002). "Global inequality, grotesque levels, ambiguous trends". *Human Development Report* (2002). p. 19.
5. Taking into account the evolution of the income shares of the richest people in the US, one can affirm that the degree of inequality in the US has gone back to similar figures as those registered in the 20s of the 20th century. Vide. Piketty, T. (2006). "The evolution of top incomes", *NBER WP* 11955. January. Concerning many developing countries, particularly in relation to China and India, there is also a general consensus on the idea that the domestic personal income distribution has worsened, following the track of the Kuznets-curve in the first stages of development.
6. The World Commission on the Social Dimension of Globalisation (created in 2001 by the ILO) suggested that between 1990 and 2002, 59 per cent of the world population were living in countries where the inequality was growing, while only a 5 per cent lived in countries in which inequality was dwindling. Stiglitz, J. (2006). "Un autre monde. Contre le fanatism de marché. Fayard." Translated from "Making globalisation work". New York: Norton. p.37.
7. On concerns about the future of the middle class in the US see, Krugman, P. (2007). "Seduced by the Wealth?" *The New York Times-Le Monde*. November 10th.

to scant natural resources (mainly oil, clean water, etc.), by worsening of the income distribution, or by environmental degradation.[8]

As proven along the second half of the 20th century, democracy is (at national level) the only system of governance capable of simultaneously solving the problems of efficient economic production—due to necessary underlying capitalism[9]—and acceptable income distribution.[10] Even more, according to recent research, national democratic systems seem also to be the best qualified for solving problems of national environmental degradation. Alternative autocratic systems, either do not deliver in terms of production (central planning systems), or in income distribution (conservative dictatorships), or misbehave in environmental protection.

To the extent that democratic governance is the key for the solution of the above-mentioned national problems, the world will have to progress towards national democracy[11] in those countries in which democracy is underdeveloped. But more important, to deal with other problems of regional and global nature,[12] the international community will have to move towards a workable global democracy to properly administrate common natural resources, and to provide with legitimacy global public goods.

Note in this regard that in the world today, the provision of some global public goods is not democratic at all. Instead of that, the so-called hegemonic power (and allies) exercises this provision

---

8. In the World today, and with reference to environmental sustainability, global warming, etc., many scientists captured by politicians, and politicians themselves, are proving that in today's politics almost everything is admitted; even to conceal the "unpleasant" environmental reality with the most abject ends (private profits for a minority against general interests of current and future generations). In this regard, vide. *Financial Times*, January 31, 2007 p.4. "Federal Agency climate scientists claim political interference". Note also that all the reports of the UN, including the scientific ones on climate change, etc., have been previously "negotiated".
9. All along this book, the world "Capitalism" refers to any self-sustainable economic system (including mix economies of market managed by social-democracies) that is capable of bringing economic prosperity mainly, although not exclusively, through the use of free markets. Note that Capitalism, as historically proven, may for long coexist with certain forms of dictatorship, but democracy cannot survive without underlying capitalism.
10. We will explain in Chapter 4 the characteristics that will have to gather underlying capitalism to be consistent with democracy and to make the latter sustainable.
11. Conditions for progress and different ways of reaching national democracy will extensively be discussed in Chapter 4.
12. The need for urgent setting up of a global democracy to legitimately and rationally provide the global community with global public goods (peace, security, environment, etc.) and to correct global externalities will be discussed in Chapters 4 and 5.

(for instance in relation to peace) without democratic legitimacy,[13] just filling a political vacuum many times at own convenience.[14] By acting in minority coalitions without a clear consent of the rest of the international community[15] (f.i. in wars against some alleged "rogue" states) or by omitting certain actions and responsibilities (in global environmental issues or in war reconstruction and conventions), the US and (some) allies have in the last years acted in a non-democratic way.

The same lack of democratic consent has also been observed in actions undertaken by some economic off-springs of the UN, in particular the World Bank and the IMF. These institutions have at times been misused by the US and allies to economically "persuade" or simply bully those countries which, in need of collective loans, have dared to disagree with the American way of managing the provision of certain global public goods (peace and security).

To conclude, we have to underline that this wrong way of governance in global issues (peace, security, global environment, etc.), which has worsen in recent years,[16] is not only authoritarian and economically inefficient for mankind—including American citizens—but also in total contradiction with the alleged aim of promotion of unconditioned democracy.[17]

---

13. As it is well known, the UN is not a democratic global body; indeed, the 5 veto-owners of the Security Council may veto any resolution and even a minimal change in the current obsolete Charter of the UN.
14. As generally admitted in economics and politics, the principle of "self-interest" is a good guide for predicting behaviour of individuals or groups (or political parties and nations). According to Adam Smith, this principle is at the core of the decision-making concerning production and interchange; and according to Machiavelli, this principle will be at the nucleus of political decision-making for "appropriation" strategies. Consequently, one has to deduce that international economic and political actions realised by any hegemonic power, will be systematically exercised in own interest. Vide. Hirschleifer, J. (1993). "The dark side of strength". p.5. *www.eumed.net*
15. Many times, even the concept of "international community" is falsified by some governments and media, intentionally reducing "membership" to just some few western advanced countries—precisely those who want to colligate to take unilateral actions—while the real international community is formed by around 200 countries, members of the UN.
16. Indeed, the emission of greenhouse gases to the global environment continues to rise, even in politically co-ordinated areas such as that of the EU (as acknowledged in 2006). In fact it would be naïve to expect other result when no one enforces the Kyoto Protocol among signing or non-signing countries. Vide. "Bilan contrasté en Europe pour la reduction de gaz á effet de serre". *Le Monde*. 23 June 2006. p.8.
17. Apparently, the US and allies only try to promote democracy at national level in selected and predefined "rogue" states; but only when they believe that their intervention is of strategic interest for the West.

Sources of Non-tenability of the Current Capitalism-Democracy Combination

As a result of the appearance of new global problems that will be explained in lines below, we do believe that the current capitalism-democracy combination is *ceteris paribus* not tenable for several reasons: 1) capitalism, which in its different forms has progressively gained ground across the world and has become global, lacks the necessary (global) democratic infrastructure to legitimately oversee and rule the global economic activity; and this while mentioned "free" capitalism tends to induce progressive degradation of the personal income distribution,[18] thus not guaranting at long-term social stability and sustainable democracy; 2) current capitalism, many a times with a dangerous trend towards excessive market orientation, particularly in the labour market, is putting at risk in many places the psychological health of (overstressed) individuals, and the basic foundations of societies: family life, socialisation and even reproduction;[19] 3) progressive degrading of global environment and depletion of some essential non-renewable resources, is threatening by itself the tenability of a capitalistic world that has made the growth mania and excessive consumption, the unique measure of economic success, be it collective or individual; 4) the inexistence of a global democracy in the world makes the legitimate and efficient provision of global public goods, as desired by the international community, impossible, thus putting in the hands of a self-defined aristocracy of nations the definition and the provision of these global public goods;[20] and

18. The IMF, in its semi-annual *World Economic Outlook* (2007), has examined how recent globalisation (1982-2002) has affected the personal income distribution in the developed world. From this report one may clearly deduce that western workers have lost income share around 0.2 per cent a year, which means around 4 per cent points in the last 20 years. Although the experienced GDP growth rate in the West has finally offset the wage loss of labourers—which means that their real income is more or less the same as that of 20 years ago—an intense negative income distribution has progressively developed, thus increasing the malaise among western workers. Vide. *The Economist*, April 7, 2007, p.72.

19. In a context of deep specialisation, absence of *de facto* working-hours limitations, unconditioned geographic flexibility, or insufficient day-care centres, when both parents are working, may be conducive, through national or international competition among labourers, to a non-tenable family life; reason why governments should treat leisure and supportive structures for families as "merit wants" to be protected.

20 The current (non-democratic) definition of global aims (f.i. in peace administration issues) enables leading Western countries to use double standards. In some cases, they define as priority targets for their political action non-democratic countries of strategic relevance for them. In other cases, non-democratic countries but with a friendly behaviour towards the West, are declared as "nominally" integrated in the general democratisation process of the world. Iraq is a good example of the first case and Pakistan and Saudi Arabia are examples of the second one.

5) human security has globally decreased and progressively become more patent in a world in which abject poverty remains, personal income distribution degrades, and political rights of minorities are not respected and enforced, due to the inexistence of a global democracy capable of reaching international peace combined with justice and respect to human rights.

We conceive democracy as an integral political system for, among other things, providing public goods and correcting externalities with legitimacy (at local, national, regional, or global levels). Observe in this regard that nowadays, the most democratic (developed) countries of the world are just in the middle of the way, thus non-considering—because it is not convenient for them—the need of a democratic provision of global public goods; and this while others have barely started the road towards local or national democracy. Both, the former and the latter will have to do significant efforts to make the world more tenable; in particular the leading western countries, which willy-nilly will have to hand over their current non-democratic global power in favour of a global governing body endowed with democratic legitimacy: a new democratic UN, that will finally work for the benefit of all.

Towards a New Ideology for the Protection of Mankind in the 21st Century

Once the main problems currently threatening mankind are listed, one should search for a new ideological framework in consistency with the collective nature of the problems to be solved.

In our view, to achieve environmental and political sustainability of capitalism in the context of a global democratic society, it will be necessary to reach optimal economic and social conditions extracted from the concept of long-term economic efficiency.[21] Only these conditions will guarantee widespread sustainable growth and indispensable global peace and security for attaining universal economic prosperity.

21. In our view, long-term efficiency concerns should take into account not only economic failures of the markets but also the social ones; otherwise free markets would not be conducive to social stability and global sustainability.

Consequently, encouragement or preservation of the mixed economy of market—in consistency with political[22] and environmental conditions for its sustainability—and development of a global democracy for the fair and efficient provision of global public goods (peace, security, global environment, global economic regulation, space and sea administration, etc.) and the correction of global externalities, will be the main lines of the new economic and political approach for the protection of mankind.

Physical Limits and Inefficient Institutional Structure for Sustainability of Capitalism

As we will see in Chapters 4 and 5, the conditions for sustainability of the current capitalism-democracy combination are complex and multi-faceted. Certainly, an apparently positive economic trajectory of the global GDP could be non-sustainable if the different intervening variables jointly make it impossible to reach a dynamic physical (natural resources) and socio-political equilibrium.

From our perspective, there are at least two groups of variables that may make sustainability of current global capitalism possible or not. The first refers to the physical ones: the natural resources involved in the economic development of nations. This process of development—mainly founded in growing industrial activities, much of them high consumers of energy and water—should in future be conducted with strict respect to the environment and available resources. Otherwise the future of mankind will be problematic and surrounded by catastrophic facts induced by global warming and climate change. These limitative aspects of the growth of nations will be developed in Chapter 5.

Note however that the existence of physical limits to growth is not the sole condition for sustainability of current global capitalism. There are also additional conditions that, belonging to the sphere of politics (developed by institutions) have (or will have) significant influence on the administration of mentioned physical limits.

It is our view that current political and economic multilateral institutions—acting as a framework of current capitalism—will not

22. The main economic condition for sustainability (both national and global) of the combination democracy-capitalism is the preservation of a "democratically acceptable" personal distribution of income.

efficiently work in future due to their obsoleteness, thus behaving as detrimental for the future viability of global capitalism. In this regard we should not forget that a few countries engineered current multilateral institutions at their own convenience when the power was practically monopolised by them (in or just in the aftermath of the Second World War).

Observe additionally that the international economic structure (production and trade) typical of the second half of the 20th century is nowadays rapidly changing mainly due to the ICT revolution and the embodiment of the two Asian giants (China and India) into the international division of labour. As a result, in next decades, industrial production will be mainly localised in Asia, as well as a big chunk of (out-sourceable) services demanded by the West.

In this new economic context, current international distribution of power will not persist, because it will become inconsistent with the new economic realities. Consequently, the power structure in current (multilateral) institutions will have to adjust to the new political and economic realities in order to induce economic and political conditions (among others, fair peace, security, environment preservation, etc.) for sustainability of global capitalism.

On the Relevance of the "Personal Income Distribution" for Gaining Security and Political Sustainability

In the context of the trade-off efficiency-equity, and to illustrate the case, we will firstly recall the domestic anxieties developed in European countries in the period 1870-1914. In this regard, one should remember that the behaviour of absolute monarchies and "liberal states" concerning wages—which directly affected the personal distribution of income—and "human rights" of workers, was one of non-consideration; or even repression when workers, commanded by Trade Unions, protested or demonstrated.[23]

In those days, the derivatives of the principle of action and reaction between Trade Unions and left opposition on the one hand, and absolute monarchies or "liberal" governments on the other, were manifold in the

23. In the name of freedom of contracting, also applicable to labour markets, these negative practices (repression) were also patronised by nascent liberal states.

political battle for taking or defending power, or simply in negotiations on working conditions. Years later, in the aftermath of the First World War and Russian Revolution, and based on the growing fear felt by industrial owners concerning consolidation of the socialist movement, fascist, corporate movements, or other purported "third ways" appeared. In the context of these movements, the role of the state was rightist, totalitarian and geographically expansionist.

Fortunately, after two human and material catastrophes (WW I and WW II), western European governments learned the lessons of history and, after 1945, started building (or enlarging) the so-called welfare state. Previous economic exploitation of masses by firms, and frequent human rights violations by the machinery of absolute monarchies or traditional-formal democracies, were no longer acceptable patterns of behaviour. The costs—constant social unrest and wars against neighbours—generated by myopic approaches to economic efficiency (which at times also included "appropriation") had been huge, and could not continue after the Second World War. With the establishment (or enlargement) of the welfare state, the social scene positively changed but, regrettably, only within Western Europe.

However, "lack of memory" of European governments (and others) made that, some decades later (from 1980 onwards), old social myopia started affecting Europe again. In fact, despite the positive effects of the construction of the welfare state in Western Europe on internal peace, security and economic prosperity, the last 25 years (1980-2005) witnessed a reversal of former trends.[24] Note that this reversal mainly materialised in the degradation of personal income distribution and in a piecemeal slimming of middle classes.

As we will explain in Chapter 4, sustainability of democracy at national level will depend *ceteris paribus* on the evolution of the personal income distribution and on establishing or maintaining middle classes; and less on reducing the number of poor under the

24. The same comment could be made in relation to the US. In fact, "during the 1950 and 1960, the halcyon days for the American middle class, productivity boomed and its benefits were broadly shared, and the gap between the lowest and the highest earners narrowed. However, productivity growth rate suddenly slowed after the oil shocks of the 70s. Some few years later, at the start of the 80s, the gap between rich and poor began to widen" till today. Vide. *The Economist* (2006). "Inequality and the American Dream", June 17th, p.25.

so-called poverty line, as it is today interestedly defended in many international fora.[25] Indeed, there is no doubt that any economic globalisation has to increase the economic efficiency of the vessel Earth and its global GDP;[26] but national democratic governance (and the global one in future) will not be sustainable if the resulting distribution of gains were not fair.

In fact, regressive movements in the national distribution of personal incomes observed in many countries (developed and developing) after the initiation of the last impulse to globalisation in 1990, have also found a parallel in the growing economic gap observed at a planetary scale. Indeed, this growing gap trend—with the exception of the period 1950-1973—has always prevailed under capitalism since 1870.[27]

Global Democracy Indispensable for Managing Sustainability

As discussed in Chapter 4, and irrespective of whether current national democracies have significant defects or not, we have to emphasise the necessity of urgently advancing towards what we will define as "global democracy".

Although national democracy is an imperfect system of selecting political and economic aims and leaders—a system that always could be improved[28]—we have to underline that, from a moral perspective,

25. In many international meetings, current globalisation impulse (1990-2007) has been 'praised' as an economic movement that has achieved significant reduction of the percentage of poor under the so-called poverty line (of one US dollar per person per day). But in fact, between 1990 and 1999 the reduction of poverty in absolute terms was very mild—moving from 1.27 billion to 1.15. (Vide UNDP (2002: 18) book already mentioned.

26. As advanced by J.F. Nash—a Nobel Prize in Economics—in his article of 1950, "The bargaining problem" published in *Econometrica*—the central issue is not to know if a particular bargaining solution is better for all participants than not bargaining at all, which is something sure; but if different possible bargaining solutions contain fairer situations for the collective than others, thus being more convenient. This message could be today translated into Global Economics saying that a certain way of additional globalisation—as that implemented under the Washington Consensus doctrine—would always be better than no additional globalisation at all; but at the same time it could be deeply unfair and inconvenient in comparison with other (till now non-implemented) ways of marginal globalisation.

27. Vide. Maddison, A. (2000: 126). Book already mentioned.

28. It is curious that while boasting of being well rooted democrats, many politicians behave reluctant to improve current Western Constitutions in relation to political parties' behaviour, elections, political responsibilities, etc. This is due to the fact that the less transparent the system is, the easier and the more comfortable will be the governance of the country.

such a system will always be preferable to dictatorship or "one party" regimes. Indeed, dictatorship at nation level is today a regime well discredited, due to its rejection to recognise as minimum certain basic human rights, as those of free speaking, free association, legal and free competition for achieving social leadership, respect to minorities, etc.

Happily, the number of democracies all over the world has significantly grown in the last 20 years,[29] although we are afraid that the quality of some of the new ones,[30] as well as some of the older, either is low or has worsened respectively.

Unfortunately for all of us, even eventual generalisation in future of internal democratic systems will not be sufficient as to solve many of the common political and economic problems that mankind have to confront. Consequently, it will be necessary to take additional steps for attaining a global democracy, capable of providing the global public goods demanded by the international community (or correcting the global externalities) with democratic legitimacy.

Attainment of global democracy supposes that in future, current rich and influential states will have to renounce their undemocratic privileges[31] in all multilateral institutions. As a result, today's privileged states will have to admit—if not a linearly weighted vote strictly conditioned to population size—at least the relevance of the demographic size of the different national communities in the formation of the "general will" in multilateral institutions.

However, it is likely that the most powerful communities, which are nowadays in patent population minority at world scale and in relative economic decline, reject to hand over their historical privileges.[32] But in the case they continue behaving like that, they

29. From 1980 onwards, 81 countries have taken significant steps towards democracy, including the replacement of 33 military regimes by civilian governments. Vide. UN Development Program (2002: 10). *Human Development Report 2002*.

30. Of the 81 "new democracies" mentioned in the former note, only 47 were "fully democratic". Vide UNDP (2002: 10).

31. Privileges of current powerful communities stem from having been old colonising powers and/or from their victory in the Second World War. These circumstances enabled them to gather mentioned privileges when the UN was created (enjoying veto rights in the Security Council of the UN, etc.).

32. The historical supremacy of former colonial powers was founded in their superior technology, which gave them military advantage, and in the "divide and rule" policy. Both instruments were successfully used for colonial domination of countries with large populations. This domination enabled a rapid economic accumulation by colonising powers, which obtained significant economic advantage in detriment of the colonised nations.

will progressively become perceived as less and less democratic from a global perspective, thus further losing prestige in a world of full and live information, resulting progressively in economic isolation.

In relation to the provision of global public goods and the correction of global externalities we should not forget that without peace, security (both stemming from justice) and a healthy environment, sustainability of capitalism and democracy will not be guaranteed. Therefore, only a reorganisation of the UN following democratic criteria for the governance of global issues,[33] will avert both "free riding" and "abuse coming from the most powerful" in economic or political matters.

As far as the world has become smaller than before and fully informed, it is completely out of reality to believe that a minority of people (1/6th of the total, the so called Western World, led by US) may continue almost unconditionally leading the world, and clearly profiting from that leadership.

It is our view that the current international political situation, which combines internal (but defective) democratic systems[34] in the West with western autocratic actions and manners[35] at global level, cannot and will not last. We do believe that, the same as thinkers brought social-democracy to old "traditional capitalism", the action of intellectuals, in a context of a world of free and live information, in connection with overwhelming collective needs and problems required of collective solutions, will finally bring global democracy to the world community.

---

33. To the extent that the current UN is a non-democratic body with veto-right owners on collective decisions, and without capacity for enforcing resolutions, this body will have to be reformed in depth. Even its headquarters should be removed to a more neutral place, out of the geography of the US. A place at the Mediterranean Sea could be a more efficient location, even from the perspective of the costs of transports and facility of connexions.

34. In Chapter 4 we will describe some of the main defects of Western democracies.

35. In front of this Western asymmetry, one could also find the opposite: countries that do not behave democratically inside, but that use to behave democratically in the UN, that is to say, do not making trouble to the rest. Note that, by definition, the action of exercising a "veto right" in the Security Council of the UN is to behave "non-democratically" at a global scale. Consequently, any reform of the UN that try to keep, or even to increase the number of veto holders in the Security Council will not be a valid reform for the 21st century (the century of Asia, and the century of the arrival to global democracy).

Main Traits of the Recent World History and Sources of Current International Tensions

From the French Revolution (1789) till the 21st century, the history of mankind in its progress towards economic prosperity and democracy has been a course of successive and multifaceted crisis—socio-economic, political and military—whose main geographical playing grounds have been Europe (Western, Central Europe and Russia), the African and Asian possessions of European countries, Eastern Asia, and Latin America in which the US interests played a central role in the 20th century.

Among the many conflicts or crisis undergone by mankind in the contemporary age, one should mention the internal European wars fought in the 19th century,[36] the independency wars in colonies along 19th and 20th centuries, the colonial aggressions carried out by Japan in Asia in the first half of the 20th century, and of course the two world wars of the 20th century, followed by localised conflicts in Latin America, Asia and Africa in the context of the so-called Cold War.

As a lateral result of the First World War fought in Europe—which unexpectedly made possible in 1917 the consolidation of the socialist revolution in Russia—a new type of totalitarian state surged: the Soviet Union, as heir of the former Empire of Tsars.

Some few years after the appearance of this threatening colossus, other totalitarian states, mainly in Germany, Italy[37] and Japan initiated or reaccelerated[38] their own geographical enlarging adventures. As it is well known, these three powers were defeated in the Second World

---

36. The most important of them were the so-called Napoleonic Wars, which were fought by the French to achieve a unified Europe under the hegemony of France. These wars, involving among others, Russia, Spain, the Austrian Empire and the British Empire, took place from 1795 (Italy campaign) to 1815 (Waterloo).
37. Observe that, specifically in Germany and Italy, totalitarian leaders and radical reorganisation of states appeared after the celebration of "democratic elections". These dramatic changes of regime, conducive to terrible killings in Europe, are even today a clear proof of the lack of stability of democracies in certain socio-economic contexts, thus fully falsifying—as we will explain in Chapter 4—the contemporary neo-cons promoted dogma that democratic elections will under all circumstances encourage political stability.
38. Japan had started years before—with its war against Russia, initiated in 1904—its own aggressive and enlarging policy.

War by a non-homogeneous political coalition, including Western democracies[39] and the Soviet Union.

The Cold War and the Decolonisation Process

As a consequence of the Second World War and subsequent skirmishes, the Soviet Union became dominant in an important number of Eastern European countries, and highly influential in many other developing nations, some of them finally falling in its political orbit, be this in Latin America, Asia or Africa.

In reaction to the support of the Soviet Union for the Communist revolution in Czechoslovakia in 1947-48,[40] a Western Union (with defence purposes) was born in Europe in 1948. For the same defensive reasons, the NATO (North Atlantic Treaty Organisation) entered into the scene some months later (1949). With the birth of NATO, commanded by the US, the so-called Cold War started.

Internationally, the most important phenomenon occurring along the first decades of the Cold War period (1947-1991)[41] was the initiation and consolidation of the decolonisation process in Asia and Africa. In this regard, we have to state that decolonisation was often reached after bloody independence wars.

Sometimes this decolonisation process was performed in a rushed and reckless way[42] by the then weakened European colonial powers, thus leaving or creating convoluted and long-lasting problems in Kashmir, the Great Lakes countries in Africa, Indochina, etc., not to quote many others, mainly in Sub Sahara Africa. Well known in this

39. It is important to remark that in 1940 the US started an unprecedented military effort to win the Second World War. Till then the US army had only 250.000 personnel, placing it at 19th position in the ranking of military powers, well behind Belgium and just larger than Bulgaria. Vide. Parker, R. (2006). *John Kenneth Galbraith*. Harper. p.124.

40. In 1945 the Soviet Army took Prague; in 1947, the Soviet Union forced Czechoslovakia to renounce to the Marshall Plan; in February 1948, the communists took over, supported by the Soviet Union.

41. Mentioned Cold War ended with the collapse of the Soviet Union in 1991, and the definite filing of its supportive Marxist economic doctrine.

42. Indeed, some de-colonisation processes were pure hasty abandonment moves, carried out by the colonising powers when the political or economic costs (military or not) of the colonial administration surpassed the economic or political advantages of colonisation. The last significant rushed abandonment of territories practically to their own survival was that of 1974, when the Portuguese dictatorship crumbled.

regard is the paramount mess created in the Palestine territory by the "international community" from 1947 onwards.[43]

Although during the Cold War, there were no direct wars between the two superpowers (US and Soviet Union), subrogated but open wars were developed in localised scenarios (for instance Korea, Vietnam, Angola, etc.), while communist guerrillas harassed governments mainly in Latin America (finally taking over Cuba, Nicaragua, etc.) and Africa. In Latin America, democratic experiments were frequently interrupted by renascent dictatorships, strongly attached to privileged local minorities,[44] and sometimes supported by the US, perhaps as a considered "second best manoeuvre" against progress of communism.[45]

Rather silently, although in a very different way, two new states—which would become relevant at the dawn of the 21st century—were respectively born in 1947 and 1949: India after a dramatic process of decolonisation and partition; and China after the final crumbling of the nationalist-republican army, which escaped to Taiwan.[46]

---

43. In 1945, after the Nazi human-rights violations against Jews, survivors from Holocaust and other Jews worldwide started a massive migration to Palestine, which was then under British protectorate, and mostly populated by Muslim-Arab people. As expectable, native Palestinians considering themselves with better right, violently opposed this operation. Finally the UN, managed by the Second World War victors, decided in 1947 the distribution of the Palestine territory between two states: one Jew and another Palestine. This was not done: at the eve of the partition in May 1948, the Jews unilaterally proclaimed Israel as a state and allegedly started an ethnic cleansing. The rest is a well-known history of wars, violence, etc. between Arabs and Israel; and all that in one of the most sensitive regions of the world, due to its huge oil and gas deposits. Vide. Dictionnaire Encyclopedique Larousse (2001:839). On the issue of the alleged ethnic cleansing (expulsion from Israel) of 800.000 Palestinians by the Israel army in the so-called Independence War in 1948, in order to guaranty a Jewish majority for the Jewish state, vide. Pappe Ilan (2006). *The Ethnic Cleansing in Palestine*. One World.
44. As we will see in Chapter 4, significant concentration of wealth and income in a small percentage of population—as it mainly occurs in Latin America—usually makes that this sociological stratum distrusts democracy, because it may brings significant redistribution of income and wealth, against their own interests. Consequently, economically privileged groups may try to arrest any initiative for creating democracy; or may try to overturn the political course, if a nascent or experienced democracy initiates a significant redistribution process.
45. This way of doing things, in which "moral authority" became subdued to the practical interests of superpowers, is even today defended by neo-cons. On this issue, one may read the comment of *The Economist* (January 20, 2007, p.18) in the article "Spurning an olive branch".
46. On the birth of these two countries, vide. Rahman, R.D. and J.M. Andreu, (2006) *China and India: Towards Global Economic Supremacy?* New Delhi: Academic Foundation. p.13.

Note that although these two countries economically under-performed during three decades,[47] from 1978(80) onwards both initiated their respective economic processes of taking-off. Particularly, that of China has been so successful that this country has become today, in 2007, a real economic and political "nightmare" for the current purported hegemonic power and its main EU-partners.

Long-lasting Unsolved Conflicts and Spill-over Effects

As a consequence of changes of borders after wars, not ended with consented agreements and of the expulsion of old dwellers from their former territories, millions of displaced people live today in tents in neighbouring countries. To the extent that these problems continue alive, nobody should affirm that the problems that originated the initial wars have been solved.

If we mix the feelings of "land usurpation" of displaced people with religious fundamentalism and derivatives—as it happens in Middle East and some African regions—a case for urgent resettlements of the displaced on their former territories appears. In absence of a strong will for resettlement of refugees in their old territories—this initiative coming from occupiers or international political institutions—resentment will remain alive. Even more, if the number of the displaced is huge, and count with some international support and financing, the violence may *sine die* continue.

Indeed, cases such as the Israel-Palestine one, which remains alive after two generations, are a real shame for the international community and an indicator that the current situation in the region is far away from a fair solution. In fact, the continuous Israel-Palestine confrontation is a clear peace-war case with huge political spill-over effects, in which the Israelites and the Palestinians are not the only involved communities, but a minority in comparison to those concerned; reason why international political institutions should directly intervene and condemn any government which supports political position based on religious fundamentalism, be this Muslim or Jew.

Lack of mutual tolerance of a few million people living in a small territory of the planet, intermittently jeopardising the world peace and

47. Vide. Our book, already mentioned, on China and India (2006: 22).

the economic prosperity of the many, cannot justify western passivity, or even worse, western biased involvement in the process.[48]

Unfortunately for the future stability of the world, the current problems of refugees and the need of resettlements stemming from past wars perhaps are not so much relevant as those awaiting us, as a result of the accelerating climate change. Advancement or geographic movement of the deserts, growing levels of the seas, significant changes of average temperatures in the most populated areas of the planet, etc. will likely generate an enormous need of human resettlements that only could be administrated rationally by a democratic global government (necessarily a new democratic UN).

A new Source of Political Instability: The Non-proliferation Treaty

The power of different states to deter violent actions against them, to undertake military actions against others or to support own diplomatic actions in different international domains, mainly depends on their different capacities for military intervention, destruction and occupation. In the classical defence analysis, and against a background of similar destructive technologies, mentioned power mainly depended on the number of the military personnel,[49] and on the power and trajectory of the underlying economy of the involved country.

Nevertheless, things radically changed in the middle of the 20th century, when nuclear weapons appeared and were tested for the first time against civilians in Japan. Proven with astonishing capacity of destruction, the "bomb" induced the initiation of a race among the global players of those days, firstly to have it, and secondly to deliver it (with special planes, submarines and strategic missiles), thus inducing a sort of "terror equilibrium" between the US and allies, and the Soviet Union.

---

48. Indeed, apart from the Jew constituency in the US, unable by itself of overturning results in US political elections, the only reason capable of explaining the long run attitude of the US on this issue—fully supported by the EU—is the convenience of keeping at the centre of the Middle East a strong ally that enables the US and the EU to keep the region (and its resources) under control, with no direct involvement. In this regard, one should not forget that Israel has launched several preventive actions against neighbours and could do the same in the future, in explicit or implicit accordance with the US.

49. On the relevance of the human factor on historical war victories, vide. Rotte, R. *et al.* (2000). "On the production of victory: empirical determinants of battlefield success in modern war" in Brauer, J. (ed.). (2000). *A Millennial View on Defence and Peace Economics*. (website).

Understanding that the world was less safe with all the accumulated nuclear armament[50] by the two main contenders, their leaders decided in a further stage to limit the volume of the then existing strategic nuclear weapons (SALT I and II treaties).

Years later, when the manufacturing of the "bomb" became "more banal", it was decided by the main UN players, already nuclear powers, to force other UN members to sign the so-called Non Proliferation (of nuclear weapons) Treaty (NPT).[51]

According to this Treaty, the global players—the 5 veto-owners of the UN Security Council—"in return for nobody else joining their club, promised to work to progressively get rid of their own nuclear weapons, as part of a process of general disarmament."[52] By this serious commitment of the five veto-owners, and in exchange of renouncing to the production of nuclear weapons by those not belonging to the club, the five UN veto-owners promised to commercially supply the signing countries with facilities for accessing to nuclear technology with peaceful purposes, mainly production of energy.

Regrettably, as explained by Machiavelli, and as usually happens in international politics, own interest and asymmetries rapidly appeared. Indeed, any neutral and serious observer should agree that the five veto-owners have not fulfilled their part of the Treaty—their progressive nuclear disarmament[53]—while they exacted to the rest, although in a selective way, to comply with the NPT. Indeed, the initiation of the nuclear disarmament by the five "seems as far off now as it ever was. And the belief among many governments that the five are not holding up their end of the bargain, exposes them to charges of hypocrisy (...) and makes it harder to encourage the three (main)

50. On the philosophy of disarmament, and different positions of relevant economists, as List, Smith, Walras, Schumpeter, and others, vide. Coulomb, F. *et al.* (2000) in "Disarmament: A century of economic thought" in Brauer, J. (Ed.) *A Millennial View on Defence and Peace Economics* (website).

51. NPT was renewed in 1995.

52. Vide. *The Economist* (2006). "The fewer, the better." June 10. p.13

53. Even more, after stopping testing nuclear weapons in 1992, the US under Pres. George W. Bush does not seem interested in ratifying the so-called Comprehensive Test Ban Treaty (CTBT), a Treaty clearly complementary to the NPT. The US refusal is an indicator that the US wants to continue with its nuclear updating (the same as the British with their Trident Project). On this issue vide. *The Economist* (2007). "America and the Test Ban Treaty", March 10. p.14.

Treaty outsiders—India, Pakistan and Israel—to curb their nuclear arsenals",[54] and to discourage others to produce nuclear weapons.

A number of countries did not sign the NPT—doing their own way, such as India, Pakistan and others—while a majority signed it. Nevertheless, after profiting from the technical supplies realised by the five UN veto-owners, some of the signing countries started breaching the NPT system, in order to finally produce the bomb. Note that the availability of the bomb practically guarantees—according to recent history—the geographic inviolability of any country.[55, 56]

In this unfulfilling and foul context, some main players defined the target to be achieved by global society as the avoidance (at all costs) of the bomb availability by the so-called "rogue states". Their argument was that "rogue states" could eventually provide "international terrorists" with nuclear devices, or could blackmail their neighbours with the nuclear threat. Note that from the 90's onwards, other powerful countries[57] or political blocks started questioning both the listing of "rogue-states" and the internal consistency of the NPT.

Letting aside the dangerous drafting of the list of "rogue states", which occasionally may depend on the international game[58] and in occasions could be concocted, we do believe that the current methodology for discouraging developing countries from manufacturing the bomb—violent pre-emptive actions or arrangements in the (currently undemocratic) UN for establishing sanctions against those

54. Vide. *The Economist* (2006). "The fewer the better." June 10. p.13.

55. After maximum political tensions in Kashmir, only the possession of the "bomb", and the assumed capacities of Pakistan for delivering it on main Indian cities, enabled Pakistan avoiding to be attacked by India in June of 2002. Concerning this and based on the Theory of Games, which studies the action of every player against the background of possible answers from others, the work of two professors Aumann (Jerusalem) and Shelling (Maryland)—winners of the Nobel Prize of Economics 2005—provisionally proved that having sufficient (nuclear) deterrent capacities is an efficient way for averting wars and domination from others.

56. A nation may choose to maintain its full conventional force, while increasing the nuclear weapons stockpile—as did the US in times of Pres. Kennedy—or to reduce the conventional destructive capacities and military personnel, while increasing the nuclear *"force de frappe"*, as did France in times of Pres. Giscard d'Éstaing.

57. We are here mainly referring to Russia, China, India and Brazil, the so-called BRIC countries.

58. In this regard, the definition of one or several Muslim countries, as a potential threat for global peace, while Israel has all the nukes it wants with no critics or intervention by the "five", all along with its non-fulfilment of many UN resolutions in favour of Palestinians, does not seem to be a neutral behaviour of the West.

that do not fulfil the NPT, or against the non-signers of it[59]—will be less and less useful in future. In particular, we think that violent actions against highly populated and/or oil-producing countries would be enormously costly in political and economic terms for the attackers/occupiers and the rest.

Indeed, given its asymmetries and its lack of fulfilment, one has the impression that the NPT is today just a mechanism to sine die keep those countries that historically first reached (at mid-20th century) nuclear-weapons technology, in their current pre-eminent international positions. Note that this pre-eminence has enabled them to continue designing and providing the basic global public goods (peace and security) without global democratic legitimacy, and undertaking international actions (at times violent) against individual states.

Note additionally that in the long term, the (national) production of the bomb will become easier and, consequently, dissuading its production will finally become completely out of range of individual or grouped actions of current UN member-states.

Therefore, the solution of the current problem of growing uncertainty, created by the almost inevitable nuclear proliferation, will necessarily have to be worked out in the context of a new multilateral democratic institution, a new UN that will have to neutrally but seriously and forcefully deal with the problem, deactivating it.

The Current World and its Polymorphic Change

The four and a half decades that the Cold War (1948-1991) lasted, not only witnessed conflicts, but also a great economic expansion[60] practically extended to the entire world.[61] This period also witnessed

59. This was the case against India, when this country started its tests in the last 90s.

60. Note that this expansion measured in GDP growth rates—that is to say, disregarding implicit environmental costs—had two velocities along the period 1950-1998. The first, at maximum speed, was registered from 1950 up to 1973; this period, called the Golden Age of Capitalism, was followed by another—the last quarter of the 20th century—of a more moderate expansion, in which Asia (ex-Japan) reaccelerated its velocity of progress, thus starting its take off.

61. Observe, however, that the last quarter of the 20th century was a period of economic stagnation in Sub Sahara Africa. In this subcontinent the per capita income practically did not grow from 1973 onwards, and new diseases (AIDS) started decimating its population.

a significant change in the philosophy of life of Western citizens[62] that progressively spread out to other less developed regions. A generalised progression in human rights definition and implementation[63] was also visualised in the West during the period.

Reconstruction of Europe, decolonisation, changes in technology and better macroeconomic knowledge made faster GDP growth[64] easier almost everywhere. Technology, by drastically reducing the private[65] transport costs, made national and international trade easier, and changed individual travelling (by car or plane) into a common thing. Trade among a growing number of GATT members experienced significant progress,[66] while in the late 60s and first 70s some concerns on the environment and exhaustible resources emerged.[67] Nonetheless, these environmental problems—particularly those of global incidence—were initially no object of significant official action.[68] Only the sharp hikes in oil prices, successively occurring as derivatives of the Yon Kippur war (1973) and the Iranian Islamic Revolution (1979), drew attention to the scarcity of natural resources. More recently, the embodiment of China and India into the international division of labour and their corresponding growing demands of raw materials, plus growing evidence on current climate change, have finally placed the environmental degradation as one of the most relevant problems to be solved in future.

---

62. Not all aspects in the change of the western philosophy of life were positive. Registered trends towards consumerism and individualism—including breakdown of family-life—mixed with a superiority complex and at times arrogant behaviour towards other cultures, are characteristics that should be considered as negative.
63. Unfortunately, human rights policies were asymmetrically implemented, and at times significantly delayed. In fact, a practise of double standard was observed in relation with the slow promotion of human rights in certain developing countries belonging to the western political orbit.
64. One should never forget the conceptual difference between the reached GDP and the attained Net Economic Welfare (NEW) (always a significant lower figure). This difference and concepts, original by Nordhaus, W., will be explained in Chapter 5.
65. If we additionally include the "social" costs of transports, mentioned reduction would have been less spectacular.
66. For a briefing on the evolution and evaluation of GATT-WTO, vide. Rahman, R. and J.M. Andreu (2004) *Responsible Global Governance*. New Delhi: Academic Foundation. p.81.
67. Analyses on environment and resources depletion became visible mainly since the Report to the Club of Rome (realised by Meadows and Meadows and a team of the MIT), as we will explain in Chapter 5.
68. If serious action had then been implemented, the current (2007) severity of the perceivable climate change could have been avoided.

Note that along the years of the Cold War, problems of under-development and difficult conditions of life of billions of human beings, although somewhat "considered" by rich countries, were clearly under-funded and, many a time, treated under geopolitical considerations. Even more, economic and political consequences of sustained under-funding of the developing world, combined with poverty and political frustration in a context of growingly informed societies, were not well assessed; but the consequences of all these failures finally emerged when in the 90s the ICT revolution gathered momentum.

Political Uni-polarisation, Democratisation, and "Unique" Economic Thinking

With the disintegration of the Soviet Union in 1991, the world became practically uni-polar in political terms. This was a new situation, favourable for western leadership but negative from the perspective of the necessary development of a global democracy, the sole system capable of providing with legitimacy and efficiency the global public goods desired by the international community, and for adequately correcting global externalities.

Many people thought in those days that the US could easily act as the sole leader and arbiter in all economic and political matters and conflicts. Irrespective of its non-desirability—remember that optimum in economics and politics will only be approached when power is distributed and negotiation is necessary—apparent US hegemony was just a transitory mirage, as it has recently been proven in the aftermath of the Afghanistan and Iraq invasions.[69]

In the decade of the 90s, some observers thought that the former huge military expenditures carried out by the main contenders in times of the Cold War, particularly by the US,[70] would be diverted

69. Although the US has enormous and high-tech weaponry piles, the human factor of its army is clearly insufficient and overstretched for its purported role of policeman of the world, without the co-operation of the rest of the international community. Indeed, this has become patent in the fight against international terrorism, when invading some predefined "rogue" states (cases of Afghanistan and Iraq).

70. In 1998, the Brookings Institution published the most comprehensive independent estimate on the US military spending in the last 60 years. According to its figures, the US had spent along the mentioned period, more than 18 trillion US$, of which nearly a third in nuclear weapons. Military expenditure was by far the largest simple expenditure of the Federal Government for the previous 60 years; by comparison the nation had spent in this period 8$ trillion in Social Security (....) Money spent on nuclear weapons alone, far exceeded the combined total spending on education, law enforcement, agriculture, natural resources, environment, science, space and technology, job training, employment, and regional development. Vide. Parker, R. (2006). *John Kenneth Galbraith*. Canada: Harper. p.220.

or retargeted towards more human endeavours, such as that of an increased development funding. Paradoxically, the reality of the 90s proved precisely the opposite: a decline in the Official Development Assistance (ODA) in real terms and in GDP terms of Donors. In fact, after some years of reduction of its defence expenditure in GDP terms, the US (and others) significantly increased it in the first years of the 21st century, mainly as a consequence of their declared war against "international terrorism".[71]

As a result of sustained economic failures of the Soviet Union from mid 70s onwards, both foundations and application of the Marxian economics pervasively entered into decadence, to be finally abandoned after the fall of the Berlin wall.

Unfortunately, the filing of the Marxian economics was accompanied—mainly in the West—by the rising of an unbalanced approach of the so called "neo-classical" economic model, according to which most internal and external markets should be liberalised hastily, and many useful public expenditures transferred to the private sector. Note that the chosen approach not only promoted a significant reduction of the size of the public sector in rich countries, but also proclaimed that the growth of the developing countries should be more a matter of freer trade and Foreign Direct Investment (FDI) than of ODA. This was the approach officially adopted by the so-called Washington Consensus.[72]

---

71. As it was devised, this war against terrorism—with frontal attacks against formal states—was not a priori easy to be gained, as we mentioned in our book *Responsible Global Governance* (2004:19). Book already mentioned. Although with a certain delay, the British Prime Minister has also confirmed our views. Vide Eaglesman, J. (2006:4) "Blair admits the West is losing the war on terror". *Financial Times*, August 2.

72. What John Williamson, of the Institute for International Economics in Washington DC, called "the Washington Consensus" describes the conditions considered as necessary for a poor country to get itself on a path of sustained development. These necessary conditions to be fulfilled were agreed and shared by a number of Washington based leading multilateral economic institutions (World Bank and IMF) and by the US Treasury, all of them in fact commanded by the same power. The main conditions of this Consensus were: no inflation; sound fiscal policies; broader tax bases and more moderate marginal rates; free internal markets and liberalisation of the external ones including the exchange rate; export orientation of the economies; public expenditure more tilted to investment in infrastructure, health and education; and fight against poverty. Fight against corruption, as a problem that assumedly conditions any development process, would only appear in the first 2000; but mainly putting the emphasis on the "corrupted" (poor countries governments) and less on the "corruptors" (private western firms and MNC, occasionally "supported" by corresponding western Embassies).

In the 90s, these ideas progressively gained ground and became "mainstream" economics, the so-called "unique" economic model for global prosperity.[73] It is our view that this radical, individualistic and dangerous ideological approach, conducive—as we will explain—to perverse (concentrated) income distribution, has capacities for derailing the process of creation of a world free of tensions; and also for arresting or overturning the development or consolidation of national democracies,[74] or impeding the setting up of necessary global governance institutions (mainly a new democratic UN).

Indeed, from the crumbling of the Soviet Union onwards, the democratisation movement at national level gathered momentum, particularly in most of the ancient Soviet Union-satellites and in Latin America. Observe that this occurred in parallel with the development of a new-neo-classical economic model, mainly applied to microeconomics (public sector reduction and freer international trade, finance and domestic labour markets), while Keynesian macroeconomics continued being applied by most governments despite its alleged scant credibility.[75]

Alleged Efficiency, Degradation of Social Protection in the West, and Consumerism

It is remarkable that in the late 80s, but mainly along the 90s and first 2000, real wages and working conditions of labourers in different (western) countries, instead of respectively increasing and becoming gentler—as a result of the technological progress and the initially expected international political stability—became quasi stagnant or unfavourable for workers; and all this even though the technological advantage in the West was comparatively large, and the big emerging countries (China and India) would not create significant problems for the West till 2004 (end of the Multi-fibre Agreement).

---

73. These ideas, combined with an incomplete democratic perspective that finishes at a state level, and with an indefinite continuation of the provision of some global public goods by a selected club of powerful-rich western countries (without any global democratic legitimacy), formed the corpus of the neo-con doctrine defended, among others, by Francis Fukuyama (in his first writings), Donald Rumsfeld and Paul Wolfowitz.

74. As far as the practise of new-neo-classical economics tends to worsen the internal distribution of income and wealth, subsistence of many current western democracies cannot be totally guarantied, as we will explore in Chapter 4.

75. Discredit of Keynesianism was to a great extent induced by reckless politicians who, progressively indebting countries up to the extreme (instead of resorting to unpopular additional taxation), forced the inflation resumption of the late 60s and 70s.

Surprisingly, the delicate equilibrium efficiency-equity—necessary for sustainability of democracy and reached after so many efforts in Europe[76] and other western countries—significantly shifted towards an overemphasised short-term efficiency in detriment of equity; and in some places in a rushed way. As a consequence, degrading of average social protection[77] at times combined with more exigent working schedules and stagnant or lower real wages,[78] became in the West, general trends in the 90s and first years of 2000; and this while traditional Trade Unions—constantly threatened by multinational firms with dislocation—were not capable to reverse mentioned trends.

Note additionally that as a consequence of the technological (ICT) progress, growing national and international competition,[79] aggressiveness of media promoting individualistic and materialistic "modern lifestyle", and lack of a balanced long-term vision on human existence, the spending orientation of western citizens veered towards short-term "consumerism".[80]

Indeed, this consumerism—requiring long working hours to finance it—has significantly changed the lives of westerners who nowadays mainly value each other by what one consumes or possesses, thus not only forgetting old ideals of brotherhood and equality,[81] but

---

76. In Europe there are different models of social protection: 1) the Centro-European model (France, Germany and others) characterised by providing generous unemployment benefits and pensions while limiting by law the capacity of firms to fire workers; 2) the Nordic countries model (including Netherlands), which is more prone to poverty reduction and dole compensation while more easily authorising firms to fire workers; and 3) the Mediterranean one, basically inclined to keep the people working irrespective of the current labour needs of firms, while giving petty dole compensations. Vide. *The Economist* (2005). "Chose your Poison". October 1. p.32.
77. European social protection and real wages are clearly in regression; particularly the wages in new labour contracts made with young people.
78. Surprisingly, the delay of real wages in a context of rocketing profits—as a generalised economic phenomenon observed in the West—has just recently started to be debated. In relation to US see. "Summers and Rubin to Highlight Lagging Wages", *Financial Times*. July 25, 2006.
79. Note that this growing competition progressively forced labour flexibility and induced precariousness.
80. Consumerism is a psychological propensity to unremittingly buying fashionable things, irrespective of whether they are really useful or not; and this while the amount of working time necessary to finance mentioned purchases, or the non-sustainable overuse of natural resources, is disregarded.
81. As recently the philosopher Régis Debray wrote, "if Freud reappeared at the dawn of the 21st century, he would find out a society embedded in consumerism dreams, while lacking utopia and project". Vide Debray, R. (2005). "Malaise dans la civilisation, suite", *Le Monde*. November 26. p.27.

also that their limited leisure time on Earth—a complementary and indispensable good to reach happiness—is the most valuable and scant asset they own.

Undeniably, this new harsh capitalism—closely related in its ideology with the failed "traditional liberalism" of the 19th century (1870-1914), has piecemeal gathered official support in the West, as well as in Asia and ancient communist states.[82]

In fact, this long-term non-efficient capitalism[83] has recently been encouraged by many states, which officially have defended the idea that significant social protection of workers and their families is rather an anti-competitive load and not a real advantage for labourers.[84] This "alleged" anti-competitive burden is mainly attributed to the fact that all subsidies are "inconvenient" (de-stimulating) and that higher taxes, required for financing social protection, will finally induce higher unemployment. According to this view, it is also believed that if social protection were privately organised, the de-stimulating effects would disappear.

Consistently with this rationale, it has become fashionable in Europe to officially recommend—even by multilateral institutions[85]—that the EU-countries should significantly and rapidly reduce social protection-nets to face Asian and US competition.

In our view, however, this way of understanding capitalism, with total pre-eminence of efficiency over equity, cannot work at long term because it would finally become inconsistent with sustainable democracy, as we will explain in the lines below.

---

82. It is understandable that workers of former European communist states, or those of communist regimes that recently adjusted to economic capitalistic rules (privatisations, flexible prices, etc.) as for instance China, etc., work (or continue working) long hours for low wages, because their perspective of access to consumer-goods at short-term is better than before, or it may significantly improve at short-mid term.

83. A somewhat overdone presentation of current ugly capitalism, in relation to the daily struggle for life in the US, may be found in the film "In pursuit of happiness" (2006) starred by Will Smith and his son.

84. In parallel to mentioned recommendation of reduction of the size of the social protection, "neo-liberal" economists also recommend that services of protection (security) should be transferred to the private sector, "always a much more efficient sector than the public one".

85. Surprisingly, in April 2005, the IMF insisted in the idea that main EU countries should not keep their current social protection systems, if they wanted to remain competitive.

Poverty, Full Information, and International Terrorism

To the mentioned armed-conflicts or political tensions, and to the already described economic—individual or aggregated—western misconceptions, we could add other manifestations of the current crisis at a global scale.

Among them, we must underline the shameful continuation of hunger and deprivation in large parts of the globe, due to local bad governance, persistence of wrong development strategies, ongoing greedy and bad organised official development assistance (ODA), and commercial protectionism in the rich world.[86]

Given the current level of information (full and live) across the world, unfair economic situations will no longer be considered by the poor as a "natural state" to which they should rationally adjust. Therefore, one should not wonder if claims from the poor become more and more aggressive, and if they start way-out actions.[87]

In this matter, we share the view that poverty, or serious economic unevenness, may under certain circumstances encourage religious radicalism and feelings of exclusion which altogether may not only unleash internal political and economic instability but also cross-border criminality and "international terrorism".[88]

In particular, the so-called "Jihad war or Islamic terrorism" whose most significant action was materialised on September 11th, 2001, is today seen as the result of convergence of diverse political and socio-economic circumstances, which at the end of the day have provoked in some Muslim communities rejection of the Western style of life, and encouraged "religious fundamentalism".

---

86. According to a remark of Mahatmas Gandhi in the famous film "Gandhi", directed by Richard Attenborough, "(politically induced) poverty is the worst form of violence."

87. Indeed, initiatives of illegal migration is a daily phenomenon at the frontiers of the US and EU; a phenomenon that is currently gathering momentum. Particularly shocking were the cases in October 2005 of Ceuta and Melilla, two Spanish cities in North Africa, where large groups of Sub Saharan migrants tried to enter in Europe by simultaneously jumping over the barber-wired fence of the border. Additionally, Sub Sahara migrants have recently stepped up their illegal moves towards the coast of Canary Islands, also a Spanish and EU territory.

88. According to Fred, Halliday—in his book, *The Middle East in International Relations: Power, Politics and Ideology*. Cambridge University Press (2005), quoted by *The Economist*, April 16, 2005, p.79—the word "terrorism" is frequently misused by politicians, "as a coded means of dismissing the validity of a political cause."

Among the possible causes of the development of Jihad- terrorism we could quote, following Halliday:[89] 1) the defective quality of political leadership in the Arab-Muslim world; 2) the traditional and low level of education[90] of its population, particularly that of women;[91] 3) the scant participation of woman in the public life;[92] and 4) the specific features of media and publications in these countries. To these primary and incomplete causes described by Halliday, we will add some more: 5) the difficult relations between the state and the religious power[93] in most Muslim-Arab countries;[94] a religious power that is always hindering the modernisation of the Muslim-Arab states by means of opposing Sharia[95] to modern civil Law; 6) the disappointment of citizens due to the negative economic results reaped after independence by Arab-Socialism in some relevant Arab-Muslim countries; 7) the existence in many Arab-Muslim countries of huge economic windfalls (oil) and related unbalanced personal income distribution, which always play against democracy; 8) the divide and

89. Halliday, Fred (2005). *The Middle East in International Relations*. Book already mentioned.

90. This low level of education—in part attributable to colonial powers—is severely compounded by the fact that the basic and secondary education in many Muslim countries is traditional, and totally permeated by references to the Koran, Sunna, etc. With remarkable exceptions, education is not based on secularism, but on religion.

91. If one observes the ranking of the HDI (Human Development Index) of the UN (2003), and compares it with that of the per capita GDP of the different countries of the world, one may deduce that many Arab-Muslim countries have a negative bias: their positions in per capita GDP are placed significantly over those of their HDI. The cause of this bias is clear: "the comparative lower level of education of 50 per cent of their populations, women". *UN Development Program* (2004). *Arab-Human Development Report*. New York. p.235.

92. Note that these two indicators used by Halliday are positively correlated. Indeed generalised secondary education of women necessary implies a greater involvement of them in economic activity and political life. An obvious example of this correlation is the case of Tunisia, a small Maghrebian country in which women are totally embodied into the productive activities and politics.

93. Note that in many Muslim countries, most of the social relations are regulated by the Sharia, and not by modern civil law promoted by politicians in parliaments. In relation to these social aspects of the human life, special religious courts administrate justice. Vide. also Note 94.

94. On the difficult relations between Islam and State, vide chapter 3 of Charfi, Mohamed. (2005). *Islam and Liberty*. Zed Books. p.102. On difficulties to achieve democracy in the Muslim-Arab countries, vide item 4.6.2.1 of this book.

95. Sharia and fiqt—that is classical-muslim Law—is a voluminous body of legal rules concerning most problems of life in society. One finds there criminal law, rules defining personal status, property law, civil law, administrative litigation, etc. This classical law is to some extent a coherent body that regulated the urban Muslim societies from 8th century (of the Christian Era) till very recently, without any historical updating. Note that during the colonial days, metropolitan law did not replaced the sharia (on the contrary, sharia was applied by colonisers when convenient). Charfi, M. (2005: 38). Book already mentioned.

rule policy for long practised by Western leadership in the Middle East, including support to dictatorships when convenient, in order to guarantee energy security; and 9) perhaps the most important, the long-lasting Israel-Palestine problem, with a "perceived" non-neutral behaviour of the West along the last 60 years, that has progressively changed mindsets of some Arab-Muslim communities into hatred, and has poisoned the Arab-West political relations.

Notwithstanding that, we believe that in the next two decades many of such characteristics of Arab-Muslim societies will necessarily change. In this regard we should remember that many of the above-mentioned traits were in other times typical in most Western (European) societies; features that were progressively overcome along the economic development process, which brought generalised education and deeper knowledge of other cultures.

Note that in the West these sociological and political changes took many decades; and that historical experience proves that externally forced acceleration of socio-political change resulted counter-productive, even in Europe, causing violent reactions, often defined by occupiers as terrorism.[96]

Finally, concerning the last mentioned cause of Islamic terrorism, a durable solution could only come from the intervention of a democratic UN, charged with the legitimate provision of global public goods and the correction of global externalities.

Economic Profile of Problematic Muslim-Arab Countries

In lines above we have suggested that "informed" poverty, extreme internal inequality, and growing economic gap between societies might be causes for conflict and even extremist behaviour.[97] If we add to these determinants, growing political radicalism and religious fundamentalism, both motivated among other causes, by long-standing political exclusion, the panorama for the worst becomes complete.

---

96. Note that already in the late 18th century, and first years of the 19th, Napoleon Bonaparte tried to bring about modern socio-political change to some backward European countries. His attempts were doomed to failure, due to the fierce internal resistance against "imposed" better governance.

97. A report by the World Bank published in May 2003 based on a study of 52 civil wars since 1960, reveals that contrary to public opinion, ethnic tensions and ancient political feuds are rarely the primary cause of civil war. Instead of that, economic forces such as entrenched poverty and heavy dependence on exports of natural resources are usually to blame. Vide Collier, P. *et al.* World Bank, Washington DC.

Looking at the Muslim world, mainly located in North Africa, Middle East and South and South East Asia, and exclusively focusing on their economies, we have to say that most of these countries[98] have a per capita GDP (in PPP terms) under the average of the per capita GDP of the world, which is well under the per capita GDP of the West. Even more, among Muslim countries, 10 communities have a per capita GDP even below 50 per cent of the average GDP of the world. As a complement to these figures, we have to add that *the Muslim world, with a 21 per cent of the global population, accounted in 2005 for only 5 per cent of the total GDP of the world,* an unbalance consistent with the fact that 39 per cent of the Muslim population is placed under the poverty line.[99]

If we now take into consideration the Muslim countries that—due to their specific political positions—have entered into conflicts, or could potentially enter in disputes with the West,[100] it is clear that all of them are below the average per capita GDP of the world. Even more, all of them, except Iran, Algeria, and Libya (three oil and gas producers), are well under the 50 per cent of the world average. And some of them are placed in per capita GDP (in PPP terms) very far below the mentioned 50 per cent.

In this regard one should admit that to accept disparities, in comparison with OECD countries, of almost 43 times in terms of per capita GDP-PPP, as it was the case of Afghanistan in 1998, and to expect no frustrations and reactions against this very unfair situation, is simply not understandable in a fully informed world. If someone in the international community had taken significant economic action long before, to avoid reaching such a state, the episode of the twin towers and subsequent events perhaps would not have taken place.

98. Only Bahrain (17,170), Kuwait (16,240), Oman (13,340), Qatar (19,844), Saudi Arabia (12,650), and United Arab Emirates (22.420) had in 2002—as expressed between brackets—per capita GDP (PPP) near those of western countries. Vide. UN Development Program (2004). Arab Human Development Report 2004. p.235.

99. Mentioned figures of 5 per cent of the global GDP and that of 21 per cent of the global population attributed to Muslim countries have been taken from the intervention of the Malaysian Prime Minister in Kuala Lumpur the 29th May 2007 in an Islamic Conference. Vide World Bank (2007) Dav-News 29.5. Doc. The fact that the Muslim community as a whole has a percentage of poor (39%) similar to that of India provides us with a serious indicator on the possible incidence of the extreme poverty on violence; in particular, when poor Muslims feel mistreated, humiliated or despised in or by the West.

100. These countries are: Algeria, Libya, Sudan, Iran, Iraq, Yemen, Bangladesh, Pakistan and Afghanistan.

Nevertheless, Afghanistan is not the only example that could generate, or that has generated, problems to the rest of the world. There are other Muslim communities with huge per capita GDP disparities (up to 27:1),[101] in which some radical groups could in future pose problems to the international community.

Facing the Big Trade Offs of New Societies

Having catalogued the problems of sustainability of capitalism and democracy, outlined the foundations of the growing uncertainty in the current world, and analysed some causes of dissatisfaction, we will now approach some of them in more detail. To this respect, we will begin with what we define as the current manifold crisis in the western philosophy of life.

In our opinion, this multi-facet life crisis—born in the late 70s and today permeating most layers of the political and economic world[102]—has to do with several disputable aspects related to human life. Such crisis deals about a new lifestyle that paradoxically few people have dared to criticise. Perhaps, the quasi-absence of this debate stems from the progressive acceptance of some "sociological trends"[103]—soaked in deep individualism and purported limitless freedom—that shapes "modernity", as understood in North America and Europe.

Nevertheless, these patterns of behaviour should not be adopted without any discussion or without considering alternatives. Particularly those which have been built on wrong principles. In this regard, we consider that a long-term generalisation of some of the current western habits (private individual transport f.i.) will likely be conducive to an impasse in the development of capitalism in the 21st century through

---

101. We are here referring to Bangladesh, a Muslim country of 150 million people, in which violence uses to combine with democratic elections. On this issue, vide *The Economist* (2006). "Bangladesh. The Hole in the Middle". November 4. p.16.

102. It is true that the Muslim-Arab population, with an amount of around 1500 million people, although in general fighting to leave poverty and become richer, consider itself as different from the people of the Western World. It seems that they would like to continue being "faithful" to their religious principles and life style, which indeed are inconsistent with some habits of westerners in their daily life.

103. This way of living is massively supported by publicity in suffocating western media systems, prone to the ongoing change towards individual "consumerism".

congestion, exhaustion of certain resources, or arrival at a radical climate change.[104]

Observe that individual transportation, often with several cars per nuclear family, implies a stage of individualism that, besides its environmental costs, has also huge private costs: need for individuals to work more hours (to finance it, or its complementary goods) in a harsher competition with others; and all this just to occasionally feel freer (only when most of citizens do not use their vehicles).[105]

Note additionally, that the current individual lifestyle of westerners—of which possession of individual cars is just one of the most visible traits—is now being imposed to the rest of mankind, without verification on its sustainability. Indeed, the implication of these impositions are multiple and range from culture (religion) to economics and politics.

In reaction to this panorama, some disputable features of our behaviour as human beings—in opposition to their respective alternatives—will be analysed in the lines below. In particular, we will discuss the cases of: 1) efficiency vs. equity; 2) income vs. leisure; 3) consumerism vs. environmental protection; and 4) uniformity vs. diversity in culture, religion, and political organisation.

Efficiency Versus Equity

In relation with the first dichotomy, efficiency vs. equity, today pervasively re-inclined in favour of (short term) efficiency, we should here remember that the ideal construction of the first rational economic model (Smithian economics) practically coincided in time with the French Revolution.

This coincidence was not totally accidental. Indeed, freedom of markets, central in Smithian economics, required the framework of

104. For a rather pessimistic analysis on what could happen in future in relation to Earth Warming and economic costs of doing nothing (up to 20 per cent of the global GDP over this and next centuries), vide Stern, N. (2006). *Report on the Economics of Climate Change*. (2006). Taken from *The Economist* (2006). November 4. p.14. Other reports, as that of the UN, February 2007, Paris, seems to be less pessimistic (although the latter was previously "negotiated").

105. In 2050, generalised individual transport at affordable costs will not be viable on a daily basis in the big cities. Indeed, in a World of 8.5-9 billion people, in which at least 60 per cent will be urban, the congestive trait of the individual transport will make it impossible at moderate costs.

a minimum of political liberties.[106] But observe that in the French Revolution the ideal of political freedom was initially[107] defined along the ideals of equality and brotherhood,[108] which nowadays may be respectively revisited as equality of opportunities and effective solidarity.

Along the last two centuries both ideals of economic and political freedom—respectively conducive to efficient production and interchange, and equal opportunities—have been at the core of political discussions, political reshaping of states, and even internal uprisings or inter-states' armed conflicts.

Note that to the extent that market freedom and political liberty could not (and cannot) be effectively exercised without a minimum background of economic resources in the hands of free individuals, some redistribution of economic assets, or income, was (or is) necessary for democratic sustainability, when democracy surges. Otherwise, the awarded or conquered political liberty would have been (or will be) useless for most citizens who, finally, would have been (or will be) prey of a minority who owned (or owns) the relatively non-human scant factors (land or capital) indispensable for production.

Note that if the new owners—the new bourgeoisie—were scant,[109] and in parallel, did not exist an extended middle class, the new economic system, although more efficient in economic terms than the former one, would be incapable of delivering a minimum of equity, thus inducing potential social instability and unstable democracy.[110]

---

106. Note that the concept of "political liberties" has historically been one of a variable geometry, without a monotonous progression in franchising and other civil rights; and even with periods in regression or breaking up. Needless to insist that after a maximum participation of the population in the Constituent Assembly and further in the Convention along the French Revolution, Napoleon took over in 1799, thus certifying that the then French society was not mature in 1789 for constructing what we will here define in Chapter 4 as a "sustainable democracy".

107. This idea varied all along the 10 years of French Revolution cycle.

108. Anyone who has studied the French Revolution initiated in 1789, must remember that, in the revolutionary period (1789-1799), there was a moment in which the "sans culottes" —the poorest of the "Third State"—played a relevant role in exchange of promised equality. Saboul, A. (1972). *Precis d'histoire de la Revolution Francaise*. Paris: Editions Sociales.

109. And, consequently, ownership of production assets was also very concentrated.

110. This phenomenon of political instability stemming from "a democratisation process without a convenient and simultaneous redistribution of assets" was clearly perceivable after the initial stages of the French Revolution. Saboul, A. (1972). Book already mentioned.

Concurrently with the evolution of the liberal states, it is also interesting to observe that in the first third of the 20th century, as well as in the last one—periods mainly dominated by economic "liberalism" in its different approaches—Darwinism appeared or re-appeared in the theories of social life in opposition to the ideals of equality and brotherhood.

Darwinism transplanted to economics, is nowadays falsely presented under the rationale that any solidarity usually results in economic disincentives for the poor, thus becoming detrimental for the speed of progression of the collective.

Note that this false rationale has gathered growing support in rich countries,[111] since most of their citizens do not expect to become poor. No wonder that most citizens of rich countries, short-sightedly focusing on own "individual" satisfaction, neglect not only their faraway poor neighbours in developing countries, but also those nearby; and—as we will explain—even themselves in the long-term.

Negative Spillover Effects when Forgetting Equality

But unfortunately for Westerners, forgetting the poor is an irrational behaviour because a stubborn and long-lasting neglect of the others, in a context of full informed societies, will be conducive to negative spill-over effects in terms of security and prosperity for all.

In this regard, one should not overlook that the alleged short-term negative effects on efficiency of many pro-equity actions have many a time been surpassed by the mid-long term induced advantages; advantages that normally have stemmed from the significant improvement in the socio-economic "climate" in which the economy and private business had to operate.

In this respect, one should not forget that in the conventional neo-classical micro-economy, the production functions—in principle defined, as technical relations among factors of production and output—have also to include the organisation of the productive activity. Logically, this organisation will have to necessarily adjust to

111. Observe, however, that in the "most liberal countries", as for instance the US, there is a significant number of poor, around 15 per cent of the total population, neglected by the System.

the dominant ideas about what is desired by society in connection with industrial relations,[112] thus imposing restrictions on the use of labour by firms.

Although these restrictions are limitations to free contracting of labour, few people—except economic fundamentalists who wrongly think in pure short-term efficiency[113]—would support the abolishment of them. In this respect, it is deducible that such an abolishment would be counterproductive because, besides its negative effects at long term on society (leisure time, family life, etc.), it would induce serious labour or political disruptions, based on the perceived unfairness of the new economic situation.

We do believe that the ideas about what are fair industrial relations have exerted a very significant and positive effect on the concept of long-term productivity of labour.[114] Note that this is a concept much more comprehensive than the cold short-term productivity of labour stemming from mere technical relations among factors and output, and sometimes from the abuse of workers.

It is not difficult to transplant these microeconomic ideas to the macroeconomic field, that is to say, to the evolution of the joint productivity of factors and global prosperity. Accordingly, what sometimes appears to be non-productive but "equity" expenditures in the context of firms, many a times results in a long-term profitable action for all parties.[115] The historical construction of the welfare state in Western Europe and the disappearance of former dramatic conflicts in labour markets (frequent general strikes) is an indisputable proof of the advantages gathered by certain social expenditures.

---

112. As for instance, working schedules, shifts, security, holidays, leaves of absences, geographical mobility, etc.

113. Instead of suggesting to help the poorest countries to initiate the building up of welfare systems to align their social security provision with that of the West, thus deactivating social complains of the poor majority, western economic fundamentalists try to degrade the current social protection system in the West for "recovering competitiveness" against the poorest economies.

114. Although internal "economic freedom" in the West probably reached its zenith in the period 1870-1914—although not for all, remember the economic situation of metropolitan workers and those of colonies—the average annual growth rate of the labour productivity was not at all the highest in the last two centuries.

115. Elson, D. (1998) "The Trade-off between Equity and Efficiency". Comment to the report "Gender and Economic Development". Netherlands Economic Institute. In this comment it was clearly stated that, "in general, all the policies that decrease social unrest also stimulate growth and efficiency."

Concluding, long-term measures taken to reduce unacceptable differences in the living standards of citizens (via public expenditure in education, health, minimal pensions, progressive taxation, etc.), or taken for the setting up of balanced rules to ease industrial disputes, should be considered as positive, and not against the efficiency of the production system.

Consequently, we firmly believe that what we could call, in a simplified way, the European model of social protection,[116] far from disappearing at a world scale, will be finally accepted—of course after indispensable corrections—and adopted in the long term by most countries in the world. This will necessarily occur because any voluntary component of any private self-protection system never will work at a general scale, thus resulting in undesired under-protection of the less prudent or poorer individuals,[117] who use to be significant in number.

Trade-off Between Working Time and Leisure

There are prosperous industrialised countries whose labourers have in the last quarter of the 20th century progressively reduced the number of their annual worked hours[118]—basically in Continental Europe (France, Germany, Netherlands, etc.)—while others, being also growingly rich (US and UK, for instance) have surprisingly increased the length of their average working time.[119, 120]

---

116. One could discuss if there is a unique European model of social protection or if there are several ones, as mentioned before; or even if it would be convenient that all EU countries adopted the "Nordic" sub-model, as defined in Note 76. But in any case the latter seems to be the most desirable one, because it is not only based on solidarity, but also on long-term progress in labour productivity.

117. Note that any operation of self-insurance carried out by individuals could neither be of general scope, nor could it profit from the optimal distribution of risks.

118. Indeed, the reduction of the weekly worked hours per person has been one of the most important targets of Trade Unions along the last hundred years; a target successfully achieved by them in the West. Nevertheless, observing the trend, one may deduce that in the last quarter of the 20th century an up-turn has been registered in some countries, particularly in US and Britain.

119. While, between 1973 and 1998, the number of per capita working hours in Western Europe decreased to 12.2 per cent, those of the US increased to 12.9 per cent. Maddison, A. (2001). *The World Economy: A Millennium Perspective*. Paris: OECD. p.132. For similar considerations, Gordon, R. (2003). "Two Centuries of Economic Growth: Europe Chasing the American Frontier". Quoted in *The Economist*, February 8. p.84.

120. In opposition to mentioned figures of Maddison relative to the period 1973-98—vide former Note—some OECD-figures recently appeared, referring to the period 1994-2005, are partially in contradiction with former comments. *The Economist* (2006). July 29. p.92.

This phenomenon of progressively increased worked hours when per capita income rises could theoretically mean that, in US and UK, either leisure was (or is) not a normal good[121] which is illogical, or the substitution effect of less leisure by more income was (or is) of a very big magnitude,[122] thus making people prone to work much more even when real wages (before or after tax reductions) just increase slightly.

But far from these theoretical explanations, the real causes of the extended worked hours in mentioned countries may have been rather different. Available data enable to affirm that in the US, the observed increase in the average worked hours per worker is somewhat consistent with a real reduction of the median wage per hour—which could have forced most workers to work more hours for the same monthly income—while the average wage per hour would have increased.[123]

Although not easy to understand, we could say that, at present, the citizens of some western countries—as for instance in the US and UK, and also in others—brain-washed by media, have dramatically acquired a very individualistic approach focused on short-term "consumerism". This means that they, to continue following current consumerism in a context of decreasing median wage per hour, would have decided to work more, thus sacrificing themselves in the short and long term, via mis-consideration of own leisure (reducing it at short term) and saving (focusing on current consumption instead of on long term capacity to consume).

This self-neglecting attitude of citizens could also be caused by the under-valuation of one of the primary objectives of community

---

121. In Microeconomics, a normal good is defined as that whose demand grows when individual real income rises.

122. This would happen if the elasticity of substitution between leisure and income were very high. This means that small relative increases in wages would induce important relative decreases of the leisure time, and relevant rise in working time. This phenomenon could laterally be connected with the psychological phenomenon of consumerism, at times consistent with growing individual indebtedness.

123. This is due to the shift of the internal distribution of income among wage and salary (non capitalists) earners. Indeed, in the US and other societies and in the last 10-15 years, top executives of firms, actors, singers, top sportsmen or sportswomen, etc. (people placed in the so-called markets of winners) have increased their incomes in a very disproportionate way with respect to normal workers, thus forcing an upward move of the average wage, in consistency with a decrease of the median wage of labourers.

life, which is to enjoy friendship, social interaction and family life.[124] At the end of the day, their current target could be an endless race to consume more than others, in detriment of their current leisure and future economic security.

More understandable than the case of overstressed labourers in mentioned rich industrialised countries, is the case of the overstressed workers in some developing economies. These labourers, in many cases without the support of a social protection net, effective trade unions and/or fair labour legislation, work more hours just to earn a minimum living, against an unfavourable framework of superabundant manpower and relatively scant demand of labourers.

Consequently, it is expectable in these developing countries that when their societies become more democratic, their demography becomes less pressing, and/or their per capita GDP becomes higher enough, the number of annual worked hours per worker will diminish, thus initiating a convergence process in this domain with rich societies (provided that the latter do not continue being involved in irrational consumerism).

On the Reduction of Leisure in the West to Gain Competitiveness

In the wake of former considerations, we could now discuss the current propensity in Continental European countries to plan or to effectively increase the annual work-hours of labourers (in the private sector), assumedly to better compete[125] with the US, Eastern Europe, or with the new big Asian challengers (mainly China and India).

In relation with this issue we have to point out firstly that the competitiveness of a country has to do with different variables, and not exclusively with the number of the annual worked hours. Indeed, the competitiveness of a country will increase when the productivity per worked hour grows in comparative terms, when the number of annually worked hours per worker relatively grows, when the annual salary (measured in internal currency) becomes smaller

124. Note that these activities (for enjoying friendship and family life, for attendance to clubs, cinemas, sports-matches, going shopping, etc.) are time-intensive.

125. The reduction in last decades of the annual working time of Western (Continental) European labourers is often judged by neo-liberals, as one of the main causes of the EU under-competitiveness. This conclusion is a serious mistake due to the fact that it does neither take into account other relevant variables that may play in favour of competitiveness, nor the value of leisure that may have also played in the interest of workers.

in comparative terms, or when *ceteris paribus* the national currency devalues or depreciates.[126]

Consequently, an increase in the number of annual worked hours per labourer in a country may *ceteris paribus* increase its competitiveness but cannot guarantee it if the rest of variables move in an inconvenient way; or if other countries increase at a quicker speed the number of worked hours. Conversely, a reduction of the annual worked hours per labourer will not necessarily deteriorate the degree of competitiveness of a country if other variables move in an appropriate way.

Having made all former comments, we may now analyse with more accuracy the recent polemic on the duration of the individual working time in EU firms. To start with, we have to say that the solution of this problem will always have much more room of manoeuvre at a macroeconomic level than at an individual one.[127] Indeed, to the extent that current level of competitiveness may be preserved[128] by favourably moving other involved variables, there is no valid reason to force—against values and interests of citizens—an increase of the volume of the annual worked hours, when in other countries workers work more hours. On the contrary, to keep working fewer hours will be a rational move, if the involved citizens accept the costs of their option for more leisure.

To put an example, a reduction by authorities of 2 per cent of the annual working time of labourers would be a legal decision that, by itself, would reduce competitiveness unless labour costs of firms would in parallel decrease by around 2 per cent; or unless the annual productivity of these labourers increases 2 per cent (while the labour productivity in the rest of the international competitors does not move); or unless the national currency depreciates around 2 per cent (or a combination of mentioned movements).

126. Note that the management (dirty floating) of the national (or the EU) currency in terms of the international ones provides to national competitiveness a total flexibility for adjusting.

127. The individuals (workers) are usually confronted with the option of working the amount of hours legally established—with some allowed seasonal variations—or not to work at all. This inflexibility does not exist at macroeconomic level (at a national one) if some lateral conditions are fulfilled.

128. In this regard we should not forget that EU-workers mainly want to work less hours and to enjoy more leisure time.

As a result, it is our view that according to traditional EU-pattern of mixing working time and leisure, the number of annual working hours per worker should be clearly defined in consistency with the desires of their citizens.[129] Indeed, this would be a relevant political decision[130] that, *ceteris paribus*, would necessarily affect the growth rates of real wages and GDP, while keeping competitiveness.

Logically, after this decision, Europeans would be less rich in per capita terms of produced or acquired goods and services, in comparison to other nations—and specifically to the US—but richer than many others in leisure time. In this regard, one should not forget that the leisure time has a very positive value in terms of the Net Economic Welfare of nations, as recognised by modern systems of accounting welfare,[131] as explained in Chapter 5.

Even more, looking to main Asian countries and considering the cheapness of labour and the huge number of the annually worked hours per person in them, a reduction of leisure time in Europe—as sometimes demanded by EU-conservative politicians—to offset the low cost of Asian labour, seems simply a non-workable policy, given the enormous gap existent today in terms of both wages and annually worked hours.

In conclusion, a hypothetical use of the total available hours per EU-worker would not enable to bridge the competitiveness gap,[132] although doubtless it would increase the profit rate of the EU-firms while likely undermining the family life of workers and their psychological health.

---

129. These social desires should be attached to a flexible interpretation of the volume of annual worked hours, for its adjusting to seasonal peaks of production.

130. Note that nowadays, rules on labour markets are not a competency of the Commission of the EU, but a full competency of member-states. Consequently, unless a consensus on the matter is build up, mentioned possibility of Euro-devaluation against reduction of working schedules, would be non-operative.

131. Although a measure of the Net Economic Welfare (NEW)—inclusive of leisure as a positive factor—has not been implemented in a generalised way, for substituting or complementing the GDP concept, there is no doubt that the per capita NEW in Western Continental Europe, would accumulate a much smaller gap than that of the per capita GDP per comparison to the corresponding aggregates in the US.

132. Let us not forget that the number of annually worked hours per industrial worker is much higher in China than in Europe, while the Chinese wages are extremely low.

Consumerism Versus Environmental Protection

We have already mentioned that, recently, many western citizens, in particular those living in economically "successful" countries, have acquired the habit—willingly or forced by circumstances—of working additional hours. Eventual additional income, plus borrowing, has enabled them to immediately increase consumption of goods, while (unconsciously in many cases) neglecting even their own future needs.[133]

Indeed, growing indebtedness and almost nil familiar saving-rate, as today displayed by the US in its national accounts,[134] in a country in which the social protection net is seriously deficient per comparison to its wealth, is a clear indicator of the current consumerism and short-termism of the American society.

Note that mentioned familiar over-consumption in the richest nation on Earth—a trait that has its correspondence at macroeconomic level with the unbalanced current account of the US—could have been caused either by the lack of confidence of Americans in their future, or as a result of the wrong economic policy practised by the US authorities in the first years of the 2000 decade.[135]

In our view, the fiscal policy recently applied in the US (reckless reduction of taxation of rich, thus increasing public deficit) has been clearly directed towards the attainment of GDP short-term results, while it unfairly and egoistically has disregarded problems of future US-governments or generations, who *ceteris paribus* will inherit strong

133. Making mockery and displaying high doses of cynicism on long-term concepts, many economists and entrepreneurs use to say that the long term "never arrives", or that when it arrives "one is not anymore in office". Indeed, long term starts at the very moment of the initiation of the analysis; and, from that moment onwards, authorities and entrepreneurs should put into practise adequate measures to reach the long-term desired targets.

134. This problem of scant or nil familiar saving rates is not exclusive of US. It was also observable in some OECD countries in the past two decades. In July 2006, familiar saving rate became negative in the US.

135. There are commentators who suggest that the said lack of internal savings of US-families is mainly due to the recently experienced "huge" wealth effect, which has apparently swollen the value of all available assets of citizens as a consequence of the rise of prices of those recently interchanged. Rise of assets prices have made "unnecessary" additional familiar savings. All this has apparently favoured the American families, although the bubble of housing and other assets bursts, "wealth effect" would play in the opposite direction.

external indebtedness.[136] Note in this regard that the current reckless treatment of the external deficit in the US is based on the wrong assumption that the dollar will sine die remain acceptable as the core of the international monetary system, irrespective of the progression of the US foreign indebtedness.[137]

Observe that current massive and obsessive consumption process in the US—partially communicated to the rest of the world—has induced a great waste of natural resources, many of them non-renewable. Over-consumption (and parallel over-production) has also been accompanied by increased emissions of greenhouse gases (CO_2)—thus accelerating climate change[138]—or by significant degradation of soil and water and sea resources, all in detriment of the environment that our descendants will inherit.

Letting aside over-consumption of the US and western countries—around one billion people—we have also to consider that the billion of poorest of the world also tend to "over-consume", thus depleting natural resources. But in opposition to what happens in the West, depletion practised by the poor is due to their pressing survival needs, mainly stemming from extreme poverty and high fertility rates.

Note that these pressing needs force the rural poor[139] in LDC[140] to overuse the natural resources at their disposal, progressively clearing their forests to meet their food and fuel needs, thus inducing

---

136. In relation to the authorship of this reckless economic policy, one must not exclude Allan Greenspan and Fed, who with their policy of cheap money to continue the party—which for a period resulted in negative real interest rates—fed a huge increase of assets prices and implicit inflation (not computable as such in the IPC) that significantly distorted the wealth distribution in the US.

137. The rapid depreciation of the dollar in 2007, to a great extent caused by capital withdrawals progressively undertaken by foreign governments, is a proof of the growing distrust towards the US dollar.

138. The case of the US is a clear overdone example of former proposition. The level of per capita CO_2 emissions of the US at the dawn of the current (21st) century (2005) was more than double the average of Europe, 6 times that of China, 15 times higher than in India, etc. World Bank (2007) *World Development Indicators.* Note that although developing countries issue a small proportion of industrial CO_2, they generate practically all the non-industrial greenhouse gases (fuel-wood, burning vegetation to clear plots etc.)

139. In South Asia more than 70 per cent of people live in rural areas, and in Sub Sahara Africa more than 60 per cent. Additionally, an estimated 75 per cent of all the poor in the World live in rural areas. World Bank. (2006: 125). *World Development Indicators*

140. The acronym LDC refers to the so-called 44 "Least Developed Countries" according to terminology of the World Bank. In this book these LDC are often included in the more general expression "developing countries".

deforestation,[141] soil degradation and some times desertification. On the other hand, in the urban areas of developing countries, the supply of public services cannot match the needs generated by the enormous increase of rural migrants that dwell in unhealthy and overcrowded shanty towns and slums.

Uniformity Versus Diversity in Culture and Political Organisation

Another perceivable trait of the recent globalisation is the strong trend towards homogenisation in consumption, social behaviour and habits. This trend has become more and more compulsory due to the fact that westerners, from the colonial days onwards, have tried to impose their culture and behaviour on others. This trend has recently been renewed by "persuading-forcing" developing countries to step up certain economic or political changes to reach "modernity".[142]

These "recommended changes" could be understandable in the field of economics[143]—provided that they were selectively, progressively and cautiously implemented—but are much more disputable in other (political and social) domains.

In relation to social domains, differentiated moral attitudes in developing countries[144] concerning roles of women and families in society, social habits, and even some human rights,[145] use to be considered by westerners as unbearable and non-acceptable backwardness.

This "unacceptable delay"—many a time caused by former colonial powers which in general refused to develop serious education systems—combined with western superiority feelings, makes that

141. Deforestation, combined with heavy rains, may induce land sliding, thus destroying assets (shelters or factories) and taking human lives.

142. Note that this forced "modernity", although wrapped in different pretexts, hides the desire of widening markets for western goods and manufactures.

143. Particularly, in relation to the liberalisation of trade and opening to financial interchange.

144. Note that these differentiated moral attitudes stem from recommendations of different religions, or by the absence or mix of other sources of moral principles.

145. Many a time one listens or reads condemnation coming from the West about the violation of human rights in certain places, due to misdemeanour of local governments or civil servants on specific citizens. These condemnations although often correct, cannot hide the fact that, in the middle of a great indifference, Western countries systematically neglect (financially) the poor, depriving them of a decent live, access to literacy and numeracy, etc., thus violating basic human rights to be educated and healthy, as defined in the Charter of the UN.

the West pose urgent political change on the others; and this, while forgetting that, after their own political independence, these changes took decades or centuries to be achieved in Western countries.

This lack of historical equity becomes even more asymmetric when the West tries to hastily and forcibly impose on certain developing countries western political (democratic) systems;[146] particularly in those (undemocratic) countries considered as relevant from a geo-strategic perspective. Amazingly, and at the same time, western countries overlook "non-analogous" political systems of others if they behave friendly, or are economically or politically irrelevant.

Apart from being historically unfair, such forced change has also proven to be non-intelligent.[147] There are few doubts that in the current case of the Muslim-Arab countries of Middle East and North Africa, the pressure applied on them by the West to rapidly force democratisation of their political systems has resulted counterproductive. Undeniably, if the socio-economic background of these countries is not mature for achieving (at short-mid term) sustainable democracy[148]—as it currently happens—forced institutional changes towards democracy, far from being effective to the purported ends, could be frustrating and cause of internal damage; and, perhaps, of the arrival of theocratic regimes.

Consequently, it is our view that it would be much more effective to continue with indirect support to the democratisation process in the Muslim-Arab world by means of contributing more significantly to the development of their human capital; in particular the education[149]

146. In relation with the long history for arrival to a (partial and defective) democracy in US (in connexion with the exigency of fast political change towards democracy in other countries), Wilentz, S. (2005). *The rise of American democracy*. Norton. Quoted in *The Economist* (2005). "American Democracy. The People´s Road." 29th October, p.92.

147. Indeed, the strategy developed by Western allies from September 11th 2001 onwards, far from solving the problem of "international terrorism", has facilitated in many countries the accession of Islamic parties to power (Iraq, Palestine), or has brought more legal political influence of Islamic parties in other places (Egypt, Lebanon, and Turkey); and this while political consolidation of sustainable democracy in Iraq and Afghanistan is far from completion.

148. Conditions for sustainable democracy will be described in Chapter 4.

149. Although one cannot say that a significant level of education is necessarily conducive to democracy, the empirical evidence suggests that in the long-term the reality is near to mentioned sequence or causation. Vide among others, Barro, R. (1999) "The Determinants of Democracy", *Journal of Political Economy* 107.

and professional promotion of women, in order to reduce the huge gender development gap accumulated by most Muslim societies.

Even more, it would be much more efficient for the cause of democratisation in Muslim countries, that the West finally plays an active and neutral role in the solution of the Israel-Palestine conflict.

Summary of the Chapter and Contents of the Book

Summary of Chapter 1

Once taken into account the main current problems of the planet—global environmental degradation, global resources depletion, lack of legitimacy of providers of some international public goods (peace and security), and almost generalised trend to the worsening of the personal income distribution induced by recent steps and approach towards globalisation—this Chapter has presented the need of looking for collective solutions to preserve or to improve the working of the binomial democracy-capitalism.

Lack of national democratic infrastructure impedes in many countries the adequate development of human rights, the economic reform for gaining prosperity and the protection of the national environment. In other countries, already democratic, exaggerated growth-mania, overdone market orientation and consumerism is significantly worsening the domestic personal income distribution, thus weakening middle classes and jeopardising national democracy. Finally, at a global scale, the non-existence of global democracy makes democratic global governance impossible, and hinders the fair and efficient provision of global public goods, and the correction of global externalities.

Former problems have driven us to discuss and define a new ideology for mankind protection, based on two main lines of action: 1) the indispensable preservation of the mix economy of market in front of the egoistic version of neo-classicism, till today in progress; and 2) the need of construction of a global democracy for the legitimate administration of global public goods and the correction of global externalities.

The above-mentioned perspective stems from our reading of the recent economic and political history. An economic history of the last third of the 20th century—based in growing individualism, growth-mania, and consumerism—has marked a trend that is currently driving the world through paths that are non-consistent with the existent physical limits (available resources) and, through shrinking of middle classes, with the sustainability of democracy. And a political history of the last 6 decades that, full of asymmetries combined with an almost triplication of the world population pushing for democracy, fully clarifies the need of democratising the global provision of global public goods, and the correction of global externalities.

We do believe that the planet will not finalise the first half of the 21st century governed by an aristocracy of western countries, that—proclaiming being internally democratic and with 1/6th of the world population—dictate to the others (with 5/6th of the population) what to do in relation to collective issues (mainly peace and security).

Attempted "international uni-polarisation", whose natural tendency is to politically abuse the others (as historically proven in every case of hegemony), and the so-called "unique economic thought" (Washington Consensus) with its practical derivatives of asymmetric goods and services liberalisation (WTO), significant downgrading of public sectors, and lower or scant supply of real ODA, have been conducive to an almost general deterioration of the personal income distribution.

In such a context, extreme and violent actions of some "losers" (particularly some groups of Muslims) have also been analysed in this Chapter, while one sub-continent (Latin America) has recently witnessed a clear veering to the left.

Finally, as related causes of the seriously unbalanced economic behaviour of the West in the last 3 decades, we have analysed some relevant trade offs that the West will have to confront in future: 1) The "efficiency-equity" combination, wrongly inclined today in favour of short-term efficiency (social Darwinism); 2) The "working time-leisure" blend, wrongly combined in many places of the world to gain competitiveness, but in serious detriment of family life, socialisation and psychological health of workers; 3) The combination of "consumption growth with environmental protection", also in urgent need of optimisation; and 4) "Uniformity *versus* diversity" in consumption, culture and political organisation," could also be seen as trade-offs that could accumulate serious dysfunctions.

Contents of the Book

Once presented the main political and economic traits of the world today and its challenges (Chapter 1), we will develop in next chapters some selected issues that, according to our view, will be relevant for the protection of mankind in the 21st century.

Making an initial comment on next chapters, we will firstly analyse in Chapter 2 the features and evolution of the world economy along the 20th century, with special reference to the second half of it. The evolution of population, GDP, and per-capita GDP of every region will be considered, as well as the shift towards Asia of the economic gravity centre of the world, with a special reference to the cases of China and India.

After making some reflections on the non-inclusion of the labour market in recent steps towards globalisation, "expectations of economic convergence"[150] of the different regions of the world will be discussed. Negative consequences of effective non-convergence, with particular attention to expectable reactions of poor societies, will also be analysed. Finally, after consideration of the recent trends of the international trade of goods and services, which additionally certificate the current economic shift towards Asia, we will describe in Chapter 2 the role of a future new UN to solve the economic and political problems of the 21st century.

After considering all such issues in Chapter 2, we will analyse in Chapter 3 the evolution of the capitalistic praxis along the 20th

150. There are at least three ways of measuring the evolution of dispersion of the different per capita incomes, and of evaluating the possible economic convergence or divergence of the different countries or regions in the world: 1) With the use of simple measures of dispersion of the per capita GDP of countries or regions, as presented by Maddison, A. in Chapter 2; 2) With the use of the so-called weighted international inequality, as analysed among others by Sala-i-Martin, as also mentioned in Chapter 2, being the latter and the former one rough measures of disparity evolution, which provide contradictory results; and 3) The most valid measure, regrettably never assayed, consisting of analysing the evolution of the Gini index of the per capita GDP or Income of the 6.5 billion people living on Earth. Note that, with the same basic data, the evolution of this Gini index could prove "divergence" while the "weighted inequality" could "wrongly" prove convergence.

century, with a special emphasis on the changes undergone by the capitalist system in the periods 1973-1995, and 1995-2007. Having described the main disputable characteristics of current capitalism and some of its trends, we will outline the evolution of the Economic Theory, along the 20th century.

Having depicted the evolution of praxis and underlying economic theory of capitalism, we will thereafter enter into the consideration of the main pending economic problems, and on reforms to be implemented to achieve a functional capitalism for the 21st century. Indeed, the necessary redefinition of the (national and international) rules for competition and the convenience of generalising social protection of workers in the context of a new and long-term more efficient process of globalisation, are basics that we will restate. Finally, the characteristics of the new global political infrastructure of capitalism—the traits of a new UN—will also be analysed in Chapter 3.

Given the interactions and crossed conditions for sustainability of Capitalism and Democracy, Chapter 4 will be devoted to a detailed analysis of the mutual dependency of democracy and capitalism. Starting with general considerations on national democracy—in particular, with the self-interest axiom, which permeates all modern analysis of politics—and after describing the limits of the debate in national democracies, conditions for feasibility of democracy under capitalism will be established. Subsequently, we will make some considerations on the recent evolution towards growing democratisation in the world, and we will warn on the delicate socio-economic equilibrium that will have to be maintained to sustain democracy; and not only in countries that have recently acceded to democracy but also in the so-called "consolidated" western democracies.

"Democracy", as a political concept, will be defined in all its levels of application in Chapter 4. After suggesting that democracy is a historically non-finished concept, or a non-completed process whose global-international projection—indispensable for the preservation of global environment and sustainability of capitalism—has barely initiated its way, we will analyse the democratic situation of the world today, and the different democratic gaps of the different countries. Chapter 4 will end with a description of the conditions for survival of the binomial capitalism-democracy in the 21st century.

After describing the current situation concerning global environment and future availability of global resources of common use (rainforests and fisheries), and following special considerations on the Kyoto Protocol and possible consequences of Earth Warming on future and massive human resettlements, Chapter 5 will enter in a theoretical explanation of externalities, and on the different ways—via markets or via direct controls—of democratically addressing these problems.

After recognising in Chapter 5 that modern economic growth is the main cause of the environmental degradation of the planet, a concept of "sustainable development" will be defined in its weak and strong versions. Complementary ways of measuring production and welfare, further the old and almost obsolete concept of GDP will also be exposed. The so-called Kuznets Environmental Curve (KEC), and a discussion on its application to different environmental problems, will also be presented in Chapter 5.

After commenting the irrelevant incidence of successive trade rules on environment (as agreed in different Rounds of GATT), by means of authorising the establishment of special barriers or compensatory duties on manufactured imports non-complying with certain international environmental standards, etc., Chapter 5 will enter into the description of alternative (suggested) policies for improving the global environment, and for a better management of the natural resources of common use.

According to widespread experiences at national level, it is our view that the scope of the democratisation processes (national and global) in the future will mainly condition the course for physical sustainability of capitalism in the 21st century. As a consequence, we will end Chapter 5 recommending global governance (in a new UN) also for the administration of the global environment and for the management of the negative global externalities.

Finally, in Chapter 6, we will present the reader our main findings, conclusions and recommendations.

[illegible]

Typeset [illegible]
Printed and [illegible]

2

Recent Evolution of the World Economy and Expected Radical Changes

To correctly project economic perspectives for the coming decades in the different regions of the World, it will be necessary to first know the economic evolution of these regions in the period 1950-2007. In this regard, we will mainly base our analysis on the figures recently presented by Prof. Maddison.[1] For comparative purposes, we will also refer to the Maddison figures of the period 1870-1914, the so-called period of the traditional "liberal order".[2]

To analyse the period 1950-2007, we have divided it in two sub-periods: 1) the period of generalised and growing prosperity, 1950-1973, also called "the golden age" of capitalism;[3] and 2) the "neo-liberal period" which, extended from 1973 to 1998 (and further),[4] has meant a certain updating of the ancient "liberal order".

Note that the analysis will be made in aggregated terms. Although this could hide interesting details concerning certain prominent countries, it will not contradict the general trends of the different regions of the world.

Trends of the World Economy in the Period 1950-2007

It is well acknowledged that in the second half of the 20th century, the world economy obtained—excluding environmental degrading and

1. Maddison (2001). *The World Economy. A Millennium Perspective*. Paris: OECD. We will also consider, as a complement, additional figures relative to the economic evolution in the period 1998-2007.
2. This "liberal order" refers to the economic system "enjoyed" by a minority group of Western countries at that time. This order, far from being really liberal, was mainly patronised by Britain and consistent with the restrictive trade rules of colonialism.
3. Observe that this "golden age", was basically "golden" for Japan and Europe, whose per capita incomes grew very fast.
4. Indeed, this period has not ended, but the available-homogeneous figures only extend up to 1998. Additional comments on the economic evolution of the world from 1998 up to 2007 will be realised in different moments of this book.

depletion of resources—its best ever results. According to Maddison,[5] the global GDP grew at an average growth rate of 3.9 per cent per annum, compared to a growth rate of 1.6 per cent per annum in the period 1820-1950. Another indicator of buoyancy of the second half of the 20th century is the average of the per capita growth rate per annum, which in this period was 2.1 per cent against 0.9 per cent between 1820 and 1950. This means that in the second half of the 20th century, the global per capita GDP grew at a rhythm that allowed doubling the global standard of living every 35 years, as compared to the time frame of 80 years that was necessary for per capita income doubling during the period 1820-1950.

Evolution of GDP and Population in the World

The former aggregated figure of 3.9 per cent of the GDP growth rate in the period 1950-1998, is the weighted average of that of the "golden age of capitalism" (4.91%), and that of the period of "neo-liberalism" (3.01%). Note that in the "golden age" the per capita GDP in the world grew at a rate of almost 3 per cent per annum, the greatest ever in history (only 1.33% in the period 1973-1998).

Entering now into regional details of the GDP growth in the "golden age", we will mention that the average growth rate of Japan was the most remarkable (9.29%). Against what one could have imagined, the European Immigration Countries (US, Canada, Australia and New Zealand, hereafter referred to as EIC group) experienced in this "golden age" the lowest GDP growth rate (4.03%) of all regions,[6] even below Africa (4.45%), Western Europe (4.81%), USSR and satellites (4.84%), Asia (excluding Japan) (5.18%), and Latin America (5.33%).

---

5. Vide Maddison, A. (2001: 125). Book already mentioned. Note that the periods selected by Maddison are arbitrary and consequently arguable. However we will not enter into discussions on this issue because identifying periods is mainly a matter of historians; and because any other arbitrary selection would not modify the results significantly.
6. It is convenient to remember that the 50s were a decade of slow growth for the US; a country that in those days was in need of changing the structure of its economy towards civil endeavours after its huge military effort during the Second World War. With the arrival of the Democrats in 1960, US started the practice of a "forced up to the limit" Keynesian policy, which was named "the new frontier economics". This policy, accompanied by the escalation of the Vietnam conflict, accelerated the growth rate of the US and meaningfully reduced the unemployment rate, although at the cost of an increased inflation rate.

Evolution of the GDP in the Period 1973-1998

Regarding the neo-liberal period (1973-98), in which the global GDP growth rate per annum was 3.01 per cent, that is to say around 3/5th of that of the golden age, we should underline the economic breaking of Eastern Europe, with an annual average growth rate turning negative (-0.56%) from former 4.84 per cent.

Also Japan decelerated its previous spectacular rhythm of growth, converging to the average growth rate of the world. Note additionally that while Western Europe had annually grown in the golden age almost 1 per cent point above the EIC, the situation overturned in the neo-liberal period, with the EIC growing almost 1 per cent point more than Western Europe.[7]

Significantly above the world average, the Asian (ex-Japan) countries not only maintained the annual growth rate of the golden age (5.18%), but also surpassed it (5.46%), reaching a figure almost twofold the world average. No doubt, this period 1973 1998 of general decline in global growth was the period of the economic resurgence of Asia, commanded by a vanguard group of 7 fast growing countries.[8] This resurgence period of Asia seems to have geared up in early 2000s.

Evolution of World Population

To continue with our aggregated analysis, we will now focus on the evolution of demography in the periods 1950-1973 (the golden age), and 1973-1998 (the neo-liberal period). We can see in Table 2.1 that the growth rate of the world population in the period 1950-1973 was 1.92 per cent per annum, which roughly meant a population doubling every 37 years. This stage was the so-called period of "population explosion" at a world scale, since there had never before been such a high global population growth rate.

Entering into details, it is remarkable that in the "golden age" the average annual population growth rate peaked in Latin America

7. This was due, among other things, to the wearing out of the reconstruction period in Europe.
8. Note that the extraordinary growth rate in Asia (ex-Japan) during the neo-liberal period should mainly be attributed to the 7 countries of fast annual growth rate, the so-called Asian tigers (Hong Kong, Singapore, South Korea and Taiwan), plus Malaysia, Thailand, and China.

(2.73%), followed by Africa (2.33%) and Asia (excluding Japan) (2.19%). In the same period the demographic behaviour of Europe land-marked a trough (0.70%), while the population in Japan grew at 1.15 per cent, USSR and satellites evolved at 1.31 per cent, and EIC group (US, Canada, Australia and New Zealand) grew at an annual average rate of 1.55 per cent.

The average population growth rate of the world lost momentum in the "neo-liberal" age (1973-1998), moving from 1.92 per cent to 1.66 per cent per annum. Most of the regions reduced their population growth rate in this period with the dramatic exception of Africa that reached an average figure of 2.73 per cent per annum, a rate capable of roughly doubling the demography of the continent every 26 years. Specifically, Latin America reduced its annual population growth rate to around 2 per cent, a little bit over the growth rate (1.86%) of Asia (ex-Japan). Amazingly, Europe halved its previous low growth rate, from 0.70 per cent to 0.32 per cent, while USSR and satellites experienced a sharp fall of their population growth rate from 1.31 per cent to 0.54 per cent.

Table 2.1

GDP, Population and Per Capita GDP, 1950-1998
(Average Annual Growth Rates)

	GDP (% Real Terms)		*Population (%)*		*Per capita GDP(%)*	
	1950-73	*1973-98*	*1950-73*	*1973-98*	*1950-73*	*1973-98*
Western Europe	4.81	2.11	0.70	0.32	4.08	1.78
EIC group*	4.03	2.98	1.55	1.02	2.44	1.94
Japan	9.29	2.97	1.15	0.61	8.05	2.32
Asia (ex-Japan)**	5.18	5.46	2.19	1.86	2.92	3.54
Latin America	5.33	3.02	2.73	2.01	2.52	0.99
Sov. Union & Satell	4.84	-0.56	1.31	0.54	3.49	-1,10
Africa	4.45	2.74	2.33	2.73	2.07	0.01
World	4.91	3.01	1.92	1.66	2.93	1.33

Source: Maddison, A. (2001: 126). *The World Economy. A Millennium Perspective*. OECD. The European Immigration Countries (EIC)*, include US, Canada, Australia and New Zealand; the group Asia (ex-Japan)** include 7 countries of fast growth rate (China, Hong-Kong, Malaysia, Singapore, South Korea, Taiwan and Thailand) plus 8 additional Asian countries with significant growth rate (Bangladesh, Burma, India, Indonesia, Nepal, Pakistan, Philippines and Sri Lanka).

A simple look at these figures enables us to identify the most problematic regions in the world. During the neo-liberal age, the case of the very high population growth rate in Africa, the poorest region of the world in terms of development and welfare, was tragic because it increased at a time when the "golden age" was over. This high rate supposed an enormous hindrance at short-mid term for the per capita income increase in the region, forcing African governments to devote disproportionate budgetary efforts to more or less maintain the already scant level (in per capita terms) of their public goods and services supplies (health, education, infrastructures, etc.).

It would be also convenient to remember that the population growth rate of Western Europe never surpassed the figure of 0.77 per cent, not even in the period of the "baby boom" (1950-1973), being the average growth rate of the last half-century around 0.50 per cent. This figure made possible the achievement of greater internal savings in Western Europe (private and public), which served to successfully finance during decades its development process and welfare state. Note also that the recent sharp fall in the population growth rate in Russia (in the period 1973-1998) continues being a cause of deep concern in this country, because—excluding oil and gas windfalls—it limits its possibilities for catching up in terms of GDP.

The Per Capita-GDP Growth in the World

As a consequence of the differentiated annual evolution of the global GDP and the population in the two mentioned periods of the last half of the 20th century, the global per capita GDP also grew at different rates. In the golden age the average per capita growth rate per annum was 2.93 per cent, while in the neo-liberal era the former rate more than halved, reaching a figure of 1.33 per cent.

In the "golden age" period, 1950-1973, the annual growth rate of per capita-GDP of Japan was the highest (8.05%) in the world. Even in this period of maximum prosperity, the per capita GDP of the African continent grew annually at the lowest rhythm (2.07%). The EIC group and Latin America registered a per capita GDP growth rate of around 2.5 per cent per annum, while the per capita GDP in USSR and satellites grew annually at 3.49 per cent. Observe that in this period—the period of the European reconstruction—the citizens of Western Europe experienced a significant increase in their per capita growth rate (4.08%) per annum, almost doubling the rates of the EIC group.[9]

Table 2.2

Evolution of the Real P.C. GDP in Prominent Stages of Capitalism (Weighted Average of Annual Growth Rates in Different Periods)

	1870-1913 Classical Liberalism	*1950-73 Golden Age*	*1973-98 New Liberalism*
Western Europe	1.32	4.08	1.78
EIC group	1.81	2.44	1.94
Japan	1.48	8.05	2.34
Total advanced countries	1.56	3.72	1.98
Asia (excluding Japan)	0.38	2.92	3.54
Total Advanced plus Asia (excluding Japan)	1.36	2.93	2.91
Other 40 countries of Asia	0.48	4.09	0.59
44 Latin American countries	1.79	2.52	0.99
Sov. Union & Satell. (27 countries)	1.15	3.49	-1.10
57 African countries	0.64	2.07	0.01
Total 168 shaking countries	1.16	2.94	-0.21
World	1.30	2.93	1.33

Note: According to specialists, the history of capitalism has evolved along 5 more or less agreed stages. Three of these stages are described in this Table. We could also have described the period 1820-1970 in which the annual p.c. growth rate of the World was 0.53 per cent, and the period 1913-1950 in which the global growth rate was 0.91 per cent.

Source: Maddison, A. (2001: 129) Book already mentioned.

Nevertheless, in the neo-liberal era the rhythm of prosperity experienced a generalised downfall[10] except in the case of Asia (ex-Japan). This region moved from an annual per capita GDP growth rate of 2.92 per cent in the golden age, to a 3.54 per cent in the neo-liberal period. In Eastern Europe, on the contrary, this period was a clear catastrophe, not only in terms of economic performance,

9. The enormous effort of European citizens for the reconstruction of war-torn Europe, initially facilitated by the Marshall Plan, made this rapid per capita GDP growth rate possible. Japan experienced a similar process. Both Europe and Japan profited from the economic battle of the US against communism in the early years of the Cold War. Main European countries also profited from the end of independence wars in former colonies.

10. Among other things, the sharp increase of energy prices, and the appearance of rudimentary internal environment legislation in Western countries, forced a significant reduction of the growth rate of the labour productivity.

which significantly reduced the standard of living of their citizens (with a negative per capita GDP growth rate per annum of –1.10%), but also in its political functioning. Note that in the middle of the period, the communist political and economic model of the region bankrupted. This bankruptcy was followed by a period of greater economic instability.

The per capita GDP of Africa did not grow at all in the neo-liberal era (0.01% per annum), while Latin America grew only at an annual rhythm of 0.99 per cent. Note that the lost of steam in Western Europe was also significant, experiencing an annual growth rate of per capita GDP (1.78%) which only surpassed those of Latin America, Africa and Eastern Europe.

Shift Towards Asia of the Economic Gravity Centre of the World

Apart from the economic derivatives of climate change and the current defective income distribution among (and within) nations, the main economic problem that many rich nations of the world are facing today is the huge structural change that is already underway. Structural change, whose process of adjustment—given the inertia induced by the inflexibilities of markets—may take decades.

Rapid Change of the Economic Importance of Asia in the World

Indeed, for the first time since the Industrial Revolution, a human mass containing around 37 per cent of the total world population (China and India), and in a very short period of time, moved from a position of being out of the international division of labour (till 1978 in the case of China, and till 1991 in the case of India) to a process of progressive integration. To the extent that reaching significant embodiment in international trade and financing took China two decades, this country did not become an obvious challenger in international matters till the end of the 20th century. Now then, in the last 7 years, and particularly after its entrance in the WTO in 2001, China has gained momentum in international trade[11] and

11. Observe that in 2004 China was already the third world exporter after Germany and the US, and before Japan.

overwhelmed the West with its rapidly growing exports, thus scaring private competitors and western governments.[12]

The case of India is currently less worrying for the West than that of China. This is due to the fact that India initiated its embodiment in the international division of labour in 1991, more than a decade later than China. This delayed (slower and less determined) economic opening of India has made that this country is currently (2007) playing an economic role[13] similar—although more tilted to the exports of services—to that played by China at the beginning of the 90s. Note that China at that epoch was more an economic and political curiosity for academicians, than a deep concern for western politicians.[14]

As we will explain later, the real GDP growth rate of these two countries along the last 25 years has been around 10 per cent in the case of China, and around 6 per cent in the case of India. This difference of 4 per cent points in favour of China, plus a more rapid population growth rate in the case of India, has made that China has today (2005) a per capita income (1,740 US$) more than double than that of India (of around 730);[15] and this while in 1978 their respective per capita GDPs were alike.

On the Duration of the Current Rapid Progress of Asia

Many observers of the current Chinese and Indian economic progress wonder on the possibilities of this two countries to continue, and for how long, with their current high rhythms of growth.[16] Some of these viewers, over-valuing the political and economic difficulties

12. In the last 5 years (2000-2005) the annual increase of the Chinese world exports share has been around 0.5 per cent points, which *ceteris paribus* means that this country will likely overtake the US exports by around 2010.

13. In relative terms, India is more inclined to the production and export of services than China. Note that the value added of the services in India was in 2005 equivalent to 54 per cent of the Indian GDP.

14. Except for the case of democracy and human rights development, whose internal support was officially crashed in the happenings of Tiannanmen in 1989.

15. Mentioned figures of per capita GDPs of China and India are measured in terms of exchange rates of Yuan and Indian Rupee with the US dollar, and referred to 2005. Vide World Bank (2007). *World Development Indicators.*

16. Note that India was growing at mid-2007 at an annual rhythm of 9.3 per cent, a rhythm that is non sustainable, because is incompatible with the current gross investment rate (33%) of India. Vide. World Bank (2007). *World Economic Indicators.*

that both countries will have to overcome in the next decade,[17] provide pessimistic prognosis suggesting that the current high growth rates will wear out in few years.

Nevertheless, serious analysts conclude that these two countries will finish the first half of the 21st century with GDPs alike to that of the US; although, of course, the citizens of China and India will be much less affluent than the US-citizens in 2050.

Additionally, the phenomenon of the very high growth rates of regional exports and imports in East and South-East Asia, and in South Asia, individually in each region and jointly in both of them, per comparison to the world figures in the last decade (1995-2005), and per comparison to those of the US and the EU, seems to confirm former optimistic opinions on the economic future of China and India.

As everybody knows, these two countries have an enormous comparative advantage in industrial (China) and service (India) wages. This has placed the US and the EU in an almost impossible position to compete with many manufactures coming from China and with (certain) services coming (or being outsourced) from India.

Indeed, given the huge differences in real wages between China and India and the West, and the alike used technology—supplied to China and India by western dislocating firms—increasing competitiveness in Western countries cannot be just a matter of increasing the annual growth rate of the labour productivity per hour (always a small percentage), or the annual growth rate of the productivity per person by means of rising the number of annually worked hours. In fact, a significant and sustained downwards correction of the western real wages will be necessary,[18] in front of the enormous tidal wave of new

---

17. We have explained these difficulties in our book about China and India. Vide Rahman, R. and J.M. Andreu, (2006). *China and India. Towards Global Economic Supremacy?* New Delhi: Academic Foundation.

18. There are already studies made by OECD and other institutions that advance shy negative forecasts for the future evolution of the median real wages in the EU in the next 10 years. Although a reduction of just 1 per cent per year is mentioned in these studies, we do believe that in next 10 years the correction will be much more significant. Note that for reckoning the effective reduction of the real wages in the US and the EU, it would be relevant to count with realistic estimations of the "rates of inflation", and not with current CPI, that cannot accurately measure the evolution of the general level of prices, including those of certain goods produced in former exercises. Note for instance that "old" residences that in the last years have been object in the West of frequent transactions among families at fast growing prices are not taken into account in current CPI.

cheap labourers that have entered or will enter—via international trade—into the global division of labour.

Unfortunately for the West, its current economic problems will not finish in 5 years time or in a decade (in 2018), as some have suggested thinking that China and India will rapidly follow a convergence process with the West in unitary costs (including wages). Conversely, it is our view[19] that, taking into account their huge reserve of active population with low productivity, currently attached to countryside activities—respectively around 400 and 350 million in China and India—and after considering the annual absorption capacity of workers by the industrial and services sectors of these two countries, the internal processes of labour-shift towards industry and services activities will *ceteris paribus* last 3-4 decades.

Bearing in mind mentioned magnitudes, we believe that if conditions of international trade keep on,[20] this new and unprecedented structural change would for long induce a rapid growth of the industrial and services employment in the Asian giants, and a mid (and perhaps long) term quasi-stagnation of the employment figures in the US and in the EU.[21]

This development could provoke disruption in western economies, which will force negotiations with China and India for timely smoothing the likely negative impact of Asian exports on Western economies. Any other solution, be this a commercial war, or even aggressions (direct or indirect) under pretexts, should be discarded because it would be a terrible experience for the whole planet.

---

19. As we have explained in our book about China and India (2005). Book already mentioned.
20. We are mainly referring to tariffs on imports, and exchange rates.
21. Recently, *The Economist* has pointed out that the current process of the industrial production shift towards Asia, will finally be a boon for the US and EU, which will see how their employment rates in the services sector will over-offset the current loses of employment in the industrial one. However, we believe that, when saying that, *The Economist* was thinking in the historical shifting process domestically observed among the productive sectors of the leading developed countries; but not in the international and massive breaking up of the current economic structure, induced by the mentioned near 40 per cent of the World population working at low wages, that recently embodied the international division of labour.

The Labour Market: A Non-considered Step for Efficient Globalisation

According to the theory of the second best,[22] it is not sure that the liberalisation of one market or a group of them, without liberalising the rest, will necessarily induce a global increase in economic welfare. It is also well known that the liberalisation applied to international trade of goods and movements of capital gathered momentum mainly along the 90s and first 2000, while in this period the different national labour markets (except within the EU) remained segmented, thus avoiding pooling of different supplies and demands of every labour speciality.

Despite of "second best" doubts and non-realised labour pooling, it seems that additional globalisation (materialised in the 90s and first 2000s) has meaningfully increased global welfare and employment at world scale, although—this is sure—non optimally and not for all.[23]

Globalisation of Labour Markets and Potential Effects

As easily deducible, from a "static point of view" and in a context of pure competence, the unification of previously homogeneous and segmented labour markets, with different functions of demand and supply and different wages in every segmented market, will generate a unique wage and an increase of the global economic welfare. Focusing on the sub-effects of this static global gain, we may say that suppliers to the market with lower initial wages (workers of developing countries), and demanders in markets with higher previous wages (firms of rich countries) will gain. Meanwhile the suppliers to the market with initial higher wages (workers of developed countries), and the demanders in the market with initially lower wages (firms of developing countries) will lose. This means that the real wages in

22. Vide. Krugman, P. and M. Obstfeld (2000). *Internacional Economics. Theory and Policy.* Asia: Pearson Education. p.225.
23. Although we have already discussed in depth the underlying problems of the current approach to globalisation—vide Rahman, R., and J.M. Andreu (2004: 49) in our book, *Responsible Global Governance*. New Delhi: Academic Foundation. Some authors are today initiating a soft critic to the recommended approach realised by the Washington Consensus. Vide to this respect, Linn, B. (2006: 13). "Globalisation must be saved from global utopians", *Financial Times*, May 30. Also well known is the sustained critical position against current globalisation—of course perfectly founded on Economic Theory—of Prof. Stiglitz, J., a recent winner of the Nobel Prize of Economics.

markets with initial high salaries, like those in the OECD countries, will experience a reduction, while the wages in markets with initial lower salaries, like those of developing countries, will register an increase. And all this will occur in parallel with a flow of workers from the second market to the first one, if authorised.[24]

To the extent that the new real wages in rich countries become lower than before, the used techniques of production will become relatively less intensive in capital. This will relatively reduce the internal demand of capital in these countries, which will induce a reduction in real interest rates. Conversely, in developing countries the newly increased wages will provoke a relative increase in the demand of capital, a movement that will bring an increase of real interest rates.

As a result of such changes in the interest rates, the effects of liberalisation of labour markets at global scale (if authorised) will induce additional movements of capital from rich countries towards the poor ones, while the real wages in poor countries will experience an upwards movement.

Looking now to the events of the last 15 years, we could say that, on the one hand rich countries have been pressing developing countries for additional liberalisation of the capital inflows coming from rich countries. On the other hand, rich countries have surprisingly moved in opposite direction by means of strictly limiting the liberalisation and de-segmentation of their own labour markets, which would have encouraged additional flows of capital towards developing countries.

This asymmetry in the external liberalisation and de-segmentation of the different markets of factors (capital and labour) is an additional example of the biased economic policies practiced by rich countries; and this against one of the main corollaries of the neo-classical model that they themselves purportedly promote. In this regard it is also paradoxical that while rich countries internally push for geographical mobility of labour in the name of market efficiency, they reject this

24. Mentioned flow of workers, with the same direction although with less intensity, will become an illegal reality when national labour markets remain legally segmented and the accumulated wages gap becomes significant.

mobility[25] when coming from abroad. Although we acknowledge the political sensitivity of this issue in rich countries, what we cannot understand is the asymmetrical use of arguments in international negotiations in the name of global competition.[26]

Migrations: History and Current Western Approach

In the context of the theoretical convenience of liberalisation of labour movements, it is interesting to keep in mind the international migration flows that occurred between 1950 and 1998. In this post-Second World War era, Western European countries received around 20 million immigrants,[27] while the so-called "European Immigration Countries"[28] received 34 million.

Note, however, that rich countries not always received net migration. Indeed, up to the Second World War, Europe was a net issuer of migrants. Specifically, between 1870 and 1949 there was a significant exodus of Europeans (Table 2.3), who tried to improve their poor living conditions by moving abroad. This trend changed significantly from 1950 onwards due to: 1) the need of workers for European reconstruction following the huge killings of males in the Second World War; and 2) the immigration "commitments" of western European governments with ex-colonies.

Concerning Western Europe, and taking into account the period 1950-2007, in which it received around 30 million immigrants—20 million up to 1998, plus another (approximated) 10 million between 1998 and 2007—we may say that total immigration represents today around 6-7 per cent of the total EU population.[29]

---

25. Normally, when developing countries pose the labour mobility problem (or part of it) in international trade negotiations (in WTO) against own concessions in trade, Western countries divert this discussion to the International Labour Organisation. And they do this as if the underlying problem was theoretically different from that of the freedom of the movements of capital that rich countries constantly defend within WTO.
26. On this respect readers may consult Legrain, P. (2006). *Immigrants: Your Country Needs Them*. Little, Brown. This is a book in which the author clearly defends a position pro free-migration.
27. Since 1950 up to 1998, Western European countries approximately received 20 million immigrants, mainly from Mediterranean and other developing countries.
28. This group of "European Immigration Countries" includes Australia, New Zealand, Canada and the US. Vide. Chart 2.1, taken from Maddison, A. (2001: 128). Book already mentioned.
29. In this 6-7 per cent are not included the individuals belonging to the second generation of migrants, because they are already nationals. Higher rates of fertility of migrant-women have also increased the visibility of some social groups, although not in fact the number of migrants.

Table 2.3

Net Migration in Western Countries, 1870-1998
(in Miles; Negative Sign Implies Outflow)

	1870-1913	*1914-49*	*1950-73*	*1974-98*
France	890	-236	3630	1026
Germany	-2598	-304	7070	5911
Italy	-4459	-1771	-2139	1617
UK	-6415	-1405	-605	737
Total West Europe	-13996	-3662	9381	10898
Japan	n.a.	197	-72	-179
Australia	885	673	2033	2151
New Zealand	290	138	247	87
Canada	861	207	2126	2680
US	15820	6221	8257	16721
Total EIC group	17856	7239	12663	21639

Source: Maddison, A. (2001: 128) Book already mentioned.

Note that these immigrants, particularly visible in some European cities and quarters, have contributed with 0.15 per cent points to the annual growth rate of the population of Western Europe that, in the period 1950-2005 was only 0.50 per cent; and this despite the "alleged"[30] higher growth rate desired by governments for the Western European population.[31]

Observe that this scant European population growth rate (0.5%), well under the population growth rate registered in the rest of the rich world, has contributed in the last 25 years to the ageing of the EU population, to the reduction of the growth rates of the European labour-force and GDP and to the growing EU-US GDP gap.

Assessing mentioned EU immigration in the last 50 years, we have to mention two main traits of it: 1) Its insufficient annual quantity in relative terms, as already commented; and 2) Its changing approach: initially encouraging just temporal migration of unskilled labourers,

30. The reality is that, although complaining on the scant natural growth of their populations, European authorities have neither practised a policy of easy entry for foreigners, nor sufficiently stimulated—with social subsidies—the fertility rates of European women.
31. The desirable growth rate of Western European population should be higher than the current one to solve problems of ageing and financing of public pensions at current levels. In this regard the figures registered by the US population in the same period, with a growth rate of around 1 per cent, are more promissory.

and from the 90s onwards, selecting only the best and the brightest coming from developing countries and LDC.[32]

Mentioned approach of selective immigration has different motivations, some of them rational, but others founded in short-term self-interest. For instance, if after the costly graduation of domestic engineers, doctors, nurses, teachers, etc.—mainly financed in developing countries by the poor via indirect taxes—most of them migrate (on invitation) to the rich world to improve their personal lives,[33] the only expectable output of the public education investment in countries of origin will be some monetary transfers to families.[34] But if these migrants settle and integrate in the receiving country, these remittances will progressively dwindle and perhaps disappear.

Analysts of brain drain additionally suggest other negative circumstances and effects, such as the possibility that heavy subsidised higher education (partially exported) coexists with a non-universally extended basic education, thus depriving the country of significant future incomes, gender equality, and more moderated demographic growth as it happens in India.

Finally, some observers suggest that, given the fact that education is a factor that has to work together with others, if the latter does not exist in convenient quantities, the additional output of marginal investment in education will be higher abroad than inside,[35] thus being convenient for the country the promotion of graduates exports during short periods of time.

Note additionally that indiscriminate brain exports from LDC to the West goes against the generalised practice of multinationals in western countries: when someone profits from the formation facilities of a western firm, the involved person will have to work in the firm

---

32. This is the policy currently promoted by relevant western countries, as for instance France (remember the recent proposal to the National Assembly (2006) of its then Home Ministry, and today President of the Republic, Mr. Sarkozy).

33. Vide to this respect Kapur, D. and McHale, J. (2005). "Give us your Best and Brightest", Quoted in *The Economist* (2005), November 5. p.86.

34. The assessment would be different if the volume of migrants were only a small fraction of the collective of candidates to migrate, as it happens for instance in India, (which has only exported a figure under 10 per cent of its graduate population. Negative assessment would be valid if the volume of graduates export were a significant proportion of graduates, as it is currently occurring in some African countries.

35. Vide. Stark, O. *et al.* (2005). "Again with a Drain?. Evidence from Rural Mexico on the New Economics of the Brain Drain", Quoted by *The Economist* (2005), November 5. p.86.

a minimum number of years, or to give back to the firm part or the total education funds invested in him or her.

Consequently, we do believe that the selective immigration approach recently practiced by many western countries, should eventually include a significant compensation to the issuing countries, which otherwise, after having invested in the education of the exported graduates—mainly paid by the poor—would be deprived from their investment, just in exchange of some temporal remittances.

Hangover in the West after Engineering Distortion of Markets

Due to the shortcomings of its approach, the new trade and financial conditions produced by the process of globalisation are already generating unpleasant financial and trade effects in the West. Note that Western countries, looking for new opportunities in the field of FDI, have in the last 17 years put steady pressure on leading Asian developing countries, for getting additional abatement of FDI admission conditions. To the extent that these pressures have succeeded, own automatisms of the market economy have induced something perhaps not considered, or at least not sufficiently analysed by western strategists: the problem of progressive "dislocation" of western industries.

Observe that in the recent past, domestic dislocation of the different industries has frequently played a positive role in the internal development of many (western) countries. In fact, this dislocation of productive assets from overcrowded and expensive cities towards "poles or hubs" of development, in search of lower wages and economies of de-congestion, followed by internal migration to these poles, was encouraged by public powers in the West. This strategy for internal dislocation forced the unemployed of overcrowded areas to emigrate to mentioned poles, or those under-employed in the neighbourhood (in the primary sector) to shift to industrial or services activities in the new poles, thus increasing the "average" per capita income, while generating additional domestic employment at national scale.

Regrettably for the West, the current FDI dislocation at international scale, is a very different one, and the governments of western countries are in split, having to grudgingly welcome at short term the increase of their GNP (not GDP) by means of encouraging FDI towards developing countries, thus indirectly creating industrial employment in these countries in detriment of the internal creation of (more expensive) jobs in the West. Of course, western international dislocation towards developing countries (mainly to China) could not be followed by migration of jobless westerners to these countries, as it happened internally in the West in other historical moments.

Consequently, if things continue as they are nowadays, there will only be few realistic options[36] for preserving industrial jobs in the West. The basic option will be the rapid reduction of real wages in the West to defend competitiveness.[37] A commercial alternative, consisting of almost arresting or reversing the current process towards freer trade would be dangerous and non-advisable.

Certainly, if the commercial liberalisation process quickly arrests or reverses in the West, large parts of the realised FDI in developing countries—previously done to export on better price conditions towards the West—will change into losses of the involved MNC, which, in addition to the contractive effects of a relative depression of trade, could additionally fuel an economic down-turn at a world scale.

However, it is likely that, in trying to meddle in the process, and paying for time, western governments embark in an intermediate strategy: putting progressively new hindrances to the industrial exports of the developing countries, with additional emphasis on quality and technical standards, spare-parts guarantees, sufficient branching for post-sale services, etc.

Following the history of the biased interpretation of the neoclassical model at an international scale, we do believe that the West will likely arrest or delay[38] the process of dismantling the barriers for agriculture

36. We have commented several times that an increase of the working schedule of Western workers to sufficiently increase western competitiveness is something out of reality.

37. Observe that if globalisation had been well implemented along the last decades, with parallel freer and progressive movements of all factors, capital and labour, the absurd situation of today would not have become real. As a consequence of greater migrations towards the West, western salaries would have not grown so much, and the current need for industrial dislocation would have not been so urgent.

38. As a result of the recent agreement achieved in Geneva (August 2004), on the elimination of export subsidies to agricultural products in the West, this elimination has compulsory started in 2007 and will be phased out... "in 2017". Indeed, in front of former pledges made in the Uruguay Round in 1995, mentioned agreement represents a continuation of the unfair treatment of the poor farmers of the South.

goods and services coming from developing countries, in particular agro-industrial goods. Of course, in such a harsh context, one could not completely rule out the possibility of a WTO bifurcation.

Summarising one may say that nowadays the Western world seems to be captured in the subtle trap that the "invisible hand" has always reserved as punishment for market-economy twisters. To the extent that the goods, services and factors markets are tightly connected, to device a partial international liberalisation as it was engineered by the West, particularly between 1970 and first 1990, had to be conducive to the creation of a mechanical monster which is today disturbing Western countries.

Instead of liberalising more or less at the same speed the markets of goods, services and factors, Western governments and multilateral institutions mainly promoted trade liberalisation of industrial goods (to increase industrial exports to developing countries) and movements of capital towards developing countries (to rise FDI opportunities), while they kept labour markets segmented. As a result and for decades, they stimulated rapid growth of (industrial and general) wages in the rich world, while keeping the immigration process towards the West almost banned. This policy of protecting middle-classes in the West, significantly limited the creation of jobs at a world scale, while it forced the maintenance of very low wages in the developing world.

After decades of practising this policy, the comparative industrial (and general) wages across the world (China-India-West) have become dramatically unbalanced; and their differences scaring because they seem non-bridgeable by means of gradual manoeuvres for increasing productivity.

Evolution of Inter-regional Differences of Per Capita GDP

The working of the neo-classical model, with its flexibility in prices of goods and services and free mobility of all factors, will in the long run automatically[39] tend to equalise the per capita GDP of

39. In the neo-classical model the word "automatic" does not imply any temporal reference to markets clearing. Consequently, the foreseeable process of convergence implicit in this model has no specific timeframe.

the different countries and regions.[40] As a result, any initial difference in prices of factors, wages and interest rates, should in time become smaller, thus generating a progressive convergence in the standard of living of all citizens. Provided that these equal (or not very different) standards of living were accepted by societies, a process of unconditional economic convergence[41] should induce political and social sustainability at global scale.

However, one should not forget that some natural barriers to trade and movements of factors exist, thus averting or delaying mentioned convergence. One of these barriers refers to the so-called transactional costs. In this case, the larger the invested resources in settling contracts are—as it happens for instance in the current process of international labour mobility—the lesser will be the profits stemming from interchange. As a consequence, an increase in the facilitation of contracting will favour the mobility of goods, services and factors, with gains for all players.

Another natural barrier to trade is the existence of transport and communication costs. These costs, defined as the value of the economic resources necessary to move the commodities or to transmit the information from one place to another, introduce an additional limitation in the working of the principle of comparative advantage, thus negatively affecting those countries that are far from the gravity centre of the world trade, or relatively disconnected. Consequently, the cheaper and quicker are the modes of communication and transport,[42] the more perceivable will be the comparative advantage of the different countries, and all the more international trade will be promoted, thus

---

40. The degree of convergence of per capita GDPs would be determined, among other things, by the initial distribution of available assets (land, capital, etc.) among countries and among different groups of citizens in every country.

41. There are at least three possible scenarios for the evolution of living standards throughout the world: unconditional convergence, conditional convergence, and no convergence at all. Following Abel and Bernanke, "by unconditional convergence we mean that the poor countries eventually will catch up with the rich countries so that in the long run individual living standards around the world become more or less the same. (In this regard) the (neoclassical) model predicts unconditional convergence (only) under certain special conditions". Vide Abel, A. and Bernanke, B. (2001). *Macroeconomics*. Pearson Education. p.228.

42. Costs of transport dramatically fall in the 19th century when railways and steamboats became of common use. In the 20th century the development of transport by road, and the introduction of containers, also reduced the costs of transport in a relevant way. The reduction of the information costs along the second half of the 20th century, particularly in the 90s (ITC Revolution), has been simply spectacular.

increasing the total gains coming from trade. Note that all this will be conditioned to the fact that governments do not erect or raise artificial barriers to trade, as tariff and non-tariff barriers (quotas, etc.) are.

Although natural barriers to trade and movements of factors have always existed, it is clear that the unitary transactional, transport and communication costs have experienced a monotonous decrease along the last 150 years (dramatically in the last 15 years with the ICT revolution); and this while in the last half a century, artificial barriers to trade have progressively, although asymmetrically, been abated in successive GATT-WTO negotiations.

Logically, if this joint progressive abatement of natural and artificial barriers had worked properly, it would have made the functioning of the neo-classical corollaries in the international field easier, and facilitated the initiation of an unconditional convergence.

Maddison´s Figures on "Non-convergence"

However, as measured by Maddison (Table 2.4), and with the exception of the "golden age of capitalism" (period 1950-1973), real convergence has not moved according to expectations stemming from the neo-classical model. Firstly, in the period 1870-1913, also called the age of "traditional liberalism", the disparity of the per capita GDP among the different regions of the world,[43] far from declining almost

Table 2.4

Per Capita GDP and Inter-Regional Differences, 1870-1998
(in US Dollars of 1990, PPP)

	1870	*1913*	*1950*	*1973*	*1998*
Western Europe	1974	3473	4594	11534	17921
EIC group	2431	5257	9288	16172	26146
Japan	737	1387	1926	1439	20413
Asia (excluding Japan)	543	640	635	1231	2936
Latin America	698	1511	2554	4531	5795
Sov. Union & Satell.	919	1501	2601	5729	4354
Africa	444	585	852	1365	1368
World	867	1510	2114	4104	5709
Disparity	5:1	9:1	15:1	13:1	19:1

Source: Maddison, A. (2001: 126). Book already mentioned.

43. This disparity is measured by the quotient of the per capita GDP of the richest region of the world and that of the poorest one.

doubled thus widening the gap between the most prosperous group of countries (EIC group) and the poorest one (Africa). This disparity became even much greater between 1913 and 1950, increasing three-fold as compared to that of 1870.

In the "golden age period" (1950-1973), when paradoxically public intervention in Western countries was more intense than before—mainly for reconstructing Europe—and Keynesian policies were openly (and at times recklessly) applied for reducing unemployment rates, the world economy experienced its quickest growth rate,[44] while the degree of regional disparities of per capita GDP downgraded from 15:1 to 13:1.[45] However, years later, in the neo-liberal era (1973-1998), which is a part of the recent period of additional impulse towards globalisation", the disparity of per capita GDP of the different regions mounted to the figure of 19:1.

As a consequence all seems to point out that in the last 15 years of globalisation—and despite expectations of unconditional convergence created by aggressive pretenders—this type of convergence has not become a reality.

Such a disappointing result does not mean that we should get rid of the neo-classical (economic) model for masterminding policies, or look for a more direct and extensive public intervention as practised in the past. In order to correct induced problems, we should get rid of dysfunctions and inefficiencies of current interpretation of neoclassicism, while introducing a more rational and comprehensive approach to it; and this with a political priority for economic catching up (by poor nations) in a reasonable time-span, conditioned to sustainability in physical and democratic terms, as defended by us all along this book.

Alternative Dubious Figures Supporting Recent Unconditional Convergence

If the trend towards per capita income divergence continues, the economic and political implications of Maddison´s figures—in a

44. In the first 2000s global GDP growth rates have also been intense, although the applied model has been one more tilted towards the market (neoclassical model).

45. After gaining independence, relative increase of public expenditure in infrastructures and setting up of public industries were strategies adopted by many developing countries. This initiative, jointly with an almost generalised implementation of import-substitution policies, directed to encourage domestic private industrialisation, (provisionally) pushed activity up in many developing countries.

frame of full and live information across the world—will necessarily be negative. It is our view that, in this context towards growing unevenness, current economic and political situations will not be sustainable in the mid-long run; and the urgent and necessary setting up of a global democracy—for reaching (physical and political) sustainability—will become more difficult.

Nonetheless, there are other scholars who have concluded the opposite: that the convergence of the per capita income among the different countries of the world has become a fact all along the past 90s and first years of the current decade. Of particular interest are the figures of Prof. Sala-i-Martin of Columbia University (New York);[46] figures that suggest that the rapid rising of incomes in those years, especially in Asia, has created a huge middle class in that Continent, thus making global per capita incomes more equal than before.

Specifically, by playing with average per capita incomes[47] of each of considered developed and developing countries, Sala-i-Martin has tried to prove that the current process of globalisation has reduced the relative per capita income gap. Regrettably, we find that his analysis is partially mistaken.

Although the methodology of Sala-i-Martin enables to deduce a certain "unconditional convergence", it is our view that such a methodology is not fully correct.[48] Undeniably, in some very populated countries of the world, that have recently experienced rapid growth rates—as for instance in China and India—the internal income distribution has worsened in the last two decades, due to the fact

---

46. Vide. Sala-i-Martin, X.(2002). "The World Distribution of Income", *NBER Working Paper* No.8933; and Sala-i-Martin, X.(2006) "The World Distribution of Income: Falling Poverty and Convergence Period." *QJE*. May. Issue 2.

47. We do believe that the idea of weighting the per capita income of every country with its population, to make an initial evaluation of the evolution of per capita income disparity of the different countries of the world, is ceteris paribus correct. Nevertheless, if internal distribution of per capita income in many countries or in the most important ones had worsened in the period, the result could be deeply deceptive.

48. Indeed, "these aggregate comparisons give an incomplete picture. When considering human development within countries, inequality must be taken into account, because simple comparisons of p.c. GDP assume that every one in a country has the same income...Long term trend in interpersonal inequality, using PPP, shows that the World has become much more unequal. Between 1970 and the 90s the world has become more unequal than in any time before". Vide. UN Development Programme (2002). *Human Development Report 2002*. p.19.

that a great percentage of their (poorest and rural) populations has been left behind.

We do believe that the lack of consideration in the Sala-i-Martin analysis of the evolution of the internal income distribution in the different considered countries falsifies the argument that in the last 15 years there has been "unconditional convergence" thanks to the "acceleration" of the globalisation process.

Really, if international movements of people are not free, those of capital are limited and asymmetric, exports of agricultural products from developing countries have no free access in the West, and poorer countries of the world have larger growth rates of population than the richer ones, unconditional convergence is theoretically unlikely. If we add to these hindrances the internal existence of higher degrees of monopoly in developing countries, unconditional convergence is today practically non-reachable.

To conclude, if one takes as more reliable the figures of Maddison,[49] one has to agree to the case of non-convergence. The regional income disparity in the world has almost monotonically grown from 1870—when it was 5:1—to a figure of 19:1 in 1998. And in the last two-three decades of the 20th century nothing less than 168 "shaking countries" experienced a per capita GDP slumping or stagnant.[50] Indeed, a panorama that makes difficult the necessary and urgent progress towards (national and) global democracy.[51]

Poverty Reduction as an Insufficient Target in the World Today

In front of the almost generalised conviction on the existence of a growing per capita income gap, which is today one of the main causes of discontent in many poor countries, multilateral economic

---

49. Vide. Maddison, A. (2001: 126). Book already mentioned. Trends extracted from the figures of Maddison are coinciding with the ideas expressed by other commentators, as for instance, by Stiglitz, J. (2006: 37), when he quotes examples of the worsening of the personal income distribution in many countries; and with the ideas expressed by studies realised by multilateral institutions (UNDP).
50. Vide Maddison, A. (2001: 58). Book already mentioned.
51. Note that, within countries, achieving sustainable (national) democracy becomes easier the more economically homogeneous the society is. Similarly—by means of progressive unconditional convergence—the more homogeneous becomes the global society, the easier will be for the international community to organise either a collective provision of the global public goods, or a correct management of the global externalities, under the aegis of new democratic UN.

institutions—basically World Bank and International Monetary Fund—and Western countries themselves, have in 2000 established a mild and short-sighted target consisting of halving the number of poor living under the poverty-line before 2015.

Observe that this indulgent target, whose possible fulfilling in time (2015) is under discussion, veils other non-pursued targets that are provoking mounting discontent (growing economic gap and exclusion) in many national communities.

Note additionally that the mentioned target of halving the relative number of poor in the world, although fulfilled, would be consistent with only a mild reduction of the absolute number of people placed under the line of two dollars a day. Consequently, although mentioned target may be useful for sedating Western governments and citizens, it will not be capable of solving the underlying problems of discontent.[52] In the new historical tempo, wherein the basic human rights have been upgraded everywhere and the information is full and live, this meagre target accompanied by other proposals (primary education for all and improving of health by 2015), even if fulfilled, will not solve the huge social problems the world is today facing.

Conversely, we do believe that the fulfilment of these paltry targets will only worsen the social situation at a global scale, since poor citizens of the poorest countries will then become more aware of their relative deprivation, which will likely provoke more frustration and irritation. Note in this respect that the degree of discontent is a positive function of the discrepancies in standards of living, and a negative one in relation to the reduction of extreme poverty in relative terms.

Economic Non-convergence and Negative Consequences for all

We have described in the lines above, the non-existence of economic unconditional convergence among the different countries of the international community, while at the same time we have affirmed that the internal distribution of income has worsened in most of the

52. In this respect, vide. Sen, Amartya (2006). "Mondialisation et Justice Social." *Le Monde. Samedi, 20 mai.*

developed and developing countries in the last 15 years, that is to say in times of the recent "additional" steps towards globalisation.

As we will see in Chapter 4, a significant degrading of the (internal) personal income distribution could jeopardise the democratic political organisation of a country, or pave the way to dictatorship. Note that although in principle this would just be an internal political matter, mentioned political shift could induce spill-over effects (through imitation) on other communities.

Likewise, as we have already mentioned and will develop in Chapters 4 and 5, a continuation of progressive economic divergence—or just sine die keeping the gap among per capita GDP of nations—could make difficult the creation of a new democratic UN with capabilities for enforcing resolutions with legitimacy, and with real power for the deliverance of global public goods and for rightly administrating global externalities.

Unfortunately, most commentators in the world ignore the delicate relations between personal distribution of income, sustainable democracy and legitimate delivery of global public goods. Indeed, some of these commentators—sustaining that "unrestricted" capitalism is the only feasible economic system, which necessarily has to be founded on significant personal economic unevenness coming from effort and efficiency—use to forget historical "non-competitive" ways of accession to wealth: appropriation of land (with parallel deprivation of others), industrial and financial concentration driving economies towards monopolisation, economic top relations between political power and corporations for changing ownership, etc.; and more important, the fact that democracy has always been a system in a delicate equilibrium between efficiency and equity.[53]

Even more, many of these commentators (neo-liberals and neo-cons) defend that the growth of the public system of protection (Social Security) in developing countries, or just its maintenance in the developed ones is a bad economic strategy for economic progress. In addition, they insist that contrary to "socialist" expectations, the

53. Neo-liberals and neo-cons should not forget that, in a democratic context, it is not convenient for the collective that an overwhelming majority of citizens results economically deprived—via markets—in benefit of a rich minority. In a democratic context, this rich minority would ultimately democratically expelled from economic and political power.

development of Social Security always has worked against the interests of own labourers, because it needs rising taxes, thus de-stimulating GDP growth and finally inducing unemployment. Symmetrically, as if the violent history of the first half of the 20th century in the West, or the civil wars in developing countries in the second half of the last century had just been a pure fantasy, they do not find in their discourse any direct relation between poverty and violence (national and international).

In this regard, although many observers—including some neo-con (or neo-liberal) prime ministers of some Western countries—nowadays assure that there is no relation among the low (or very low) levels of the economic development of certain communities and the recent outburst of violent activities, and even international terrorism,[54] we firmly believe that there are direct or indirect relations between these two variables.

Longstanding feelings of frustration and indignation may change into protests, riots and violent actions,[55] when groups of poor, after becoming well aware of their unnatural economic disadvantage, take conscience of their incapacity for getting justice through peaceful means; and this while (national or international) rich communities or groups, using economic advantage in their own benefit, torpedo any peaceful initiative of the poor for improving their lot.

Although huge economic gaps within or among communities may be at the core of the frustrations of the poorest, one cannot discard political or sociological exclusion as complementary motives for violent outbursts. Conversely, the rich of the world, though belonging to different ethnic or religious communities, rarely feel excluded by other rich.

---

54. Some people absurdly blame Islam for international terrorism, while ignoring longstanding political frustrations suffered by some Muslim communities.

55. Indeed, most violent revolutions in history have started in the same way and at similar moments: when the majority of the population—for long poor and mistreated by a privileged minority attached to their wealth and incapable of solidarity—decides that the current state of affairs cannot continue. For an extended explanation of this argument, vide. Saboul, A. (1972). *Précis histoire de la revolution francaise*. Paris: Editions Sociales. Vide. Introductory Chapter titled: “La crise de l’ancien régime”.

Economic Divergence (1870-1914) and Results

History is to be analysed. If we observe the economic and political history of Europe, we may deduce that many of the negative events that occurred in the last years of the 19th century and the first half of the 20th century could have been averted by the rich, without significant long-term economic sacrifices. In particular, if the then economic and political powerful groups had acted with a rational long-term prospect—thus considering the negative political consequences of their lack of economic solidarity—history would have rolled in another manner.

Going back in history, one may remember the watertight agricultural labour markets, typical of the pre-industrialisation age. These markets were almost completely segmented. This segmentation made possible that wages in the different markets were diverse and in general placed at very low levels.[56] We will add that in this context, almost the entire economic surplus was for the landlords, the owners of the then sole scant factor: the land. According to David Ricardo, the different surpluses obtained by landlords had to do with the difference in quality of their plots.[57]

This unfair social situation, typical of agriculture societies, could indefinitely remain because: 1) the different labour markets were not connected; 2) there was no accessible and truthful economic information, thus poor workers believing that theirs was the natural state of things; and 3) the egalitarian philosophies that so much would change the world in the future, had not appeared or become popular.

56. The theory of "subsistence wages", developed among others by Smith, clearly reflected the idea that the labour market in the long term will always tend to generate subsistence wages. According to the ideas of Smith it would be possible that these wages grew for a while, but the incidence of this growth in the evolution of population (increasing it), would force future reductions of wages, thus making them to converge again to subsistence rates. Note that this theory was abandoned many decades later because it did not consider the growth rate of labour productivity and the evolution of modern demography (practically independent of economic fluctuations).

57. The theory of the land rent is original from David Ricardo. This classical author explained that if it was possible to freely find non-exploited land of acceptable quality, then no one would pay a rent for using others´ land. However, if this was not the case, since all arable land was already exploited (as it happened in Britain at the beginning of 19th century), everybody who wanted to take over a plot would have to pay a rent to the owner. This rent would be variable according to the quality of the plot. As a consequence, competition between tenants, resulting in increased rents for better plots, would deprive them in the long run of any surplus, which would instead only be enjoyed by owners.

Consequently for centuries social injustice and political stability could coexist, and many times coexisted (although with some "political" changes of seigniors).

This unfair and—not so "naturally"—balanced world, collapsed with the arrival of industrial-urban societies. In these societies, the wages of every market were known by all players while the idea of abuse (exploitation) of labour by the owners of the new scant factor (capital) started gaining ground.

In this new and informed context, the second industrial revolution witnessed some of the direct results of the neo-classical model when non-competitive behaviour is the rule—in particular in abusive labour markets—or, simply, when free competition in labour markets generates famine wages.[58] Note that these styled facts occurred in parallel with an unprecedented industrial growth rate in Western European countries and North America.

To the extent that the Marxian analysis was capable of explaining some causes of the observed problems of income sharing and working conditions, this new perspective easily gained ground; in particular, among trade unionists who used this new approach as a foundation in their struggle for conquering better wages and working conditions for workers.

In those days, Trade Unions acted primarily as a mechanism of information dissemination among their associates, and used certain tools to support negotiations, such as strikes, pickets, and so on. The derivatives in Europe of actions and reactions among trade unionists and left politicians on the one hand, and entrepreneurs and governments on the other, were manifold; in particular, in negotiations on working conditions and, at times, in the political battles for taking over.

In the middle of these new and threatening political stances, the then liberal states (the most advanced ones in national democratic terms at that time), prone to mainly defend formal rights of owners without paying significant attention to social aspects, had to necessarily remain unattractive to the masses in most European countries.

58. These facts are nowadays well observable, for instance in South Asia, where many people do all kinds of jobs they can do to earn a minimal living. It is interesting to visit these areas. Just by seeing reality, extreme defenders of the current approach of the neo-classical model could reconsider their aloof intellectual positions.

The result of the stubborn blindness of the rich (concerning social rights of the majority), who were in control of key positions in liberal states and traditional societies, drove Europe to a social and political escalation with a tragic outcome of two world wars. Let us here insist that if the European masses had not been so deprived, these wars probably would not have become a reality. Instead, growing middle classes and faster arrival to more franchised democracies to soften the "struggle of classes" and to create more opportunities to those deprived, would have likely been the political roads of the European societies.

Emergence of a Welfare State Inside Europe

After two human and material catastrophes, the European governments learned a lesson of history and started building or enlarging the so-called welfare state. Previous economic exploitation of masses by firms, and frequent human rights violations by the machinery of traditional "democratic" states or dictatorships, should no longer be a pattern of behaviour. The costs (two European wars and constant social unrest) generated by mentioned myopic political and economic behaviour had been huge and could not continue after the Second World War.

The construction or improvement of the welfare state, significantly changed the social scene; but mainly within Western Europe. Indeed, the behaviour of this sub-continent in relation to the rest of the world continued being economically short-ranged although to a lesser extent than that of the US.

Delayed Win-Win Solution: The European Welfare State

In fact, soon after the Second World War, the different Western European countries started the construction or the expansion of their welfare states. The creation of more sufficient and fairer fiscal systems, in parallel to an unprecedented growth rate of the western economies in the "golden age" of capitalism (1950-1973), encouraged the different European states to construct or complement public systems of pensions, national health services, and systems of public education for the promotion of equal opportunities for all.

Indeed, few of the rich who at the beginning of the 20th century opposed the construction of the welfare state, could have imagined that some decades later the alleged "huge costs" of building the welfare state would result in a highly profitable strategy for European societies. In fact, this economic effort done in the name of internal solidarity proved its relevance, enabling the rapid increase of the long term labour productivity. This rapid productivity growth was the result of the guaranteed social stability, the huge increase of human capital due to generalised education, and also the cheap imports of raw materials from developing countries.

The European democracies also introduced or consecrated the concept of the minimum wage. The establishing of this minimum wage, although criticised by many economists in the 70s—because it introduced an element of inflexibility that decreased the availability of jobs in some situations—for decades played an important social role in some Western European countries.[59]

The new financial possibilities of the states in the "golden age" period also enabled the setting up of internal regional policies, mainly dealing with the creation of sufficient infrastructure to improve connections among markets of different regions. This new public search for correcting internal geographical imbalances, although it had its enemies too, reaped significant good results in terms of economic homogenisation within European countries. The same could be said in relation to the inter-regional transfers of funds later organised by the European Union to facilitate the catching up of the poorest new member-states.

It has been said all along the last 25 years that the setting up, or the completion, of these welfare state systems brought inefficiencies, and this is true. Although the intentions of legislators were good, in some cases the possibility of misusing public funds appeared. However, as in any "trial and error" procedure, the initially committed mistakes should not encourage the scrapping of the welfare systems, as some

59. When "minimum wages" were legally established in Europe they were welcomed because, in many cases, market wages were under their levels of competitive equilibrium, thus generating less employment than the potential one. This means that some former labour market situations were oligopsonistic or, at least, non-competitive. Consistently, with the introduction of minimum wages in those days the average paid salary rose and the level of employment increased.

non-neutral observers demand, but its progressive correction, thus making efficiency and equity to co-exist to the maximum extent.

In this regard, the current observable trend in Europe to degrade the role of public sectors and welfare systems—supported by market fundamentalists—is something that should be carefully analysed from a multi-disciplinary perspective, because it could jeopardise future social peace, and even consolidated democracies. To sacrifice social peace for encouraging short-term efficiency would be an absurdity conducive to mistakes in timing and aims that would sacrifice general long-term prosperity and opportunities for all.

The West and its Disappointing Relation to Developing Countries

For decades (from 1950 till today), the Western countries, including the European ones, were not capable of organising a decent financing plan to solve, in a reasonable period of time (2 or 3 decades) the economic problems—including building up Social Security—of the poorer developing countries, mostly former exploited colonies.

Letting aside the US—which for decades continued doing its own way[60] in its relations with LDC—Europe overlooking its own historical experiences of the first half of 20th century, also renounced to make a sufficient effort for the promotion of growth in developing countries. In the 90s western selfishness even increased and progressed in the wrong direction. This was a decade in which the spreading of a new US-lead neo-liberal capitalism, combined with fragmented, insufficient and non-organised development aid and inconvenient trade rules, worsened the problem of the growing economic gap.

One should not forget that in the "golden age" (1950-1973) there was a significant difference in approach between Europe and US concerning the economic promotion of developing countries. Later on, although with exceptions, the European economic policy towards developing countries became similar to that encouraged by the US and the Washington Consensus. Note that in its latest version, the

60. In this period, the US was the leading "donor" in absolute terms, although very modest in GDP terms. Note additionally that the US donations were mainly geopolitical and just accidentally connected with poverty alleviation. Perhaps all this happened because the US, despite having implemented the Marshall Plan after the WW2 did not trust "international public transfers" of funds to poor countries as an effective mechanism for enhancing development and avoiding future international political problems.

Washington Consensus policy deals with transplanting to LDC an economic model of international relations that, in our view, only can work efficiently after long periods of transition; and always conditioned to the setting up of enabling infrastructures.[61]

Due to the fact that such economic approach was defective in the application of some crucial corollaries of neo-classicism,[62] it had necessarily to generate sub-optima outcomes. In this regard we do believe that few academic economists would agree on the possibility of reaching an optimum in global welfare, by means of encouraging international flows of capitals, whereas international flows of labour are forbidden and access to western agriculture and services markets are limited.

From our perspective as outsiders, we wonder why important professional economists or academicians have not devoted more time to explain the problems contained in the Washington Consensus. The answer seems to us quite clear and was explained three decades ago by Feyerabend, a famous methodologist of science.[63] Indeed—as he could have suggested—whoever goes against the mainstream runs the risk of becoming isolated not only in academic circles but also in the race for obtaining research funding or political postings. Circumstances that many a times create among scientists an invincible fear to exhibit discrepancies, particularly on relevant issues. Regrettably, and during a certain period that may be long—that is to say, till the moment in which the former situation becomes unbearable—this fear uses to be a drag for the progression of knowledge and action.

61. As a proof of the defective strategy exclusively based on private initiative, as recommended by the Washington Consensus, one could refer to a recent report of the UNCTAD. In this report it was said: "the 50 poorest countries of the World will not develop if they do not create—or if others do not help to create—production and employment capacities". Indeed, the strong growth (5.9%) experienced by LDC in 2004, after decades of semi-stagnation, has been based on exports of raw materials and increased agricultural production; a growth that has not created employment. Vide. *Le Monde* (2006: 9) 22 *Juillet. La CNUCED denonce une croissance "sans employ" dans les pays le plus pauvres.*

62. It is curious to note that some contemporary communists, who in other times defended political stances very far away from those stemming from the neo-classical model, have today started defending international free movements of labour within the neo-classical model, as a more consistent approach for reaching a fairer income distribution at a global scale.

63. This author, in his famous contribution, denounced the fact that, against believed, the way of advancing in science is not so linear, objective, and based on falsification of former theories, as proposed by Karl Popper, but permeated by limitative sociological components. Vide. Feyerabend, P.C. (1975). *Against Method: An Outline of an Anarchistic Theory of Knowledge*. London: New Left Books.

Expectable Reactions of Poor Societies to the Behaviour of the West

It is surprising to see how current Western governments—who should be well aware of the catastrophic results of exploitation of informed poor, as it happened domestically in Europe before the Second World War—are repeating today the same mistakes in their economic relations with developing countries, which—let us not forget—are in demographic majority. Indeed, after observing the (international) growing economic gap registered since the 70s, one becomes bewildered when observing the indifference and lack of acumen exhibited by successive Western leaderships.

Perhaps the distance in time and civilisation made this international neglect more understandable in the first decades of the second half of the 20th century. Much more incredible has been the maintenance of this stance in the 80s and 90s. Particularly in the last decade in which the historical tempo accelerated its rhythm as a result of the great leap forward registered in information technology and communications. It seems as if the rich countries were barely concerned with the fate of the rest of human beings in the world, under the wrong assumption that the destiny of the poor could not affect their lives and communities. This is a clear misconception, since the negative effects of the economic oblivion of the poor are already pervasively perceivable in terms of human security.

It is surprising that at this turning point in history, no relevant Western country or multilateral organisation has tried to seriously project current trends, and to suggest some measures to significantly correct[64] the *ceteris paribus* non-brilliant economic future of poor countries. Only some individuals and private institutions have made undertones on the convenience of using different or complementary strategies, founded on effective[65] and sufficient commitments, for the promotion of fast development of the poor.

---

64. The most elaborated proposal to correct the present economic and political problems of the world was presented in 2000 by the UN, in the context of the so-called UN Millennium Targets. However, this was a limited proposal, whose targets will not likely be reached even in 2015 by the lack of sufficient and effective financial transfers of funds and technology by the West.

65. At times these commitments, mainly signed for internal political consumption in Western countries (reports in TV on trips of European Prime Ministers in Asia or Africa) do not materialise, thus creating more hopelessness in the LDC.

We have to say that, against general opinion, these approaches for fast development of the poor, are affordable,[66] could improve the standards of life of the many, and could save, in the mid-long term, millions of human lives from wars, poverty related diseases and environmental disasters.

Individual Way Out of Deprivation: Increase of Illegal Migration

One may hear at times in western democratic countries that the easiest way of eliminating certain illegal activities with a strong demand in society, is to liberalise them, while keeping them under state supervision. The underlying rationale is that banning these activities will automatically induce the appearance of illegal organisations, or Mafiosi, that will try to take advantage of the existence of highly unsatisfied demands for corresponding goods and services. Observe that these crooks intervene, irrespective of whether these banned activities are intrinsically perverse or not. An example of intrinsically perverse activities (due to their very negative spill-over effects) is drug-trafficking. Conversely, illegal migration is a clear example of a non-intrinsically bad activity. Note that migration is an initiative based on the human-rights of people to earn a living by means of working abroad, although this activity has been declared illegal at the receiving end.

In our view, the current problems of growing illegal migration into Western Countries or its lateral derivatives, as that of "bogus asylum seeking", are to a great extent a consequence of the lack of sufficient economic co-operation of rich countries. This deficient co-operation has particularly been visible in WTO issues and in development financing (ODA).

With the exception of the "golden age" period (1945-1973), rich countries have kept their frontiers watertight to the reception of low-skilled foreign workers. And this, although neo-classical economists have always emphasised that in a context of informed societies, public powers will never be successful in their battles against the law of supply and demand. Indeed, this lack of success will occur due to the

---

66. This will be discussed in Chapter 4.

existence of an "invisible hand" against which, neither the police nor the missiles of Western countries can result victorious in the long term, as one cannot fight against the law of gravity.

The migration processes have never been easy, neither for migrants nor for hosting countries. In principle, migrants are often (unwillingly) forced to move out from their countries by circumstances of poverty and lack of job opportunities. In this context, if Western countries had been capable of implementing an adequate development financing for poor countries, while they had been less egoistic with developing countries in WTO negotiations, many current problems of illegal migration could have been avoided.

To conclude, illegal migration is a by-product of underdevelopment in the countries of origin of migrants, and of prohibitions of labour movements (to the West), that affect ordinary people in need of work and in search of a better world for their families. Consequently, to legally impede the international movements of people, without taking complementary measures in the fields of development financing and trade facilitation to LDC is a sterile manoeuvre of unsustainable protectionism. We hope that future democratic global governance, implemented by a new UN, will significantly increase development financing for bridging current gaps, while at the same time rationalising migrations.

Emergence of National and International Terrorism

Longstanding frustrations, often induced by endless suffering due to sheer exclusion and/or abject poverty, are sometimes conducive to violent reactions. This phenomenon may generate, under certain conditions,[67] internal or international terrorism. Observe that internal terrorism, coming from separatist movements or due to political

---

67. Terrorism—targeting also or mainly civilians—uses to appear when there is an enormous difference between the small destruction capacity of the insurgency and that of the so-called "oppressors" or "occupiers". When insurgency has enough power to oust governments, they normally uses plots or "*coups d état*"; they may also present internal open battles to the legal power of the state, without significant civilian disturbances.

One should not forget that targeting of innocent civilians to crash the moral of the enemy was introduced by all belligerent countries in the Second World War. Note finally that, as we have mentioned before, the word "terrorism" often contains a code used by certain politicians against some "freedom fighters". Vide Halliday, F. (2005). Book already mentioned.

uprisings, does not produce concern at international level, because their targets are always pursued within own national boundaries.

A cause of more concern for Westerners was the appearance in the 90s of terrorism based on religious-fundamentalism (so-called Jihad). Note that this terrorism fights a new type of war carried out internationally by small cells mainly against the so-called hegemonic power and allies. These groups act against citizens or economic interests of the countries declared as targets, seemingly at random, in any part of the world and at any time.

The emergence of this type of terrorism, with its spectacular and dramatic attacks, as for example those of "September 11", the "Bali blast", the "Madrid trains", the "London underground", etc, is highly feared by citizens in targeted countries. Note that the widespread fear among westerners is also based on the presumed progressive easiness of making or acquiring weapons of mass destruction (WMD) by terrorists, who may even be nationals (home-grown) targeting fellow citizens in crowded public places and transports.

The big question that arises nowadays is how to halt this phenomenon. In fact, there are growing doubts on the success of the current war against international terrorism as practised by the US and allies by means of invading states, kidnappings of suspects for interrogatories, etc. (thus neglecting international conventions).

It is our concern that while economic and technological gaps continue to grow,[68] cultural and religious peculiarities of Muslim-Arabs communities continue not being acknowledged by the West and some of the long lasting international problems continue unsolved (Israel-Palestine issue, etc.), the ground for frustrations will increase. To the extent that the fight against terrorism[69] continues being practised in a frontal way—thus inducing huge lateral damages, as has been the case in Afghanistan and Iraq—its results will likely be counterproductive.

---

68. We should here remember that the Muslim community counts for 21 per cent of the total population of the world while its GDP only reaches 5 per cent of the global production. As a result 39 per cent of total global population living under the poverty-line is Muslim.

69. Note that in the jargon of the US-military involved in the Iraq war, the word "terrorism" has recently changed into "insurgence", this meaning that the US Army—granting to insurgents certain legitimacy—probably wants to negotiate with them.

Note additionally that when terror actions occur, they are always based on *"coups de main"*, with no space to defend, and never with publicity in advance. Consequently the prevention and reaction against this sort of actions should be a matter of intelligence instead of frontal attacks against states that allegedly protect terrorists; and this in parallel with a much more visible and effective collaboration in development and commercial issues by Western countries and a more neutral political behaviour of the latter in international disputes (mainly the Israel-Palestine issue). We do believe that under those premises, neither LDC governments nor local communities would protect international terrorists.

Potential Reactions of Developing Countries if Bridging the Gap Fails and Multilateral Trade does not Progress

In the lines above we have depicted some natural reactions (migration) of LDC citizens in order to individually escape the nasty effects of the growing economic gap. Thereafter we have described current international terrorism as violent actions of fundamentalists against citizens and assets of targeted countries.

In lines below, we will detach from previously described practises implemented by individuals or groups. Instead of that, we will conjecture some (potential) official and non-violent reactions of developing countries, to counter the endless global growing gap and its negative effects.

To begin with, we will here refer to a *ceteris paribus* likely increase in the frequency of skirmishes[70] or economic battles among different players, the rich and developing countries. This increase in agitation may start from the present situation, which is one of fatigue and irritation among leadership of developing countries, after years of greedy behaviour concerning development financing and practical

70. One of these skirmishes took recently place in a leading developing country, India. In the spring of 2003, this country decided to refuse bilateral development grants and loans from the West, due to its small amount in terms of India's GDP, and because its implementation was time consuming, due to its fragmentation and over-conditionality. In fact, this was an expected decision since India itself gave in those days almost a similar amount of aid to neighbouring countries, and clearly showed interest to become a global political player.

deadlock in international trade negotiations.[71] Even in 2003, the rich countries remained aloof to the call of the "Non Aligned Movement"[72] for a better behaviour of the West. At this meeting in 2003, remembrance of the dark times of colonialism reappeared, and messages on exploitation of developing countries, currently practised by rich countries purportedly in the name of market freedom, were also mentioned.

We do believe that in the future, in absence of multilateral progress and in search for additional regional trade gains, the formation or deepening of trade agreements at regional level could be more rules than exception. To the extent that in the next 10-15 years, and as a reaction from frustrations, regionalism continues prevailing over multilateralism, the global trade gains will result sub-optimal.[73] Observe additionally that although the current tendency towards trade regionalisation is criticised by WTO officials, this non-multilateral behaviour has always been at the playground, enhanced among others by the European Union.[74]

Even more, one should not rule out that, from one moment onwards, relevant developing countries invoke some principles of GATT, for diverting relevant western exports. Western countries should acknowledge that an eventual unleashing of such manoeuvres could be disruptive for the evolution of their own GDP.[75] Depending on the duration of the action, the number of involved countries

---

71. In relation with negotiations in WTO, the main criticism made by the developing countries has been the lack of "implementation" of commitments that the West had signed in the Uruguay Round in relation with agriculture and services. According to these commitments, developing countries should reduce their industrial tariff duties, in a phased way, in exchange of a meaningful improvement in access to Western markets in the fields of agriculture, garments, and services. Although Western countries had not fulfilled mentioned commitments, they forced the launching of another Round at the Ministerial Conference in Doha.
72. Sessions celebrated in Kuala Lumpur (Malaysia) in the third week of February 2003.
73. A solution that encourages regional trade cannot be optimal. This is because the formation of trade blocs is prone to induce "trade diversion" from the cheapest sources to more expensive providers; and to increase intra-bloc commerce, the so called "trade creation", by the artificial mean of keeping external common tariffs while eliminating the internal ones.
74. Note that this regional trade, as a midway between bilateralism and multilateralism, is completely legal in the context of WTO rules.
75. The West should bear in mind that as early as 2009, four larger developing countries (China India, Brazil and Russia) could generate an expenditure increase larger than that of the so called G-6 Group (US, France, Germany, Italy, Japan and U.K.). Goldman-Sachs (2003). *Global Paper 99*. October 1.

and the number of diverted items, a turning point in the Western economic business cycle could be forced.

It is clear that in economic wars there are no absolute gainers, while in economic co-operation long-term gains for all (although uneven) are expectable. Notwithstanding that, the country or group of countries that called for the war (selecting the ground and the moment for initiation) may lose less than those that have to react; in particular when the internal cycles of the former are to some extent de-coupled from those of the West, and their economies are large (in PPP terms) and less dependent. Even more, the countries that initiated the war could even gain, if all sides finally acknowledge that the departure position (previous to this economic war) was unfair.

Trade of Goods and Services, and Movements of Capital in the Second Half of the 20th Century

The above-mentioned higher GDP growth rates at a world scale in the period 1950-1998 were mainly due to the reconstruction (up to the 60s) of war-torn European countries and Japan, and to the increase of public investments (up to the 70s) in the newly independent countries. These higher GDP growth rates were also founded on the registered advances in the productivity of labour, induced by the application of the human effort to more productive capital goods. As a complement, mutual commercial and financial relations among the different regions of the world experienced a sharp increase, thus giving a further push to the process.

Specifically, the growth rate of trade in raw materials surpassed that of the GDP; and, as an average, the quotient between exports and GDP at a world scale moved from 5.5 per cent in 1950 to 17.2 per cent in 1998. Founded in new technologies, transport and communications also experienced an accelerated development, which enabled cheaper transports and faster spread of knowledge and information concerning markets, thus increasing the opportunities for interchange.

The international flows of capital also increased significantly. Although the bulk of these flows were concentrated (in the period) in the developed world, capital also flowed to developing countries of Asia, Latin America and (less to) Africa. As a consequence, the gross value of accumulated foreign capital in developing countries, increased from 4 per cent of their GDP in 1950 to 21.7 per cent in 1998.[76]

This growing interchange was also promoted by some institutional developments. In particular, successive international negotiations within GATT enabled the reduction of tariff and non-tariff barriers to international trade, which encouraged it. On the other hand, progressive liberalisation of international movements of capital triggered a process of de-segmentation of former narrow financial markets of nations, thus improving the efficiency of the international use of capital.

However—and this has to be underlined—the flows of private funds (basically FDI) from the developed world to the developing countries were mainly directed towards a limited group of them, namely to those endowed with enough economic assets (strategic raw materials, infrastructure, educated population) to generate non risky and short term capital gains.

In the first decades of the Cold War, and for political reasons, some developing countries (South Korea, etc) received significant amounts of public foreign funds (ODA), mainly in order to strengthen walls between the communist world and the West. Other developing countries that were not selected for any of the former (economic or political) reasons were left to their own financial possibilities, which meant leaving their growth rates far from those of catching up.

In recent decades, China has been the most successful and remarkable developing country in initiating convergence. In 1978 it started a fast process of economic reforms and development, being the latter mainly pushed by high domestic investment rates basically financed through domestic savings.[77] Note that, although in the last decade this country has additionally received FDI (external savings)[78] reaching figures up to 3.5-4.5 per cent in GDP terms, these

76. These are figures of Maddison, A. (2001). Book already mentioned.

77. It is convenient to remember that in 2005 the Gross National Savings rate of China was around 50 per cent in GDP terms. Although this figure published by World Bank (2007), World Development Indicators, has recently been put into question, its extraordinary high level is evident.

78. Note that a significant part of the FDI invested in China comes from the Chinese community living abroad (in Taiwan, Singapore, South Korea, Indonesia, US, etc.).

capital receptions have become more relevant by their annexed new technologies than by the economic figures themselves.[79]

New Direction of the International Trade of Goods (1995-2005)

Continuing with our analysis of the main economic trends in different regions of the world, we will now consider the recent evolution of the international trade of goods. But, before realising this analysis, we will refer to the regional structure of the international trade of goods in 2005. These data will enable us to have a better knowledge on trends and potentials of the involved countries and regions at mid-long term.

International Economic Structure of the Commerce of goods

According to recent figures provided by the World Bank,[80] at the end of 2005 the structure of commerce of goods had the following profiles: 1) The exports value of the high-income countries was 70.4% of the total export of goods;[81] and 2) the exports value of the low and middle-income countries, that is to say the rest of the world, only reached 29.6 per cent of mentioned total exports,[82] although with a rapid trend to improve its share. To this unbalanced profile, one could add another meaningful features: 3) the volume of the total exports of Asia (excluding Japan) were of the tune of the 53-55 per cent of total exports of the developing world; and 4) once eliminated mutual commerce, the total exports of mainland China plus those of

79. Strictu sensu, with its overwhelming domestic savings rate, China does not need foreign savings to grow at a double-digit rate. A good proof of this is the magnum accumulation of foreign reserves in the last years, well over the volume of received FDI.

80. World Bank (2007). *World Development Indicators.*

81. This implies a loss in the last three years (2002-2005) of more than four per cent points (4.2) in their world trade share.

82. According to figures of IMF, provided by the Direction of Trade Statistics, Yearbook, 2006, the share in 2005 of total exports of the Industrialised Countries was 61.8 per cent, and that of the Developing Countries 38.2 per cent. Following this source the share of Asia (ex-Japan) in total exports was 19.5 per cent. If we alternatively used figures of the WTO, the export-share of Asia (excluding Japan) in 2004 would have been similar (20.4%).

In front of all these statistical differences, and looking for the consistency of our analysis, we have chosen the figures of the World Bank commented in the text. This is because in a long term analysis as that realised in this item, differences in departure positions are less relevant than the speed of variation of the involved variables. Notwithstanding that, one has to acknowledge that current higher positions of Asia (ex Japan), reflected by figures provided by IMF and WTO, could speed up the arrival of the possible economic and political derivatives that we will comment lines below.

Hong Kong represented in 2004 around 44 per cent of total exports of Asia (excluding Japan), that is to say 7.5 per cent of the world, thus overcoming the export figures of Japan (5.9 per cent), which till recently was the third exporter of the world (behind Germany and US).

Note additionally that, from the mentioned share of 29.6 per cent of the total exports of goods realised in 2005 by the low and middle income countries—4.2 per cent points more than in 2002—21.4 percent points were exports directed towards high income countries, while the developing countries only mutually exported 8.2 per cent points, which means less than 1/3rd of their total exports.

General Trends of Commerce Along the Period 1995-2005

Although the magnitude is small—we are here referring to the mutual trade of goods of the low and middle-income countries, which in 2005 was 8.2 per cent of the total world exports—this does not imply that this magnitude cannot grow, or that it cannot grow very quickly. On the contrary, looking to trends, we are convinced that this figure is going to experience a fast growth rate in future, as well as that of the share in total exports of the developing countries (mutual trade plus that directed to the industrialised world), today reaching 29.6 per cent of the total world exports. In consistency with former statements we are also convinced that the share of high-income countries in total world exports is already quickly decreasing.

To be specific, high-income countries have generated all along the last 10 years (1995-2005) growing total exports at an average nominal rate per annum of 6.4 per cent, a figure below the world average that was 7.8 per cent. If this disparity of growing rates continues up to 2015 the share in merchandise trade of high-income countries could reach approximately 60 per cent of the total, from current 70.4 per cent.[83]

Conversely, along the last 10 years (1995-2005) the exports of goods of low and middle-income countries have moved in an

83. If we had used for calculation the figures provided by IMF, the mentioned total exports shares, forecasted for 2015, as 60 per cent and 40 per cent for respectively developed countries and developing ones could change into others, respectively around 50 per cent and 50 per cent.

accelerated way. Their total exports have grown at an average annual rate of 12.3 per cent, a figure well above the world average (7.8 per cent). If these trends and disparities are confirmed in next years, the total exports share of the low and middle-income countries could reach in 2015 a level of the tune of 40 per cent of total exports, from current 29.6 per cent.

Intra-Regional Trade of Goods in the Period 1995-2005

Letting aside the industrialised countries and dividing the "developing world" in six geographical areas, we may observe that in the period 1995-2005 all developing regions have registered annual (nominal) growth rates of their total exports of goods well above the annual growth rate (7.8 per cent) of the world. In fact, in all developing regions[84] total exports of goods have grown between a minimum annual rate of 9.6 per cent in Latin America-Caribbean and a maximum of 13.1 per cent in Eastern Europe and Central Asia.[85]

A relevant detail of the commercial figures (goods) in the late 90s and first 2000 is that referred to the average "intra-regional" export growth rates per annum in the different regions of the world. In this regard, only the "high-income economies" have experienced mutual intra-trade growth rates[86] below the world average (5.8 per cent *vs.* 7.8 per cent).

Conversely, the "intra-regional trade" was more than extraordinary in two developing regions of the world that share borders: East Asia-Pacific, and South Asia. Particularly outstanding was the intra-regional growth rate of trade in the East Asia-Pacific region, which grew at an average annual rate more than two times the world average (16.0 per cent *vs.* 7.8 per cent), while the intra-regional growth rate of commerce per annum in South Asia was also almost the double of the world average (14.9 per cent *vs.* 7.8 per cent). These high growth rates of mutual trade in the last 10 years are clear indicators of the

---

84. These regions are: Eastern-Asia and Pacific, Eastern-Europe and Central Asia, Latin America-Caribbean, Middle East-North Africa, South Asia, and Sub Sahara Africa.
85. Observe that the annual growth rate of some of these macro-regions uses to experience certain volatility as a result of the variability of prices of raw materials and oil contained in their exports.
86. This intra-trade growth rate refers to the mutual trade of the high-income economies, mainly US, EU, Japan, etc.

present and future trade performance of these two regions, of course commanded by China and India.[87]

Even more, if we consider the mutual import-export relations of these neighbouring two super-dynamic regions, we find something extraordinary: 1) that East Asia-Pacific region has exported to South Asia in the period 1995-2005 at annual growing rhythms of 16.5 per cent, while 2) South Asia has exported to East Asia-Pacific at an annual growth rate of 17.7 per cent. These figures jointly with those "intra-regional" mentioned above, have generated along the late 90s and first 2000 an average annual growth rate of exports, inside the common perimeter of these two regions, of the tune of 16-17 per cent, which means more than doubling the growth rate of total world exports.

If we turn now to the "high income countries" we may deduce some additional clarifying profiles. First of all, we have to mention the fact that the US and Japan have exhibited along the 90s and first 2000 growth rates of their total exports (of goods) well below the world average. According to figures provided by WB, the total exports of goods of US and Japan along the period 1995-2005 grew respectively at annual rates of 3.8 per cent and 3.0 per cent, well under the world average (7.8 per cent); and this while total exports of goods in the EU grew at an annual rate of 7.2 per cent (also under the world average).

Underlying Automatism of the Growing Asian Trade

Although the drums of fear are already sounding in western countries, particularly in part of former EU-15, in relation to the quick gain by China[88, 89] of total (world) exports share, the worst for them perhaps has not started.

87. The exports of China to the rest of its region grew along the period at an annual rate of 18.3 per cent, and those of India to its region at 13.0 per cent.

88. Some comments unofficially realised by authorities of relevant western countries, suggest that their registered imports from China are larger than corresponding exports declared by China to WTO. If these undertones were correct, the world exports share of China in 2005 could have been significantly higher (perhaps around 8.5 per cent) than the 7.5 per cent stemming from the official figures of WB.

89. Observe that the rapid annual growth rate of exports of goods coming from China is enlarging the imports in the West. This rapid growth relatively reduces the western aggregate demand against internal production, thus *ceteris paribus* diminishing the internal job opportunities for westerners.

We do believe that Asia (excluding Japan) has entered in a self-sustained process of exports at a high (or very high) rate of growth. The causes of this rapid gain in export share of Asia are differently rooted. Firstly, mentioned Asian regions (East-Asia and Pacific and South Asia) are gaining quota in the internal markets of almost "all high income countries" due to their high competitiveness, based on their comparative low industrial and services wages. And this despite the low GDP growth rates of western countries in comparative terms—particularly in developed Europe and Japan—which induced limited growth rates of their total imports all along the 90s.[90]

Note for instance that while former EU-15 countries have shown total annual import growth rates of 7.5 per cent along the period 1995-2005, the export growth rates towards the EU-15 coming from East Asia-Pacific, Eastern Europe and Central Asia, and South Asia have respectively been of 14.1 per cent, 15.1 per cent, and 8.7 per cent. These growth rates of exports of many Asian countries, as well as those of Eastern Europe towards former EU-15—well above those of the average EU-GDP and EU imports—explain by themselves the difficulties for the creation, or simply for the maintenance, of industrial employment in the EU.

Almost the same could be said with respect to the US, which registered along the period 1995-2005 annual growth rates of 8.1 per cent in total imports, while its imports from East Asia-Pacific and South Asia respectively grew at 13.9 per cent and 10.6 per cent.

Although former figures project serious doubts about the long-term stability of the current geographical distribution of international trade and support our predictions on rapid shift, there is a second argument perhaps more detrimental for the economic future of western countries. As we have already mentioned, Asia (excluding Japan) counts as a whole with an enormous potential for additional growth during decades, given the low level of its development and the huge absolute (and relative) figures of people attached to agriculture

90. Annual growth rates of total imports of the US and Japan along the last 10 years (1995-2005) were respectively 8.1 per cent and 4.7 per cent, while the growth rates of the total exports of US and Japan in the period were respectively 3.8 per cent and 3.0 per cent. These figures of imports and exports display clear unbalance, which is a clear indicator of the lack of competitiveness of the US and Japan economies in the analysed period.)

with nil or very low marginal productivity, particularly in China and India, the two gigantic countries of the continent.[91]

Summarising, the two main factors supporting mentioned automatic trend to increase the international trade share of these two regions are: 1) the declining capacity for competition in US, Japan and EU, which is inducing rapid growing exports from Asia to mentioned industrialised countries; and 2) the huge and expectedly long-lasting GDP growth rates of these two Asian regions, which will continue inducing rapid growth of mutual imports in these two neighbouring macro-regions.

Note additionally that forecasted higher growth rates of the two involved regions, led by China and India, will *ceteris paribus* induce significant higher growth rates of their total imports. Notwithstanding that, given the current trend of the intra-regional trade growth of the two mentioned regions, their mutual growing commercial co-operation,[92] and the lower competitiveness of the West[93] in these two sub-regions, western countries will have serious difficulties in the future to keep their export share in the Asian markets, which will favour mutual Asian imports-exports.

Note finally that, conversely to what is remarked by some western economists in relation to the assumed automatic maintenance of the western shares in global trade, the expected magnum GDP growth rate of the Asian region and its rapid growth in mutual trade in the first half of the 21st century, will not significantly profit the West. Consequently, to the extent that the westerners do not adjust (mainly through reductions of their real wages) to this new situation, a new factor of economic conflict and political non-sustainability could emerge in consolidated democracies.

---

91. To this respect vide our book *China and India. Towards Future Economic Supremacy?* (2006). New Delhi: Academic Foundation.

92. Note that in October 2004 China signed a Free Trade Zone (FTZ) agreement with the ASEAN countries. One should not rule out the future addition of India (with or without SAARC) to the mentioned FTZ. On the other hand, China and India have in the recent months signed a frame-agreement for the development of a FTZ among themselves.

93. In particular, we have to underline that while the US exports to East-Asia and Pacific, and South Asia, respectively grew in the period 1995-2005 at rates of 8.7 per cent and 9.1 per cent, the total growth rate of imports in these two regions were respectively 10.1 per cent and 10.7 per cent. Logically, all these figures point to a fall in the exports share of the US in the two mentioned Asian regions.

Economic and Political Conflicts in the 21st Century Require Global Solutions through Democratic Global Governance

We have described in the lines above the recent evolution of the World economy and its trends. Specifically, we have paid attention to two main trends that doubtless will have long reaching and durable effects in international economy and politics: 1) the rapid shift towards Asia of the economic gravity centre of the world; and 2) the lack of economic convergence on the planet, induced by an ill devised globalisation. Additional relevant problems, also with serious economic connotations, will be explained in Chapter 5: global environment degradation and progressive depletion of common natural resources.

Indeed, some of the economic and political problems of the world today—those of free trade and migration on the one hand, and those connected with the disputed frontiers of some countries on the other—have mainly to do with the natural immobility of land and enrooted natural resources, and with the lack of mobility of population and labour across the world, mainly due to the existence of restrictive immigration rules; and all that in a context of different stages of accumulation of human and non-human capital.

Against this backdrop, and in a full and live informed world, frustrating negotiations in the context of the WTO,[94] lack of internal opportunities for individual progress due to insufficient private investment, and simultaneous and pervasive non-acceptation of legal immigration, except for highly qualified professionals, have shattered all hope of many poor citizens in many developing countries. Indeed, without human capital (education) and productive land, with wobbly health systems, and with bad infrastructures which hinder exports, poor citizens in many developing countries (mainly Africans) have only one way out: illegal migration.

---

94. These frustrating negotiations refer to the denied access of poor countries to certain agricultural and services markets in the rich world. Note that against the rationale of the market economy, which defends the principle of the comparative advantage, the developed countries have for long rejected the access of developing countries to certain own markets in which the former have comparative advantage.

As an alternative to frustrating underdevelopment, growing economic gap and induced illegal migrations, we have years ago suggested[95] the convenience of implementing a win-win solution founded on the promotion of trade of agricultural goods and services, and on significant increase and reorganisation of the public international co-operation (ODA).

But unfortunately, one cannot expect too much from the individual solidarity of rich countries: they do not want either to increase the ODA up to the necessary level for generalised taking off of poorest LDC, or to give them access to western agricultural or services markets, or simply to accept them as immigrants. Indeed, rich countries—although making propaganda on aid to poor countries for internal political consumption—do not want to share but peanuts.

Nevertheless, we do believe that in a global and full-informed context, lack of attention for the mentioned three ways out from poverty will not be acceptable. As a consequence, the problems of "uneven development" that rich western countries do not want, or cannot individually solve,[96] will have to be arranged by a new multilateral institution with full powers on financing and provision of global public goods (global peace and security) and on the intermediate economic targets (financial co-operation) to reach mentioned public goods. Without this multilateral institution the world will become in future less and less liveable and safe.

Role of the UN in this Context

Mentioned multilateral institution will necessarily be a renewed and democratic UN. This new UN will have to have full capacities for the administration (funding and provision) of the so-called final global

95. Vide Rahman, R.D. and J.M. Andreu (2004). *Responsible Global Governance*. New Delhi: Academic Foundation. Note that our suggestion of increasing the ODA up to a level equivalent to 2% of the GDP of rich countries (Donors)—over at least one generation—to place LDC in its way towards sustained growth is not new; it was proposed nothing less than more than 35 years ago by JanTinbergen, the first Nobel Prize of Economics. We shall recall that our main contribution in mentioned essay was to propose the creation of UNICO, in the context of a new UN, for reorganising and administrating multilateral ODA. In Chapter 4 we will make a proposal for financing ODA, basically using inheritance taxation.

96. Note that western countries behave as free riders in relation to the financing of the required faster development of LDC (really an intermediate target for de-activating violence and achieving peace and human security, the main final global public goods).

public goods (peace, human security, healthy global environment, etc.) and for the enhancement of economic co-operation, as well as for the correction of global externalities, thus bringing economic justice for the poor and security for the rich by means of effectively delivering economic convergence.

One has to admit that the idea of setting up a real democratic UN, endowed with funding and functions to provide the necessary global public goods and to correct global externalities, could be considered today as a mere dream; but perhaps not after the next two decades, when the "current non-delivering system" has finally proven failure and has been recognised as untenable.

Observe that the non-existence of an international institution with global democratic legitimacy for providing such public goods enables the current hegemonic power (and allies) to realise this provision in their own interest and some times in detriment of the welfare of the rest.[97] Indeed, this way of providing global public goods while forgetting the intermediate economic target (development co-operation) for facilitating peace and security, and while rejecting pooling of partial sovereignty in a new UN, implies a non-democratic behaviour that in the current life and full informed world will not be acceptable for long.

As outlined in Chapter 3, our proposal for setting up a new democratic UN implies the creation of new UN-agencies and the reshuffling of other multilateral institutions (WTO and International Monetary Fund).

Referring to the Bretton Woods institutions, it is not understandable that, in the 21st century, institutions that have to deliver global public goods (global economic and monetary stability) with significant spill-over effects on all nations, are commanded by a selective group of countries that mainly finance the institutions. This is similar to a hypothetical case in which the richest citizens of a country administer the central bank of the nation, as it actually but wrongly happened

97. Indeed, to allege that the conducted international policy of Britain, will be presided by the general interest and not by that of Britain—as expressed by Toni Blair in his speech on the future of Britain in Mansion House the November, 14th, 2006, is just pure rhetoric's. This has not been the historical way of doing politics by politicians, as clearly expressed in Hirsleiffer (1993). If they acted like this, they would have been automatically expelled from power in following elections.

one century ago (central banks controlled by private shareholders) at the dawn of some European democracies.[98]

In relation to the Security Council of the UN, the core of the UN system, we have to say that this organism, with its veto-owners and all that, makes of the "democratic" General Assembly just a place to talk and to vote, but not to decide or to really act. Indeed, this General Assembly, which is today a multilateral Parliament without correct representation and functions and only with some moral "authority",[99] will have to be radically reshuffled for endowing it with supremacy over national parliaments (of members) on the financing and deliverance of global public goods and correction of global externalities.

To design a new scheme of globalisation for its progressive implementation, including reformulation of ILO, etc.; to piecemeal but seriously reorganise the ODA[100] for bridging the economic gap (UNICO); to redesign a new and neutral International Monetary Fund; to create a World Environment Organisation (WEO), also charged with the correction of global externalities; and to indirectly control the evolution of the world population, will be the relevant and exclusive functions of the new democratic UN and agencies.

Summary of the Chapter

In Chapter 2, we have briefly analysed the current economic framework of the world, its recent history and its expected evolution, as a whole and by regions. This has been done because some of its current trends (towards worsening income distribution) could introduce elements of economic and political untenability that—in our view—could only be overcome with the development of democratic global governance. This system of governance based on global

98. The reader should remember that in the 19th century and part of the 20th, most of embryos of future central banks in Europe were private (banks). Arrival to national democracy, or simple growth or rationalization of public sectors, changed them into public institutions.

99. The General Assembly of the current UN in relation to the Security Council or some veto-owners, reminds us the Assemblies of the Nobility in the Middle Ages which, after being carefully listened by monarchs, could expect a positive result, the opposite, or simply a non-reaction.

100. To this UNICO (United Nations Institution for Cooperation) would converge the current WB and all interested NGO.

democracy, will be indispensable for the legitimate provision of global public goods (among them global economic regulation), and for the legitimate correction of global externalities.

To consider current economic trends we have made use of the historical and credited figures of Prof. Maddison, completed with additional economic information up to 2007. After considering the evolution of the main figures of GDP, population growth, and evolution of per capita GDP in relation to the different regions of the world, we have deduced that an important economic shift towards Asia—which will last several decades—is today underway.

The main cause of this shift is the recent entrance of China and India in the international division of labour; countries that, with a huge comparative advantage in industry and services—stemming from their very low wages—may keep mentioned advantage for three or four decades. This foreseeable and protracted advantage of China and India is due to the huge amount of their active populations attached to rural activities (400 and 350 millions respectively), and to the limited capacity of employment absorption per annum of their non-agricultural sectors.

We have also analysed in Chapter 2 the effects of the non-consideration in the process of globalisation of the labour markets, whose segmentation continues being a fact. Indeed, while engineering a self-interested and partial globalisation (not all sectors and factors were included), the West nurtured for decades a global monster whose main results are already at sight: 1) existence of a practically unbridgeable wage gap at mid-term; 2) accumulation of an artificial excess of industrial jobs in the West that from now onwards and for long will have to be shifted towards Asia; and 3) an ever growing "illegal" migration to the West, stemming from: a) the lack of opportunities in many LDC;[101] b) the existence of a huge wage gap; and c) the very biased and selective Western policy for "legal" immigration.

Note that mentioned partial globalisation developed by the West in the second half of the 20th century and in particular in the last

101. This absence of opportunities is mainly due to insufficient internal and external financing (ODA or FDI) in poor countries.

16 years—which did not follow all prescriptions of the neoclassical model, but only some of them—has induced, as expectable, growing economic gap and hazardous personal income distribution.

Against mentioned negative results in times of recent additional globalisation, ill-advised western politicians have focused their attention solely on the "positive" reduction of the volume of poverty, which—as suggested by the WB—has mildly diminished in absolute terms in the last 16 years. Nevertheless, we do believe that this is a paltry target that, even though fulfilled, will not deactivate the increasing malaise in developing countries and LDC against (non-neutral) practiced policies by industrialised countries, conducive to the registered growing economic gap and worsened personal income distribution.

We have also underlined in Chapter 2—making an advancement on what will be explained in Chapter 4—that perverse evolution of the personal income distribution, if sustained, could in future hinder the internal promotion of democracy in developing countries; or change western consolidated democracies into non-sustainable. And what is worst, mentioned trend of income distribution could also hinder the setting up of an international democracy—necessary for the legitimate provision of global public goods and the correction of global externalities—thus working in serious detriment of the preservation of the environment.

Despite unfair commercial rules and biased globalisation, developing countries—particularly Asians—are in last 10-15 years rapidly gaining share in total world trade, reaching today a figure of 29.6 per cent. On the other hand—as suggested in Chapter 2—the intra-regional growth rates of exports of goods of all developing regions have in the last 10 years been higher than the total world average, while corresponding figures in the West have been inferior to mentioned average. In particular, in the last 10 years two neighbouring Asian regions—Pacific and South-East Asia, and South Asia—respectively commanded by China and India, have increased their mutual exports at annual rates of 16-17 per cent, around the double of the average growth rate of trade; a circumstance that combined with the rapid growth rates of GDP of China and India confirms the unavoidable shift of the economic gravity centre of the world towards Asia.

We have also concluded in Chapter 2 that, as far as the acceleration of the Asian economic growth has not been capable of reversing the trend towards growing international economic gap (per capita GDP gap) while masses of poor have been left behind within most developing countries, increased illegal migrations and violence have been, and will be, automatic derivatives in a full informed world.

As an alternative to these absurd "ways out", induced by the current economic non-system, Chapter 2 suggests the rapid modification of the international rules of trade (in WTO), and the reorganisation and increase of net ODA.

Finally Chapter 2 recommends the creation of a democratic international institution—a new UN—with supremacy on member states for the provision and funding of global public goods and the correction of global externalities. As suggested, all new reorganised multilateral bodies (WTO, IMF, ILO, etc.) or those of new creation (UNICO, WEO, etc.) would depend on the General Assembly of this new democratic UN.

3

Capitalism: Evolution in the 20th Century and Indispensable Corrections for Sustainability

In order to assess the possibilities of survival of capitalism, as it is today understood, we will first analyse the main characteristics of "traditional capitalism", which significantly differed from those of the current one and from those developed in the West in the period 1945-1995 in the context of the mixed economies of market. Note that although we usually refer to all mentioned approaches as capitalism, their historical divergences in implementation and results—beyond pure market concepts and theories[1]—have been huge.

As anyone may observe, the number and relevance of players and intervening institutions in the development of capitalism has significantly changed along the 20th century. These changes were influenced by the huge advancements registered in science and knowledge, infrastructure, energy production, and transport and communications. These mutations have made that the current experience of life of citizens in large parts of the world has become totally different from that felt at the beginning of the last third of the 19th century.

Letting aside the period 1914-1945, which encompassed two World Wars and a scantly representative period in between, it is possible to establish a long period of transition of around half a century, between the "traditional capitalism" period (1870-1914)[2] and the time of emergence of current capitalism.[3] For analytical purpose, we

1. The underlying economic theory that describes the working of capitalism, the so-called neo-classical economic model, has always been praised by capitalists and governments of the rich world. However, this economic model has always been interpreted in a biased way, and never practised in its integrity for achieving maximum efficiency.
2. This period (1870-1914) is rather arbitrary, as always happens in the delimitation of historical phenomena, but acceptable to our purposes. This period has been baptised as "Traditional Liberalism", among others by Maddison, A. (2001). Book already mentioned.
3. We do believe that capitalism will radically change in next decades in order to make physical assets (nature) and political and social life sustainable.

will divide this transitional period (1945-1995) in two sub-periods: the first one (1945-1973), including practically all the decolonisation processes and the years of cheap energy; and the second one that lasted from 1973 till mid-90s, when the so-called ICT revolution gathered momentum.

In our view, the between-wars period (1918-1939), with its two heterogeneous stages, one of rapid growth (the 20s) and another of deep economic crisis (the 30s), does not form part at all of any transition period among the diverse forms of capitalism. Mentioned period was one in which two very different political and economic conceptions of life, defended by different groups or countries, tried to impose their criteria over the others', thus finally resulting in devastating violence (Second World War).

We have to additionally underline that capitalism of the 21st century will have to be very different from the current one, as a consequence of diverse phenomena: 1) the huge structural economic change, already underway, that will overwhelm a meaningful part of the today's rich West; and 2) the significant global changes that necessarily will have to be introduced in the current economic and political systems to face not only the economic challenges of our days (reversal of the degraded personal income distribution and maintenance of a healthy global environment) but also the political ones (need of setting up a system of democratic global governance). In particular, the first half of the 21st century will witness progress towards what we will define—in Chapter 4—as "global democracy".

"Traditional-liberal" Capitalism: International Competition, Internal Social Warnings and Collapse

A first feature of "traditional liberal capitalism" ruling along the period 1870-1914 was that, despite the enormous fragmentation of the domestic supply in many activities, there was a limited number of independent players at international scale in most crucial sectors;[4] players that, of course, were protected by metropolitan colonial powers.[5]

4. We are here referring to firms capable of initiating economic ventures abroad in relation with the development of infrastructures (railways), industrial activities (energy), or massive exports or imports.

5. Metropolitan army and navy, which played a major role in the development of colonies, constantly protected mentioned firms.

Let us not forget that in that period, great parts of South and South-East Asia were controlled by the British,[6] while Central Asia was under the aegis of the then economically delayed Russians. Although France also had colonies in Asia and Africa, its influence was smaller than that of Britain, who controlled, Australia and New Zealand as well.

The African continent, largely unknown in those days, was also colonised by the British and French, as well as by the Germans,[7] Belgians and Portuguese. The so-called "scramble for Africa", till then exploited only at the coastline, took place at the end of the 19th century.[8] Other European colonisers, relevant in former centuries—as the Spaniards—played a minor role in the colonisation of the huge African continent.

Latin America countries, although mostly independent from Spain or Portugal since the first decades of the 19th century, were for long incapable of reaching significant industrialisation—always in need of an initial big push[9]—thus remaining attached to agriculture productions.

Note that international competition, in a context of preferential commercial relations between colonies and metropolitan powers—was limited and, most of times, tinged by underlying commercial mistreatment of colonies. Often, products of the metropolis were protected by the existence of a huge technological gap,[10] and by the asymmetric commercial relations (preferential agreements), based on political domination.

6. Let us remember that practically the entire Indian sub-continent was under the British rule, as well as Burma and Malaysia, including Singapore. Additionally, as a result of the defeat of China in the First Opium War of 1839-1842, UK profited from the cession of Hong-Kong.
7. Although the Germans lost almost all their influence in Africa at the end of the 1st World War (1918), the British and the French continued with their colonies in the African continent till the 50s or 60s of the 20th century.
8. Meredith, M. (2005: 1) The State of Africa. Free Press
9. This "big push" theory is original by Rosenstein-Rodan, P. (1943). "Problems of Industrialisation of Eastern and South-Eastern Europe," *Economic Journal*. Vide also Nurkse, R. (1953). *Problems of Capital Formation in Underdeveloped countries*. Oxford University Press.
10. The Industrial Revolution was born in Europe (Britain and Germany) and it spread later to the US. The reasons of the delay of the industrialisation in other continents (Asia, Latin America or Africa) were frequently: 1) the asymmetric economic relations between colonised nations and colonising states; 2) the comparative low population densities in colonies; 3) the denied access to industrialisation and knowledge (education) in colonies; and 4) the scantly developed infrastructures which hindered economic traffics.

Along a good part of the 19th century, the continuation of the difficulties in the maritime transport[11] gave the few nations that controlled the seas, mainly Britain, a supplementary advantage for economic and political domination abroad. In function of all former commented advantages, the British Empire reached the zenith of its influence, dominance and relative wealth, in the last decades of the 19th century and the first one of the 20th.

In context of political stability in Europe—after the France-Prussia war and against the background of the international monetary stability provided by the gold standard—the mechanics of economic development automatically worked in Europe,[12] thus generating a significant growth rate in the so-called "traditional liberal-capitalism" period.

Regrettably, as mentioned before, and as expectable from the development process in its first stages,[13] the distribution of personal income worsened, and the spark of social unrest ignited a process of social change and political reorganisation. Progressively, the social boiler took pressure, and in the first decades of the 20th century the exploitive socio-economic situation became unbearable in many cities and regions of Europe.

Traumatic Events in the "Traditional Liberal" States

Growing social pressure inside states in connection with political tensions in some of the empires—remember that three[14] European Empires were absolute monarchies—finally unleashed a continental war, in 1914. This was a war in which the political (even religious) economic and social targets of some contenders were completely

11. Note that the maritime transport experienced a huge thrust in the last third of the 19th century with the growing use of steam as propeller of boats.
12. This development process worked through the rapid transfer of human factor from countryside to industrial-urban activities. This human shift, combined with comparative quicker processes of investment registered across the continent, made that the GDP of the different western European nations grew at significant speed.
13. Remember to this respect the Kuznets curve, which relates the degree of development of a country (measured by the reached per capita income) with its domestic income distribution (measured f.i. by the Gini Index), as described in any handbook of Economic Development. Vide. f.i. Ahluwalia, M. "Inequality, poverty and development", article published in Meier, G. (2000). *Leading Issues in Economic Development*. 7th Ed. Oxford University Press. p.387.
14. We are here referring to the German, Austrian and Russian ones.

entangled,[15] while an ever growing share of conscripted soldiers became disaffected to the cause their countries were fighting for: among others, the defence of an economically "liberal state", not sensitive to social demands and completely out of touch with the masses.

In such a socio-political context, the end of the war which lasted 4 years (1914-1918), brought a traumatic outcome for the three intervening European monarchs and for two of their empires.[16] The Austrian-Hungarian divided in a mosaic of small states, many of them later becoming an easy prey for the successor of the other failed empire, the Russian one, transformed in 1917 into the Soviet Union. Finally, the third one, the Prussian empire, became a reduced version of itself and changed into a liberal but fragile republic (Weimar). German citizens, fearing communist escalation, finally handed all power over to a gang of enemies of democracy who founded the 3rd Reich.[17]

Period Between Wars (1919-1939)

Soon after the signing of the Versailles treaty, a new and dangerous European cocktail was again in the making. The main components of this cocktail were the unstable German Republic of Weimar, and the 'red' revolution-exporting country, the Soviet Union. Additionally, an aggressive reaction against the communist threat, took over in Italy. Note finally that in the Far East, Japan continued with its aggressive geographical expansion.

Observe that two basic and opposed conceptions of politics had recently re-appeared or became re-shaped in Europe: dictatorship

---

15. Probably it was not so much the political assassination of a royal in 1914 which ignited the war, but a combination of several factors: the political non-tenability of the Austrian Empire, the irrational policy of alliances between states just to balance military power, and the disproportionate retaliation of Austrians after the murder.
16. As a result of the First World War, the Ottoman Empire also collapsed and was occupied by the allies. From 1918 onwards, Mustafa Kemal initiated the construction of a Turkish state, basically in the Anatolian peninsula.
17. In Germany, concurrent or successive negative developments such as the hyperinflation of the 1920s, the great depression of the 30s, the frustrations over the outcome of the First World War, the irresponsible alliances among political parties, and the fear felt by capitalists in front of the communist threat, drove into power an unscrupulous extremist group with a racist and geographical expansionary doctrine. After democratically taking power, this group commanded by Hitler, choked the democratic system and started huge human rights violations, political aggressions and forced annexations.

(in its different versions) and "limited" democracy. Note that the latter was just national (defined at a state level), formal, defective in franchising,[18] and not concerned with growing social demands. Observe that these demands were based on information on the worsening of the personal income distiibution, which quickly degraded at that time in Europe, as normally occurs in the first stages of the industrialisation process.

Competition to gain social support for the mentioned (opposed) conceptions of life became fierce; and the debate among contenders focused on ownership of production factors, as well as (in some cases) the rest of private ownership. As a result, industrial relations—under the tutelage of populist trade unions and socialist and communist parties on the one hand, and under stubborn and myopic entrepreneurs associations backed by conservative political leaders on the other—became difficult and often violent.[19]

From an economic perspective, the 20s were years of a new significant expansion of trade and production in the West. In those years, most of the traits of traditional capitalism remained, including the partially restored "gold standard". Nevertheless, the arrival of the so called "Great Crisis", starting in 1929, brought huge levels of unemployment in the then leading countries (US, that had recently started its role as a global player, Germany, Britain and France).

To "protect" domestic jobs—in decline due to the recession—the main economic powers embarked on a counterproductive "beg your neighbour" policy, mainly consisting of rising direct or indirect additional barriers to imports coming from abroad. Logically, this policy depressed the exports of all of them, thus generating reduced aggregated demands (external and internal) and more unemployment in the above-mentioned countries, as well as in others.

---

18. Observe that, in 1919, most of the scant western "democracies" had huge levels of adult illiteracy, had not given voting franchise to women, and the state had not developed a significant level of social protection for their citizens: states hardly guaranteed health and pensions, while full employment of citizens was not even an economic target, because—according to conventional wisdom—the free market system would "automatically" provide jobs for all. Indeed, full employment would only become a serious economic target in the 30s.

19. As we will explain in Chapter 4, this was due to the fact that in that moment of the European history, the "equity system" provided by "traditional capitalism" was incompatible with sustainability of democracy.

Second World War and Political Results

The policy of alliances among the different European countries made that with the German invasion of Poland in 1939, the "dice were already cast". This invasion automatically placed the British and the French in front of the Germans; after a while, the Soviet Union and the US also colluded with Britain and France.

The US, which also waged a war in the Pacific against Japan as an answer to the pre-emptive aggression of the latter in Pearl Harbour, surprisingly entered (with other allies) in coalition with the Soviet Union against the Germans. The fascist authorities of Italy, expecting territory gains in the Balkans and Africa, embarked the country in an alliance with the other two aggressors. The final result of the above-mentioned facts is well known: millions of people died in Europe, Asia, Africa, and Pacific, and the destruction of physical assets was huge.

Some months before the end of the war, (nationalist) China,[20] Soviet Union, France, UK and US, met in Dumbarton Oaks (US), to draft a Charter for the United Nations. In June 1945, the representatives of 50 nations signed this Charter; and the United Nations officially started its activities in October 1945, when the Charter was fully ratified.[21]

From "Traditional-liberal" Capitalism to "Capitalism of the 21st Century"

Undeniably, capitalism of the last decades of the 20th century and early years of the 21st has several common traits with "traditional liberal" capitalism (1870-1914) already analysed, and also with capitalism from 1945 to 1973. Nevertheless, there are relevant differences among them that will be portrayed in the lines below.

---

20. Note that in 1945, the "official" government of China was patronised by the Kuomingtang (KMT). This government, after the defeat and withdrawal of the Japanese in 1945, was also defeated in 1949 by the Popular Army of Mao Tze Dong, and flew to Taiwan.

21. In the Preamble of this Charter, the founding members expressed their determination to avert more wars, to reaffirm the dignity of people, their fundamental human rights, the equality of men and women, and of nations large and small... and to promote social progress and better standards of life in freedom. To fulfil these aims the Preamble encouraged the practise of tolerance, good neighbourly relations and to unite forces to keep international peace and security, while employing the international machinery for the promotion of economic and social prosperity for all peoples. Regrettably, letting aside significant success in the field of human rights development, the following sixty years proved that mentioned Preamble was mostly a set of good intentions.

Disappearance of Colonialism and Reorientation of International Trade in the Period 1945-1973

Shortly after the Second World War (1939-1945) a new wave of decolonisation started.[22] Logically, after the two or three decades that this decolonisation process lasted, the international community radically changed its morphology.[23] This was due to the embodiment of many old colonies of Western countries into the UN, many of them with historical claims against former bosses.

Observe that although the period 1870-1914 was baptised by professional economists and historians as the period of "traditional-liberal capitalism", the pure truth is that, in those years, the practised international trade was completely tinged by commercial asymmetries. Typically, the bilateral trade[24] among relevant western countries and their colonies was mainly founded on ideas of another age: the age of Mercantilism.

As an example of what we are saying, we will here focus on the commercial relations of a typical metropolitan coloniser (Britain) with a relevant colonised nation (India). Indeed, according to many Indian historians, the history of the "British rule" in India was a long story of political neglect and systematic economic exploitation of the population through a typical policy of "divide and rule".[25] As a consequence of the asymmetric and non-neutral applied policies by the colonial power, the benefits of the British rule for the Indians were rather incidental.[26]

Observe that in those days the Industrial Revolution had heavily reduced the unitary cost of machine-made goods in Britain; goods that

---

22. Note that the so-called first wave of the decolonisation took place in the 19th century, mainly in Latin America.
23. One indicator of this change of morphology was the rapid increase in the number of member-countries of the UN: the founders in 1945 were 50 countries, of which only some few were democratic (not even all the veto-owners in the UN-Security Council); currently the number of member countries in the UN is around 200, of which 140 hold in time multi-party elections.
24. Most of the authorised exports of colonised nations were with the metropolitan power. When exports to other countries were not prohibited, they were de-stimulated by means of the establishment of preferential agreements with the metropolitan power.
25. We believe that this comment could be applied to almost any colonisation in the World History.
26. Datt, R. and K. Sundharam (2004). *Indian Economy*. 49th Edition. New Delhi: S. Chand & Company. p.29.

previously had been handcrafted. The temporary synchronisation of the Industrial Revolution in England with the colonisation of India gave the Brits the opportunity of selling machine-made goods to India, placing this country in a clear manufactured-goods disadvantage, in particular in textile handicrafts, the then most relevant "industrial" activity in India.

Paradoxically—although in historical consistency with the asymmetric way of doing international politics by western colonisers—while the British emphasised the convenience for India of a bi-directional free trade system, which could have meant that the latter exports raw materials and imports machine-made goods[27] and also machinery, the British did not allow India to import machinery coming from Britain, thus averting the industrial modernisation of the country. In fact, the British rulers of India mainly oriented this country towards the commercialisation of primary Indian products and the exports of raw materials.[28]

As a consequence of the former manners of the British, when India gained its independence in 1947, it inherited a crippled economy with a scant industry, a stagnant agriculture and a peasantry immersed in poverty (typical trait of many LDCs in the epoch). Indeed, it inherited an economic structure that, in order to reach industrialisation, "forced" India to practise the so-called "import substitution" policy (the same occurred in many other de-colonised developing countries).[29] Remember that this "import substitution policy", was also one of the main features of the industrialisation process in many capitalistic countries during the first transition period (1945-1973).

Other Traits of the First Transition Period (1945-1973) of Capitalism

Additional traits of the first transition period of capitalism in the 20th century were the following: 1) growing economic public sector

27. This process enabled the swamping of the Indian textile market with British textile manufactures.

28. As a result, the Indian agriculture started to work for world markets, while the village's production of handicrafts meaningfully declined across all India. Even worse, in some years of bad crops, the compulsory fulfilment of the export quotas established by the British rulers compounded the contemporary problems of rising prices and famines, typical phenomena of years of bad monsoon and short agricultural productions.

29. The "import substitution policy", as for decades practised by independent India, was extremely overdone reaching one of the highest levels of protection against imports.

and (further) development of the welfare state in the context of the reconstruction of war-torn Europe; 2) practise of fiscal and monetary activism;[30] 3) piecemeal progress of international trade liberalisation (initial Trade Rounds of GATT in which only a selected group of developed countries participated);[31] 4) use of the US dollar as an effective pattern for international settlements;[32] and 5) steady and cheap price of energy. Note that precisely the sudden alteration of the oil price in 1973-74 marked the end of the first transition period. As a result of this alteration and its initial derivatives towards stagflation,[33] many economies starting moving towards less intervened and allegedly more efficient micro-markets.

Capitalism as practised in the period 1945-1973, additionally differed from the "traditional-liberal" one, on two other aspects. First of all we have to mention that, although growing, the degree of international interchange of goods in GDP terms was lower than that experienced in some moments of traditional "liberalism" (1870-1914), and in the 1920s.

On the one hand, it occurred that in the period 1945-1973, the international restrictions were much more relevant than in times of old liberalism. Indeed, the Cold War and the induced political distance between capitalistic and socialist economic systems made that trade between the West and the Communist world practically disappeared. On the other hand, independence of many developing countries since the end of the Second World War, and their interest in developing their own industry, made that most of them practised the already mentioned "import substitution policy", which made Western

---

30. We have already mentioned all these aspects in Chapter 1.
31. The initial aim of GATT was to liberalise international trade. This has been gradually achieved along successive negotiations among participants via reduction of custom tariffs and progressive elimination of other barriers to trade. Of the 8 celebrated negotiations, the so-called Trade Rounds, the first 5, which took place between 1947 and 1961, just focussed on reduction of tariffs, and this while the number of involved countries was very small (ranging between 13 and 38).
32. Along this period, currencies that in other times had played a relevant role, particularly in interchanges with former colonies (sterling pound, French franc, etc), progressively lost their relevance, even in relation with transactions with mentioned territories. This practically changed the US dollar into the sole reference of the International Monetary System.
33. This phenomenon of stagflation—a mix of economic stagnation and monetary inflation—appeared in the second half of 70s.

industrial exports to developing countries more difficult.[34] Observe that at the same time the West—allegedly for strategic reasons—practically banned agricultural imports from LDC, thus compressing exports of poor countries. All this made that in this period, the growth rates in many LDCs—among them the most relevant and populated ones—were really disappointing.[35]

Secondly, we have to underline that in the first transition period (1945-1973) although with some temporary exceptions (France), the US indirectly "controlled" western economies at international level through the so-called Bretton Woods institutions. The appearance of the World Bank and the International Monetary Fund, and the financial and political structure of these two institutions based in Washington, gave the US the opportunity of getting economic and political dominance in the Western Hemisphere. The Soviet Union did the same with its satellites and other socialist-communist countries.

Note that during this first transitional period, it was not obvious that the Soviet Union would finally lose the arms race and scientific competition[36] in which the two ideological leaders of the world were involved.

The Second Transitional Period (1973-1995) of Capitalism

The overwhelming rise of petrol prices along the 70s, developed in two stages,[37] plus the contemporary economic stagnation, unleashed—

34. After having hindered—practically all along the Traditional Liberal Capitalism period—the export of machinery and other industrial products from the metropolis (and from other rival countries) to colonies, thus obstructing the economic development of the latter, when colonies reached political independence western countries tried to rapidly and vehemently increase their industrial exports to LDCs. In this new context, although in some cases in a mistaken way, many LDCs initiated industrial (machinery) "protectionism", thus "artificially" reducing the volume of interchanged goods.

35. The cases of China and India are remarkable. Note that these two countries although for very different reasons, economically under-performed in times of the first transitional period (1945-1973) of capitalism. Rahman, R. and J.M. Andreu (2006). *China and India: Towards Economic and Political Supremacy in the World?* New Delhi: Academic Foundation.

36. On the contrary, the launching of the Sputnik by the Soviet Union in 1957 brought the US into a political crisis in times of Pres. Eisenhower. This event was a first pointer of the then relative delayed position of the US, in its scientific competition with the Soviet Union. Mentioned warning triggered a US reaction to speed up the economic development of the country (new frontier economics) to further gain the weapons race. Parker, R. (2006: 324). Book already mentioned.

37. The first stage developed in 1973-74 in the aftermath of the Yon Kippur War, and the second one in the aftermath of the Iranian Islamic Revolution. In the second stage the oil price reached a historical maximum that, measured at US dollars of 2004, was around 100 US dollars per barrel. This record price was overcome in 2008.

after a period of bewildering[38]—a first attempt of paradigm shift. The related economic policy change was manifold: it not only affected the way of implementing economic policy, as we have explained in Chapter 1, but also enhanced the production and trade in geographical areas that, till then, had not entered in the international division of labour.

Following the wake of Japan, some then non-democratic countries of East and South-East Asia (South Korea, Taiwan, Hong Kong and Singapore) took the leadership in the implementation of a new approach for industrialisation, opposed to the "import substitution policy": the so-called "outward industrialisation strategy". This new policy, prone to the opening of the economies, mainly consisted of internal liberalisation of markets, to some extent including the labour one (for gaining internal efficiency), and the progressive dismantling of barriers to foreign imports. This new approach rapidly spread all over the region, affecting, against political expectations, even mainland (communist) China.

This country, against negative economic forecasts coming from the West, started a fast development process, generating average annual growth rates of around 10 per cent during the following 25 years. This rapid growth rate did not worry the West during the period 1978-1995; indeed, in those days, western economic think-tanks considered the economic development of China as a mere scientific curiosity.

Although without external opening (which only took place in 1991), India also initiated in 1980 a process of liberalisation of some internal markets, giving much more chance to the corporate private sector in some industrial activities, till then practically monopolised by the public one.[39]

Former economic phenomena enabled Asia as a whole to grow quicker than in the period 1945-1973; and more than the rest

38. The years 1974-1976—which witnessed the resignation of the US president Nixon and the accession to power of his vice-president Gerald Ford—plus the years of the presidency of Mr. Carter (1976-1980), were years in which the economic ideas on how to face the current challenges of the "stagflation" phenomenon, were shaky. Then onwards, biased neo-neoclassical ideas, in some cases based on unrealistic assumptions, started gaining ground.

39. Vide. Rahman, R. and J.M. Andreu (2005). *China and India: Towards Global Economic Supremacy?* Book already mentioned.

of continents of the world in the period 1973-1998 and further. Remember that in the period 1973-1998 the rest of continents grew, as an average, ostensibly less than in the first transition period (1945-1973).

On arriving to the 90s, the most important political phenomenon of the second transition period occurred: the collapse of the Soviet Union and the initiation of an economic transition in Russia and former Soviet Union satellites.

Current Capitalism, Recent Trends, and Necessary Corrections

When the political countervailing power—the Soviet Union—disappeared in 1991, the behavioural model that had supported the US international policy during the Cold War became obsolete. Indeed, the collapse of the Soviet Union gave the US the opportunity (more apparent than real) of becoming the last global "hegemonic power" on Earth; and, as a derivative, of emphasising their traditional international policy, founded on own interest and implemented on a case-by-case way.

In fact, this new "hegemonic" position and actions of the US increasingly accentuated among third countries the perception of being abused, thus making the US progressively losing moral authority.[40] Even more, from 1991 onwards—but particularly in the first 2000s—the US lost in some international actions even the weakest justification for its foreign policy, based on the "theory of the second best" as applied to politics.[41] Indeed, by the summer of 2008 the international prestige of the US had reached a historical minimum.

Among other economic and political conceptions, an off-spring of Reaganism appeared in the first 90s: the so-called Washington Consensus, enhanced by the US government as a new way of understanding national and international economic relations and criteria for the development process in LDCs.

---

40. Note that in current times of full and live information, acting in international policy on a case-by-case basis, without any predefined and stable rule or model, or even worse with pre-defined rules bypassed at convenience, is and will be counterproductive.
41. Mentioned theory of "the second best", transplantable from economics to politics, would justify non-transparent and/or non-consistent behaviour of one of the two superpowers, if the political adversary behaved the same way.

This consensus solemnly introduced the liberalisation of the internal and external markets, the monetary and fiscal discipline, and the absence of corruption, as "sufficient conditions" for gathering additional and essential FDI in LDCs, and for achieving growth;[42] and all this irrespective of whether the internal savings of the developing countries were sufficient or not for promoting development, whether these countries could accede or not to certain western markets (agriculture goods or services), or whether minimum levels of education, health and infrastructures for steady growth attainment had been reached or not.

However, if we analyse what happened in former decades, the recipe of the Washington Consensus for economic development should be considered as a mockery of economic history. Promoters of the Washington Consensus should have noted that after the initiation of the de-colonisation process only a minority of developing countries had gathered most of FDI directed to them, while the rest were practically bypassed by the private international investors[43] and left to their own financing capacity; and to the very scant, fragmented, disorganised, and over-conditioned Official Development Assistance (ODA) provided by donors.

Financing Developing Countries in the Period 1990-2006

As it is well known, growth rates of developing countries do not only depend on their domestic savings, but also on their ability to gather foreign savings in order to increase their domestic rate of investment.[44] In this regard, the two most important and stable

---

42. We should not forget that in this issue of alleged corruption in LDC, there always have been corrupted and corruptors; and that some EU and US multinationals have gained international contracts by means of corruption (of course using middlemen, whose fees have for long been legally deducible from corporate taxation, etc.). Even more, till recently, the US, UK, and other states have practised a business-policy of twisting arms to local governments, through their embassies; and what some people could in such a case name as lobby or economic pressure, others could call corruption, because in most cases the objective of the corresponding embassy is to get a contract for the national firm, although it has not made the best offer.
43. Today, similarly as what happened in the last half a century, the concentration of Direct Foreign Investment in some few developing countries is a logic and clear trait of the current private Development Financing. To this respect, Todaro and Smith (2003). *Economic Development*. Pearson Education; also Faujas, A. (2006: 15) "Record d'investissements pour les pays en developpement en 2006", *Le Monde*. 31 Mai
44. Note that total foreign savings have to be in absolute value equivalent to the current account balance, but with opposite sign.

items to raise foreign savings have historically been Foreign Direct Investments (FDI), and Official Development Assistance (ODA).[45]

In relation with international private long-term flows of funds (FDI), we have to underline that along the years of the Cold War (1948-1991) these flows increased quickly, although from a low initial basis. Note that the great bulk of FDI flows concentrated in the developed world, although private capital also flowed to some developing countries of Asia, Latin America and Africa. However, mentioned flows of private funds from the industrialised world to the developing countries, were mainly directed towards a limited group of them.

Complementary to FDI, developing countries also received along the period 1950-1990 foreign public financing (ODA), although most of times for political reasons. Consequently, in those days, the developing countries that were not selected for any of the former reasons (political-ODA or economic-FDI) were left to their own domestic possibilities for financing their development, which often meant reaching growth rates far from those necessary for catching up.

In the 90s of the 20th century, FDI directed to developing countries overcame the ODA received by these countries; and this while ODA entered into a situation of nominal stagnation. To be specific, FDI received by developing countries experienced a rapid increase in the 90s, reaching an unexpected huge figure of 185 billion US dollars in 1999. After a brief period of reduction of FDI, developing countries registered again record figures in 2005. Although one could have expected that these growth rates of FDI had worked according to the suggestions of the Washington Consensus, the naked truth is that 60 per cent of this FDI went to Asia, of which half went to China. Observe that this concentrated regional distribution of FDI, completely matched with the logic of free markets. Given the fact that the risk of losing money put at stake was higher in LDCs with serious problems of foreign indebtedness, insufficient infrastructure or socio-political problems, private capital was channelled towards the most advanced developing countries and not to the rest.

45. The reception of short-term foreign capital, although sometimes convenient for short-term balancing the balance of payments, uses to be unstable. This is the reason why this source of funds should not in general be used for supporting development processes.

Note that the value of ODA—as complementary and stable source of external funds for financing development—although nominally multiplied by more than 10 times from 1960 to a magnitude of around US 50 billion in 2002 (and to a magnitude of around 75 billion in 2004),[46] for long declined in donors' GDP terms, from 0.51 per cent registered in 1960 to 0.23 per cent in 2001.[47] Already in 1971, and based on the successful experience with the Marshall Plan, the UN established a target-figure of 0.7 per cent of donor-countries GDP as a relative minimum of ODA. Note however that along last 3 decades only a few countries reached this 0.7 per cent GDP target, namely Denmark, Norway, the Netherlands and Sweden.

What is even more revealing than its scant volume[48] is the arbitrary distribution of ODA among developing countries.[49] If we consider the distribution of foreign aid by individual receiving countries, we will have to conclude that the correlation between the geographical allocation of foreign aid and the level of poverty of recipient countries (measured by their p.c. GDP) is amazingly non-existent.[50]

To finalise this item, we have to say that in the logic of the development process, private and public investments cannot, in general, substitute one another since the sequencing of their appearance into scene is not a matter of choice, as neo-liberals use to suggest. Normally, FDI only flows to countries or enclaves when

46. In the last two years (2005 and 2006), more pollution of the concept of ODA occurred: introduction in it of post-war reconstruction expenses in Iraq and Afghanistan and debt forgiveness by many donors. Consequently the nominal increase of ODA in mentioned years was misguiding.

47. Perkins, D. *et al.* (2001). *Economics of Development*. 5th Edition. Norton. p.409

48. In relation to other sources, we can say that although Japan and the US remain being the most important donors in absolute terms, the case of the US is rather disappointing. The amount of its foreign aid is very low in terms of its GDP (0.15 per cent), and strongly tinted with geo-political targets and not with the idea of bridging economic gap.

49. In terms of regional distribution, we can say that although nearly 50 per cent of the world's poorest live in Asia, this continent receives ODA only for 3 US dollars per capita per annum. This is in sharp contrast to the Middle East (in particular Israel and Egypt), where the received per capita foreign aid is six times higher than that received by South Asia; and this while the per capita income in the Middle East is five times higher than that of South Asia. All these comments reveal that this so-called "Aid" is basically an instrument of geopolitics.

50. To cite another example we could say that only 31 per cent of foreign aid is allocated to the 10 developing countries in which 66 per cent of the poorest of the world live; and this while the 40 per cent rather well-off developing countries receive the double in per capita terms. To finalise this list of irrationalities we could add that those developing countries that spend more than 4 per cent of their GDP in defence, receive twice as much foreign aid in per capita terms as compared to LDC that spend much less in this item.

in these countries/enclaves a sufficient infrastructure, energy, and healthy and educated manpower are available.

This enabling environment will initially have to be promoted by the public sector, since in this initial stage the private sector will not significantly intervene. The problem is that in poor LDCs, while the private sector does not intervene, there is not enough internal public saving as to finance the required public investments. This generates a vicious circle, almost impossible to be broken without resorting to significant public external capital (ODA).

Summarising, we could say that for stepping up the economic development in many developing countries, in particular in LDCs, it is necessary to increase the reception of foreign flows. Note that in opposition to some statements of the Washington Consensus, the correct sequencing is to firstly receive public foreign transfers (currently ODA) in order to facilitate public investment in infrastructure and human capital, and only thereafter it would be rational to expect the arrival of significant FDI. An adequate opening of internal markets to international trade (if reciprocal) would also facilitate the arrival of FDI.

Huge Amount of Indirect Newcomers to the Global Market

In the last two decades of the 20th century, and in particular in the last 16 years up to 2006, the potential volume of people that entered in the international division of labour (up to 2.4 billion, if we just count China and India) has by far been the most important one (in absolute and relative terms) since the First Industrial Revolution.

Observe that in 1950 the total world population was around 2500 million while at that time China and India—for different reasons—did not enter into international economic interchanges. Today, we may say that these two nations have massively entered into the international trade of industrial goods (mainly China) and services (also India). Even more, given their enormous reservoirs of people in countryside—progressively transferable to other sectors at rates of 10-11 (China) and 8-9 (India) millions a year—and their current joint population near that of the total world in 1950, it is no wonder that many nations of the world feel scared.[51]

51. Such scaring ideas has been expressed recently in the book of Prestowitz, C. *Three Billion New Capitalists: the Great Shift of Wealth and Power to the East. The Economist*, July 29, 2006. p.73.

Indeed, the action of putting in communication two vessels with different levels of liquid (personal incomes or wages) was necessary to initiate a convergence phenomenon between Asia and the West.[52] It is true that the convergence process could be overlapped with a generalised trend to grow, which could mitigate in rich countries the negative effects of convergence, as in fact it has occurred in the last two decades, as recently reported by the IMF.

Role of Full Information in "Economic-Industrial" Relations and in International Economic Affairs

Starting with microeconomics, and going back to economic history, we may remember that when Capitalism progressed from Mercantilism,[53] and pioneering European economies grew more than before as a result of the first Industrial Revolution, former rural populations began concentrating in urban areas,[54] mostly earning their pitiable livings in dehumanising sweatshops.

In the name of freedom of contracting, also applicable to labour markets, these negative results were accepted, as natural, by nascent liberal states which, for long, were not concerned with the income distribution and living conditions of workers.[55] Although mentioned industrialisation-urbanisation process enabled a significant growth

---

52. In other geographical areas or continents (Africa and Latin America), the convergence process seems more difficult because the synergies are less influential and the general parameters of growth are much less favourable than in Asia.

53. Mercantilism is a doctrine that defended that all the economic measures taken by states should exclusively be directed to the enrichment of the states themselves. In order to reach Mercantilism-targets, industry and commerce were intervened by public sector and guilds. In particular, the game of economic international relationships was based on encouraging trade mainly to colonies, while imports from other countries were highly restricted. This kind of policy allowed the states to increase their gold and silver reserves, useful to finance expansionary adventures in benefit of the then great mercantilist states in conflict (France, Spain, UK, etc.). This economic approach entered into crisis some decades after the writings of new economic philosophers, such as Smith and Ricardo. These authors stressed the idea that the wealth of nations was based on the richness of their citizens (and not on that of the state), thus encouraging free economic relations among citizens and companies.

54. The percentage of urban population in Western Europe in 1820 was 12.3 per cent. In 1890 this figure had increased up to 31.0 per cent. Maddison, A. (2001: 40). Book already mentioned.

55. This implicitly supposed the making of a choice for efficiency while neglecting many social aspects of the economic life. This is more or less what is happening today in the context of current neo-liberalism.

rate of GDP,[56] it negatively modified the personal income distribution and drove the new urban workers into living conditions often worse than those in countryside.

Note however that in the last decades of the 19th century a countervailing power, trade-unionism, came into being, enhanced by three main factors: 1) the better information on working conditions now known at national level; 2) the new socialist-Marxist ideas on profit and exploitation; and 3) the feasibility of spreading these ideas and information among workers concentrated in manufacturing cities. Indeed, this was the first historical experience of the application of "better information" on geographically joint mistreated collectives.

Observe that these historical negative micro-relations among social agents within western nations could be considered similar to the current economic and political macro-relations at global level, between the western world and the poor countries.

It seems to us that the long period of 50-60 years wasted by western "traditional-liberal" states in addressing their internal social micro-problems caused by the abuse of the working class—a by-product of a non-restricted freedom of contracting—should not be replicated at a global level, reason why the West should invest in the catching up of LDC by means of promoting ODA and by facilitating trade. However, in the past 25 years the practise in international trade negotiations, and also in ODA, has tended to replicate old biased relations.

Summarising, we do believe that implementation of a complementary, boosted and reorganised ODA,[57] improvement of trade accessibility of developing countries to agricultural and services markets in the rich world, and upgraded efforts for the correct understanding of the political demands of the "today informed" poor of the world, may altogether result in a more effective solution for the achievement of

---

56. The average growth rate experienced in the 19th century by the GDP in Western Europe was around 1.5 per cent, while the annual growth rate of the European population was around 0.7 per cent, thus facilitating a real per capita GDP growth rate per annum of around 0.8 per cent. This last figure enabled more than doubling the European per capita GDP in the 19th century. Note that the velocity of prosperity was higher in the so-called EIC group of countries.

57. In relation to the reorganisation of ODA by UNICO. Rahman, R.D. and J.M. Andreu (2004: 135). *Responsible Global Governance*. Book already mentioned.

peace and human security than a continuation with the Washington Consensus recipe plus the war against international terrorism.

Decadence of the Trade Unions?

After having played a historical role in the formation of wages and working conditions in western labour markets, western Trade Unions seem today doomed to progressively disappear.

In effect, recent steps towards "globalisation" (based on growing freedom in international capital movements, in connection with practical immobility of labour) has made possible that multinational firms (MNC) may choose the place they want to invest in. Under these new location options, workers of MNC in rich countries have progressively been forced to accept lower or quasi-stagnant real wages.

On the other hand, weak or inexistent trade unions in the "South", combined with scant capital and huge supply of labour pouring to cities from rural areas, have made that wages remain very low in developing countries. Logically, under these circumstances, MNC may initiate new activities in the "South", or abandon the old ones in the West, thus profiting from the existing wages gap.

Clearly, this is a new unbalanced situation favourable this time to MNC that, however, will not last forever. After the industrial progress of developing countries—mainly in Asia—and the relative industrial decline of the developed ones, the world will approach towards a new equilibrium. In our view, trade unions will progressively gain clout in developing countries; as they will recover their lost role and influence in the West when wage convergence steps up.

One could also visualise in future a change in size and influence of trade unions, which will become multinational; that is to say, institutions that will deal with labour affairs at trans-national and sector level, thus progressively recovering countervailing power.

Evolution of the Economic Theory and Ideologies in the 20th Century

For around a century (1870-1970), two main economic models were in competition for explaining the economic behaviour of workers and entrepreneurs: the Marxist one and the Neo-classical one.[58] In order to explain the "non-sustainability" of capitalism, the Marxian analysis focused on private owners of capital goods, who in their industrial relations with workers obtained a surplus, thus depriving the employed masses of part of the value generated by them. According to Marx, this unfair distribution would historically produce progressive discontent among workers and ever growing economic cycles and unemployment, finally resulting in the crumbling of capitalism and its substitution by socialism, followed by "communism".

Marxian and Neo-classical Economics

The economics of Marx was essentially a dynamic theory (rather a dynamic hypothesis) partially based on the classical value of labour (formulated by Smith and Ricardo) that, jointly with components of sociology and politics, was "capable of explaining" the evolution of the organisation of production, in historical stages. When arriving to the stage of socialism, the former way of production based on free markets and on the exploitation of workers (capitalism) would disappear, and would be substituted by the socialisation of assets of production.

When the implementation of the Marxian economy started, the economic planning emerged.[59] The need of establishing prices for goods and salaries, and the required mutual consistency of the different industrial productions, forced the appearance of mentioned central planning. However, this approach, lacking the flexibility of decentralised markets, became more and more untenable when the number of goods and services to be produced increased along the economic development process. Finally, it became clear that this approach lacked the necessary stimuli for increasing productivity, private savings, and for timely taking new economic initiatives, thus being condemned to perpetual inefficiency.

Paradoxically, when the Marxian model started gaining ground, mainly in workshops, an opposite conception of the economic science,

---

58. Note that after the 30s of the 20th century, previous "neoclassical ideas" were complemented by the Keynesian contribution for the rationalisation of the applied macro-economic policy under certain macro-economic conditions.
59. After the Soviet revolution in 1917 in Russia, the revolutionaries needed several years to develop a central planning strategy in order to make the model operative.

neoclassicism, appeared and grew in the last third of the 19th century. This new neoclassical paradigm, enhancing the idea of giving the maximum relevance to the demands of goods (not analysed by Marx) and markets, as suggested one century ago by Smith and later by Ricardo, started gaining ground at a world scale.

In fact, in the most "civilised" part of the World at that time, Europe, domestic free markets had already flourished for goods, services and factors, including labour, while significant limits existed in relation to international trade: asymmetric commerce with colonies, and "convenient" barriers to the entrance of raw materials or manufactures coming from other European countries. This market system in connection with the Industrial Revolution and the development of the railways—as stated in Chapter 2—made possible an acceleration of the economic growth in the West, which of course underwent cyclical oscillation, and generated negative distribution of income[60] and growing social anger.

Despite the interruption of its working during the First World War and the non-consideration of externalities and income distribution problems, this model based on "free markets" worked rather "efficiently" in the West for almost 60 years (1870-1929), while accumulating huge social tensions.

Keynesianism and Return to Neo-classicism

The Great Depression of the 30s seemed to be the prelude of the end of capitalism, as predicted by Marx. However, capitalism of those days found in the macroeconomic ideas of J.M. Keynes—based on public intervention on the demand of goods and services of new production, mainly infrastructures (and also weaponry)—a way to compensate the then scant private demand. This Keynesian approach, a mix of free market economy and juncture state interventions, later on complemented with the implementation of welfare economics and the development of the welfare state, generated in the following decades, a significant growth of public sectors.

---

60. This trend towards negative income distribution in the first stages of the development process has for long been considered as normal in the literature on Economic Development. Remember in this respect the so-called Kuznets curve, already explained.

Unfortunately, the Keynes approach, as later explained by Keynesians and Monetarists, contained certain non well-defined and imprecise areas. Particularly in relation to the long-term effects of public deficit on inflation, when it was financed with new printed money; or on the real interest rate when it was financed by issuing public debt. On the other hand, initially recommended increases in public expenditure by naïve Keynesians paid practically no attention to its efficiency, since it was initially thought that efficient or less efficient increases in public expenditure were a better policy than no increase in public expenditure at all.

In many cases, growing public sector combined with reckless succession of public deficit provoked the increase of the internal outstanding public debt in GDP terms, thus limiting future application of this kind of policy.

Summing up, although for a period the western world became absolutely Keynesian,[61] one may say that imprudent and inefficient application of the Keynesian recipes by politicians finally drove this policy to a loss of prestige, although not to its filing.[62] Nevertheless, the more the above-mentioned dysfunction became clear, all the more criticism on public intervention gained ground. In fact, different groups of theorists, all belonging to the most liberal (neo-classical) tradition, started criticising Keynesianism. Some pioneers, among them the so-called "Monetarists", already in the 60s criticised economic activism of governments, due to its possible pro-cyclical inconvenience, its eventual crowding out effect,[63] and the oblivion of its inflationary bias.

---

61. In 1965, the *Time* magazine put John M. Keynes on its cover, and declared America's post war affluence to be the consequence of its choosing to live in "the Keynesian era". It even quoted the (late) conservative economist Milton Friedman, as saying that "we are all Keynesians now", a stunning admission (...) exceeded only by the Republican President Richard Nixon's announcement a few years later that, "now I am a Keynesian". Parker, R. (2006: 167). Book already mentioned.
62. Indeed, public deficit—often caused by the deliberate reduction of taxes payable by rich (income tax) or firms (corporate tax)—has continued their existence across the World in the last 30 years; even reaching record figures in some countries as the US in 2004.
63. This "crowding out effect" refers to the possibility that public deficit financed by means of issuing public debt induces interest rates increases, thus negatively affecting the private sector.

Some years later, in the 70s, the so-called "new neo-classical economists"[64] after building up a new micro-macro model—a mix of rigorous maths, acceptable hypothesis and some fancy-whimsical assumptions—according to which the market system would automatically guarantee a steady growth with internal and external equilibrium, once more condemned the occasional political interventions of the state, due to its purported ineffectiveness.

A third group, the "theorists of the Public Choice" (Buchanan, Tullock),[65] attacked the ever growing public sectors, arguing that its development was mainly due to the personal interest of politicians and bureaucrats, and not so much to the interests of citizens, which would be better served by means of transferring public activities to the private sector.

Needless to say that most of these "new neoclassical contributions"—many of them for long kept in the fridge of the Chicago School—only gained credibility when the world economy entered in relapse in the second half of the 70s and first 80s, as a result of the two oil crisis registered in these decades. In this bewildering period, modern conservatives recovered their engagement with one of the oldest exercise in moral philosophy; that is, the search for a superior moral justification of selfishness.[66]

The New Neo-classical Movement and the Law of Pendulum

As a consequence of the reformulation in the 50s of former quantitative theory, and the appearance of "monetarism" and new-neoclassicism in the 60s and 70s, both approaches defending economic non-interventionism, the pendulum started moving; but then again to the other extreme.

---

64. Among these economists we could mention the Nobel-awarded R. Lucas, and T. Sergeant. Specifically in their article "After Keynesian Macroeconomics", and certainly overdoing it, they suggested that "existing Keynesian macroeconomic models cannot provide reliable guidance in the formulation of monetary, fiscal or other types of policy...There is no hope that minor or even major modifications of these models will lead to significant improvement in their reliability." The contributions of N. Wallace and R. Barro were also relevant in the "restatement" of the neo-classical model.

65. These two authors, plus other political scientists as Downs, reached the same conclusion about the increasing ineffectiveness of governmental interventions. And all of them did it through the well-known neo-classical assumption referring to the radical individualism of the economic agents (firms, individuals acting as consumers, voters, politicians, etc.) as the main foundation of their actions.

66. Parker, R. quoting John K. Galbraith (2006: 522). Book already mentioned.

In those days (70s), supporters of the new-neoclassical movement, far from only attacking ineffective public interventions (such as some subsidies to production or consumption, permanence in public sector of non strategic public firms, or some direct interventions in financial or real markets), attacked almost the entire public sector. They even put into question the convenience of keeping inside the public sector services such as health, education, pensions, and provision of infrastructures. Of course, at the foundation of this overdone pro-private sector movement, Darwinism and disrespect for the poor was once again underlying.[67]

Following the appearance of new technologies, public provision of certain goods and services that for long had unanimously been considered as a matter of natural public monopolies (railways, telephones, electricity, water, etc.) was also put into question. Note, however, that while some of these public monopolies had lost arguments to remain in public sector, they were often not correctly privatised and thereafter not efficiently supervised and maintained; while the results of the privatisation of others (mainly railways) became a real nightmare.

Let us additionally remember that, in the 70s, the Bretton Woods system of fixed exchange rates had crumbled, and that a sudden multiplication of oil prices, with high potential for inflationary acceleration, had appeared onto the scene. In this regard, some years after the first oil crisis (1973-74) it was correctly thought that a continuous (upwards) monetary adjustment to the high and growing prices of oil would change into a global galloping inflation, which could jeopardise the political and social stability in Western countries;[68] hence, the urgency in those days of fighting against inflation.

Coinciding with this macroeconomic urgency, conducive in the early 80s to a rapid contraction of the growth rate of the monetary aggregates in the US, the new neo-classical economists also proclaimed

---

67. The old "Darwinist" ideas that suggested that "the wealth was the God's way of blessing those who put Him first", or that "millionaires were a product of natural selection", changed in the 80s into something less imaginative and much more brutal: "common people are not entitled to any (public) services", as remarked by Reagan's Budget Director who was charged with the implementation of massive cuts in social spending. Parker, R. (2006: 574). Book already mentioned.
68. Maddison, A. (2001). *The World Economy: A Millennium Perspective*. Paris: OECD. p.131.

the convenience of recovering the full freedom of markets, distorted by previous (and according to them frequently overdone) micro and macro interventions, which allegedly had induced growth of unemployment.[69]

Observe that the new neo-classical economists based their liberalising ideas on the assumptions that prices and wages would easily reach total flexibility in future, and that the economic agents would always use all the available information to fully anticipate government actions.

One has to admit that some of their ideas were valid.[70] Other assumptions however, were clearly biased and unrealistic.[71] Even more, exaggerated privatisations of traditional public activities (education, health, pensions, etc.) could at mid-long term become socially or politically destructive, if they—as expectable—induced negative distribution of income and wealth.

Notwithstanding the weakness of some of its basic assumptions and the non-consideration of its negative results in relation to income distribution, the new neo-classical economic model quickly gained ground, and came into the forefront as mainstream economics, calling everywhere for liberalisation of markets, zero inflation target[72] and downsizing of the public sector.

The Thatcher-Reagan Experiment

Against this doubtful intellectual background, complemented with some non-accurate ideas in the field of public finance (supply-side economics), two governments decided to pioneer the implementation of the new neo-classical ideas.

---

69. At least for a while, the reality proved the opposite. The rate of unemployment steadily grew in the periods 1974-1983, 1984-1993 and 1994-1998 practically in all regions. Maddison, A. (2001: 134) Book already mentioned.

70. The replacement of backward looking "adaptive expectations" by the new forward looking "rational expectations" was one of the main contributions of the new neoclassical economists.

71. For instance, the implicit assumption that a fast clearance of all markets—based on the assumed full-flexibility of prices and wages—would quickly result in full employment without distorting the personal income distribution was really a fantasy.

72. Only two decades later, this recommended optimum zero inflation became a serious concern for mainstream economists. This is because this target can provoke a problem much more dangerous than that of inflation: the deflation of prices conducive to depression or stagnation of real GDP, as it occurred in the 90s in Japan.

In the early 80s, the governments of Margaret Thatcher (UK) and Ronald Reagan (US), conveniently using just a part of the reformulated model, took the first steps to hastily correct the somewhat oversized public sector, and to facilitate the clearance of markets. Both of them started a de-escalation of public intervention in private markets, and a rushed privatisation of public firms and some public services, disregarding further problems of industrial concentration and personal income distribution. In parallel—mainly in the US—tax reductions in line with the Laffer recommendations, increased defence expenditures, and severe monetary corrections to choke current inflation were implemented.[73]

Leaving aside doubts on the economic and political long-term validity of this approach, two external and independent developments seemed to support successful "expected" results. First, the economic recovery that started in the West in 1983-84 appeared as very strong[74] after a long period of standstill, thus apparently "validating" the new economic approach. Second, the crumbling of the central planning system—a case of extreme public intervention—as practised by the Soviet Union and satellites, additionally seemed to confirm the supremacy of the new approach as the only way to produce a steady and generalised growth process.

Not surprisingly, this new economic theory and policy quickly spread to many countries of the world, and also permeated the philosophy of the Bretton Woods institutions, devoted to assess policies and financing external deficits and development. In particular, autarky was condemned, and outward-oriented policies were indiscriminately defended and hastily promoted by IMF and WB.

Paradoxically, and against basic political corollaries deriving from the neo-classical model, the accessibility of exports of developing countries to agriculture and services markets in Western countries, as well as freer international movements of labour, remained denied (thus depriving western consumers from important gains of trade,

73. We should note that in parallel with tax reductions, Reagan significantly increased the US defence expenditure, a combination of policies that, against recommendations of new neo-classical economists, finally drove the US economy to a huge public deficit and to much higher interest rates.

74. This was not new in economic history: it had been registered in many expansionary phases of former economic cycles.

while employment in developing countries was forced to remain undersized).

Asymmetrical Application of the Neo-Classical Model with Doubtful Economic and Political Results

In order to provisionally assess the working of the above-mentioned approach, we should firstly take a close look into the economic results of the applied model. First of all, it should be underlined that the rate of unemployment in Western countries (as average) was higher in the neo-liberal period 1973-1998, than in the "interventionist" one (the so-called golden age of capitalism, 1950-1973). Nonetheless, continued application of the neo-classical micro-recipes in western countries finally improved the unemployment situation in the period 1998-2006, although at a high social cost in terms of the degradation of the personal income distribution.

On the other hand, expectations of generalised prosperity, stemming from the undertaken approach, were not met in many other countries.[75] Finally, the increase in the last 15-20 years of the per capita GDP discrepancies among nations additionally proves the long-term deficiencies of the recently adopted approach of neo-classicism.

Even without rejecting some of its undeniable advances, the new approach also accumulated meaningful weakness from social and political perspectives. One of them was the indiscriminate degrading of the social protection of western citizens, a trait which compounded in the West the observed trend towards worsening of personal income distribution induced by "private sector". Note that at the same time and in the international field, in the name of alleged "inefficiency", some public transfers to LDC (ODA) also underwent exaggerated reductions in real terms, particularly in the 90s, with insufficient results in the fight against poverty.

75. Maddison, A. (2001). *The World Economy. A Millennium Perspective*. Paris: OECD. p.129. In this publication it is explained that, as a whole, 168 countries (40 countries of Asia, 44 countries of Latin America, 27 countries of Eastern Europe, and 57 countries of Africa) experienced in the so-called neo-liberal period (1973-1998) an average annual growth rate of their per capita GDP of minus 0.21 per cent (negative growth rate). Note that the 57 countries of Africa experienced no growth at all in their per capita GDP in this period, while the per capita GDP of Eastern European countries slumped to an annual rate of minus 1.1 per cent. Even more, the per capita GDP of the selected 40 slow-growth countries of Asia experienced in this neo-liberal period a growth rate (0.59%) almost similar (0.48%) to that reached in colonial times (1870-1913).

From the perspective of applied macroeconomics, we have to underline that just a few countries tried to follow the new-neo-classical recipes completely, in particular that referred to the maintenance of balanced public budgets. Contrary to the recommendations of the model, and amazingly, we find the case of the US, a country that in the period 2000-2004—by significantly reducing direct taxation—reached the largest public deficit of its history, thus behaving as a super-Keynesian state of the 60s, while at the same time it behaved as a neo-classical one in microeconomic terms. Indeed, this contradiction proves that Western leadership has not trusted some implications of the new neo-classical model, thus only applying a microeconomic part of its recipes (forgetting for instance the international free movements of labour).

In conclusion, the application of the new economic policy was partial,[76] and played again as a pendulum. This time it moved from the naïve macroeconomic Keynesian policies applied in the 60s (f.i., the New Frontier policy in the US, etc.) and early 70s, to a purported extreme market liberalisation with oblivion, and sometimes contempt, of some vital public sector interventions;[77] and also with oblivion of the political effects of this policy on the degree of equity required for the democratic acceptation of capitalism.[78] Note in this regard that a low degree of equity provided by capitalism could everywhere undermine democracy at mid-long term, even in Western countries.

In fact two decades and a half after the initiation of its implementation, one may today perceive the economic and political

---

76. Note however that mentioned reduction of taxation, besides non-fulfilling one of the new neo-classical recipes—zero public deficit—recklessly and intentionally reduced the fiscal burden of the have's, thus in parallel forcing a reduction of funds to finance social goods and services.

77. Observe that all along these two waves of theoretical and political change, one form of public expenditure never ceased to grow in the US: the defence expenditure. Its rapid growth in the 60s drove to significant inflation, and in the 80s to significant degrading of the social protection (the same could be said in relation to the currently programmed US budgets till 2012). Taking into account the evolution of the personal income distribution of the US from the 80s onwards, one may conclude that the middle class and the poor (in the US) have paid for the rearmament.

    We could additionally affirm that, in the US, while the debate on economics among politicians has always remained open, the "required" growing in defence expenditure for trying to maintain the role as military dominant global super-power has always remained out of question.

78. This basic issue of acceptability of capitalism, which will depend on the attainment of a minimum degree of equity, will be explained in Chapter 4 of this book.

limits and fragilities of the selective conservative interpretation of the new neo-classical approach. Remarkably, the same happened in the case of Keynesianism, which after two or three decades of naïve and reckless implementation, also entered in a blind ally.

One could easily draw some lessons of the last two pendulum movements in the application of economic policies: new neo-classical and public choice economists should not have attempted to bury Keynesianism and the public sector at all costs. Similarly, political leaders in the 60s should not have abused public deficit expenditure by means of indiscriminately increasing the public sector, while financing this operation by means of printing new money (inflation) or with rapid expansion of public debt thus crowding out private sector.

Consequently, as the correct economic policies should have moved along the last 50 years in the "middle of the road", the optimum policy should have moved on the coordinates of the mixed economy of market, giving maximum relevance to the private sector when it really behaves in a competitive way (unfortunately this is not so common as thought), while public sector should have been charged with the provision of public goods and the correction of the rest of economic and social failures (externalities, production of information on markets, and redistribution of income). But all this provided that it would have been funded mainly with current revenues.

Main Economic Problems of Current Capitalism

Once described in this Chapter the main traits of the historical stages of capitalism—"traditional-liberal" capitalism (1870-1914) and the post Second World War transition towards contemporary capitalism (1945-1995) developed in two stages—and briefly depicted the evolution of the economic theories and ideologies along the 20th century, we will now enter into the analysis of the main economic problems of capitalism in its recent phase (1995-2007).

Among them we could mention the following ones: 1) The magnum economic shift favouring Asia, a shift that will change in one or two generations the current political and economic power play in the World; 2) The worsening of the personal income distribution in many countries, including the rich ones, a problem that may undermine democracy, as well as making difficult the creation of a "global democracy"; 3) The wrong social consequences of certain competition rules, particularly in the labour market, which are inducing long run negative spill-over effects on the foundation of societies, the families; 4) The deterioration in the rich world of social protection nets of workers and the delay in the development of these nets in poor countries; 5) The liberal oversimplification of the playground of the public sector and its consequences for human security; and 6) The non-sustainability of the global environment and the lack of efficient administration of the scant natural resources of common use. Note however that the latter two issues will be developed in Chapter 5, reason why we will not insist on them here.

Asian Take-off and Western Adjustment to the New Economic Structure of the World

Although one cannot ignore the difficult economic position of a good part of Asian citizens (mainly those living in countryside), in particular those living in China and India who only count with limited per capita GDPs—1,740 US dollars in China and 730 in India (2005)[79]—one should not undervalue the capacities of progression of Asia, commanded by the two mentioned giants, assumedly called to become, along the 21st century, global powers in all matters.

Concerning predictions on the future of these two countries, one has to move in two tiers: the economic one and the political one. Specifically, the foundations of any economic prediction on the future of China and India have to rely on theories of economic development, applicable to those developing countries that experience rapid structural changes,[80] and on the conventional theories of economic growth.[81] This economic approach, with the help of econometric exercises, may show us a trend of China and India (less in the case of India) to quickly gain world shares, being this in GDP or in international trade or financing. In this pure economic and partial

79. These figures of 2005, taken from WB (2007), "Development Economic Indicators" are expressed in terms of dollars at current exchange rate.

80. These foundations are mainly based on the model of Lewis for rapid industrialisation, and on that of the opportunities coming from backwardness, as explained by Gerschenkron. Vide. Todaro, M. (2003). *Economic Development*, 8th Ed. Pearson Education.

81. These theories are mainly based on the neo-classical model, with the complement of the endogenous growth perspective.

context, the recent study published by Goldman-Sachs[82] is illustrative. According to conclusions of the Goldman-Sach study,[83] as early as 2009 a small group of four countries (China and India, plus Russia and Brazil) will have a joint absolute growth of their production (in US$ terms) greater than that of the 6 currently more advanced countries altogether: US, France, Germany, Italy, Japan and the U.K. This means that in 2009 the mentioned group of four will become the engine of the economic growth of the world.

As suggested by mentioned study, this catching up process of the four countries commanded by China and India will continue, thus generating *ceteris paribus* in 2050 a surprising picture in relation with the economic potentialities of the analysed (four plus six) countries. China, US and India, and by this order, would then be the economically and politically most powerful countries of the world. Behind them, but far away in the economic game, and in some cases also in the political one, would be Japan, Brazil and Russia. Finally in the last wagon, and by this order, one would find UK, Germany, France and Italy.[84]

In our view, the trend of recent economic history may mark an evolution for future catching up not faraway from the mentioned one, and mainly in the cases of China and India. These are two countries with pressing populations, with huge reserves of labour force currently stuck to agricultural activities with nil (or almost nil) marginal productivity, with a great margin for technical improvement in their physical and human capital, and with a great capacity for generating internal savings, particularly in the case of China.[85]

---

82. Vide. Wilson, D. and Purushothaman, R. (2003). "Dreaming with BRICs. The Path to 2050," Goldman Sachs Global Economic website. *Global Economics Paper* No. 99. October.
83. Logically, the longest the period of econometric prediction, the lesser the credibility of the results because they will not include new national and international political and economic changes, that currently cannot be envisaged accurately, or that cannot be foreseen at all.
84. Note that, long before 2050, some of the mentioned Euro-Zone countries, plus other current EU-partners, may have become EU Federation. In our opinion it is expectable that with the attainment of a voluntary EU Federation, the federated economy will reach significant economies of scale, reap economies of integration up to 2 per cent of its joint GDP, and significantly gather momentum, which could partially contradict the results of the commented Goldman-Sachs study.
85. In 2005, the gross internal saving of China was 50.4 per cent in terms of its GDP and the gross internal saving of India was 32.2 per cent. Vide World Bank (2007). *World Development Indicators*. On the other hand, the domestic rate of investment of India has recently increased from 23 per cent (2002) to 33 per cent (2005), making possible the rise (up to 7.5-8 per cent) of the long-term growth rate of India, till recently positioned around 6 per cent.

We do believe that—conversely to the successful cases of Japan, Korea and some other Asian tigers in the 20th century—at the beginning of the 21st century China and India seem to be faraway from the typical positions of diminishing returns suffered by some of the above mentioned countries, just two or three decades after the initiation of their take off processes.[86] In fact, China and India "started" their development processes in 1978(80) at significant lower levels in per capita GDP terms than many of their current Asian competitors, and with a delay of two to three decades. Even more, these two countries count with huge potentialities for transferring labour from their rural areas to the industrial and service sectors, which may protract the current rapid growth for three or four additional decades.

But perhaps more important than the final results of the mentioned Goldman-Sachs research is what it conceals: a) the fall or stagnation of real wages of western labourers combined with growing profit rates of western firms (and their owners), thus inducing a significant shift in the personal income distribution that could deteriorate Western democracies; and b) the necessary repercussions of the economic success of China and India on the political power play at a global scale. In particular the case of China and its rapidly growing influence in Africa and Latin America is simply spectacular, causing already growing concern in the West.

Globalisation, Distribution of Personal Income and Democracy

Clearly, in the last 15 years, if not before, financial capital has acquired a great comparative advantage in geographical mobility in comparison to that of labour. For family reasons (note that two or more family members working in different firms or sectors cannot move at the same time), due to technical barriers (languages and skills) or due to political ones (immigration rules), labour has traditionally found significant limitations to move.

In this context, western firms looking for better opportunities have abandoned—or have threatened with abandoning—old settlements,

86. On the reasons why China is today seen as bringing a superior level of economic threat than that experienced with the rise of Japan in the 80s: Vide. Enderwick, P. (2007). *Understanding Emerging Markets. China and India*. New York: Routledge. p.48.

thus forcing a *ceteris paribus* reduction or stagnation of real wages of western workers; and this while GNPs of relevant western countries[87] have tended to increase, partly due to the growing investments realised abroad at expected higher earning-rates. Of course, mentioned industrial dislocations, have induced a significant change in the personal income distribution in western countries, as a derivative of the existence of lower real salaries in developing countries.

Observe that this change in the personal income distribution in western countries induced by globalisation, plus other registered changes,[88] if long-lasting as foreseeable, will be non-neutral in relation to sustainability of democracy. Note however that current good times for western investor-capitalists may not last forever, because the current situation—being economically one of non-equilibrium—will in future trigger the introduction of stronger taxes on the richest residents, looking for more equitable personal income distribution.

The personal income distribution in poor countries has also registered a negative trend, in particular in China and India. The causes of this negative redistribution in developing countries have been different from those in the West, and can be explained by the evolution of the pattern of internal distribution of income in the first stages of the development process, as depicted in the model of Lewis and described by the Kuznets curve.

As a consequence, incidence of globalisation on the distribution of income in rich countries—and also in poor countries if many people are left behind (in rural areas) as usually happens in the development process—could be harmful for their (consolidated or not) democracies; reason why a system of surveillance on income distribution should be set up everywhere.

---

87. The difference between GDP (Gross Domestic Product) and GNP (Gross National Product) has to do with the differentials in transfers of remunerations of national factors working abroad, and those of foreign factors working inside the country. As a consequence, a country with a lot of capital or labour (in net terms), respectively invested or working abroad, will have a higher GNP than GDP. And vice versa.

88. To mentioned change today underway in the personal income distribution between western capitalists and workers, we should add as a cause of the worsening of the personal distribution of wealth, the almost generalised maintenance in the West of very low (or negative) interest rates in the last years. This phenomenon has hugely favoured citizens with previous significant wealth (assets) used as collateral for taking new loans.

On the Redefinition of Competition Rules in Capitalism

As readers know, all competitive sports have rules which define the limits of competitiveness (duration of the game, targets, specific way of doing things, treatment of adversary if there is personal contact in the game, no use of drugs to take advantage, etc.). Transgressions of limits will be declared fault and penalised by referee for the adversary to take compensation. Transgressors could even be expelled from the playground if the committed mistake had been serious. Of course, participation in the game is always voluntary and no one believes that the existence of rules is detrimental for the competitiveness deployed by participants.

In the economic activity under competitive system, things are like in the sports: there are rules or there must be rules for fair competition; rules that, of course, and after agreement, will be susceptible of modification.

Note however that in the economic sphere there have always been economists, the so-called market fundamentalists,[89] who prefer total absence of rules, alleging that any hurdle or limit to economic freedom will be detrimental for the collective;[90] and this without taking into account either the negative incidence of total economic liberty on the quality of life of individuals (and families) at the mid-long term—which should be the main target of any economic reform—or the negative spill-over effects affecting current and future citizens. It seems as if mentioned fundamentalists neglected these extremes because they believe that the consequences of the eventual freedom excesses will not affect them (because they are rich or because negative spill-over effects will only be felt in the future).

As an example, let us analyse what is currently happening in part of western labour markets (for instance in US and UK). In these markets, after a generalised trend all along one century towards the reduction of the annual worked hours per worker, from the 80s onwards a reversion of mentioned trend started. While this happened, other

89. We here refer to "market fundamentalists", following the ideas defined by Stigliz, J. in his book of 2006. Book already mentioned.

90. Note that "market fundamentalists" usually defend the (discredited) "self-regulation" in front of any governmental regulation, because in their view public (external) regulation is always detrimental for the economic activity.

western countries, mainly in Continental Europe—those disdainfully defined by neo-cons as "Old Europe"—continued with their trend of the past century, with France reaching a working-time schedule of 35 hours, Netherlands of 36, etc., this apparently signifying that workers of "Old Europe" preferred more leisure than more income.

The pretexts to break the long run trend in some Anglo-Saxon countries—and today in France under Sarkozy—have been manifold. The most frequently quoted has been the "necessary increase in the productivity per labourer", achievable by means of increasing the working hours per week, in order to reduce the unitary costs of production. As it is usually alleged, this would improve the competitiveness of western firms against overwhelming imports coming from East Europe or Asia.

In front of this wrong economic argument—already debated in lines above—we oppose two main counter-arguments. The first one of a practical order, and the second one deeply rooted in the philosophy of life and the convenience of preserving the core of human life on Earth: the family.

Starting with the first, we have to mention that, although an increase in the productivity per worker in the West is convenient to preserve or increase competitiveness, the reality of our days is that the unitary costs are much lower in Eastern Europe and Asia than in the West, being the current differential—based on much lower real wages and longer schedules—non-bridgeable at short term.[91] In this practical context, lengthening the working schedules is a rather useless and costly operation.

Note that neo-liberals, encouraging freedom in labour contracting, thus stimulating the lengthening of working schedules, do not see but profits (for firms and also for workers) with the change. Indeed, "working till extenuation" seems to be the new creed for "good western workers", who should only pay attention to their squalid marginal income increase and not to what they give up in exchange: their scant leisure time all along their working lives.

---

91. Note that if globalisation continued, one should also expect convergence in working schedules and social protection nets. One cannot reasonably expect that labourers in Asia continue with extenuating working schedules and without a minimum of social protection when higher wages enable them to buy more leisure time and social security, as it historically happened in Europe.

The non-consideration of the spill-over effects of the lengthening of working time is our second but main argument against the so-called total flexibility of schedules. Note that significantly lengthening the schedules may produce in the mid-long term irreversible damages in family life and gender equality, and in the social and cultural life of labourers (cultural expressions, adult education, recreation, sports, travelling, etc.); and this irrespective of the additional damages that additional consumption—financed with supplementary incomes coming from protracted working schedules of labourers and profits of capitalists—may provoke on the environment and health.

Indeed to the extent that, in a given context of division of labour, specialised technology and reproduction, human beings cannot be totally flexible and mobile (in their activity and geography), the governments should practise some agreed intervention to deal with the mentioned spill-over effects.

Generalising former arguments, we should recognise that in fact, there are few aggregated markets without spill-over effects. Let us remember that national or international financial markets, if totally free, could be used for speculative activities, thus inducing more volatility than convenient; likewise, a sudden setting up of total freedom in the trans-national movements of workers would also be harmful for all parties; equally, a hasty and total liberalisation of commerce, if implemented for all goods and services, would also be dangerous for many communities, etc.

Of course, the combination of liberty with the public administration of the spill-over effects will not be easy, but forgetting the latter will surely be a non-profitable operation for mankind. Undeniably, all this will force in the 21st century a redefinition of competition rules in many markets that should be worked out in democratic multilateral bodies depending on a new democratic UN.

Redefinition and Global Agreement on Social Protection Net

All human beings may along their lives unwillingly enter in situations of misfortune—illness, unemployment, etc.—that may negatively affect them and their families. People also become older and incapable of continuing working to cope with their needs. In front of these possible or sure events, many people take insurance policies. But not all the people will do so for different reasons. Some of them will have no economic means left after meeting the current needs; and others will underestimate their future needs, thus not saving enough.

Note in addition that even those citizens with economic possibilities and keenness to take insurance policies or make savings for the future, may eventually fall in deep need. Sharp falls in prices of their assets (residences or stocks), and/or bankruptcies of firms, banks, pension funds, etc. in which they deposited or accumulated funds, are also events that may occur. All this means that human insecurity coming from other (unpredictable) causes than violence are all the time in front of us. Consequently, this human insecurity (for individuals) is a "bad" that governments should try to offset by directly producing the corresponding services—at least until a certain minimum—or by indirectly supervising or guaranteeing the insurance or risk coverage provided by private insurance companies.

Although a philosophical debate on the private or public provision of insurance against illness and other misfortunes, or of pensions for the old age, still remains, the reality has constantly confirmed that health and pension systems cannot be exclusively left to the private sector. This is due to the fact that—despite of its eventual security problems—there will always be a significant group of people that, having scant capacity for saving, cannot pay private policies for access to decent pensions or health systems.

Obviously, every country may have a different feeling in relation to the amount of risk to be covered by public sector, in relation to health, unemployment or pensions. But since different sensitivities will have a clear effect on taxation, and consequently on the competitiveness of firms, a fairer international competition will force in future an agreement at a global scale on the minimum degree of coverage and on the way of financing the Social Protection Net. Minimum to which every system of protection (placed under mentioned minimum) should arrive after a phasing period.

Note that in this issue, as it also occurs when calculating wage-differentials among nations, expenditures made by the Social Protection Net, should be considered as part of the gross salary-cost of workers, that will have to be withheld (from all of them) and simultaneously spent[92] when the hazardous individual circumstances appear.

As to the definition of the minimum level of the social Protection Net, we consider that this is a global issue that in future should have to be discussed and agreed upon in a new ILO, depending on a new democratic UN.

Although today poor countries cannot afford a higher social protection net, this does not mean that the dwellers of these countries do not desire stronger Social Protection Systems. However, as far as mentioned convergence in social protection and wages arrives, a good policy for helping to partially bridge the existent international "insurance gap", could be offered by a multilateral institution.[93] This policy should include a minimum compensation against some misfortunes of individuals; a compensation that should be collectively guaranteed.

Talking about convergence, it is our view that Social Security protection in Western countries should not converge to the current minimum levels of developing countries—as is openly and frequently suggested by western neo-liberals in order to "gain competitiveness"—but to a position somewhat in the middle of the way. It is important to add that mentioned convergence should not be hastily forced in Western countries, to significantly and rapidly cut current social advances, because this could damage democracy.

Redefinition of National and Global Public Sectors

Although there is nowadays a significant debate on the size of the public sector, there always will be a minimum of activities to be developed by it. In a context of progression towards global democracy, defence, justice and police—which are public activities traditionally

---

92. This would happen in the case that the Social Protection System closes the economic exercise with a balanced budget. A deficit of the Social Protection Net financed with funds coming from the general budget of the state would imply an additional redistribution of income.

93. We are here referring to rapid and organised reaction in cases of catastrophes, etc.; cases in which UNICO should automatically intervene. Shows in media asking for charity, filming families in ruin and cry, pledges of funds realised by relevant western politicians that may finally never arrive to its destination, or the geopolitical administration of the ruin of the poor, are traits of current post-catastrophes interventions, that should be avoided.

and exclusively provided by national states—will have in part to be globally reorganised, depending on a supranational authority with global democratic support (a new UN as we have many times suggested).

Indeed, defence activities, whose partial but collective (global) provision would induce significant economies of scale enabling public savings up to 1 per cent of the global GDP,[94] should indisputably fall into the global public sector sphere. Note that this transformation of the defence, partially but progressively organised under the auspices of a new democratic UN, would have a decisive influence in conflict resolution and on de-activating arms race, thus by and by changing current unilateral practises into things of the past.

Although to a great extent, Justice is a national or local activity,[95] it has also a global dimension that should be provided at global scale by a democratic multilateral public sector (special international courts, etc.). The same could be said about police in relation to trans-national crimes.

Nevertheless, mentioned partial shift of parts of the national public sectors activities towards a global public sector, will not be easily implemented. First of all, by the enmity of the different (national) conservatives to give up an inch of their national sovereignty (in the US or in other countries); and secondly, due to the recent and successful attack of neo-liberals to the public goods provision in the fields of defence,[96] justice and police at national level. The promotion of private arbiters for cases of private dispute; the multiplication of private companies of security to substitute the police; the rise in subcontracting of vital elements for national defence and emergency aid, etc. are proofs of the success of the mentioned attack.

Note additionally that, of these public activities related to defence, justice, and police, the profitable ones have tended to be privatised

94. This amount of 1 per cent of global GDP, added to other funds, could be used through UNICO for financing the development of LDC

95. Public provision of Justice is in crisis everywhere. Justice is slow and expensive, thus mainly favouring the rich, the criminals—who enjoy "free defence"—and the public sector.

96. Note that in the Iraq war not least than 30,000 men contracted by the American private security firm Blackwater, are involved in paramilitary activities, which implies a certain privatisation of the US military forces.

in some western countries, while the rest have remained in the public sector, at times undergoing—with exceptions—more restricted funding.

Observe additionally that the funding of public activities—privatised or not—have progressively been based on indirect taxation,[97] mainly in order to avert progressive taxation of the rich. As a consequence of the former combination of privatisation and progressive financing through indirect taxes, access to general security, emergency aid, and justice services have today become degraded while mainly financed by middle classes and poor in many rich countries.[98] This is the reason why mentioned activities, after being reorganised, should fall again into the public sphere. Of course, something alike could be said about other traditional public services as the Mail-Postal Services, Public Transports, Social Protection Net (already discussed), etc.

Consequently, it would be important to redefine and agree at a global scale the main activities that should fall into the sphere of the global public sector. Note that size and contents of public sector at national scale should be consistent with the maintenance of a minimum of equity—the so-called equity system for acceptation of capitalism—necessary for developing or preserving democracy.

Under the aegis of a new democratic UN, the global public sector should also be involved in the administration and provision of other global public goods (environment, space and sea exploration, global economic regulation, etc.) and in the correction of global externalities. Note that these global provisions and corrections would be cheaper, fairer and more efficient than the current ones, which are poorly and fragmentarily provided, while lacking democratic legitimacy.

---

97. Again, to introduce in industrialised countries a copycat taxation taken from the developing countries to allegedly gain competitiveness, mainly against Asia, and particularly against China and India, seems to us a backward move designed in the interest of the rich; and, as a result, an attack to the "equity system" of capitalism which in due time could undermine democracy.

98. As examples of the consequences of overstated privatisation in the field of security, we will quote the chaos that followed the flooding of New Orleans in the summer of 2005, or the alleged (in autumn of 2007) misdemeanours in Iraq by Blackwater (a US private company which keeps deployed 30,000 armed individuals doing military activities).

Multilateral Political and Economic Framework to Correct Great Problems of Capitalism in the 21st Century

Although history has always moved with inertia—thus relevant political and economic reforms taking a lot of time since the appearance of the first expressions of discontent—we strongly believe that the recent ICT Revolution and the overwhelming magnitude of the recently unveiled global problems, have changed the historical tempo in a non-reversible way; and, consequently, former long delays in reaction will have to become dramatically shorter.

Bearing in mind this acceleration of history, and the current economic "structural change" coming from Asia, it is not difficult to deduce what components of the current institutional framework, political or economic, will not survive at mid-long term; at least in their current conception.

In a world in which "democracy", or a more intense popular participation in the political process, is progressively permeating practically all-political systems,[99] current United Nations will have no space to survive; and this because current UN—although having been useful for some decades in different fields of concern—continues being a non-democratic institution, and consequently, an invalid machinery for fulfilling many aims assigned to them in the current UN-Charter.

One has to acknowledge that in the 21st century, and in the overcrowded and geographically limited world in which we live, it will progressively be more difficult to justify the pre-eminence of the individual on the collective in most of the relevant economic decisions to be made. In the world today, and with the available and foreseeable technology, the export to developing countries of the current wasteful American way of living is non-recommendable because it is unsustainable. Indeed, this individualistic style of living, typical of pioneers of 19th century, is today clearly inconsistent with the control of global warming or the correct administration of the common natural resources.

---

99. Even China is nowadays starting its political reforms with elections at local level, although with restrictions concerning acceptation of candidates. In March 2007, private property rights in China have also experienced a significant leap forward.

Certainly, in the option "individual vs. collective" consumption, the so-called "composition fallacy" is today more perceivable than in many other historical moments. This paradox, which frequently emerges in economics, suggests that what is true for an individual is false for the collective.[100] Indeed, it is not realistic to think that in 3 or 4 decades every one of the foreseen 8.5-9 billion inhabitants of the planet would reach a standard of life similar to the current American one, with its derivatives of tremendous squandering of energy and egoistic recklessness with the environment.

Biased globalisation as that conceived in past decades, particularly in the 90s, based on private firms (MNC) and individualistic behaviour will not be tenable in the long run in a "global" democratic framework. In addition, in a global democratic world, and in front of the probable need of relevant human resettlements, due to climate change or other political causes, limitations and criteria for the mobility of people (migrations) will not be the same as the current ones. Of course, all these new aspects and conditioning circumstances will force the adoption of new collective policies that will have to be considered by new multilateral institutions, in the context of a new democratic UN.

Relevance of New Global Governance for the Delivery of Global Public Goods and Correction of Global Externalities

From our perspective, the main (final) aims to be achieved with priority by mankind in the next two or three decades, and in a democratic context, are global peace and human security on the one hand, and a healthy global environment on the other.

Note however, that the first two quoted public goods could only be reached if some indispensable global policies—that will have to act as intermediate goals—were previously implemented. These intermediate objectives, economic in nature and designed for significantly bridging the economic gap and promoting welfare, will have to do with the

100. In this regard, the "composition fallacy" may be defined as any "wrong generalisation based on individual experiences". For instance, to increase the saving rate of a specific individual in a cyclical downturn would be positive for him, but negative for the collective if all individuals behave the same way. This is due to the fact that if everybody acts in the same way—increasing savings—the aggregated consumption would decrease, as well as the employment, which would induce an additional fall of the GDP. Vide. Samuelson, P. and W. Nordhaus (1999) *Economics*. 16th Ed. Mac Graw-hill. p.6.

reorganisation and multiplication of current development financing—by means of the instauration of UNICO[101]—with the democratic renewal of the IMF, with the restatement of the WTO rules to create a fairer international trade, and with the reform of the ILO, mainly for the attainment of efficient international movements of labourers. Issues on global environment and global externalities will have to become dependant on WEO.[102] Of course, all these policies will have to be accorded in a multilateral-global and democratic context.

Similarly, long-lasting and burning problems, such as those of the Middle East and Kashmir, should be dealt with in a global democratic institution. As repeatedly proven, self-appointed mediators in many international conflicts, have not delivered any clear-cut and totally acceptable solution in more than half a century. Indeed, one should have not expected otherwise since these mediators were at the same time judges and interested parties.

Since in our world today it is unthinkable that relevant regional conflicts have no negative spill-over effects elsewhere, we do believe that the key for future resolution of general problems of humanity lies in treating them in a democratic global-multilateral context. Consequently, it is necessary to urgently "reorganise and democratise" the UN.

Besides its huge democratic deficiencies, we should not forget that the current UN, from the time of its inception with the choice of New York[103] as headquarter, up to the last created committee in our days, has basically followed a step-by-step alluvium accumulation process in which rationality has not been present many times.

It is true that there have been several attempts to reorganise the UN and its specialised agencies, but these attempts have not fructified either by their lack of opportunity, or by the suffocating rules for

101. We are here referring to the UN Institution for Cooperation (UNICO), as defined and described extensively by us in Rahman, R. and J.M. Andreu (2004: 143). Book already mentioned.

102. We are here referring to a World Environment Organisation (WEO) which would embody existing UN programmes on environment and climate change.

103. Note that the geographically non-centred city of New York was chosen as headquarter of the UN at a time in which the ruling insecurity in Europe and North Africa did not allow to establish the UN-headquarter in this area, when it was then the gravity centre of international commercial traffic. Besides, keeping the UN headquarter in the economic capital of the apparent hegemonic power does not seem to be politically neutral.

change as contained in its Charter. Although in 2005 the former UN General Secretary, Kofi Annan attempted a modest reform, it was suffocated by the main Security Council veto-owner. Note however that mentioned reform, although trying to reach a more balanced representation of the world, was not intrinsically more democratic than the current one, and consequently insufficient to improve the required global governance on global issues.

Changing the UN is Urgent

In our view, and for several political and economic reasons,[104] the moment for the initiation of a drastic change in the UN has finally arrived. The world cannot go ahead without solving the most important political problems that hinder the achievement of serious pending objectives;[105] that is to say, without changing the UN organisation and its decision-making process, including voting systems in different organs. Note, that a continuation of the current organisation and decision-making process in the UN would not only be irrational, but also a mockery of the democratic principles that most of veto-owners proclaim to defend.

We are conscious that, given the current chaotic political situation of the world, the creation of a democratic UN may be considered as a metaphysical impossibility. Nevertheless, we are convinced that rationality and common instinct of self-protection of mankind will finally impose its superiority on any alternative based on selfishness.

Consequently, when in next decade(s) the tremendous risks in which the world could be involved become patent,[106] today privileged

104. We are here referring among others to: 1) the breaking down of the old political equilibrium at times of the cold war; 2) the growing economic gap; and 3) the IT Revolution.

105. To reach some final objectives (mainly, peace and security) it will be necessary to boost, pool and efficiently reorganise (in the context of UNICO) the transfer of official funds from rich countries to the poor ones (current ODA); and to do it under the aegis of a democratic UN. Other basic current multilateral institutions as the WTO, ILO and IMF should also undergo significant democratic corrections to ultimately favour peace and security. For achieving other targets (keeping global environment and correcting global externalities) it will be necessary to create a World Environment Organisation (WEO) depending as well on the new UN.

106. In one or two decades global risk may have meaningfully increased on the planet. This could be due to the existence of an easier availability of nuclear weaponry, and the perceivable climate change implying continuous catastrophes.

countries will be forced to hand over part of their sovereignty—also materialised in their defensive systems—to a common democratic and supranational organism: a new democratic UN. In this regard, one should note that—although on a smaller scale—the same happened at the end of the Middle Age, when army capacities of lower instances were handed over to nascent, more powerful, national "states".

On the other hand, we have to say that a UN—like the current one—incapable of solving the economic and political problems of our global village, deserves neither its present budget (which is very small) nor any additional comment. Good intentions or mere political tactics, as currently deployed by the powerful in the UN, are not enough to solve current global problems.

We should not create or keep alive organs with inadequate financing for the functions assigned to them. This only generates frustrations. For instance, the function of stimulating the development of LDC, committed in the Charter of the UN, cannot be achieved by just making minimal contributions,[107] as for long the rich countries have been prone to believe, in opposition to the corollaries of the theory of economic development. Much more public foreign financing for development is absolutely necessary to avoid future problems related with peace and security since—as it currently happens—private funds do not go to most LDC.[108]

In the last decade multilateral (public) funding of development has gained ground over the bilateral, fragmented and over-conditioned one. This desirable change towards multilateralism in parallel with indispensable multiplication of funds devoted to this activity—which to a great extent could come from savings in (eventual) collective common defence—would per se require a democratic reorganisation of the UN, the only institution capable of providing with legitimacy the above mentioned global public goods and correcting global externalities.

107. Note that the allocation of resources to this activity by donors, including multilateral institutions, hardly reach today the figure of 0.3 per cent of the GDP of donor countries, as compared to the UN proposal of 0.7 per cent in the 70s, or the 2.0 per cent proposal of Tinbergen and us.

108. Indeed, in the decade of 90s and first 2000, the percentage of FDI directed to Africa, never surpassed the 2 per cent of the total; and this per comparison to the African population, of around 15 per cent of the World. Vide. Ajayi, S.I. (2006). *L'IDE e le developement economic en Afrique. Congrés International sur l'acceleration du developement de l'Afrique le 5 premieres annees du 21 siecle*. Tunis. 22-24 November.

Concerning this reorganisation, we think that it would be preferable not to compromise on current privileges of the powerful, since this would be in detriment of democracy, the final aims of the institution, and the survival of mankind in the long run. In this regard it would be preferable to have a democratic UN with a smaller number of represented countries than all represented, but some of them taking (non-democratic) advantage of the decision making process, in own interest.

Nevertheless we believe that, due to rationality and basic instinct for survival, current privileged countries will finally accept a new non-privileged status—that is to say representation depending basically on demography—instead of remaining outside of the multilateral management of world developments.[109] Indeed, eventual loss of prestige of the industrialised world stemming from its non-democratic global behaviour, relative decline of its economic relevance, and progressive growing export difficulties towards developing countries as a feedback effect of their international political behaviour, would force them to joint the new democratic UN.

Directives for the Reorganisation of the UN

As mentioned in paragraphs above, a new democratic UN will be the core institution for the legitimate provision of global public goods and the correction of global externalities. As a first outline, we will here refer just to the indispensable reforms of the UN (mainly its Security Council). All along this book (Chapters 4 and 5), we will also refer to the reform of its agencies (IMF, ILO, etc.), to the re-inclusion of WTO in the new UN, and to the setting up of new offsprings (mainly WEO and UNICO). Logically, we will not enter here in comments on the reshuffling of the rest of the UN complex organisation (special agencies, committees, and other bodies).

In our opinion, to achieve peace and security, a two-fold strategy is required. On the one hand, and as an intermediate target, bridging the economic gap will be essential; and on the other, solving current

109. Note that a new democratic UN, or a new democratic UN agency, as f.i. a modified WTO—with direct or indirect control on commercial flows, via resolutions on embargoes, extra-tariffs applicable to non-member states (among them, expelled countries from the UN as a consequence of violations of UN resolutions) etc.—could introduce stimuli for proper behaviour of powerful but reluctant countries.

violent conflicts and preventing future political and economic snags should be main priorities. As a consequence, it will be indispensable to modify the Security Council, including its rules for membership, financing and voting system.

On the Security Council Reform

The first issue to be discussed here is that of membership and, as a derivative, the regional representation of member-countries in the Security Council. At this moment the structure of the Security Council is one still rooted in the outcome of the Second World War, with the "victors"[110] as permanent members of the Council (Russia, US, France, UK and China[111]). In addition, there are ten members in rotation every two years, proposed by the General Assembly.

It is clear that the UN Security Council has serious problems concerning democratic global representation. The current small number of members, "necessary to gain efficiency" according to the existing Charter, may encourage some permanent members to buy wills in exchange for financial or political promises. Thus our call for increasing the number of represented countries to 24, and for changing the way of decision-making. A fixed number of countries per continent or region, according to its political and economic importance, should make up this representation.[112] This would be the only way to obtain a more balanced geographical representation,[113] more regional co-operation and less dominance of current permanent members.

110. Indeed, no one should consider "Nationalist China" as a victor of the WW2, due to the fact that the withdrawal of Japan from China was basically the result of the victory of the US in the Pacific War.

111. At the moment of the inception of the UN Security Council, a civil war was going on in the Republic of China. In 1949 Mao Tze Dong took power in Mainland China, while the nationalist government flew to Taiwan. Between 1946 and 1971 the Chinese seat in the Security Council was occupied by the so-called Republic of China (Taiwan) and not by the People's Republic of China (Continental China) controlled by the Chinese Communist Party (CCP).

112. In May 2003 the British Prime Minister, in trying to repair the damage inflicted by the UK and US to the Security Council, in relation to the Iraq war case, suggested some changes in this body. Specifically he suggested the inclusion of Japan, Germany, India and Brazil as new permanent members, while the body would enlarge up to 24 members. As anyone could have expected, his enlargement proposal did not suggest the elimination of veto rights of current permanent members in the Security Council.

113. Nowadays China is the only Third World country and only Asian nation among the permanent members of the Security Council. At the same time, Germany and Japan —losers of the WW2—contribute much more to the financing of the UN than Russia, China, UK and France, without playing a minimum role.

In second place, membership of the Security Council should be divided in two categories: long term membership (for instance 10 years tenure), extracted from prominent countries of every region; and short term membership (two years) extracted democratically from the rest, and also selected on a regional basis. This would imply the disappearance of permanent membership that, having been logical in the cold-war era, today seems counterproductive.[114] A tentative distribution of seats between long tenure and short tenure could be 8 and 16 respectively.

Thirdly, concerning the decision-making process, all members of the Security Council should have a weighted vote—defined by the General Assembly—connected with their relative population. Resolutions should always be passed by qualified majorities (for instance two-thirds or three-fifths of the total votes-value at stake) and in a fixed time-span.

All this would imply the disappearance of veto rights; an institution that, established (in 1945) for consensus building, has proven not to be the most effective for attaining peace and security, but rather paralysing.[115] Note additionally that quite a number of adopted resolutions were neither implemented nor enforced.

All this means that the Security Council and the UN Organisation have to be reformed as soon as possible to provide: 1) a fast and effective resolution system when peace and human security are threatened, or have entered into a situation of likely breakdown; and 2) an enforcement mechanism for peace making or keeping, based on the existence of a multi-base military system at a world scale (in all continents), in which the UN military forces would be stationed.

---

114. The Charter is extremely inflexible and non democratic in terms of decision making for Charter reforms. In article 108 of the Charter it is written "Amendments to the present Charter shall come into force ... when they have been adopted by a vote of two-thirds of the members of the General Assembly and ratified in accordance with their respective constitutional processes by two-thirds (...), including all the permanent members of the Security Council". These last 9 words are, in our view, defy the logic of global democracy. Opting for maintaining the decision making structure as devised in 1945 will necessarily avert rational updating.

115. It is remarkable that, in the last 60 years, and based on particular interests of one or more vetoing permanent members, the Security Council almost vetoed 250 (15 per cent) of around 1750 proposed resolutions.

On the Financial Problems of the UN

As one may deduce from economic theory and history, without enough multilateral funds allocated to the UN, the world will not be capable to push its peace and security agenda forward with a minimum of rationality.[116] Consequently—apart from the budget for the UN army which should be significant—if the UN wants to overcome the development problems of LDC, as an intermediate target for the deliverance of the main global public goods (peace and security), to become more fair and efficient in its voting and decision-making processes, and to be the core institution for the provision of other global public goods (global environment, global economic regulation, space and sea exploration, etc.) and the correction of global externalities, the contributions of member states will have to be multiplied.[117] Note that a significant part of this multiplied funding—devoted to bridging the economic gap—should be administered by a new UN agency (UNICO), with renewed criteria and perspectives.[118]

In contrast with former considerations, and concerning its size,[119] one should note that the total current UN budget is really insignificant, thus by itself expressing the intrinsic incapability of the UN to solve the basic problems the world has assigned to it. Indeed, with this petty budget, UN partners cannot expect from the current UN much more than exerting the right to talk, listen, and vote (on issues that could be vetoed).

The current formula for defining contributions to be made by member countries is evaluated every three years mainly according to the GDP of members, their per capita GDP, and their ability to obtain foreign currencies. At the inception of the UN, the US paid

116. Vid. Rahman, R.D. and J.M. Andreu (2002: 49). *Financing Economic Development*...Book already mentioned.

117. We have suggested, 30 years after the proposal by Nobel Laureate J.Tinbergen that the amount of ODA should move towards a figure equivalent to 2 per cent of the GDP of current donors, and be sustained at this level at least during one generation. Note that part of this ODA amount would also be financed by rich people of poor countries via the global introduction of a common recharge on the inheritance tax.

118. On the outline of UNICO, vide. Rahman R. and J.M. Andreu (2004: 135). Book already mentioned.

119. Note that the current regular UN funding includes budgets for the administration, major organs, and auxiliary agencies and programmes. Peacekeeping expenses have a separate budget, as do the specialised agencies (including World Bank and IMF).

40 per cent of the regular budget, while it pays now 22 per cent. The minimum assessed rate was initially 0.04 per cent for the poorest developing countries, although this figure is today even lower, just 0.001 per cent.[120]

In the wake of these figures we have to underline that, apart from the very scant amount of the total UN funding, its contribution structure is unfair and inefficient. We may additionally illustrate the financing mess of the UN by clarifying that, in 2000, 88 UN members, slightly less than a simple majority, all together paid less than one per cent of the assessed budgets. Conversely, of the five top contributors, US, Japan, Germany, France, and UK, who financed around two-thirds of the budgets, three are permanent members of the Security Council and the rest (Japan and Germany) only paid without playing a significant role.

Summary of the Chapter

After describing the huge changes undergone by the world economy along the 20th century (significant improvements in technology, infrastructures, energy and industrial production, transports and communications, etc.), and after dividing the period 1870-2007 in three relevant sub-periods for analytical purposes—those of "Traditional Capitalism" (1870-1914), "Transitional Period" (1945-1995), and current Capitalism (1995-2007), Chapter 3 has clarified that the main problems that current capitalism will have to confront and solve in the 21st century are: 1) the structural change, that will force the West to an economic adjustment of enormous magnitude; and 2) the great political and economic changes that current political system and underlying capitalism will have to undergo for encouraging or preserving democracy and environmental sustainability.

Traditional-liberal capitalism (1870-1914) has initially been depicted as an economic system of domestic freer enterprise and contracting (even in the labour market), combined with a limited number of political actors at a global scale, the colonial powers. These

120. We have serious doubts on the efficiency of the allocation of resources, when it is possible to be a member of a club, without paying practically anything (a typical case of free riding); and/or when one single member (out of around 200) pays 22 per cent of the budget, thus creating strong vested interest and lack of neutrality in organs.

colonial powers, managing their international trade with colonies in an asymmetric way—often through preferential agreements and authorised firms—and profiting from the monetary stability induced by the Gold Standard, unleashed a rapid growth of the international trade. As expectable, this sort of capitalism induced a high concentration of income and wealth in few hands at national level in the West that, progressively, generated discontent and violence which co-induced the First World War.

The period "between wars" (1918-1939) has not been considered in Chapter 3 as a transition period between traditional-liberal capitalism and current capitalism. This lack of consideration is due to the fact that in this period there was no gradual modification of the capitalistic paradigm, but an open confrontation between three opposed concepts of life: communism and nazi-fascism, both organised in autocratic regimes, and limited democracy; and this along one decade of rapid (average) economic progress, the 20s, and another (the 30s) of deep global crisis. The result of that confrontation is well known: the Second World War and the appearance in its aftermath of two superpowers (US and Soviet Union), which for long were trapped in mutual countervailing and Cold War.

One of the main traits of the first transitional sub-period (1945-1973)—towards current capitalism—was the disappearance of colonialism. Additional traits of this sub-period were: welfare state building or enlarging (in Western Europe), growing economic interventionism—including monetary and fiscal activism—and piecemeal progress in trade liberalisation (first GATT Rounds).

As a consequence of the post-war partition of former Northern hemisphere economy in two big blocks (the West and the Soviet Block), and the pervasive import substitution policy implemented in the South (by developing countries) to encourage industrial production and growth, the global volume of trade (in GDP terms) remained almost frozen during a good part of the period (despite mentioned piecemeal commercial liberalisation). In the political field, the US blatantly commanded the West with the sole and temporal exception of France (of General De Gaulle). Of course, the Bretton Woods institutions—mainly WB and IMF—moved also under the guidance and command of Americans.

The Second Transition sub-period (1973-1995) to current capitalism started with an overwhelming rise in the registered prices of energy. Specifically, at the end of the 70s (in times of the Iranian Islamic revolution) the price of oil per barrel moved up to 100 US dollars (in dollars of 2004). This tremendous hike in crude-oil prices, which firstly unleashed a generalised "stagflation", finally forced a change in economic policy, mainly focusing on microeconomics,[121] thus moving again the economic pendulum, this time towards a "radical but partial" form of neo-classicism.

In this second transition period, China (1978) and India (1980) started their different ways towards rapid development, much more tilted towards exports in the case of China, which made this country to reach an annual GDP growth rate of around 10% during the following three decades.

Paradoxically, when the Soviet Union collapsed, the "perceived" new hegemonic power, the US, entered into a process of losing moral authority. This was mainly due to the fact that the US could no longer blame whatever non-solved matter to the "wicked" Soviet Union. Consequently, it became responsible of every international snag, thus suffering from the non-existence of a multilateral-global democratic institution. Even more, by further undermining the existing non-democratic UN, the US shot itself in its own feet.

At the beginning of the 90s, a so-called Washington Consensus for fast growth of developing countries was defined by WB, IMF and the Treasure Department of the US. This Consensus proclaimed liberalisation of internal and external markets (of the developing countries), minimisation of their public sectors, monetary and fiscal discipline, absence of corruption, etc., as sufficient conditions for growth.

On the wake of this insufficient and consequently wrong economic philosophy, national or international subsidies and public transfers towards LDC—as part of an "old failed strategy", resulted frozen or downscaled. Certainly, the new economic policy fully trusted exports

---

121. Although pioneers of the new neo-classicism also built up a new macroeconomic system of analysis, its main corollaries were not followed by Western politicians who preferred to remain attached to Keynesian macroeconomic policy.

for accelerating economic growth while distrusted ODA, which decreased in terms of donors GDP: ODA figures in GDP terms moved down from 0.51 per cent in 1960 to 0.23 per cent in 2000.[122]

Regrettably, developing countries lacking sufficient infrastructure, educated and healthy population and sound and credible monetary and fiscal systems did not receive significant FDI, which was mostly channelled towards Asia (60% of total FDI directed to developing countries), and mainly to China (25-30%). At the same time, many developing countries—contrary to expectations—could not accede to the super-protected western markets for their agricultural products.

The decade of 90s was characterised by the massive arrival of newcomers at the global market. Note in this regard that, in the year 2000, China and India had altogether a joint population of more than 2.3 billion people; a figure which was almost the same as that of the total population on Earth 50 years before. This means that almost suddenly—in little more than one decade—the volume of (potential) individual competitors in the global market multiplied significantly. Even more, if we take into consideration the high volume of active people in these two countries, attached to rural activities with nil marginal productivity (400 and 350 million in China and India respectively), and the limited absorption capacity of their non-agricultural sectors, it is deducible that the new stage of rapid growth in these two countries could easily last three or four decades more.

Based on the theory of communicating vessels, our description of Contemporary Capitalism (1995-2007) has also made a reference to the consequences of the recent steps towards globalisation, especially in relation to the future trajectory of the relative real wages in the West (downwards) and Asia (upwards).

Facing new unfavourable trends stemming from a sort of biased globalisation as engineered by the West, the latter could be tempted to commercially castle itself in order to arrest the foreseeable relative decline of western industrial production and employment. But any

---

122. In the last two years, 2005 and 2006, the budgets for ODA significantly increased; but this increase was partially a pure statistical fiction, due to the inclusion in them as part of the ODA the condonation of old loans to poor countries, and the reconstruction expenditures realised in Afghanistan and Iraq, budgets wrongly included as part of ODA.

commercial castling would jeopardise the stability of the world economy, thus being negative for the West.

On the other hand, we have underlined that in the period of contemporary capitalism (1995-2007), the ICT revolution has made possible a radical change in the evaluation of poverty by the poor in developing countries, thus triggering more reaction than in the past. The analysis of traits of current capitalism has ended with a comment on the future of Trade Unions, which in the last years have become bewildered by the process of industrial dislocation carried out by MNC. Nevertheless, it is our view that, after a while, internationalised Unions will recover relevance, thus favouring workers across boundaries and global democracy.

Subsequent to the review of the evolution of the economic theory and ideology along the 20th century, Chapter 3 has entered into the description of the income distribution induced by the new economic policy undertaken since first 80s, marked by: 1) a fall in the equity degree of capitalism in the West, that, if continued for long, could turn hazardous for the sustainability of democracy; and 2) a worsening in the income distribution in the main Asian countries (China and India), due to the fact that rural people attached to agriculture have not yet embodied into the rapid urban-industrial-services development process, while they have also been left behind in terms of social benefits. This unfavourable distribution trend could pose political problems to mentioned big countries, with uncertain consequences on internal democracy (in India), or difficulties for progressing towards domestic democracy (in China).

In Chapter 3, other main problems of current capitalism have also been listed, and some corrections for getting environmental and democratic sustainability have been formulated. The mentioned problems and suggestions have dealt with: 1) The need of redefinition and homogenisation of current competition rules, many of them favouring industrial concentration (at global scale) and perverse distribution of income, while generating negative spill-over effects not beheld by the ruling economic policy; 2) The redefinition (or setting up in developing countries) of a (minimum) Social Protection Net, as well as its funding with taxes, in order to guarantee an adequate equity degree of capitalism and to facilitate sustainability or arrival to domestic democracy; 3) The ex-novo definition of a future global public sector, that in coming decades will administrate the global externalities and the provision of global public goods (mainly peace, security and global environment); of course under the political direction and control of a new global democratic parliament (a new UN General Assembly) to be set up.

On the bases of current socio-political trends and conditionings, Chapter 3 has finally depicted the progress towards global democracy and future pre-eminence of the global collective over individuals and nations for the correct provision of global public goods. It has depicted as well the profiles of a new democratic UN, its Security Council, and some UN subsidiaries.

Underlining that the UN change towards global democracy is urgent and indispensable, Chapter 3 has also put on the desk, among other issues, the creation of UNICO—a UN subsidiary for development financing—and the setting up of a world environment organisation (WEO); both of them with capacity for seriously dealing with the problems assigned to them and for enforcing resolutions. And not only to talk about the problems or to sign protocols that at the end of the day only few would really comply with.

We do firmly believe that relinquishing to this collective or global democratic approach would be equivalent to renounce to sustainability of environment and democracy.

4

Global Capitalism and Democracy

Having described the main economic trends of the world in a disaggregated (regional) way, and taken for granted the *ceteris paribus* continuation of the current trend towards economic internal and external divergence (Chapter 2), and analysed the diverse stages through which doctrine and practice of capitalism has moved along the 20th century, in particular, in the period 1973-2007 (Chapter 3), we will now enter into the analysis of the mutual interrelations between capitalism and democracy. And we will do it not only from the current narrow perspective of the states (national economies and democracies), but also from the point of view of the democratic global governance on global issues.

In this regard we do believe that the 21st century will witness a political reorganisation of the planet towards bigger political entities, capable of reaching "economies of integration" in the provision of regional public goods and the correction of externalities. In addition, these bigger unities and the rest of smaller nations will have to necessarily co-operate in the context of a democratic multilateral governing body, a new UN, capable of organising the supply of the so-called global public goods, of administrating global externalities, and of defining rules for cross border economic activities and interchanges.

Resolutions of this new UN will have to be adopted and enforced for reaching environmental and socio-political sustainability—the latter implying the attainment of acceptable personal income distribution at a global level—targets that after corresponding fulfilment will induce a more rational (capitalistic) way of production, distribution, and interchange.

Note that democracy at national level will be non-sustainable if the obtained economic results[1] in relation to gross-net growth

1. We are here referring to the results of extreme neo-liberalism or to unrestricted capitalism.

rates[2] and income distribution, do not match the required conditions for reaching sustainable democracy (among others, existence of a wide middle-class).

Additionally, it is our view that current global capitalism will need global democracy—today in existent—for global environment sustainability and for the correction of global social failures; and that democracy, at national and global level, will need for its tenability a social approach to capitalism, opposed to the current interpretation of the neo-classical model, as done by the Washington Consensus and neo-liberals.[3]

In order to analyse mentioned interdependence, we need to enter in some previous comments on what democracy is, on the different levels in which it has been developed along history, and on the necessary conditions for its tenability. Then, in the final part of this Chapter we will discuss the necessary conditions for the simultaneous tenability of capitalism and democracy.

Democracy: On Its Definition and Working

As known, democracy is a political system for the selection of leaders and goals at any level,[4] and for the control of the correct use of means to reach the desired goals. This political system is based on the distribution of power,[5] the majority rule, and the popular participation in governance through periodical free elections and parliamentary representation. And all this in an environment founded in political

2. These gross or net growth rates refer to the growth rates resulting before or after discounting the natural resources depleted or misused.
3. The neo-liberal ideology "is based on a believe in the virtues of markets and private ownership that is not justifiable in the light of the contemporary economic theory... (and facts). It values efficiency over distribution to the extent of justifying social horrors... This (ideology)... is based on a conjecture..., on a mixture of evidence, argument from first principles, self-interest and wishful thinking. Przeworski, A. (1995: ix). *Sustainable Democracy*. Cambridge University Press.
4. When people talk about democracy they mainly refer to the one at national level and not to lower (regional or local) democratic levels, or to the highest one: the "global democracy" as described in this book.
5. Political power works as a natural monopoly, which exhibits increasing returns to scale: directly, to the extent that incumbency gives advantage; and indirectly, to the extent that political power can be used to acquire additional economic power, which may be used for extending the political power. Hence, if democracy wants to avert dictatorship, democratic institutions must provide the opposition with instruments to counteract mention accumulative effects of power. Lane, F. (1979). *Profits from Power*. State University of New York Press.

liberties (of speech,[6] association, etc.), respect to minorities, total subordination of the military to the civil power,[7] and separation of religion and state.

Consequently, we should firstly underline that democracy will be much more than the mere realisation of periodical elections.[8] Note that the history of the 20th century has known cases of tyrants who reached power by means of general free elections—then onwards scrapping them—or after "fake-free" balloting in which basic democratic rights were not respected.[9]

Indeed, democracy is what John Rawls[10] defines as "the exercise of the political reason" through discussions by citizens in different ways (parliament, media) for the responsible governance of nations. Of course, the existence in time of open and fair elections will be the *sine qua non* condition for the validation of any democratic regime.

Undeniably, democracy (national or global)—as it will be described lines below—is a system whose philosophic principles, due to its moral superiority, cannot go against the values of any secular society.[11] This does not mean however that sustainable democracy may successfully be developed everywhere, irrespective of the fulfilment of certain conditions. A proof of the relevance of the fulfilment or not of these conditions—discussed extensively in the lines below—is the temporal

6. The limits of freedom of expression are not well defined. Note that the playground of the freedom of expression cannot invade the playground of freedom of religion and conscience, the respect to minorities, and the right to protect one's image. Note also that the limits of freedom of expression should be somewhat restricted if underdevelopment, slowness, and expensiveness of the justice systems do not enable to timely fight against eventual transgressions of such a freedom.
7. Note that in Latin America, there have been "democratic constitutions" that have given the military a special role, even superior to that of civilians, in issues such as the defence of the "constitutional order". In some cases, military prerogatives have remained so extensive that elected civilian governments never have become integral domestic powers. Przeworski, A. (1995: 47). Book already mentioned.
8. Indeed, the realisation of elections in absence of the rest of democratic conditions—sufficient physical security, freedom of speech for all, significant economic freedom, etc.—is a pure masquerade directly conducive to political failure, as it is occurring in Iraq.
9. The action of voters may be falsified or invalidated if public debates on public issues are degraded by censorship, if political opposition is suppressed or degraded, or if other fundamental political rights are violated.
10. Rawls, J. (1999). *Collected Papers*. Harvard University Press. p. 579.
11. Theocratic—or religion founded—political systems, which consider that simple majority should not define principles and policies, cannot be considered as conventional democracies, since these regimes will not respect either minorities or majorities once theocrats have reached power after free elections.

non-sustainability of many democratic experiments attempted in history, either before the French Revolution (1789) or after it.

As history has proven, economic underdevelopment with extreme internal differences of per capita income,[12] or non-integrated heterogeneous societies (with different tribes, races, religions, languages, etc.) will make difficult or extremely difficult the survival of an integrative democracy. Consequently, rushed and forced introduction of democracy or forced elections by external powers, irrespective of the socio-economic traits of concerned societies, although it has today become fashionable,. will likely fail.[13]

Even more, the opinion that a forced introduction of democracy will always promote quicker economic development than former political systems—as defended today by some politicians—seems to us a non-realistic proposal;[14] and a hazardous one, because it may be used for the "scientific" support of military adventures, "nominally" undertaken for changing political regimes, in pursuit of the happiness of nationals.

National Democracy for Economic Prosperity?

About 3 or 4 decades ago, it was mostly admitted among economists and political theorists that, at low levels of per capita income, the economics of development posed a cruel dilemma between a rapid and self-sustained economic expansion[15] without democracy, and the implementation of a democratic process conducive to slow growth.

12. As Przeworski says—in his *Sustainable Democracy* (1995:2) Book already mentioned—if we are to believe in the immense body of literature following Lipset´s seminal work of 1960 (*Political Man*) the organisational, social, and cultural prerequisites of sustainable democracy are largely a matter of the level of economic development.

13. On the "advantages" of intervention in foreign countries with the intention of bringing democracy and state building, Fukuyama, F. (2004: 69). *State-building, Governance and World Order in the 21st Century*. French version: *La Table Ronde*, Paris.

14. The example of "democratic" India and its slow economic progress up to the 80s, amidst huge poverty, does not support precisely mentioned theory. Nonetheless, the example of "democratic" India has been used by certain authors to defend the position that development or underdevelopment has nothing to do with democracy. On this consideration, Vide Sen, A. (2005). *Les racines globales de la democracie*. Editions Payot. Vide also Bhagwati, J. (1995). *Democracy and Development: New Thinking on an Old Question*. Rajiv Gandhi Memorial Lecture. Rajiv Gandhi Foundation.

15. The strategy of rapid and purported self-sustained economic expansion promoted by the state and public sector has at times played a crucial role; in particular, by means of setting up capital-intensive public firms behind high protective barriers (the so-called import-substitution strategy).

In particular, the idea that democratisation of political systems would reduce the saving and investment rates of the developing countries,[16] thus reducing their GDP growth rates, was at that time part of mainstream macroeconomics.

Conversely to this approach, it is today defended—although without strong arguments—that mentioned cruel choice is just a fiction, because democracy does not handicap economic development, but promotes it.[17] Although the idea that freer markets and limited public sectors may, under circumstances, support more rapid growth is essentially correct, this could also occur under authoritarian regimes.[18] Consequently, what is a serious mistake is to relate in a deterministic way multi-party elections with economic prosperity. In our view, the idea that elections will necessarily and automatically drive to liberalisation of markets, economic prosperity[19] and sustainable democracy, is simply a *non sequitur*.

Against the backdrop of thousands of years of history, in which epochs of growth or slump were almost exclusively combined with absence of democracy, the recent study of Summers and Heston[20] is frequently quoted in support of the idea that democracy may favour economic growth much more than dictatorship. In their study, 229 regimes were observed in 139 countries over the period 1951-1988; some of them with alternated regimes, and others with consolidated democracies. Considering all the data in terms of regime-years, of which 1,731 were democratic and 2,981 under dictatorship, the outcome was that the per capita annual growth rates of GDP (PPP)

16. It was supposed that democratisation, by subsequent processes of privatisations and liberalisation of markets, would rapidly implement significant income redistribution policies that would reduce the (internal and external) savings rate, the domestic investment, and the rhythm of growth.

17. Vide Bhagwati, J. (1995) Article already mentioned.

18. Dictatorships or incomplete democracies may for long well be consistent with the promotion of market economy. Indeed, the cases of the 4 Asian tigers—South Korea, Taiwan, Hong Kong and Singapore, which up to the 90's grew quickly in a non-democratic context—or the current case of China and Vietnam, are proofs of this.

19. The case of democratic India between 1947 and 1980—the period of its economic underperformance—proves that a democracy of poor, illiterates, with population explosion, and with basically free internal (at state level) markets of labour and goods for its most relevant activity, agriculture, is not necessarily conducive to prosperity.

20. Summers, R. and A. Heston (1991). *The Penn World Table (Mark4): An Extended Set of International Comparisons, 1950-88*. QJE.106. Note that in this publication, mentioned authors classified the countries as democratic or not in function of some conventionally accepted traits.

of democracies was 2.4 per cent and that of the authoritarian regimes was 1.9 per cent, thus apparently implying that democracy was more efficient for economic development than dictatorship.

The outcome of this study, although still used by neo-liberals, has been widely criticised. A first critique was realised by Przeworski *et al.*,[21] who underlined the fact that any temporal classification of countries, as democratic or not, would be endogenous in relation to their temporal economic performance. This means that a democracy, when working badly could change into a dictatorship—as history has proven in many occasions—thus favouring as an average the per capita GDP growth rate of democracies. Conversely, when a dictatorship is doing well, a likely democratisation process could favour again as an average the per capita GDP growth rate of democracies. As a result of this criticism, it is easily deducible that the main implication of the data-study of Summers and Heston is not correct.

As a second critique, one should not overlook the fact that the study of Summers and Heston included consolidated democracies (in Europe, US, Japan etc.) which, as an average and in per capita GDP terms, grew in the period 1950-1973 much more rapidly than Africa, Asia (excluding Japan) and Latin America[22] altogether. Note additionally that consolidated democracies, which for long had been colonial powers—thus profiting from superior technology and biased commercial relations—extended these asymmetric relations along the considered period, 1950-1973, which again favoured the economic growth of Western consolidated democracies, therefore polluting the analysis of Summers and Heston. Observe as well that many countries in Africa, Asia (excluding Japan) and Latin America were involved in continuous "regime changing", which always implies significant economic costs, while the western ones did not. This again implies that the conclusion of Summers and Heston that democracy favours growth is not correct.

Finally, we could also say that if, in the mentioned study of Summers and Heston, one eliminates the effect of population growth

21. Przeworski, A. *et al.* (1994). "Democracy and Development", Presented at the Nobel Symposium, Upsala. August.

22. To this respect, the reader may remember the figures of Maddison presented in Chapter 2. Maddison, A. (2001) *The World Economy. A Millennium Perspective*. Paris: OECD. p.126.

rates—significantly higher in developing countries, many of them dictatorships and with extended poverty—the result would become indifferent.

As a consequence of all mentioned critiques, we do share the view of Lal and Srinivasan[23] who believe that there is no necessary empirical relationship between the form of government and successful economic development. This is because non-democratic countries, by means of economic reforms, may establish significant economic liberty, as it happened for decades with the four Asian Tigers, while some consolidated democracies may, at times, be reluctant to make markets more flexible, as it happened in the analysed period in many OECD countries and India.

In addition, when discussing democracy as a possible cause of economic prosperity, one should not forget that the world as a whole did not behave democratically in the last half a century[24]—with a sequencing of two political poles during the Cold War and just one afterwards—while it registered its ever best economic results. In an opposed sense, one could wonder why those neo-cons who want to promote democracy in certain countries to bring economic prosperity, are so reluctant to promote democracy in the UN to bring global economic progress and political and environmental sustainability in the world.

Nature of Democratic Governments and Political Parties

The way in which democratic governments behave to fulfil their economic and political purposes, was traditionally presented in economics in two main forms.[25] The first one considered the state as a separated moral person, with its own ends, not necessarily related to those of citizens; an approach which was rapidly scrapped due to its lack of functionality.[26]

---

23. Lal, D. (1994). "Participation, Markets and Democracy". *Working Paper* 20, Human Resources Development and Operation Policy. World Bank. Vide also Srinivasan, T.N. (1995). *Democracy, Markets and Development*. Ámsterdam. Homage to Prof. Tims.
24. Indeed, the world as a whole has never behaved democratically in History.
25. Buchanan, J. (1949). *The Pure Theory of Government Finance: A Suggested Approach*. JPE. December.
26. This would mean that the state has its own welfare function to be optimised. Unfortunately, as far as no one—except absolute monarchs or dictators—is capable of "defining" the welfare function of the state, this way of thinking proved to be useless as a guide for democratic decision-making.

The second approach, apparently more realistic than the former one, considered that only individuals could have a structure of political ends. As a result, governments—which have no welfare function of its own—should try to collectively optimise the desired consumption of public goods and services expressed by "individual" citizens,[27] while simultaneously financing (more or less) the cost of its public action; funding that should mainly come through taxes to avert "free riding".[28]

Observe that this second approach contains to some extent the same mistake as the first one, since it bases its logic on the assumption that a "moral entity" may have targets—although in this case derived from those of the "individual" citizens—when in fact the interpreters of the social needs are the individuals who are in charge (the cabinet ministers).[29]

Indeed, as far as in democracy a group of people has to govern, to some extent taking into consideration the preferences of individuals, there will be a relation between the individual ends or values, and those of the coalition (or party) that has to run the country.[30] But this connection has proven to be elusive to economists.

Irrespective of the elusiveness of this relation, we have to additionally clarify that till the second half of the 20th century economists were not busy at all with an essential part of the democratic process: the political foundations on how to reach office for practising the wanted politics.

Even more important than former considerations, is the traditional and still alive disinterest of economists in the social and political consequences in the long-term of the implemented economic policy.[31]

---

27. The essay of Bergson, directed to construct a social welfare function from the individual ones, was a failure from a practical perspective, while the Nobel-awarded Arrow explained the difficulties to move in a consistent way from the individual values to the social ones. Scitovsky, T. (1951). "The State of the Welfare Economics" *AER*. p.303-315.; Arrow, K. (1951). *Social Choice and individual Values*. NY: John Wiley and Sons.
28. On the foundation of taxation as a system for financing public goods, vide. Samuelson, P. (1954), "The Pure Theory of the Public Goods". RES. Nov.
29. Vide. Downs, A. (1957). *An Economic Theory of the Democracy*. New York: Harper. p.17.
30. When a political party or a coalition, takes over, the new government will change into an apparatus of decision-making. In case of coalition governments, the resulting priorities could be very different from the values of the median voter who have elected the parliamentarians.
31. Usher, D. (1981) *The Economic Prerequisite to Democracy*. Basil Blackwell. p.2.

This is attributable to the fact that economic theory has been basically concerned with the analysis of government actions in the context of a short-term analysis, thus taking as a datum—among other variables—the initial personal income distribution, while practically paying no attention to the final one; and this despite the fact that the worsening of mentioned distribution could in the long term undermine the sustainability of democracy.

In particular, we do believe that most (national) governments of the world—focused on the economic competitiveness of their nations—have ignored the effects of the recent liberalisation of labour markets on the behaviour of individuals in society (family life, reproduction, consumerism, etc.); indeed an important aspect for sustainability of democracy.

Modern Political Behaviour: The Self-interest Axiom and Rules of the Game

In the following paragraphs we will describe the foundations of a model of political behaviour, which is far away from previous conceptions about how to design social priorities. Recently exposed by political scientists and "public choice" economists, this model, moving away from concerns on social priorities based on individual values, has focused on the analyses of how to gain elections and influencing the voting choice of citizens.

Modern theory of politics assumes that every agent acts in accordance to his or her own interests; this means that individuals—as voters, politicians or bureaucrats—act in their public life in an identical manner as they do in their private economic activities, although with some exceptions.[32]

This theory assumes that political parties and politicians will act basically to attain the prestige, income and power that they will enjoy when reaching office.[33] Consequently, the main argument of the political action of a party will be directed to gain elections, and

32. In extraordinary cases (mainly in international issues), politicians could undertake actions (in interest of the nation), which could be detrimental for the interests of their own party, thus losing internal political support.

33. This assumption, although not totally realistic, is operative and explains most political actions of politicians. On the aspect of the relevance or the irrelevance of the realism of the assumptions, Friedman, M. (1956). *Introduction to Positive Economics*. Chicago: University Press.

if possible to fulfil political pledges as contained in its manifesto. As a result, political and social functions of general interest will be by-products, while private "legitimate" ambition will be the main end of their human action.[34]

Having said that, we could define a modern democratic system as one that fulfils the following conditions:[35] 1) Elections to form parliament are held during periodic intervals, the duration of which is constitutionally defined; 2) A single party (or a coalition of them) is elected by popular consent, thus obtaining majority which entitles it to govern the country; 3) All adult residents behave rational as electors or eligible in each election; 4) Every voter may only cast one vote per election; 5) The losing party or parties will not try to avoid the governance of the winning party by means of illicit manoeuvres to take office; 6) The party in power will never restrict the political activities of members of other parties, while the latter will not make attempts to violently overthrow the government, and 7) There always are two or more parties competing in every election.

Fading of Confidence in Political Parties?

Whatever its causes, one should note that militancy and political support of political parties is experiencing today in the rich world a continuous decline. In many rich countries, the existence of specific electoral laws practically induces a two-party system, which forces parties, leading coalitions, or possible heads of coalitions to present similar, centred and hardly innovative political programmes,[36] thus not offering any workable solution to the challenges of the 21st century.

Even more, due to current globalisation, these parties do not dare to put into question the foundations of mainstream economics and western centred policies, even though it is patent that these national policies cannot solve the current global problems of deteriorating internal personal income distribution, growing gap, environmental sustainability and human security.

---

34. In politics happens the same as in the private sector economy; actions of private sector will be directed—by an invisible hand—to produce what people want to eat, drink or dress; and this although the end of the entrepreneur is profit and not benevolence or charity. Schumpeter, J. (1950: 282). *Capitalism, Socialism and Democracy*.
35. Downs, A. (1957). *An Economic Theory of Democracy*. New York: Harper. p.23.
36. Downs, A. (1957: 117).

On the other hand, in most of incipient democracies in the developing world, political parties use to be fragmented, weakly organised, and internally non-representative, which could negatively affect popular opinions on democratic systems. In particular, when in developing countries property rights and fiscal conditions are being modified, people hesitate to what party to give political confidence.[37]

Despite these mistrusts in both developed and developing countries, we fully support secular democracy as the less bad of all political systems for national governance, and as the only one capable of solving at global level the pending global problems of mankind (efficient and legitimate provision of global public goods and correction of global externalities).

Limits and Conditions of Decision-making in Democracy

As it is well known, democratic decisions on new rules are made in parliaments adjusting to a pre-defined majority rule,[38] while daily government actions have to adjust to law and parliament supremacy. However, this does not mean that the majority rule can be applied to any subject; indeed it will only be applied to issues that fall within the constitutional limits[39] established in "democratically elaborated" constitutions.[40]

One of the main constitutional limits established for the preservation of the market economy—a *sine qua non* condition for survival of democracy—is that referring to the redistribution of income and wealth in its different manifestations. Indeed, to be

---

37. Przeworski, A. (1995: 57). Book already mentioned.
38. This rule uses to be a simple majority (or 50 per cent of votes plus one). For some prickly or momentous decisions stronger majorities are, or should be, required (constitutional changes, changes in electoral law, devolution of power to regions, etc.).
39. Democratic constitutions assure minorities (which may control up to 49 per cent of seats in parliament) that their vital interests will not be violated by transitory shifts in power relations. Przeworski, A. *et al.* (1995). *Sustainable Democracy*. Cambridge University Press. p.50.
40. Indeed, "the democratic or non-democratic nature of constitution making, its timing, and its style, plays an important role in determining the stability of constitutions". Ozbudun, E. (1992). "Constitution Making in Democratic Transition", *East-South Systems Transformations*. University of Chicago. *Working Paper* No. 20. An example of a non-democratic process for constitution making has recently taken place in Iraq, in which interferences of external powers have been crucial in its elaboration.

acceptable, decisions on the political redistribution of income will have to be carried out in a piecemeal and moderate way. Consequently, (hasty) re-assignation[41] of income and wealth among citizens should be forbidden by constitutions, since it undermines or demolishes sustainability of democracy. The same could be said in relation with: 1) hasty and immoderate increases of the public sector as a result of nationalisations, and/or rushed growth of public interventionism; 2) aggressive actions in favour of (private or public) monopolies or production concentration; 3) elaboration of rules which, encouraging new technologies, severely penalise contemporary ways of production, thus significantly reducing the current volume of employment, etc.

Indeed, the voting mechanism, indispensable for starting democracy or for sustaining it, will ultimately result counterproductive when the winning party uses its power to hastily redistribute income and wealth among voters. Consequently, a "system of equity"—or a way to distribute income and wealth, basically independent of political action—must pre-exist to preserve democracy.

One of these systems of equity is the income distribution realised by capitalism when competition is "really" operational, when existent competition is complemented with anti-monopoly laws and government action, when economic externalities and social failures of the market system are taken into account by public powers, when the state promotes economic transparency, and when the public sector is not oversized.

Capitalism and "Equity System" for Acceptability

Observe that, in a pure capitalistic framework—with no intervention of the state—there will be an almost automatic trend to worsen the income distribution.[42] This is the reason why this automatic trend should be offset by a policy of public redistribution (moderately progressive income tax, moderate inheritance taxes, policy of transfers to the more destitute, social expenditures, etc.) to keep

41. Re-assignation of income or wealth stands for a movement in which those that initially were poor replace the rich, while the latter become poor. Observe that these re-assignation movements will not always be reflected by movements of the Gini-index, thus at times confusing economic observers.

42. There is little doubt that pure capitalism—without practical intervention of the state, as defined by first neo-classics—favours accumulatively those who have capital, if this is the relatively scant factor, while indefinitely keep workers in relative poor condition, if the labour factor remains *sine die* over-abundant.

democracy alive. This policy of redistribution will make capitalism more acceptable for those who at birth received nothing, in relation to those that inherited a lot (silver spoons) without any previous personal effort.

In fact, as far as the initial distribution of assets is taken as a datum by the neoclassical model—irrespective of the personal merits[43] of anyone—democracy will have to keep a system of redistribution to avert temptations of the more destitute of society to open the "Pandora's box" of the "unfair initial distribution", and to seek justice.[44] The government should also offset market failures mainly with a system of subsidies and indirect taxes in order to make the "equity system of capitalism" acceptable.[45]

Talking about the acceptation in other times of the equity of capitalism, we have to remember that, despite the unfair initial distribution of wealth and income—inherited from feudalism—and the continuation of the bad distribution induced by "traditional liberal capitalism", this form of capitalism was initially consistent with the "incipient democracies" existing in 19th century and first half of the 20th. Note that in this early stage of democracy, citizens without assets (or illiterates) were not franchised,[46] thus not having, through the democratic process, any option to put claims on the distribution of land, etc.

This strategy of delaying franchising—useful for traditional liberal states in past times of lack of information—could today result dangerous because non-franchised citizens, if they are large in relative numbers, could become enemies of a democracy with constitutional limits (on "franchising") for them, thus trying to undermine or destroy it.

---

43. It is true—as mentioned by Von Mises, a rightist economist of the old Austrian School—that theft, appropriation, inheritance, gifts, and (ulterior) sale, may have all played a role in creating the initial distribution of (physical and human) assets of any generation.
44. It is important to embody the more destitute into the democratic system by means of implementing a system of equal opportunities for all. Indeed, when a democracy is not sensitive to the aspirations of wide layers of society (the poor in majority), it will not reach political stability and sustainability. Note that in this case the poor could organise non-democratic parties to overturn the system.
45. A "system of equity" only will be acceptable if at least the 50 per cent of the population—the 50 per cent poorest—who could use their political majority to overturn the current pattern of distribution—believe that the cost of reorganising the current "equity system" is higher than the cost of remaining in it.
46. This means that they had no voting right.

Nevertheless there are situations in developing countries—existence of cultural (religious), ethnic, or regional heterogeneities—that could justify the setting up of certain temporal limitations in franchising, or in the authorisation of certain political parties. An example of such limitations would be the prohibition to establish political parties based on religion, ethnicity or geography as long as the nation building process after independence has not matured. Otherwise rushed full democratisation could be conducive to civil wars as experienced in many Sub Saharan countries and recently in the Middle East.

On Fractional Decisions which Undermine Democracy

Having defined some economic issues, mainly reassignment, that cannot be voted in parliament without jeopardising democracy, we will describe different types of debatable subjects which may keep alive or undermine democracy: 1) The matters of general interests, 2) The so-called single peaked issues; and 3) The so-called fractional ones.

The "matters of general interests" have to do with issues in which all parliamentarians, regardless of their political colour, have a common interest, as for instance the appointment of a non-executive President of the Republic.[47] Likewise, to vote the reform of some civil or commercial contracts (urban hires or life insurances), to correct the severity of penalties in the penal code, or to outline the framework of the international policy, are additional issues in which all the main political parties could agree on proposals, thus resulting in matters of general interests.

Alternatively, a "single-peaked issue" is one whose voting results may be associated to numbers of a scale, in such a way that every parliamentarian or party—having a preferred number on the scale—will always vote a possible outcome closest to his preferred number.[48] Single peaked issues have three special traits: 1) Propensity to reach

47. In this case, the political profile of the candidates should be irrelevant. Consequently, the capacity of every candidate to represent the country or to intervene in negotiations among different parties in the domestic political game is what parliamentarians should evaluate. Note however, that this election for the appointment of a President could change into a singled peaked or a fractional decision when the different candidates are identified with different policies, or supported by different political parties or groups.

48. The concept of "singled peaked issues" is original by Duncan Black, and it was carefully analysed in his book titled *The Theory of Committees and Elections*, Cambridge University Press.

a unique and stable result after a voting procedure; 2) Consistency of the reached result with the preferences of the median voter; and 3) Reached result will not be affected by alternative strategies (coalitions among parties). As the reader may imagine, there are a lot of debatable single peaked issues, as for instance, the age of retirement, the amount and length of the unemployment insurance, the degree of progressiveness of the fiscal system, etc.

Finally, "fractional issues" are issues neither of general interest nor single peaked (with unique solution). They will be those in which the positioning of every voter or party will depend on the benefits to be extracted from colligating with others, thus inducing individual positioning, which could be far away (up or down) of their preferences. In this case, it will be impossible to identify the median voter, and hence no "unique" and stable result will be produced by the parliament. In fact, the result could vary according to the different potential coalitions formed for gaining majority. Consequently, in "fractional issues" the result of the political process will not be predictable in advance, as it happens with the well-known "paradox of voting".[49]

One example of a fractional issue could be the case of a communist party voting with the right in relation to (low) pensions in exchange for minister postings and against a socialist party claiming increased pensions. Another could be the case of a rightist regional party supporting national fiscal policies proposed by a socialist party in exchange for political devolution to its own region. Finally, we could quote the case of a decision making process in parliament, in which the left (or the right), without overall majority, colligates with a small party (which defends re-assignation of income to a social group) to produce a result favourable to it.

In consistency with former lines, we have to conclude that all the more political actions are undertaken through strategic political means (by setting up artificial coalitions)—and, consequently, far away from

49. For an interesting example of this "paradox of voting", Usher, D. (1981: 28). Book already mentioned. In this case, in which a society of three voters (1, 2, and 3) votes on three issues (A, B, and C), it could result that following the preferences of the voters, A could socially be preferred to B, and B to C—that is to say A to C—while at the same time C could socially be preferred to A, thus making a rational transfer from individual preferences to the social ones impossible.

the singled peaked rationality, the more undermined will democracy result and the least sustainable it will be.[50]

Production Structure Effecting Tenability of Democracy

Additionally, democracy will be relatively more fragile in those societies in which a great part of the income has a "windfall" origin—stemming from the mining of a globally scant raw material (oil, diamonds, etc.)—while at the same time, there is not sufficient socio-economic homogeneity. This non-desirable combination may encourage some political groups, representing regions or ethnicities, to scramble for the windfalls.[51]

Conversely, the existence of a more diversified capitalistic production will normally imply the existence of much more economic groups involved in the economic activity. This context of "diversified" activity and competition among multiple groups, including competition among owners, will successively generate a reasonable and positive flow of human transfers across mentioned groups and economic activities, thus making the individuals and economic groups less dependent on politics (region or ethnicity).

Logically, if there were many economic groups and a diversified capitalistic production (no windfalls), no one could initiate any political manoeuvre to economically privilege its own group (regional or ethnic) by means of controlling the windfall. Consequently, competition, information, factors mobility, and economic diversification should be promoted by the state for sustainability of democracy, especially in the context of non-homogeneous societies.

---

50. Note that the distinction between singled peaked issues and fractional ones may sometimes become blurred by means of logrolling manoeuvres. Different authors differ on whether logrolling actions may improve or worsen the democratic governance through the strict application of the majority rule. Buchanan, J. and G. Tullock (1962). *The Calculus on Consent*. University of Michigan Press. p.198; or Brams (1975) in *Games Theory and Politics*. Free Press. p.129.

    Indeed, singled peaked issues as the age for pensions, the amount of the unemployment insurance, or the amount of transfers to the poor, may become fractional if poor, retirees and unemployed, after founding political parties, colligate with other groups to gather majority in parliament for economically exploiting the others. This political action will clearly undermine the current "equity system" of capitalism.

51. This political fight all the more will undermine democracy the greater is the mentioned windfall in GDP terms. Indeed, this political fight uses to be one of the implicit causes of political instability in the big oil producing (developing) countries (in particular when a full democracy with total franchising is established). In fact, this quasi-monopolistic "windfall" production and its implicit perils for democracy, may also explain the slowness of the democratisation process in part of the Arab world (The Gulf countries).

In this regard, previous diversification of capitalistic production would be advisable for the promotion or strengthening of democracy in developing countries. However, we do believe that externally imposed democratisation in non-homogeneous societies with or without previous economic diversification may significantly raise the risk of political failure, at times resulting in civil wars.

Relevance of Social Forces in the Democratic Debate

After elections, and once formed parliament and government, the latter being supported by a majority (of one party, or a coalition of represented parties), the government action will start. But, this government action directed to correct problems in specific fields, could at times be problematic in the short run.[52]

Note that in case of a previous landslide electoral victory resulting in "dominance" in parliament, the new government may be tempted to initiate economic reforms without any consult of the opposition or social forces, in particular trade unions, but solely based on own economic considerations.[53] Many a time, as a result of mentioned omissions, reactions of trade unions could drive economic reforms[54] to failure.

Both "parliamentarism", defined as a political manner based on previous and systematic consultation of other political groups in parliament, and "concertation"—in which the affected groups by economic reform are systematically consulted—are political styles that make the undertaken policies much more effective; and this although the agreed policy may lose some of its initial coherence. Indeed, many a time less coherence with reliability will be better than theoretical consistency without social support.

---

52. We are here basically considering economic reform, from former interventionism towards more open market positions, or vice versa.
53. At times, an economic blueprint may be considered as technically correct; but if it counts with the enmity of the social forces—even in the case that the latter tend to behave irresponsible—the initial blueprint should be considered as "bad economics", because it will lack credibility on its potential success. Przeworski, A. (1995). Book already mentioned, p.76.
54. Although Dominique de Villepin—Prime Minister of France in 2005-2007—could technically have been right, his Contract Premiere Embauche sent to the parliament in the first quarter of 2006, suffered a dramatic failure because it lacked consultation of the involved social forces.

In fact, one reason why the opposition to economic reforms may use non-democratic ways—violent actions, confrontations in the streets, etc.—is the "incomplete" democratic behaviour of the executive. It is true that according to many democratic constitutions, governments are not required, *strictu sensu,* to call for previous consults to political opposition or social actors. But doubtless, previous negotiations on blue prints, seeking approval or consent among the different democratic forces, may make the devised policy much more credible and consequently successful.[55]

Conditions for Sustainability of Democracy under Capitalism

Having explained in the lines above, the limits of democratic decision-making, we will now discuss the conditions for the long-term consistency of capitalism with democracy. Likewise, we will also discuss if, and under what circumstances, socialism could be compatible with democracy. Although in both cases we would finally end up talking about the same system: the system of "mixed economy of market" supported by democracy.

Today, there is general consensus that a "full equality distribution system"—in consistency with a full socialist distribution of income—cannot work in a modern interactive economy. This is because a socialist egalitarian distribution of income, or even wealth, would destroy incentives for individual economic initiatives[56]—be this in the fields of education, work, savings and investments—and would be inconsistent with any hierarchical human organisation, as required in modern economies and firms, thus altogether inducing the GDP to fall well under its potential.

These considerations notwithstanding, we have to underline that neither is capitalism a system in which free markets necessarily induce acceptable distribution, nor is socialism a system that completely condemns free markets, while practising some "equality

55. This has been the case in the Netherlands in last decades (polder model), in particular on the issue of labour market flexibilities.

56. Note that a fully equalitarian distribution would deprive individuals from the prize of their special efforts. This would drive most of them towards free-riding behaviour and, consequently, towards a social catastrophe.

distribution" through political channels. In fact, "socialism" is today a word with many meanings, ranging from very lukewarm social positions—in which socialism just defends progressive tax systems while implementing some programmes for poverty alleviation—to a "full socialist state" in which all productions and distribution are decided by state bureaucrats.[57]

Under this multiplicity of meanings, socialism will only be compatible with democracy if the economy, at least roughly, basically determines through markets the income distribution.

It has been said in handbooks on political theory—and we agree—that some explicit[58] re-assignment of income or wealth is unavoidable; and that this will occur even in the most conspicuous capitalistic system. Otherwise it would not be possible to keep the lid of the distributional "Pandora's box" closed which—as we have before remarked—contains all the nasty and even bloody history of the current personal income distribution of nations.[59]

On the other hand, one should not forget that a capitalistic system of "free markets" might generate a system of prices and wages that may be considered as unfair by a majority of voters;[60] particularly in cases of bad governance, unfair (inherited) structure of property, and high degree of monopoly. In such cases, capitalism could be contradictory with sustainability of democracy, reason why public powers should urgently intervene to redistribute income and to break

57. This form of extreme socialism is clearly inconsistent with democracy, because all incomes and assets of every citizen would have a political origin. This would make that all political decisions change into re-assignments of income.

58. Besides the explicit re-assignments of income, one should not overlook the implicit ones contained in the big purchases of the state in fields of defence, infrastructure, energy, etc. which, without any content of transfer, undeniably favour determined economic groups. We could also consider as implicit re-assignment the unbalanced contracting of civil servants, when ethnical, religious, or political majority dominates the government.

59. Even a very well known economist, not at all suspicious of being a socialist, as Ludwig Von Mises, declared that "all ownership derives from previous occupation and violence". Von Mises, L. (1951). *Socialism*. Yale University Press. p.43.

60. Although many analysers of income distribution have said that it has never been proven that a "perfect competitive system" may be conducive to unacceptable distribution of income, the reality is that in countries in which the non-organised sector includes the majority of population, the overabundance of people in relation to capital has driven to a bad distribution of income (perhaps because a real free competition has never existed). On the other hand, the birth of Trade Unions and socialist parties in the West in the last decades of the 19th century, is a clear proof of the perceived unfair distribution of income at that time; a time in which many markets, including the labour one, were freer than today.

monopolies (although, if possible, without directly entering in the productive activity).

Note that in the last years of the 20th century, particularly in the 90s, the registered movement towards consolidation in big unities of production, transport, communication, accounting, etc. at an international-global scale, could have ignited a new process towards monopolisation of the global markets, thus in future possibly undermining national democracies.

Observe also that in the so-called "mixed economies" there will be a margin for "re-assignment of income" without political risk; of course, provided that the amount of funds politically allocated is a small fraction of the GDP, and that the bulk of the economic activity is realised by the private sector.

As a consequence, the larger is the middle class (promoted by a majority private sector in a public redistributive context), the less relevant will be the political bargaining and re-assignment of income; and the lesser will be the number of economically affected individuals by the political process (at alternation of power), all this protecting the democratic system.

Note that, conversely to what is today preached by market fundamentalists, the private sector should not to be as large as to kill or seriously deteriorate the public services and the welfare system. A sufficient public sector will be essential for keeping the infrastructures in shape and to avoid the worsening of the income distribution that totally free markets would automatically induce, as it has historically occurred.

Consequently, if economic power is well distributed and several political parties are in the game, if there is a wide middle class, if the private sector generates the bulk of the national GDP, and the public sector corrects economic and social market failures, internal democracy will be sustainable.

Growth of the Public Sector and Possible Undermining of Democracy

Although it is clear that a fully socialised system of means of production is incompatible with democracy, it will be convenient to analyse to what extent a growing public sector could jeopardise democracy.[61]

The answer to this question is not simple, because its alternative, a fully privatised economy—with its possible derivative of a long-term worst distribution of income and wealth—could also undermine democracy. In general, the wideness of the public sector in GDP terms will have necessarily to do with the particular history of the income distribution—the problem of the Pandora's box—with the interests of citizens expressed in successive voting procedures, and with the existence of different externalities.

There are certain activities of the government that, although increasing the economic base of the public sector, will profit all citizens and will improve equity. We are here referring to the generalisation of basic education,[62] the general provision of basic health services,[63] the supply of sufficient infrastructures and communications, etc. Public equity could also come from the other side of the budget, by means of implementing moderate progressive taxes,[64] thus both sides of the budget redistributing income and de-activating eventual historical claims of the poorest.

Even more, public sector should also play an important role in the market economies when the so-called "market failures" appear. In these cases the public sector should offset the inefficiencies induced by markets in which only the private initiative intervenes. To illustrate this argument, we could say that subsidies directed to partially financing[65] public transport in cities (for avoiding congestion

61. Note in this regard that overgrown bureaucracies in Latin America—induced by successive economic re-assignments and existence of weak fiscal systems, prone to accumulate public deficits and consequently to accelerate inflation—have in some cases been the main cause of democratic failure, conducive to dictatorship.

62. In the cases of secondary and higher education, the principle of merit for poor combined with private financing, could play a certain role, thus discharging the public sector of part of the responsibility.

63. In the health service it would be also convenient that the private sector play a certain role; and not only in initiatives for the creation of private health institutions but also in the co-financing of public sector practises, just to avert abuses.

64. Note that overdone progressive taxes could stimulate tax evasion and-or reduction of the number of economic initiatives, both being counterproductive.

65. This partial financing will have to be positioned between two extremes: between the position of the rich who will push for a full private financing of mentioned public services—thus forgetting the positive externalities of the service—and the extreme position of those who claim for the total public financing, thus forgetting private benefits induced by the public service, and its likely overuse at nil price.

and environmental problems), or to facilitate the mobility of people across the country (trains) could be advantageous for an overwhelming majority of people. Of course, between the free provision of some goods (as for instance basic education) and the almost full priced provision of others (as for instance transports), there are multiple approaches for the intervention of the public sector in order to make the "equity system" of capitalism more acceptable.

Is Total Liberalisation Conducive to Prosperity?

In front of the dangers for democracy of growing (or big) public sectors, some neo-liberal economists have defended (and defend today) an alternative approach based on the quasi-total liberalisation of markets as the only way for unleashing fast economic development. Unfortunately, the perspective of neo-liberals is incomplete and consequently mistaken. This is due to the fact that long-term economic or social "market failures" are barely considered in the underlying neo-liberal analysis.

Neo-liberal economists opine that trade liberalisation; privatisation of public firms; implementation of antimonopoly measures;[66] and reduction of subsidies to industries and consumers will necessarily induce in any country prosperity and employment growth. However these neo-liberals tend to forget the possibility that these policies may play a negative role in the short run, provoking eventual socio-economic turmoil, or in the long run by means of inducing negative distribution of income, which could undermine democracy.

In our view, this neo-liberal approach allegedly directed to provoke rapid growth in LDC, is either a simple mistake or just a manoeuvre consisting of turning a blind eye to reality in interest of western elites. Observe that this neo-liberal perspective concerning LDC is contrary to evidence because economic prosperity in these countries requires the previous existence of a minimum of infrastructure, as well as a healthy and decently educated population, a stage hardly achieved in LDCs mostly in need of increased budgets in these fields. To say it blank, we have to underline that the development of human resources and infrastructures in LDC, and their financing, is mistakenly not on the neo-liberals agenda.

66. However, in the name of attainable economies of scale and "convenient concentration", anti-monopoly measures are often recommended but hardly applied by neo-liberals.

In relation to the convenience of increasing competition at all costs as recommended by neo-liberals, we should here remember that the neoclassical model of growth—in particular the Solow-Swan-Meade model—despite assumed competition, will only drive to significant economic growth of the per-capita income when technological change grows continuously and exogenously. Consequently, if for any reason mentioned technological change becomes exhausted, saving and investment efforts in a context of free competition will be conducive in the long run to economic stagnation of the per capita income or GDP.

Conversely, recent models of endogenous growth provide an explanation of the observed phenomenon of continuous per capita GDP growth, also based on the technological change, while competitive equilibrium is declared as no longer efficient for stepping up progress.[67] In these models the engine of growth is the technical progress, which will not be any more exogenous but depending on education, research, etc.; variables that will have to be publicly encouraged (subsidised) to reach their maxima contributions to growth. Otherwise, existence of non-subsidised positive externalities[68] would reduce the positive contributions to growth of mentioned variables. Additionally, the existence of incomplete markets or serious defects of information in others,[69] may make that pure market solutions become non-optimal, and so in need of public correction.

All the above-mentioned arguments enable us to conclude that the arrival to a pure competition system by means of dismantling public sector and interventionism,[70] as suggested by some pro-market

---

67. Vide to this respect the writings of Lucas, R. (1988). "On the Mechanics of Economic Development". *JME*, 22; Becker, G. *et al.* (1990). *Human Capital, Fertility and Economic Growth. JPE*. 98; and Romer, P. (1990). *Endogenous Technical Change*. JPE, 98.

68. The existence of positive externalities—as for instance in education—makes that a pure private provision (realised at pure private market prices) under-provides the amount of the involved goods or services.

69. Vide. Stiglitz, J. (2000). *Economics of the Public Sector*, 3rd Ed. Norton. p.38.

70. Economic growth requires a significant and sizable role of the state. Barro, R. (1990) showed that the present utility of future consumption, or the rate of growth, are maximised when the share of the public productive sector in the output, equals the marginal elasticity of substitution of public and private capital. Findlay, R. (1990) presented a similar result with regard to public employment. Hence, some intermediate role of public investment and employment—very far from 100 per cent but also far from zero—will be optimal for the economic growth. Vide Barro, R. (1990). "Government Spending in a Simple Model of Endogenous Growth". *QJE* 106; and Findlay, R. (1990). "The New Political Economy: Its Explanatory Power for the LDC", *Economics and Politics* 2.

fundamentalists, will not be conducive to optima, but possibly to environment destruction, economic stagnation, deterioration of the personal income distribution, and in the long-term to the undermining of democracy.

Relevance of Private Property for Sustainability of Capitalism

It has many a time been said that capitalism can only be consistent with democracy, if government guarantees the total security and inviolability of private ownership. Of course this statement is not correct.

Observe that when thinking on ownership, one has to agree that there is little difference if people make efforts either for achieving income—that is to say, for the fruits of the existent productive assets—or for getting ownership of the productive assets as sources of income. Consequently, the same what happens with the income and its eventual political redistribution—not really hazardous for democracy if it moves piecemeal and within a critical limit—will happen with the productive assets, if they are moderately redistributed or affected.

In fact, governments of most capitalist democracies use to make economic re-assignment; and not only on certain incomes, but also on certain assets, although mainly[71] after compensation.

In this regard—due to the eventual existence of monopolies; over-accumulation of assets by a limited group of families; oversized real estates; etc—current capitalism, opposing the expected results of the model of pure-free competition, uses to introduce limitations to inheritance,[72] to free contracting in certain markets,[73] and even

71. Recently, western governments have generalised environmental rules that establish limitations on ownership rights.

72. Note that rules on inheritance taxation are a compromise between the intergenerational transmission of inequality, defended by traditional forms of capitalism that rejected inheritance taxation, and the modern interpretation of private property not totally extensive to the heirs. Observe in this regard that tax exemption to inheritance, a very fashionable movement today in the West, is an exaggerated and dangerous post mortem complete extension of property rights that, in our view, plays against the "acceptation" of capitalism.

73. This happens for instance in the labour market—with rules on maximum working annual schedules, etc.—in water and land contracting (assets whose ownership is subordinated to the public interest), in publicity (cigarettes), etc.; and all this while hoarding of essential commodities is an activity normally forbidden, etc.

to the availability by creditors of certain (own) assets in case of bankruptcy.[74]

As a result of mentioned limitations in freedom of contracting, democracy will not be undermined but indeed enhanced and strengthened. In this regard, it should be underlined that keeping a certain level of "equality" counts in democracy as much as keeping property rights. As a consequence, politicians will have to negotiate the existing political trade-off between these two goods.

Note that in capitalistic-democratic societies, the wealthy or well connected, and those who manage important chunks of the national assets, will try to extend the field of the private property rights, while the poor or the powerless will try to move them in opposite direction, thus trying to socialise part of the productive assets. As the reader may imagine, as far as the number of relevant owners is small while the less wealthy are in majority, a "democratic limitless defence" of private ownership will become a pure defence of the privileged.

Observe however that this conception of limitless "private property" as a "privilege" only reflects part of the reality. In fact, competence among the richest will constantly make possible a change in the internal composition of the wealthier, while the general increase of productivity due to competition and accumulation of productive assets (by the wealthier) will positively affect most of the poor (generating jobs for them), who normally use to be risk-averters.

As a result of former mixing of "privilege" and competition, combined with additional redistribution policies, mild forms of capitalism will *sine die* successfully combine with sustainable democracy. This will occur because, in general, the poor or middle class people will accept a system that, although privileging some of its riskier individuals, will in exchange provide the majority of the population with a sustained improvement of per capita income. This successful combination only will survive if successive doses of monopolisation, socialisation, or contracting limitations do not alter the essence of the stimuli of capitalistic societies; and this while the size of public sector remains in a minority position in GDP terms.

74. This type of rules exists everywhere, because otherwise no one would take economic initiatives associated with the risk of losing assets.

Indeed, there are three basic reasons by which capitalism has been progressively accepted in western societies: 1) Because capitalism (in its moderate version of mixed economy of market) is the sole economic organisation compatible with sustainability of democracy in complex societies; 2) Because moderate capitalism has induced an almost generalised feeling of prosperity; and 3) because moderate capitalism has tended[75] to reduce the internal disparity of incomes and wealth between rich and poor, thus de-activating claims against capitalism and democracy.

Other Necessary Conditions for Sustainability of Democracy

As proven, existence of an economically rather homogeneous society is a necessary condition for sustainable democracy, but its fulfilment will not guarantee such a sustainability. As a first additional condition for sustainability of democracy, governments will have to fulfil some crossed checks and balances to remain democratic: a proper division of powers among parliament, executive and judicial, is commonly considered as a guarantee to avert dictatorship.[76]

To guarantee sustainable democracy, the fulfilment of other conditions will be also indispensable. For instance, co-existence of capitalism and democracy will result complicated when an extremely high number of civil servants,[77] mainly extracted from the constituency of the party in power, makes up the administration. Note that in such a case the party in charge will have an additional share of power: that of civil servants and their relatives, who will owe their jobs and living to the current government. This "interpretation of democracy" uses to develop a cobweb of vested interests through which the party in power may tyrannise the rest, not having the other parties the opportunity of attaining power in successive elections.

---

75. This tendency was clearly perceivable in the so-called "Golden Age" of capitalism (1950-1973), but it reversed in the last 25 years.

76. If the division of power dwindles, democracy degrades and the political system moves towards successive dictatorships, in which the winning party, after elections, exercises the power in an unbalanced way, trying to undemocratically succeed itself.

77. In this issue of the number of functionaries, there could be two extreme positions: the case of existence of almost nil number of civil servants; and the case of a suffocating majority of the labour force in the civil service or alike. Logically the line not to be trespassed should be placed in between these two extremes. Possibly, this line should not be over 20-25 per cent of the total labour force.

Besides former phenomenon, the existence of social fractions within a defined country will complicate the sustainability of democracy;[78] and this even though the fractional groups as a whole gather a significant but mixed middle class.[79] Social fractions, based on ethnicity,[80] religion,[81] language,[82] and geography,[83] may drive governments to biased behaviour—when clearly favouring own constituencies[84]—thus undermining democracy. Observe that in the case of existence of mentioned social fractions, one way of solving the subsequent problems would be the attainment of a constitutional consent on banning parties based on these characteristics.

Indeed, situations of permanent inferiority of minorities induced by a fractional-sectarian government may be conducive to the adoption of a pro-independence position by the minority fraction, or to the formation of alternative *contra-natura* coalitions, just to oust the sectarian government.

If there is full and live information, as it happens in the world today, and provided that the nation building after independence has become a fact, the existence of total franchising will be another additional condition for survival of democracy.[85]

---

78. Indeed, the creation of democracies will inherently be more difficult in multi-communal states than in states in which all people see themselves as members of the same society.
79. While economic integration is possible in a multi-communal society, cultural integration—of socio-political fractions—uses to be significantly more time consuming. At times, existence of socio-political fractions hinders progress towards democracy.
80. Discrimination of ethnic minorities makes a country not entirely democratic. This is to some extent still the case in the US.
81. Discrimination between Hindus and Muslims, or between Protestants and Catholics has respectively placed Muslims in India, and Catholics in Northern Ireland in a second class citizenship.
82. This is for instance the case of Belgium.
83. These are the cases of the Basques and Catalans in Spain, Corsicans and Bretons, in France etc.
84. When a multi-communal society is involved in a process of independence from former colonial power, it is possible to gather provisional consensus on certain pro-independence matters. But once finalised the independence process, geographical, social and ethnic fractions use to appear.
85. Note that in today's western democratic countries, democracy historically grew under limited franchising. This was done to pay for time till the moment in which education and middle classes had become sufficiently extended. If, alternatively, the poor had earlier received franchising (thus placing them in political majority)—as it was the case in the first stages of the French Revolution—they would have voted in general for the expropriation of the rich, thus making democracy less tenable. Observe that Aristotle already recognised this problem. Vide *The Politics of Aristotle*. (1958). p.206. Oxford University Press.

Finally, it is important to underline that although in some contexts the behaviour of political parties could undermine democracy,[86] normally they will make democracies more resilient. Nevertheless, we have to affirm that this resilience will depend on the relative strength of the national or regional loyalties of mentioned parties.[87]

Indeed, if all or some of the above mentioned necessary conditions for sustainability of democracy were not fulfilled, either the dominant political party or groups in minority could seek non-democratic political change: 1) The dominant party by means of appointing a leader who in advance promises to assume dictatorial powers if he takes over with sufficient majority as to change the constitution; and 2) The minority group(s) by means of declaring independence of the territory under its control.

Special Consideration on Regional Breaking up

It is clear that the existence of a common language has in the West historically been one of the main reasons behind the promotion of nationalities. Ethnicity has also been frequently invoked for reaching independence, as well as religion.

As far as society trespasses the first stages of economic development, tolerance in religion and ethnic differentials become a less relevant matter. Reason why in these societies regional attempts of breaking up may have more to do with the per capita income disparities of every region within a country, than with the other mentioned arguments, at times used as pretexts.

In current times in which solidarity is a value in relapse—as we have described in Chapter 1—one should not be surprised if the richest region of a country, under pretext of a special identity (ethnic majority, religion, language, or a combination) rejects the idea of continuing "fully" financing the poorer ones through the central public

86. For instance, this may occur if a constitutional party enters in coalition with a separatist one in order to remain in power (a fractional strategy), as recently happened in Spain; or if an extreme right party colligates with another of the extreme left, just for jointly governing the country.

87. Similarly, if some regional voters, regardless of the contents of the political manifesto of a regional party, automatically vote in favour of it and always against national parties (mainly interested in national and international politics), mentioned regional party and voters would also undermine (current) national democracy. Vide. Usher, D. (1981). p.46. Book already mentioned.

finance system.[88] Note in this regard that a more comfortable—for the rich—degraded solidarity may be partially reached by means of a progressive reduction of the direct tax rates, and a reduction of public transfers granted to the poor.

As far as "regional interests" and demands of rich regions—as for instance, mentioned rebates of central taxes and subsidies to the poor—are satisfied by the central government, phenomena of imitation will appear in other regions and the logic of democracy—based on general interests and singled peaked voting actions—will vanish at a central-national level. In fact, regional interests may finally prevail (over the general ones) thus being used to fulfil the purposes of regional leaders—even the call for independence—in detriment of the nation as a whole.

Observe that under conditions of constant regional demands for privileges, the central government should be aware of the risks coming from the military and national security apparatus. Indeed, if state rulers concede an ever increasing regional autonomy, military and security elites—who may see themselves as protecting the unity of the state— may initiate manoeuvres for breaking up the established order in detriment of democracy.

Blossoming of Democracies in the 20th Century

Although sporadic, limited in franchising, and ephemeral forms of democracy were already developed many centuries ago,[89] their destiny was for long to remain sidelined from the normal governance of nations, which in general moved in a context of absolute (monarchies), despotic or authoritarian regimes. The same could be said about some

88. This geographical reading of the regional balances induced by the state finances uses to be a distorted interpretation of the reality, because the public transfers received by the poorer individuals, or the higher direct taxes paid by the richer ones—irrespective of the place in which they live—are consequences of the individual position of every one in the social scale at a state level, and not the result of a deliberate regional policy. Now then, as far as a region accumulates a lot of richer inhabitants, the visual financial effect is that mentioned region is *sine die* transferring public funds to the rest. As a consequence, and for supporting their demands for autonomy, regional parties of rich regions, use to exploit this unbalanced "regional" perception.

89. One could go back to ancient Greece to see the democratic scope and working of some geographically very limited republics or city-states. Or even to Rome in times of its Republic. Note however that all these "republics" were not very democratic while they legally supported slavery.

crucial democratic developments of the second Millennium, such as that of the Carta Magna (1215), or even the French Revolution (1789), which did not result in sustainable democracies.

Although along the 19th century and first half of the 20th, franchising became slowly, but progressively, larger across a good part of western Europe and North America, it is clear that only in the second half of the 20th century, democratic forms of government[90] blossomed in other parts of the world.[91] In fact, the idea that all peoples have the right to converge to democracy is an intrinsic output of the last decades of the 20th century.

As mentioned before, along the 19th century and the first half of the 20th it was accepted that some nations were economically or socially mature for (limited) democracy, and others not. However, this conditioning maturity was abandoned in the second half of the 20th century; particularly from the 80s onwards, when an opposed view—which defended the idea that any country could reach political maturity and subsequent economic prosperity by means of implementing democratic elections—gained ground.

However, this new approach[92] often gathered disappointing results. Amazingly, mentioned naïve idea that making multi-party elections would automatically result in sustainable democratic societies and economic progress was again launched at the early 2000s by the US, in the context of its "war against terrorism".

However, as described in this Chapter, the key to political success in establishing democratic governance lies almost entirely on the right sequencing of the democratisation process in combination with the specific characteristics of the involved societies. Although democracy has today an indisputable moral superiority over other forms of

---

90. Note that this blossoming is exclusively referring to internal or national democracies, just a step—although relevant—in the human trajectory towards full democracy.

91. Since 1980, 81 countries have taken significant steps towards democracy, although only 47 are fully democratic. Note that today, 140 countries of around 200 existing in the world, have timely multiparty elections. Vide. UN Development Program (2002: 10). *Human Development Report 2002*.

92. The idea that setting up "global democracy" could be a more useful instrument to reach national democracy (in some developing countries) than firstly doing national elections without any guarantee of maturity, seems to us plausible.

government,[93] the velocity of progress in implementation will be substantial for reaching sustainable democracies.

National and Global Democracy: A First Evaluation

As we have mentioned before, democratic political systems are those that—in a context of political freedom—use the rule of majority for the selection of leaders and programmes, through the celebration of general elections which define, for a limited period, who is in power and who exercises opposition.

In these democratic societies, people are represented by politicians who, grouped in political parties, reach power to govern a political entity (state, region or town) by means of organising the provision and financing of the public goods and services, and the correction of externalities.

Note that mentioned public goods (and services) and externalities have different levels of provision or correction:[94] 1) the local one, organised either at level of towns and cities for the provision of local public goods and services such as the gathering and treatment of local garbage, public lightning, water provision, etc., or at the level of counties, provinces or regions for the provision of more general goods and services such as the maintenance of the local road net, the net of the regional public transport, etc.; 2) the national one, organised at the level of states for the provision of national goods and services, such as defence and external representation of the state, administration of the national currency, national and borders police, national systems of health and education, etc.; and 3) the global one.

Observe that in recent times the existence of certain global public goods has become patent. For instance, the problem of the

93. Vide. Sen, Amartya (2003: 50). *Democracy and its Global Roots*. For a French version vide. *Les racines globales de la démocracie. Pourquoi la liberté n´est pas un invention de l´ Occident* (2005). Editions Payot and Rivages.

94. Note that according to the theory of Fiscal Federalism, different levels of public goods and services should be provided by different authorities: those who could supply them more efficiently. Vide Musgrave, R. and Musgrave, P. (1984). *Public Finance in Theory and Practise*, Mac Graw-Hill. Former theory implies that, "mutatis mutandis", global public goods and services should be provided by a global government, because it will be the only one that could legitimately and efficiently provide them.

environment,[95] which in certain aspects has many years ago overcome national frontiers (thus inducing global externalities), clearly requires a common democratic treatment supported by all nations of the world. Consequently, any nation that would refuse a global treatment of this problem should at least be qualified as a free rider. But observe additionally that this negative political positioning should also be considered as a non-democratic behaviour at global scale. The same could be said in relation to the abstention or insufficient co-operation in international financing of development or in other global issues. Note that under-financing of basic education, health and infrastructures in LDC, in connexion with other political variables, may induce extreme violent behaviour with negative spill-over effects for all.

In the world today there is also a clear need for a fast, effective and democratic mechanism for the solution of international violent conflicts that, alive for decades in certain parts of the planet and having considerable spill-over effects on the entire global community,[96] should be democratically solved by co-operation of all nations. In this case, the auto-proclamation of certain states as mediators for the resolution of the problem without a clear delegation from the global community is another form of abuse and non-democratic global behaviour. And, even more so when such self-appointed mediators behave as partisans.

Having made all former considerations, we could affirm that a country only could be considered as totally democratic if its citizens decided and agreed to behave democratically at all the above mentioned levels, including the global one.

However, it is perfectly possible that a country behaves democratically at a state level, and less democratically at local level, if for instance the degree of autonomy at such a level is scant (majors

95. To the extent that the global problems of the environment affect all citizens of the planet, decisions on the issue should be made taking into account all the interested parties, and not only the interests of rich countries.

96. Of course, we are here referring to cases such as that of Israel-Palestine. Indeed, more than half a century of violence and negotiations resulting in nothing, is a clear indicator that the methodology and approach for advancing has been totally wrong. The explanation of the long lasting negative evolution of this problem has to do with the absence of neutrality of the self-appointed mediators, who since the very beginning played a self-interested role.

of important cities appointed by the central government).[97] And vice versa, if some democratic concessions are given at local level, while the state is totally or partially closed to general elections and/or other democratic manners.

It is also possible that a country—perhaps by its lack of international power—behaves democratically at an international level; and not only when it votes in multilateral institutions[98] but also when accepting and complying with their resolutions, while internally it has non-democratic institutions and performance.

We could say that it is also possible to be internally democratic, while externally exhibiting abusing manners; and not only in international forum when using veto rights (in the UN-Security Council, for instance) or producing foul play manoeuvres by logrolling or twisting arms, but also by getting involved in external aggressions, sometimes disguised of preventive actions. Or alternatively, while being small and internally democratic, they systematically ignore unfavourable resolutions of the UN, since they feel protected by a veto owner.

Finally, as a complement to this gallery of "democratic" pretenders, we could also imagine countries, which behave non-democratic at all the above-mentioned levels. Fortunately, this absolute lack of any democratic trait is marginal in the world today, as are the countries that behave democratically in all senses.

As anyone may have noticed, we have not put names to the portraits, but we are sure that intelligent readers could easily put several names to match mentioned profiles.

---

97. For instance, "power in democratic Britain has for long been more centralised than in America and other European countries, but it has become so in the last 50 years...Local government lost importance in the last few decades. In the 80s Margaret Thatcher´s Tory government applied a fiscal arm-lock to restrain loony left councils, capping the taxes they were allowed to charge...Following the failure of the poll tax..., in the 90s the local power to set levels of taxation on business was also taken away". Vide. *The Economist*. (2006: 37). February 25.

98. We have here to insist that the UN organs and agencies—as devised in the Charter of the UN—are not democratic because their power structure is not based on popular representation. In particular the UN General Assembly, the head of the current multilateral system, was mainly born as a chamber for consensus building—at times achieved by arms-twisting—and for avoiding violent confrontation. Note that in this organisation, the "winners" of the World War II reserved a "veto right" in their favour in the so-called Security Council; but observe that "democracy" and "veto-rights" are antithetical concepts. Observe additionally that, theoretically, any UN-resolution may be bypassed by members; and, after bypassing, corresponding sanctions to non-fulfilling members may be vetoed by (friendly) veto-owners. Indeed, a mockery of democracy.

Two-Track Promotion of National Democracy

Having realised the former description of the different conceivable "democracies", and once recognised that the concept of total (national and global) democracy is something to be achieved to guarantee physical sustainability (healthy global environment and common natural resources availability) and social justice to make global capitalism acceptable, the next issue to be analysed is how to promote national democracy, effectively and successfully, at a world scale.

In our view there are two convergent ways to promote national democracy: 1) The first has to start from the bottom within nations, that is to say at the level of municipalities, in order to gain experience for further entering into higher national and global democratic endeavours; and 2) The second should be top-down by means of organising a truly democratic UN with capacities to make decisions on global issues and to enforce them, and also to create a complete set of stimuli for encouraging (national) democratisation of non-democratic (small) members.

While the bottom-up promotion of national democracy should mainly be an internal process in countries, the top-down approach inclusive of an effective global economic cooperation policy— seriously committed to education and health, as well as to the creation of infrastructures in LDC[99]—could significantly accelerate the internal process. Observe that once a sufficient level of education and health is reached in connection with better infrastructures, a growing middleclass and a diversified economy will trigger the automatic blossoming of democracy and its values (participation, tolerance and mutual respect).

Alongside with the development of infrastructure, the necessary social homogeneity (nation-building) for achieving sustainable democracies could become a fact in no more time than one generation; of course, provided that the financing of development of LDC carried out by a reorganised UN-Agency for Development (UNICO) become sufficient as to provoke the necessary acceleration of the economic growth for, at least, achieving a partial catching up.

99. This new UN agency (UNICO) for the promotion of development of LDC, and annexed considerations, are extensively described in Rahman, R.D. and J.M. Andreu (2004). *Responsible Global Governance*. New Delhi: Academic Foundation. p.150.

History of Democracy in the West and Attempts to Export Democracy

As we have mentioned before, one should not forget that the western democratic systems have not been constructed in one hour, but along generations; and not in a linear way, but often combined with step-backs, at times moving towards dictatorship, as a consequence of the non-sustainability of the previously established democracies.

A sparkling example of a non-sustainable democracy is the case of the French Republic created in 1789. In fact, after years of instability, the revolutionaries finally handed all power over to Napoleon. More recent examples in Europe are the experiences of Italy and Germany in the 20th century, countries that at one moment also shifted towards dictatorship from previous non-sustainable democracies. In fact, processes towards tenable democracies have been long lasting and rather painful in many western countries; and this even though they enjoyed along the process huge relative economic and technological advantages in comparison to the current economic situation of many developing countries.

Against this background, it seems to us rather cynical, that some western countries put strong pressure on developing countries (even seriously threatening them) to force rapid progress towards national multi-party elections; in particular on those countries suspected of political radicalism when they behave unfriendly and are in possession of scarce raw materials (energy).

Note that this manoeuvre is not only undemocratic—since the pressing western countries often lack global democratic legitimacy for exercising pressure—but also irrational because to force the celebration of elections in countries that do not minimally fulfil pre-conditions for democratic sustainability, is just to ignore political theory and history, and to condemn these countries to instability and political failure.

Democratic Relapse in the West: Bad Examples for Imitation

In the context of the blossoming of national democracies in the second half of the 20th century—which firstly followed the decolonisation process in the 50s and 60s, and recently continued after the fall of the Berlin Wall—one should not forget that the introduction of democracy in a society, although desirable, could be non-sustainable in the long run unless the corresponding society fulfils—and continues for long fulfilling—some prerequisites, as explained in the lines above.[100]

One should not forget either that the consolidation of democracy in countries newly arrived to this form of government, or initiatives for progress towards democracy in non-democratic countries, could be spoiled by the imitation of wrong behaviours and defects in certain western democracies.

Entering now into the observed defects in "advanced" western democracies, we should make a first reference to the weakening of the division of powers, in favour of the executive and in detriment of parliament and democracy itself; and this not to quote the historical under-development of the judicial power in the West.

Indeed, the judicial power in most western democracies is an institution which has not been updated and whose slowness has always worked in favour of some minorities: the rich, the executive, and the criminals. This is the reason why the majority of individuals have always preferred not to enter into juridical claims, be these for civil actions or for battles against the Administration, since the financing of long procedures by simple citizens is almost unaffordable.

In this regard, we have to clearly affirm that to keep untouched these degraded judicial powers in the West does not encourage the setting up of democracy by developing countries. Indeed, if eventual condemnation of the administration occurs long after the government has been replaced, or if the recovering of funds in case of private contracts takes 4-6 years after maturity, one has to deduce that the current organisation of justice is a farce.

Once mentioned the judiciary delay and the lack of effective supremacy of western parliaments during the legislature period, we will enter now into the analysis of some additional dysfunctions that will also confuse the countries today in retarded franchising positions, and with more democratic aspirations.

---

100. The examples of democracies that some few years after their birth, collapsed to fall provisionally (or not) in the hands of dictators, have proliferated in the last 55 years in Latin America and Africa.

Indeed, serious dysfunction appears when political power is exaggeratedly distributed[101] in the context of a multiparty system;[102] or when bad governance comes from the existence of a federal (or autonomic) political system with majority regional parties in every state or region, endowed with constitutional vetoes; a situation which normally requires political consensus on many items for decision-making, as it happens f.i. in India, not to mention the case of a non-unitary political entity, as the European Union is.

Meaningful dysfunction is also observable in Western democracies when a serious regime of incompatibilities for acceding to top postings does not exist, thus allowing multi-billionaires, or global economic actors, to confuse their own (or familiar) interests with the economic aims of the nation.[103] Difficulties in Western democracies also use to appear when there is no political responsibility and reliability,[104] resulting in politicians promising certain targets in the electoral campaigns, to do the opposite once taken office, with the alleged pretexts that the inherited political or economic situation was not really known, or that the needs of formed coalition has forced a change in the political programme, etc.; or simply when politicians lacking integrity, vote individually in parliament—in exchange of bribes always difficult to prove—against the ideology of the party which promoted them to their parliament seats.

Dysfunction may also appear when logrolling operations pass rational political limits, thus enabling politicians, at very high cost for the nation, to remain in power without calling for new elections; or when lacking a minimum of decency, party in power misuses its majority to change electoral rules—from a more proportional to a

---

101. This problem could easily be solved by means of establishing a minimum of gathered votes (f.i. 5%) for access to parliament. Establishing a high limit for access, f.i. 15 per cent of the votes, would be also counterproductive because it would limit political competition among parties.
102. As far as political parties could serve as an instrument for fractional activity in the sense already explained, it would be convenient that the number of parties were not too high and not "single-issued". In particular, existence of ethnic parties, religious parties, geographical parties, professional parties, etc., aside of general parties (conservatives, socialists, etc.), will complicate the governance because they always will give priority to their ethnic, geographical, or professional problems over the general ones, thus defending programs exclusively devised to favour themselves which will tend to undermine political stability.
103. Vide. Rousseau, J.J. (1994). *Du contract social*. p.71. Cèrés Editions. Tunisie.
104. Vide. Downs, A. (1957). *An Economic Theory of Democracy*. New York: Harper. p.105.

majority system of representation, or vice versa—without the consent of the others, to sine die remain in power or to avoid significant failure in following election.

And what to say about the so-called sacred "freedom of expression" in the West, in which mockery of politicians and even religions is allowed, thus directly or indirectly promoting domestic or transnational religious hatred and rampage, and progressively discrediting politics as an honourable profession.[105] Indeed, in this matter of freedom of expression almost all the red signals have been crossed in early 2000, while its exercise should basically imply freedom to criticise governments in power, thus letting aside private and conscience matters.

Apart from the above mentioned dysfunctions, we could list other additional defects of western democracies: 1) Corruption or misdemeanour of top executives of large Western republics who, instead of resigning, use legal exceptional protection of their top-jobs to escape their responsibilities; 2) Control or harassment of media by dominant parties which simultaneously avert access of others to the media; 3) Unfair financing of political parties which falsifies reached representation; 4) Reckless political coalitions to govern which, although legal, escape the logic of good governance; 5) Lack of consideration of the rights of neighbouring countries, when some western polluting countries do not compensate for the negative spill-over (pollution) effects suffered by others; 6) Generalised mockery and systematic rolling over parties in opposition by arrogant parties supported by overall majorities; 7) Use of lies—disguised of half-truths—to concoct political actions, be these national or international;[106] 8) Tendency to manage the public issues with a short term perspective, irrespective of whether some public issues have only a possible correction at long term; or vice versa, when taking economic initiatives beyond "one's grave", thus depriving future elected politicians of their right to govern efficiently; 9) Trend, in case

---

105. In this respect, a historical parallelism between perverted "advances" in the freedom of expression and average fall in the quality of politicians has been observed, this being an indicator that the external costs of being a politician have significantly increased, thus discouraging the best to enter in the career.

106. We suggest the readers, as an interesting exercise, to try to guess the involved individuals in the above quoted misdemeanours.

of overall majority, to disdain any collective multiparty governance, thus increasing partisanship and destructive opposition instead of loyal collaboration; and 10) Trend to minimise main underlying principles of democracy (privacy of communications, privacy of financing, right of own image, etc.) allegedly to defend democracy against non-defined enemies (external or internal).

We do believe that former list of democratic vices have a common root based on the so-called "professionalism of politicians". Bearing in mind that a first derivative of democracy is alternation in power, a life career as a democratic politician is to some extent a contradiction in terms since the number of postings when the party is in power is by far more abundant than when the party is in opposition.

Many misdemeanours of western politicians are today directly related to their need of unduly protracting their political careers or unduly enjoying privileges. Indeed the fear for a sudden interruption of their careers, which often would be a personal drama, may force them to enter in illegal actions or trying to get postings in private sector if next elections are expected to be lost. Regrettably, the general loss of morals observed in western societies has also contaminated politicians when they, as leaders of societies, should have adopted total transparency and legality in their actions.

After visualising the above-mentioned (national) democratic problems—which proliferate in the West—and after considering the relative lack of respect of some relevant western countries to others (developing ones) in relation to the administration of global public goods, it is no wonder, that many countries that could accede to national democracy may feel somewhat discouraged.

Indeed, the bad examples of the West with internal democracies in relapse, and with no interest in promoting global democracy for solving the main common problems of mankind, but on the contrary, auto-proclaiming themselves as policemen or mediators (while being at the same time parties in the game)—and this in a time of global and live information—is not the best of scenarios for promoting democracy in traditional or medieval LDC.

Costs of Irrationally Enforcing Democracy

Although we have already exposed the way for promoting democracy from within, with the enabling support of the international community along one generation, we will now review the recent failing attempts by western governments to impose democracy in the Muslim world and its costs.

The first question that western leadership should have answered on this issue is whether the democracy they wanted to export to non-democratic nations, should precisely be the one described in the former paragraphs—including its vices and dysfunction—or just a system of government based on direct population representation. Experience has repeatedly proven that to forcibly export political systems (democracy or others) to other countries is often just a loss of time, money and, probably, a lot of human lives. Consequently, before initiating any manoeuvre for promoting democracy in the Arab-Muslim world, the West should at least have reviewed the sociological and psychological conditions of the involved populations,[107] their homogeneity in terms of religion and language, the existence of a significant windfall production, the existence of a well spread middle class, etc.

Of course if many of these conditions were not fulfilled, as it was the case, the shortest way for promoting sustainable democracy in these countries would have paradoxically been to initiate a crash programme for improving education, health and infrastructures over one generation, which to some extent should have been financed by the international community. Indeed, education (particularly that of women) and information on the one hand, and economic development with a diversified private sector on the other will make up the best platform for gaining progressive internal acceptance of democracy in these countries.

Against this background, and in front of the facts of September 11, 2001, the US administration, mainly for internal consumption

107. Acceptance (or not) of separation of religion and state is a crucial point that affects a great part of the Muslim World (near 1.5 bn. people, that is to say, 21 per cent of total world population). Non-separation implies that God's rule has primacy over human political choices. Note that eventual dissociation of state and religion would force, in a vast majority of the Muslim World, a domestic redefinition of the family rights of the population.

but also for ignorance, initiated a policy of military aggressions for regime change in two Muslim countries, Afghanistan and Iraq, while sending warnings to others.

From then onwards, the world has shockingly observed successive errors leading to chaos in these two countries: hastily formation of fractional political parties (based on ethnicity and religion, etc.); partially boycotted elections performed under curfew and controlled at gunpoint by foreign occupiers; sub-representative parliaments and forced formation of (unity) governments to approve semi-western constitutions; huge loss of private assets and infrastructures; systematic violation of human rights; over-killing (lateral damage) of nationals by occupying forces and contracted private para-militaries combined with unstoppable actions of the insurrection, etc. Indeed, not good precedents for the consolidation of democracy; and all that to a very high price for the US tax payers. Indeed, a 100 per cent regrettable initiative.

Not sufficiently satisfied with the disastrous political output obtained since 2001, a new line of action—in this case almost childish—was announced by the US Administration in relation to the need of "urgently" exporting democracy by means of the so-called "transforming diplomacy" for regime change. We have to say that this is another simple and non-meditated strategy, which is also doomed to fail.

Summarising, we have to affirm that in the operation of promoting democracy there are no shortcuts, violent or not. This is because the democratisation process is a conditioned and time consuming process, as western countries experienced themselves in the last two Centuries. Indeed the West has no other option than to facilitate the achievement of the necessary conditions for establishing a feasible democracy. In the meantime, the West should preach with the example, by improving own democracies getting rid of their current vices, and by promoting the democratisation of the UN.

Democratic Situation in the World Today and Perspectives

Once described the different theoretical forms of democracy and its variations, national and global, we will now review the different "democratic behaviour" of certain countries, individually or classified by groups.

Democracy Temperature of "Democratic" Societies

In relation with the degree of democracy attained in rich countries—those of Western Europe, North America (US and Canada), Japan, Australia and New Zealand—we could underline the following characteristics: 1) In all these countries, citizens (except some immigrants) enjoy full franchising; 2) The honouring of human rights is high, in particular the so-called civil and political rights, but the honouring of the socio-economic and cultural rights, both internal and in relation to developing countries, is in decline; 3) In many of these countries, internal democracy, as explained before, has entered in relapse, and new rules enacted by their parliaments, particularly in the last 15 years, have introduced a growing bias towards a radical interpretation of economic freedom, which has undermined the social protection net and the personal income distribution in many of these communities; 4) Progressively, some of these countries are misusing or violating international laws; in particular, those dealing with immigration and with the consequences of occupation (reconstruction, prisoners of war, arbitrary arrests, etc.), not to quote the recent shameful scrambling for the future exploitation of raw materials in the Poles; and 5) Most of these countries, while internally democratic behave non-democratically in global issues despite the fact that they altogether only count with 16 per cent of the population of the world.

This abusive behaviour has also been extended to the domains of NPT, WMD, pre-emptive actions, war against terrorism, war crimes prosecution, Kyoto protocol, etc. Note that the US has refused in the past 40 years to sign any international treaty since Americans consider their national laws as above any international form of democratic control.

Democratic Features of Some Developing Countries

The Case of the Muslim World

To start with the analysis of achieved democracy in developing countries—a description that will necessarily have to be selective—we will begin with some considerations on Muslim nations. 1) A first characteristic of these countries is their stagnating democratisation process. This stagnation has mainly to do with the constant tensions among secular political modernisers (at times democratisers) on the one hand, and the defenders of the Muslim identity and religious law (Sharia) on the other. Note that the latter, sometimes include radical groups who promote the construction of Islamic states, allegedly following recommendations of the Sharia.[108] Mentioned stagnation has also been induced by the political uncertainty created by dominant global powers[109] which for half a century have been involved in a partisan way in the Palestine-Israel conflict, while at the same time they have become more visibly concerned with their access to oil. The last two factors—Palestine-Israel issue and oil—have induced incoherent relations of Western leadership with theocratic or secular dictators, while at the same time the West has called for democracy when convenient;[110] 2) A second political characteristic in these countries is that Islamist parties—with an explicit goal for establishing a theocratic government (Islamic state)—enshrine as a principle "limited democracy" in combination with Sharia law. Hence, "democratic" developments promoted by these parties encompass the risk of the so-called "trap of the one-off elections" referring to the possibility that once an Islamist party reaches power via election, it may change the constitution and electoral system for protecting theocracy; 3) A clear pre-democratic characteristic of these countries is the non-consideration or the half-hearted treatment of 50 per cent of their population: women. Indeed, although with some few exceptions, the role of women in Muslim societies is unequal, having

108. Many Muslims believe that the Koran makes neither recommendation for construction of an Islamic state, nor does it mention anything about politics. The state is consequently for them a non-religious institution, and state and politics are not part of the religion. However others—some of them in power (Iran and Sudan) or constituting minorities in other Muslim countries—defend or promote the opposite. Among the latter there are some who consider themselves as moderate Islamists, capable of adjusting to democratic alternation even after reaching power. Vide. Charfi, M. (2005) *Islam and Liberty*. Book already mentioned. p.104.

109. Note that current Arab States, as many other developing countries, grew up at the shadow of colonial arrangements. Although in the 1950s occupation-administration of Arab Territories (by France and Britain) had come to an end, some of the legal structures and practises, limiting freedom under occupation, were adopted in the political and legal architecture of the newly independent Arab states. Vide UNDP (2004) *The Arab Human Development Report 2004*. p.66. New York.

110. Vide UNDP (2004) Book already mentioned. p.66.

to accept legal restrictions in public-social life, on the work-floor, in education, and in family life (parenthood, divorce, inheritance, etc.). It is our view that these gender restrictions, together with the former experienced colonisation, have been severely detrimental for the socio-economic progress of these countries; 4) Another peculiarity of Muslim communities is the delay of their education systems—mostly traditional and underdeveloped in terms of access—a bias that, could take one or two generations to be corrected; 5) Delayed industrialisation is also a clear deficiency of these countries; note however that this deficiency is not an exclusive trait of the Muslim-Arab countries but also of the rest of developing ones that have suffered biased administration from colonial powers;[111] 6) The existence of large deposits of gas and crude oil in the subsoil of some of these countries, has not only conditioned their relations with the West—as already explained—but has also stressed the problem of the personal income distribution; 7) We could also refer to another specific aspect of most of these countries: the lack of separation between religion and state. Note however that this trait was overcome, with difficulties, by some Western Mediterranean countries only in the second half of the 20th century; 8) We have to also underline that total franchising, even for male citizens, is far from being introduced in some of Muslim countries; and 9) Last but not least one should not forget the cynical political double standards recently played by the West in these countries: recommending free access to elections of Islamist parties, while at the same time rejecting their access to government if these parties reach electoral victory (Algiers, Palestine), using after election non-recognition or boycotting tactics.[112]

The Case of China and India

Looking into the democratic profiles of large emerging countries as China and India, we may observe the following remarkable features. Starting with India, which since its independence in 1947

111. The administration of colonies by colonial powers was mainly focused towards the provision of raw materials for the metropolis, with generalised disregard of education and industrialisation of "protected" territories.

112. Bearing in mind the multiple and contradictory shifting in alliances, and the selective use of international law and UN resolutions by the West, neutral observers have necessarily to deduce that the political actions of Western leadership (military and diplomatic) in the Middle East have not been driven by democracy promotion but by self-interest.

has always been a (national) democracy—although, to say the truth, a non-fully informed democracy due to the existing high number[113] of illiterates—we cannot hide its convoluted national governance, its widespread petty corruption, and its very slow justice machinery.[114] Indeed, as a derivative of its organisation as a peculiar Federal State—the decision-making process in India is enormously time consuming in comparison with other political systems, in particular with that of China. Specifically, in many economic reform issues, which at least partially fall under the constitutional competencies of the states, a rule of consensus is needed in India,[115] thus resulting in exasperating slowness. Observe additionally that India used to behave very democratically in international matters, having for decades been one of the leaders of developing countries in international negotiations, at times leading as well the "Non Aligned Movement".

In relation to the democratic progress of China, it is frequently said that, although lacking basic democratic institutions today, from one moment onwards the growing political demands of a society progressively richer,[116] will generate a pro-democratic movement that finally—probably channelled by the CCP—will change the current Chinese style of doing politics. As expectable, after the creation of democratic institutions—with parliament open to all

113. Indian illiteracy reached a figure in 2006 of 28 per cent of the male adult population, and other of 52 per cent of the adult females. Vide World Bank (2007). *World Development Indicators*.

114. Concerning politics in relation to the juridical machinery of India—one of the slowest of the world—we should add that that alleged criminals have reached parliamentary seats in successive elections in order to gain personal immunity. In this regard, a former President of the Republic of India, Mr. Narayanan several times called the political parties (in 2003) asking them for the exclusion of alleged criminals from electoral lists. According to a recent statement of *Outlook*, a weekly Indian magazine, not less than 100 parliamentarians of the Indian Lower House were involved in penal procedures against them. As an example, we could here quote the case of the former Union Coal Minister, who resigned in December 2006 after getting a life serving condemnation, allegedly for killing his secretary in 1993. While the ex-minister appeals, he continues with his parliamentary seat, even 14 years after such alleged crime. Vide. *The Economist*. December 9, 2006, p.58.

115. This is a similar problem as that currently experienced by the EU in comparison to the US. The time-consuming and paralysing EU mechanisms for decision-making in common issues have additionally become compounded after the enlargement from 15 up to 27 members.

116. Note that in comparison to the Maoist period, the current Chinese citizens, particularly those living in urban areas, may travel inside and outside the country, may choose their own studies, may move from one job to another (mainly in the urban private sector), may start private businesses, may access to a variety of cultural expressions, may buy apartments, etc.

parties, independent trade unions, etc.—China would politically and economically homologate to the West. According to some observers, mentioned homologation would deprive China from its current "comparative advantage" of rapid decision-making and management of the core economic variables for development, as the domestic saving rate, labour wages, etc.[117]

Indeed, despite the apparent standstill political situation of nowadays, and being difficult to conceive a more and more capitalistic economy in the context of a socialist political framework, we do believe that China will ultimately advance towards a more democratic political system: towards a social-democracy, which could have some peculiarities as many democracies in the West.[118] Steady and significant economic growth, progressive international integration and, above all, freer information will be variables which will doubtlessly bring internal democracy to China.[119]

Finally, we do believe that for supporting own progress China and India[120] will necessary have to promote multilateralism and democratisation of the UN, as a healthy way out to avert temptations of the today powerful. Note that this convenient (especially for China) democratisation of the UN will also force China to democratise itself. And it will do so when the necessary conditions for achieving democracy are fulfilled.

---

117. While in the West it is categorically affirmed that democratisation will deprive China from its comparative advantage in decision-making, thus cutting current rapid growth rate, western "neo-cons" constantly suggest that progress towards democracy will accelerate growth rates of most developing countries; something totally opposed to the former argument.
118. Note that in the West there are countries that following the so-called "first pass the post" system may get huge majorities in parliament with 30-35 per cent of popular votes, while in others majority requires 45-50 per cent of popular votes. And no one protests against these peculiarities.
119. According to some observers, this transition towards democracy could be managed in due time by the CCP itself. In this respect we have the reference of Taiwan—another Chinese society—in which the transition to democracy was done in the beginning of the 90s by the KMT, a rightist party that after decades of conducting dictatorship in Taiwan, gained the first free general elections. It is plausible that in the People' Republic of China a similar process takes place in due time. On the other hand, the convenience for China of encouraging UN democratisation, will additionally force this country to speed up its own domestic democratisation process.
120. On the possible hindrances that western countries could put in front of the economic progress of China and India Vide. Rahman, R.D. and J.M. Andreu (2006). *China and India. Towards global economic supremacy?* New Delhi: Academic Foundation. p.191.

Besides making a case for the democratisation of the UN, we have to additionally mention that China and India are already becoming more and more involved in development co-operation and funding (in particular China in Africa).

The Case of Russia and Brazil

After the crumbling of the Soviet Union and the difficulties of its economic transition towards a market economy, Russia initiated in the first years of the 2000s a process of rapid economic recovery, strongly supported by a period of sustained high prices of energy. This economic revival of Russia, mainly in the last five years, has given the country an increased clout in international politics.

Observe that along the past 15 years, Russia passed through two different political stages: 1) the first one included two sub-periods: a first sub-period of political transition from the Soviet Union into a federation of independent states lead by a "democratised" Russia, as implemented by President Gorbachev, and a second sub-period, economically unstable, under President Yeltsin; and 2) a period of economic consolidation combined with a perceived slowdown in the democratisation process, in times of President Putin.

Precisely in this second period of nation rebuilding, provisional movements of approaching Germany and France in relation with certain Middle-East issues (Iraq war, Palestine), mediation in the Iranian nuclear issue concerning the NPT, and recent joint military manoeuvres with China and India, are indicators that Russia has recovered part of its lost international influence and—in collaboration with others—seems to be prone to the creation of countervailing powers, while rejecting uni-polarisation.

In relation to democratic Brazil, we have to say that, although showing ambitions for international political leadership, its current economic take off is not satisfactory—with average growth rates of the tune of 2-3 per cent in the last years—while presenting one of the worst distributions of the personal income in the world, as measured by the Gini Index.[121] These indicators create doubts about the future sustainability of democracy in this country.

---

121. According to the last figures published by the World Bank in its World Development Indicators (2007), the worst (among the published) Gini Indexes of the World was that of Brazil. According to recent information it seems that mentioned Gini Index has slightly improved in the last two years.

Independent in international political issues, particularly from the US, and ready to play a relevant role in global environmental protection, Brazil[122] wants, like India, to become a permanent member of the Security Council. Brazil, jointly with Russia, India and China make up the so-called BRIC countries, which in two or three years will become the engine of the (additional) economic growth of the world.

Of course the rest of developing countries, with their peculiarities in governance, demographic size, internal composition of population—be this homogeneous, or heterogeneous in terms of distribution of income, language, race, geography, etc., which complicates the democratisation process—economically behave as described in Chapter 2, while politically adjust in international issues more or less to the powers on which they economically or politically depend. Observe that in the last ten years many developing countries are politically under surveillance of the West, which at its own convenience is using the "degree" of reached democracy and good governance in these countries as main conditions for obtaining development funding.

On the Absence of Global Democracy in the World Today

After several decades in which the UN was mainly a baffle for the cold war, the crumbling of the Soviet Union gave the United Nations a clear opportunity for progressing towards an effective global democracy. Amazingly, what happened in the following 15 years (up to 2006) was rather the opposite: a self-considered hegemonic power (US), using or bypassing the political structure of the UN when convenient, hindered any progress towards global democracy.

Reflecting on global democracy, one has to admit that the legitimate provision of global public goods, as peace, security, environment preservation, space and sea exploration, etc.—or the administration of intermediate variables to achieve peace and security, as for instance sufficient development financing of LDC—has to come from the global will of the majority of citizens of the planet, democratically represented in a new UN; and not as it currently occurs from the will

---

122. As explained in Chapter 3, we believe that India and Brazil should be "long tenure" members of the Security Council, as well as Germany and Japan, but all of them without veto rights—as the rest of the current veto owners—and for a fixed period of time.

of some powerful countries (in military terms), particularly the US, which has a minor share in the population of the planet.[123]

Note that when their national interests are not directly involved, these powerful countries use to act in agreement with the world majorities, as expressed by voting procedures in current UN General Assembly. But when their own interests are directly at stake, they often behave in an abusive way, disregarding opinions or desires of others. And this although the latter forms the vast majority of the world in terms of demography, and the matter in discussion refers to global public goods or externalities.

Undeniably, at the UN inception in 1944, in a world in War, the concern of UN founding-members was neither the degree of the internal democracy of current or future members of the institution, nor the establishment of a global democratic body. Indeed, the top interest of the founders was then to finish the Second World War and to avoid future generalised wars.

From those days onwards, the decolonisation process progressively added new members to the UN, some of them democratic, and others not. Unfortunately, many of these new democracies proved to be non-durable because they did not fulfil the earlier explained pre-requisites to become sustainable democracies. As a result, they veered to different forms of dictatorship, both rightists and leftists. Note that in the second half of the 20th century and for many years, a significant chunk of the developing world was the stage on which the Cold War became warm.

With the crumbling of communism in the Soviet Union (and satellites), opening of markets and pro-democratic movements gathered momentum at international scale. Indeed, in the last 15 years the efficiency of the market economy and moral superiority of democracy significantly gained ground.

Note however, that in the last 15 years some developing countries have delayed their democratisation process, while working on

123. In particular we should here mention the fact that the US, with less than five per cent of the total world population, spends in weaponry and military personnel near 50 per cent of the total military expenditure of the world. This is a figure that annually represents around US$ 350 bn, that is to say near five times the annual average ODA of all the donors of the world, and around 20 times the US expenditure in its so-called Aid to Development.

economic progress and on the solution of their religious and cultural peculiarities. Although they hoped for some tolerance from the West during a period of transition, they have found incomprehension and at times suffered political harassment.

Taking into consideration all the arguments above, we do believe that the time of starting the construction of a global democracy has finally arrived. Indeed, it is absurd to defend (domestic) democracy as the best (or as the least bad) political system for the administration of national public goods and services—and to aggressively promote this system when and where convenient—and at the same time rejecting this system for the administration of global public goods. This is exactly what some western countries do today: torpedoing democratisation of the UN while using non-democratic multi-lateral institutions for administrating global public goods in their own interest. Observe that this practice politically ignores the majority of citizens of the planet, when most of them are informed and concerned with peace, human security, protection of the environment, etc.[124]

Consequently, rejection of democratisation of the UN by permanent members of the Security Council, although individually understandable in terms of a second best policy,[125] cannot be considered as fair, and it will play against the prestige of the rich western countries. Note that the administration of the global public goods by superpowers, without being democratically entitled to do so, is—even if well intentioned—just to practise dictatorship, something in principle detestable.

We think that, in times of full and live information and growing democracy, to play the role of the good and the intelligent person "because the others are bad or stupid" (and small in military capacities) is simply not acceptable. As a result, persistence during a decade or more of current (traditional) behaviour of the West in

124. For instance, it is evident that the Israel-Palestine conflict—with its economic derivatives (oil)—is a global issue in which every citizen of the World should desire reaching a fair and democratic solution. But what in fact happens, is that the self appointed main mediator of the conflict, the US (with less the 5 per cent of the World population) is a close allied of Israel, while at the same time the Americans are the main demander of oil in the region, being both circumstances clear causes for abstention in mediation in a democratic context. The case of CO_2 emissions and the non-signing of the Kyoto Protocol (by US and others) is also a global non-democratic behaviour.

125. If others do not relinquish their veto right, or act unilaterally against resolutions of the UN, why should other veto-owners renounce their veto-right? Nevertheless, this option, although understandable, is far away from the logic of democracy.

global political or economic issues could, in our view, be conducive to a bifurcation of the current UN and agencies. Indeed, a scenario not very positive for the international community, reason why it would be worthy to take actions to avoid it.

Should Non-Democratic States Participate in a New Democratic UN?

Indeed, the sole way of deactivating the currently unfair treatment of the provision of global public goods—almost always directly or indirectly defined and implemented by main western countries—is the creation of a new democratic UN, with supremacy on national parliaments in relation to the provision of global public goods and the correction of global externalities. If this creation became effective, unilateral or minority actions of individual developed nations[126] against some emerging countries should from then onwards be considered as selfish and non-democratic initiatives, and consequently condemned.

Having said that one could wonder if the most powerful Western nations would hand over their current individual power in relation to the provision of global public goods, etc. and to submit it to a democratic global body—to a new and democratic UN.

Indeed, one elemental source of criticism to the creation of a democratic UN could come from western countries, which would not admit national non-democratic countries—for instance China—to form a part of this new UN at the same level as them since, in their view, the "representatives" of these countries would lack national democratic legitimacy for representation.

Although, apparently, this argument based on the lack of national representation, could be considered as rational from a democratic perspective, the reality is that it is not entirely valid at a global scale for the following two reasons: 1) the first stemming from an incorrect interpretation of what a global democracy is; indeed, those

126. Note that Western veto owners (US, UK, and France) and followers (mainly EU countries plus Canada, Australia and New Zealand) use to say that their opinions and actions in relation to the provision of the described global public goods and the correction of global externalities are those of the "international community" when they only represent a 16 per cent of the total population of the planet, and when in many occasions they ignore the rest (the 84 per cent of the world population living in developing countries, of which 37 per cent live in China and India).

who defend exclusion of non-democratic countries from a democratic UN confuse their national democratic behaviour with democratic behaviour at global level to which often they do not adjust at all, since they provide (or disregard) global public goods without any global democratic representation; and 2) the second coming from the urgency to solve serious threats for the survival of mankind (mainly climate change, correct administration of natural resources, proliferation of civil wars and massive violations of basic human rights, and growing terrorism); in fact the argument of the urgency and the impossibility of provision of global public goods and the correction of global externalities[127] by individual nations or even by (non-inclusive) multilateral treaties, should carry us to the acceptance of most countries in the new democratic UN.

In fact, small countries[128] without internal democracy could acquire a transitory legitimacy for their participation in the new democratic UN if they behave properly at global level. Note that—if agreed—any (nationally) democratic or non-democratic country, accepted as a member of the new democratic UN, could lose its membership if it behaves non-properly at a global scale, that is to say, if it rejects or does not comply with the resolutions of the General Assembly. Even more, we do believe that the participation of non-democratic countries or countries in transition in the new UN will actively stimulate their transition to democracy, as it has been proven in the past 60 years in which most of them went into organising regular elections.

Note however that the big non-democratic countries, as for instance China, should be a particular case for admission. In this

127. We do believe that in case of the existence of a global democratic UN, global public goods and externalities would be more efficiently provided, irrespective of the lack of democratic legitimacy of the representatives of small non-democratic countries. Most likely these non-democratic countries, with divergent interests in many domains, would act rather independently in this new democratic UN in relation to the solution of common global issues. This means that these countries would in general support rational solutions for global issues as already proven by the experience in the General Assembly of the current UN.

128. Non-democratic countries with less than 100 million inhabitants (equivalent to 1.5 per cent of global population) could be unconditionally acceptable as members of a democratic UN. Of course, the case of China is very different because its entrance as a member could distort the system of representation in the new democratic UN. Do not forget that China is a country that, according to its relative population, should have around 20 per cent of the population representation in the UN, which should be based on popular mandate.

regard, we consider that to favour the creation of a new democratic UN, the prior democratisation of big non-democratic countries will be indispensable. With China and India democratic (altogether 36% of the global population), the creation of a democratic UN would be almost automatic in the current circumstances of non-sustainability and additional threats to mankind. In such a context, also the current self-appointed representatives of the "international community" would have to necessarily adjust.

Concluding, we do believe that conditionally inviting non-democratic countries to form part of the new UN would not only be positive from the perspective of the rights of their populations in a global context, but also to speed up their national democratisation processes.

Towards a More Efficient and Fair Capitalism-Democracy Combination in the 21st Century

Given the theoretical conditions for tenability of democracy, and despite the current disappointing trajectory of Western democracies, the delay in democratisation of some developing countries, the failures of imposing democracy from outside, and the current difficulties for the democratisation of the UN, it will not be complicated to make a reasonable prognosis about future political trends. The outcome of the prognosis will enable us to list both the conditions that current democracies themselves will have to fulfil to be sustainable, and the conditions that capitalism will have to accomplish for preserving democracy.

Conditions for Survival of Capitalism and Democracy

We have assured in the lines above that a fair system for the economic distribution of income and wealth is essential for the sustainability of democracy. We have also settled that a pure system of market –without any government intervention—will likely result in monopolisation, concentration of income and wealth, and non-acceptable income distribution. We have also underlined that a worsening of the income distribution may provoke disloyalty to democracy both among the rich and among the masses.

In the last 15 years up to 2006, most countries (rich and poor) that entered into the process of (additional) globalisation, thus liberalising many external and internal markets while reducing their public sectors, have experienced a worsening in their personal income distribution.

As far as an overdone move towards inequality tends to degrade middle classes and undermine democracy[129]—because high inequality uses to induce the poor to "democratically after elections expropriate the rich"—politicians in power should administrate capitalism in such a way that it is acceptable for all, including the poor, who should be convinced that any alternative economic system would be worst even for them.

As a consequence of this reflection, current trend in western countries, particularly in Europe, to reduce direct taxes and to degrade the existing social protection net (Social Security)—coinciding in time with an almost generalised stagnant, or even negative evolution of the real wages[130] induced by globalisation—should be reversed. This implies that the fiscal system[131] and the social protection net should be reorganised in Western countries in order to gain efficiency, but also to avert disloyalty of citizens to democracy.

The same considerations, *mutatis mutandis*, should be valid for the current developing countries which, not enjoying today a decent social protection net, should fight to achieve it if they want to count in future with tenable democracies. This consideration should take them to a piecemeal rising of their income taxes, although without moving beyond a certain degree of progressiveness.

---

129. Remember that acceptable capitalism (which should include an equitable distribution of the personal income) is a pre-requisite for sustainability of democracy. Any other economic organisation (socialism) based on economic re-assignment coming from public sector, will be incompatible with sustainability of democracy.

130. Remember that the recent report of the IMF (*Economic Outlook*, 2007) on the incidence of globalisation on real wages in western countries, suggested an average stabilisation of these real wages along the period 1982-2002. However, it is our view that this result is not realistic because the evolution of these real wages have been calculated using official western CPIs, which do not gather the inflationary effects of the recent bubbles on assets. Besides this, "calculated" stabilisation of wages in a context of rapidly growing GDP in the world and in the West implies itself a clear worsening of the income share of western labourers.

131. According to new trends of taxation in the West, the income tax is losing its progressiveness—allegedly for reducing des-incentives to work and save—while private income redistribution also worsens. On the other hand Corporate tax rates are also moving down "to improve the degree of competitiveness of the firms" and for attracting FDI; and all this in coexistence with a trend towards elimination of the inheritance tax, and a trend to increase indirect taxes. Note that all these developments favour the rich in detriment of the poor, thus altogether reducing the degree of "acceptability of capitalism" and consequently undermining democracy.

Generalised national privatisation in simultaneity with international consolidation of capitalism, via cross-borders take-overs of corporations, is currently conducive to a fundamental mutation of the former equilibrium for the acceptation of the "equity system" of capitalism. Note that this mutation towards "global capitalism" has moved in parallel to the melting down of domestic Trade Unions that so much helped in the past to promote acceptability of capitalism in Europe and, consequently, national democracy.

Observe that today's Western governments not only accept unbalanced developments in capital and labour markets at national and international levels[132]—thus admitting a trend towards additional monopolisation of capital—but they also neglect (or just ignore) the dangerous political consequences of such a development, which could jeopardise national democracies.

Towards a Fairer Global Distribution of the Per Capita Income

As a derivative of former arguments, we understand that, although recent additional globalisation has been as a whole convenient for the World economy, its approach in the last 16 years[133]—which has significantly favoured Western firms and shareholders[134]—should change to reach a more balanced geographical production and a better personal income distribution.

For reaching these targets, a first change to be introduced is that related to the necessary substantial increase of public (ODA) and private international financing (FDI) directed to the poorest developing countries, since this development financing was highly insufficient all along the last 60 years. To the extent that current internal financing of LDC is insufficient for their taking off, and given the fact that FDI hardly flows to these countries, the volume of the annual foreign public funding (ODA) should multiply from around 0.25 per cent of the GDP of the Donor Countries registered in the

---

132. From a global perspective, the evolution of capital markets has been one of progressive liberalisation, while that of labour has pervasively remained selective and one-sided.

133. A comprehensive analysis of this issue may be found in Rahman, R.D. and J.M. Andreu (2004). *Responsible Global Governance*. New Delhi: Academic Foundation. p.38.

134. Recent globalisation also favoured: 1) industrial and service workers mainly in Asian developing countries (while most workers in agriculture have been left behind); and 2) high skilled and top managing workers in the West.

first 2000 up to a figure of around 2 per cent.[135] Only an initiative at this scale could significantly bridge the current rich-poor per capita income gap, thus deactivating in one generation many conflicts in the world, including international terrorism.

In relation to this necessary and multiplied increase of the volume of the Official Development Assistance (ODA), some politicians have made non-well meditated suggestions. The adaptation of the so-called Tobin tax on movements of capital, as a new fiscal source for increasing the budget for development financing in LDC, or the suggestion (partially implemented) of establishing a tax on plane tickets, are two non-neutral proposals[136] that would negatively affect the involved economic activities.

Perhaps a general, unified and agreed additional taxation on the inherited wealth all over the world[137] would be the most convenient and neutral source to make the new required financing consistent with the optimal allocation of resources. Let us not forget that this inheritance tax is precisely one of the most relevant taxes for the acceptance of capitalism by the poor. Indeed capitalistic globalisation would be much more acceptable for all if poor countries received significant compensation under ODA, in proportion to suggested figures.

Note that the suggested increase in taxation on wealth inheritance would be a high-powered and neutral way of revenue gathering. In fact, an additional taxation of just 5 per cent on the annually transferred wealth among different generations (mainly of westerners) would reach an annual figure of US$ 100bn.; and of US$ 200bn if the additional taxation amounted 10 per cent; or of US$ 400bn. if the

---

135. Vide Rahman, R.D. and Andreu, J.M. (2004). Book already mentioned, p.143. Vide also Rahman, R. and J.M. Andreu (2002). *Financing Economic Development and Human Security*. New Delhi: Rashtriya Printers. In 2006, mentioned percentage of 0.25 per cent has almost doubled according to certain publications. However, this doubling, is partly due to the pollution of the ODA by including the costs of forgiveness of the debt, reconstruction of Afghanistan, Iraq, etc., and the expenditures of fielding military peace missions.

136. Mentioned proposals, affecting two specific economic activities, and not the rest are economically non-neutral, reason why they should be discarded.

137. This taxation should also be compulsory in developing countries, although its revenue should be very low in comparative terms.

additional taxation on inheritances was 20 per cent;[138] certainly, not an unbearable effort for individuals because inheritance has always had an element of unexpected windfall, while mentioned additional taxation is not recurrent.

A second strategy for reducing the current rich-poor per capita income gap would consist of improving the access of developing countries to the agricultural and services markets of the industrialised countries. In fact, after promises on mentioned matters realised by the West in the Uruguay Round (in 1995), instead of rapidly implementing these commitments, the West hastily launched another round in Doha (2002), in order to gain new commercial advantages. Since some developing countries (in particular China and India) had changed their economic potentialities from 1995 onwards, and had become more aggressive in negotiations, the Doha round was doomed to fail, as proven in successive ministerial conferences of the WTO.

Although, asymmetric trade concessions, as proposed by the West, will probably enhance the inter-regional trade in Asia—now already growing at a double speed in comparison to the world average—limitation of access to agricultural markets in the West would continue hindering the economic modernisation of many non-Asian developing countries, thus making more difficult their arrival to internal democracy, or the consolidation of their recently acquired democratic manners.

Though current neo-liberals constantly insist on the slogan "better trade than aid" (of course to "save" on financial public transfers abroad), the reality is that lack of infrastructures (roads, railways, and ports) and deficient education and health systems hinder potential (agricultural) exports of LDC, and avert arrival of sufficient FDI for the industrialisation of these countries. Consequently, the correct

---

138. This figure of US $ 400-450bn, equivalent to 2 per cent of the GDP of donor countries—although not exclusively payable by them—was already defended by us in "Responsible Global Governance" (2004: 145). To rationalise these figures, and given the fact that traditional donors would finally be the biggest contributors via additional taxation on inherited wealth, we have started our projections from the GDP of donors in 2003 which was around US$ 20,000bn. Assuming that the net wealth of donors is three times higher (US$ 60,000bn.), and that as an average the total wealth changes of hands every 30 years, the annual volume of inherited wealth within donor countries would be US$ 2000bn, which if, additionally taxed at 20 per cent in all rich countries would generate a revenue of US$ 400bn. for financing development, as mentioned above.

policy sequencing for LDC will have to start, despite wrong neo-liberal opinions, with much more ODA. As explained in Chapter 3, to be efficient, this ODA should be reorganised under the aegis of a new democratic UN Agency, UNICO.

Mentioned suggestions on policy changes, in magnitude and sequencing, would also allow the deactivation along one generation of the current global problem of illegal migration. Finally, we have to additionally underline that (legal) movements of people should have been freer. This is probably the main shortage of the engineered globalisation in the past 60 years, which has certainly helped to increase the economic gap among nations and to compress the creation of jobs in the developing world.

Summary of the Chapter

Along this Chapter, we have analysed the mutual interactions between capitalism and democracy; and not only from a national perspective but also from a global one. The indispensable reorganisation of power at a world scale in order to provide with democratic legitimacy "global public goods" (peace, human security, environment, etc.) and to correct global externalities has also been considered. Note that this reshuffling of global power is something that—in our view—will necessarily occur before the end of the 1st half of the 21st century. Otherwise physical sustainability (environment and non-renewable resources) of the planet will be in danger; violent conflicts in the world will increase; democratisation processes in developing countries could halt; and conditions for tenability of democracy in currently industrialised countries will deteriorate.

Willy-nilly, global capitalism will need global democracy for survival (to minimally rule trans-national economic transactions); and democracy, as always, will need for sustainability mild forms of capitalism: mixed economies of market, far from those desired and devised by neo-liberals.

In order to reach mentioned conclusions we have started defining democracy which, being a political system with moral superiority with respect to any other alternative will be much more than the mere realisation of timely general elections. Indeed, to be sustainable, national democracies will have to fulfil some conditions, while extreme economic differences among social groups or individuals, or other meaningful heterogeneities will complicate reaching national democracy or keeping it.

After discussing the wrong (*non-sequitur*) idea that making elections will necessarily bring sustainable democracy and that democracy will necessarily drive to economic development and prosperity, considerations on the nature of democratic governance and political parties have been made.

Leaving aside historical but obsolete ways of understanding democratic governance, the approach in this Chapter has been one based on the "self-interest axiom" applicable to voters, politicians and bureaucrats, as understood by the "Theory of the Public Choice", the most modern and better founded perspective we have on the issue.

To understand democratic working and sustainability, we have analysed the limits of the debate in democracy, stressing the importance of concepts such as the inconvenient "political re-assignation of income"[139] vs. its marginal redistribution". We have also defended the convenience of the existence of a fair "equity system", independent of political action, for the acceptation of capitalism. Different types of democratic decisions have also been analysed—those of "general interest", the so-called "singled peaked", and those "fractional"—being the latter hazardous for the tenability of democracy.

Analysis of conditions for sustainability of democracy under capitalism and its foundations has been our main aim in Chapter 4. Taking for granted that "re-assignation" of income is incompatible with durable democracy Chapter 4 has also asserted that socialist or capitalistic systems with big public sectors will also undermine democracy. In this Chapter we have also affirmed that pure free market systems with very limited public sectors, will generate progressive and unfair concentration of income and wealth (monopolies, property concentration, etc.), leading to deterioration of middle classes and consequently to the undermining of democracy.

---

139. Let us remember that economic "re-assignation" implies fast political redistribution of income and wealth through substitution of citizens in government and public postings.

With reference to private property, it has been pointed out that sustainability of democracy does not require a "sacred" respect to private property. Indeed, to the extent that some income may be "re-assigned" in democracy without undermining it, "re-assignment" of some property will also be positive for sustainability of democracy. For instance, inheritance taxation, public rights on water and subsoil, limitations on labour contracts, etc., are instruments that, being apparently against private property and freedom of contracting, ultimately will play in favour of democracy because they, while introducing more "equity", will make capitalism "more acceptable".

These considerations should not make us forget that private property is consubstantial to capitalism, because ownership is in fact the materialisation of the economic success of individuals, necessary for stimulating risky investments and entrepreneurial initiatives, indispensable for increasing productivity and reaching prosperity. Note additionally, that under capitalism, competition among entrepreneurs will make that owners of property and wealth appear and disappear, thus making the system work efficiently.

Existence of a high-extended number of civil servants, particularly when they belong to the same political party, will not play in favour of democracy, because in this case political "re-assignment of income" will (or will have) become relevant. Existence of political parties based on "social fractions" (ethnicity, religion, geography, etc.) will also be dangerous for the sustainability of national democracy. This is due to the fact that these parties may participate in coalitions-contra-natura, thus voting "fractional" and against general interests, in order to obtain own economic or political advantage.

We have also considered the negative repercussions on the geographical income distribution (in some provinces or regions), stemming from the existence of localised "windfall" resources in certain countries, particularly in those with non-homogeneous ethnic or cultural populations. Since the existence of windfall resources combined with fractional societies may avert reaching democracy or weaken it, we have recommended the convenience of diversification of the productive structure for facilitating democratisation in these societies.

We have underlined that the existence of different levels of public goods—local, national and global—in the context of a general and progressive democratisation in the world, makes that a legitimate provision of global public goods has also to be democratic. Consequently, any interpretation according to which one or a group of aristocratic countries has the right to take initiatives for delivering global public goods—as it happens today mainly with the US in issues of global peace and security—is biased, self-interested, and essentially non-democratic.

As exposed in the text, the history of building up democracy will not finish when all countries of the world become national democracies as some recommend, but when the World as a whole becomes democratic, that is to say when policy decisions on common global issues are adopted and implemented democratically, thus big powers finally respecting majorities and minorities.

Although the formation of this global democracy could today been interpreted as a mere dream, overwhelming new realities on the ground (climate change, scarcity of some natural resources, expected massive migrations, international terrorism, civil wars, pervasive worsening of personal income distribution, etc.) will force its formation in the first half of the 21st century for the survival of mankind.

We have also underlined in Chapter 4, that imposing democracy by means of military intervention is an immense mistake that should not be repeated in future. Indeed, spreading democracy is something that finally will occur from within, although it could be encouraged from outside; but only by means of friendly multilateral policies coming from a new democratic UN, which should focus on education, health and infrastructures. Economic support (development financing) by a new democratic UN for the creation of the necessary conditions for democratic sustainability in developing countries could result in a generalised democratisation in the world within one generation.

After reviewing the state of democracy in the World today, in particular in the West, Muslim-Arab countries, China and India, as well as in Russia and Brazil, Chapter 4 has ended with proposals to promote development with a more balanced and fairer distribution of income and wealth. Chapter 4 has also clarified the conditions for sustainability of capitalism and democracy and their necessary mutual support for reaching indefinite tenability.

5

Democracy and Environmental Sustainability

Introduction

In Chapter 4, when writing on history of democracy and on the conditions that capitalism has to fulfil to co-exist with sustainable democracy, we have clearly distinguished between the concept and scope of "national democracy", and the notion of global democracy. We have also concluded that in absence of a global democracy in the world, the democratic process is today far from being finished.[1]

Let us remember that democracy is a political system to, among other things, administrate with legitimacy the market failures by means of providing public goods and correcting externalities. Consequently, only a global democratic system could legitimately administrate the so-called "global public goods"—among which we have included the preservation of global environment[2]—and the correction of the so-called global externalities (correct administration or protection of some natural resources of common exploitation, as rainforest, fishing in international waters, etc.).

As we will conclude in this Chapter, lack of development of a global democracy is nowadays the main reason underlying the deficient performance on global environmental protection by many

1. As we have already mentioned and will repeat, the current forum in which multilateral affaires are today discussed (UN) is not a democratic one; and its functionality for providing global public goods and for correcting global externalities, if not in frank decline, is at least not progressing; indeed, a situation extremely worrying and negative.

2. Global environment basically includes generalised clean air and water (fresh or salted) and a stabilised temperature of the planet; all these environmental resources and conditions should be preserved in the interest of all human beings living on Earth. In this regard, we should not forget that the humans themselves also belong to the system to be protected, and consequently its amount should not be considered as an exogenous variable to which the rest should adjust.

countries—in particular those industrialised, lead by the US,[3] and some emergent ones (led by China and India).[4]

Understanding the behaviour of every group of countries (industrialised, developing, etc.) in relation to issues connected with physical sustainability (global environment, administration of relevant scant resources of common exploitation, etc.), and realisation of proposals for solving sustainability problems, will be the main aims of this Chapter. To this respect, one should not forget that the environmental behaviour of countries will differ depending on: 1) their degree of industrialisation; 2) their level of democratisation combined with their income distribution; and 3) the nature[5] (internal or external) of the provided public goods and corrected externalities, thus affecting or not the entire international community or a significant part of it.

Indeed, a proposal to rapidly progress towards global democracy, in order to solve with legitimacy the problem of the physical sustainability of the planet, will be the main and clear-cut message of this Chapter. Note that this solution coincides with our proposal realised in Chapter 4 to make capitalism and national democracies sustainable.

Data on Environment and Natural Resources of Common Use

As recently explained by the World Bank, "economic development and growth have improved the quality of life of many people on Earth", in particular along the second half of the 20th century. However, as mentioned before (Chapters 2 and 3), these gains have

3. The annual US emission of CO_2 to the atmosphere amounts to around 6,000 million tonnes; note that these emissions are, in GDP terms, the double than those of Japan, Germany or France, this implying the existence of dirtier processes of production in the US; and this while the US government has for long acted as if nothing should be done to correct mentioned exaggerated volume of emissions. Vide. Stiglitz, J. (2006: 232) *Une autre monde. Contre le fanatism du marché*. Fayard. Note also that the US emissions in per capita terms, are 6.2 times those of China and 16.5 times those of India. Vide World Bank (2007). *World Economic Indicators*.

4. In general, the annual emissions of CO_2 per unity of GDP are higher in the developing world than in the West. This is due to the use of dirtier and older production systems of energy.

5. Observe that, many times, industrial emissions into the rivers—in principle a case of domestic externality—may become a global one if finally these emissions end up in the sea.

been unevenly distributed and the economic growth has had negative consequences on the environment and on the availability of natural resources, with profound impact on poor people.[6]

As far as problems of environment preservation and natural resources availability have many aspects to be considered, prior to their analysis we will make a general description of the subject. To give an idea of its complication, one should note that the environment problem—besides its specific urban (air quality, waste recycling, etc.) and rural aspects (soil erosion and degradation)—has mainly to do with the issues of pollutants into the air and waters, and with the conditions for the maintenance of forests and landscape; and all this with differentiated local, national, regional[7] and global repercussions.

On the other hand, a correct management of natural resources has to do with the right administration of the renewable ones, and the rational and phased exploitation of those extinguishable.

Environment, Natural Resources, Countryside and Poverty

Before studying any relevant aspect of the environment, we should firstly underline that despite the rapid and generalised process of urbanisation,[8] almost half of the world population still lives in rural areas;[9] and what is more important, around 75 per cent of the poor of the world live in the countryside.

We have to clearly state that the rural poor population is currently the most negatively affected by environmental problems and overexploitation of natural resources of common use (be these internal or global). Deepening into geographic details, we have to

---

6. World Bank (2006). *World Development Indicators*. p.125.
7. Mentioned repercussions at regional level have at times been solved by means of establishing Regional Environment Agreements (REAs), as for instance the one signed by US and Canada on air quality. This REA was signed in order to balance the effects for Canada of the acid rain stemming from coal burning in thermal electricity factories in the American Mid-West. For attempting to overcome—some times without success—other global environmental problems, other Multilateral Environment Agreements (MEAs) have also been signed.
8. Note that in the last three decades (1973-2003), and in many cases, this process of urbanisation has not been accompanied by significant growth, as we have explained in Chapter 2.
9. In South Asia more than 70 per cent of people live in rural areas, while in Sub Saharan Africa the figure nears 60 per cent.

highlight that while 44 per cent of the work force in the world is attached to agriculture activities, the corresponding figures in South Asia and in Sub-Sahara Africa reach 60 per cent.[10] These figures explain by themselves why physical-global sustainability and proper management of the main natural resources are vital for the future of the poor villagers of the world.

Note that the current environmental problems affecting the countryside of many poor countries are not exclusively[11] created or induced by the significant growth rate of their populations and the corresponding pressing needs on food and fuel (over exploitation of forests, etc.),[12] but to a great extent by the global warming induced by the increased use of fossil-based energies by industrialised countries. Indeed, the resulting climate change—that will be discussed in the lines below—has added a plus of vulnerability (natural disasters and environmental risks)[13] to the rural poor of the world.

For instance, due to Earth warming and climate change, insufficient availability or serious scarcity of fresh and drinking water has today become a relevant problem for the rural-poor of the world. Indeed, this is a problem that is likely to worsen in future,[14] thus negatively affecting crucial food productions, particularly, in Sub-Sahara Africa (the region of the world with the most serious problem of scarcity of clean water in per capita terms).

---

10. This figure also includes the labourers working in fisheries and livestock rising. Note that the corresponding figures in most developed countries are positioned well under 5 per cent.
11. Although the fast evolution of population—the so-called population explosion registered at a world scale between 1950 and 1980—has not been the only confluent variable, we have to underline that the rapid growth of the number of humans has automatically introduced an additional and significant pressure on the biological and geological systems of Earth. In this regard, we should not forget that mankind—to eat, to dress, to shelter and to move—is the most important predator of biological and geological resources on Earth.
12. Most low-income countries depend on biomass energy for cooking and eating. This constitutes some times a health hazard for millions of people. More than three million deaths are annually caused by the air pollution generated while cooking or heating in developing countries. Many of these deaths are among children, who die of acute respiratory infections due to indoor air pollution resulting from burning fuel-wood, crop residues, or animal dung. World Bank (2006: 128). Book already mentioned.
13. Indeed, cyclones, torrential rains, etc., affect much more the rural poor of the world than the rest, due to the rudimentary construction of their dwellings.
14. The Food and Agriculture Organisation (FAO) of the UN has estimated that, due to climate change, the land suitable in 2080 for rain-fed agriculture may shrink in developing countries by 11 per cent. World Bank (2006: 125). Book already mentioned.

Note however that this difficult situation, related to scant water availability, may in future also affect other regions. In particular, there are estimations which suggest that by 2020, around 2/3rds of the world will live in water-stressed countries, firstly due to climate change and secondly to growing population.[15]

Natural Resources and Evolution: Water and Energy

The main variables that determine the demand of fresh water in the world are the necessary expansion of irrigated agriculture to meet the needs of the growing population, and the industrial development. In particular, we have to emphasise that agriculture globally demands 70 per cent of the available fresh water in the world; a figure that in Africa, due to its scarcity in per capita terms[16] and its low level of industrialisation, mounts to 85 per cent.

In addition, in a significant number of developing countries (and regions) water quality is a problem even more important than water availability. Indeed, lack of adequate treatment of the available water is the cause of serious diseases that shorten the life expectancy of people and reduce the productivity of workers in many developing countries.[17]

Urbanisation in many developing regions of the world, which induces qualitative increase in food demand—enhancing the consumption of meat and dairy products—is a phenomenon that, added to growing population, has additionally increased the pressure on the forest masses,[18] which is currently undergoing a significant annual decline[19] in the world. Africa and Latin America are today the largest net

15. The world will have around 8.5-9.0 billion inhabitants in 2050.
16. Vide World Bank (2006: 126). Book already mentioned.
17. Although the share of people with access to healthy-improved water source increased from 70 per cent in 1990 to 82 per cent in 2002, even today 1.1 bn. people lack access to safe drinking water, most of them living in Africa and Asia. World Bank (2006: 127). Book already mentioned.
18. The need of producing additional food in developing countries sometimes forces the logging of extended areas of forest to put them into agricultural exploitation
19. In the period 2000-2005, the annual net change of the forest area in the world was negative. This supposed an annual loss of around 7.3 million. Ha, an area equivalent in size to the surface of Panama or Sierra Leone. This global annual loss of forest surface has been however smaller than that experienced as an average in the period 1990-2000 (8.9 mill. ha).

losers[20] of forest in the world, while Europe has recently started the expansion of its (formerly over-exploited) forest masses. A favourable forest expansion has recently been registered also in Asia (China), thus reversing the former negative trajectory undergone by this continent.

Against the background of mentioned negative trajectory, we have to underline that the maintenance, or better the growth, of the total available forest surface should be one of the crucial aims to be reached by individual and global governments of the world, for arresting or reversing the current global warming.

Growing Energy Consumption and Emissions

In relation to energy, it is well known that economic growth and power consumption are variables directly correlated. In particular, the level of per capita consumption of electricity is one of the most relevant indicators of the standard of living of communities.

According to the more recent figures of the World Bank,[21] high-income countries use in per capita terms more than five times the energy used by the developing ones. Consequently, with only 16 per cent of the world's population, mentioned industrialised countries use more than the half of total consumed energy.

In relation to the sources of power, we have to say that despite the currently high and growing (at mid-long term) cost of energy—due to the appearance of new, large and rapidly growing consumers (China and India), and due to the restrictions in the West on thermal-nuclear production of electricity—fossil fuels (mainly oil, coal and gas) continue being the main source for energy production.

Note that the generation of power from combustion of fossil fuels (oil, coal, gas, and others) induces emissions of CO_2, allegedly the substance that mainly contributes to Earth global warming and climate change. Observe additionally that the combustion of coal is the dirtiest of all fossil combustions, being natural gas the cleanest one. Paradoxically, the poorest countries or regions in the world mainly

20. Net change is the difference between the losses of forest due to fires and conversion of forest soil into agricultural land, and the expansion of forest due to forest planting, landscape restoration and natural self-reproduction.

21. Vide World Bank (2006: 127). Book already mentioned.

use coal (Sub Sahara Africa, East Asia and Pacific, and South Asia) which, besides contributing to Earth warming, additionally generates localised problems of "acid rain", a phenomenon that tends to ruin neighbouring forests, thus re-stressing the climate change problem.

Although the low-income countries only produce 8 per cent of the total CO_2 emissions,[22] agriculture production of many of them will result seriously affected by earth warming and climate change; a phenomenon basically induced by the high-income countries, which today generate around half of the total emissions of CO_2.[23]

Logically, the use of cleaner energy sources,[24] indispensable for the protection of global environment, is growing, though at a very slow speed. Observe that in 2003, although 13 per cent of the energy production came from renewable resources, only about 4.5 per cent came from modern renewable energy sources, up from 3.1 per cent in 1971.[25] Latter figures prove that—in opposition to which one could have expected from the growing trend of energy prices—technological efforts for the substitution of dirty energy sources by cleaner ones have been small, mainly by lack of sufficient stimuli;[26] and this against naïve (or interested) expectations of some neo-liberals who even today, reject to seriously consider the earth warming as a real problem, stating that "when the moment is there, any difficulty will be solved by scientific-technological advance."[27]

Earth Warming and Climate Change

Although some stubborn scientists and politicians continue

---

22. Vide. World Bank (2006: 128). Book already mentioned.
23. Although the US is currently the world's biggest producer of greenhouse gases on Earth, around 2020 it will be overtaken by China (in absolute terms but not at all in per capita terms). *The Economist* (2006). "The Heat is On", p.9. September 9.
24. Clean energy sources (hydroelectric, solar, wind-mills, thermal, biomass, etc.) are those that, avoiding fossils burning for the production of energy and being renewable, avert global warming.
25. Modern renewable energy sources are those mentioned in the former Note, letting aside the traditional hydroelectric one.
26. Hydropower is the largest renewable energy source; but large-scale hydropower exploitation, when possible—that is to say in countries with sufficient rains, appropriated orography, etc.—may induce major adverse environmental and social costs. Modern biomass and geothermal energy are other major renewable sources that have a substantial growth potential. Wind and solar energy, although growing rapidly, still only provide with an insignificant share of the total supply of energy.
27. We consider as irrational this intellectual position consisting of doing nothing, while confiding the future of the planet to alleged automatism of market and induced successful research.

rejecting the case of Earth warming as a problem[28] caused by the industrialisation process, the reality is that while in the past 10.000 years the Earth climate remained stable, man-made greenhouse gases along the last two centuries seem to threaten former stability.[29]

Indeed, projection of future developments concerning climate change is a complicated and uncertain task. Nevertheless, extrapolated results of scientists suggest that, *ceteris paribus*, average temperature will increase along the 21st century by between 1.4°C and 5.8°C.[30] Note that increases over 2°C could lead to catastrophic rises in sea levels, rapid increase of the number of extreme weather events such as hurricanes, flooding and droughts, falling agriculture production, and probably famine and mass population movements.[31]

Due to the fact that global warming has countless indirect effects on the climate system, no one can be sure of the total costs of Earth warming. Consequently, the benefits of doing something in future to prevent additional warming will also remain uncertain.

However, former considerations on uncertainty should not drive us to inaction. Indeed, similar to the fact that most advanced countries spend a figure between 1.5-2.5 per cent in defence although the probability of being attacked is almost nil, and that western individuals mostly take insurance policies to protect their assets against a fire when this is also unlikely—nations and individuals should similarly

28. Other neo-liberal scientists and politicians "fully trust" in the so-called "geo-engineering" as a way of using advanced technology to counteract climate change. Some supporters of this "Plan B for facing global warming", whose ideas are highly controversial, believe that global cooling could also be possible although expensive. Note that in this case, only a global democratic body could undertake a global action. On the issue, vide *The Economist* (2007). Technology Quarterly, March 10, p.4.

29. Fifty million years ago, there was no ice in the poles and crocodiles lived in Wyoming. 18.000 years ago there was ice two miles thick in Scotland, and because the size of ice sheets, the sea level was 130 m. lower. (Then onwards) dramatic changes happened, remarkably swiftly in some places: temperatures rose by as much as 20° in a decade. After that the temperature fluctuations stopped. Vide *The Economist* (2006). "The Heat is On", p.9. September 9.

30. Recently, in February 2007, the UN has published a report of scientists (a report apparently neutral) that has introduced mild corrections on the expected rise of the average temperature, commented in the text. Surprisingly, and against other former scientific studies, this report suggests that the level of the seas could rise (only) around 0.5 m. at the end of 2100.

31. These possible massive movements of people would induce a magnum problem of human re-settlements, without any possible comparison with other former movements of people in the history of mankind. A World Authority would in this case be absolutely indispensable to solve the resulting problems of land redistribution.

take measures to fight against climate change, just to avoid eventual highly catastrophic results.

Although economic evaluations on the annual costs of doing nothing to reduce emissions of CO_2 range from 5 per cent to 20 per cent of the total GDP by the end of the 21st century,[32] it would be wise if the world starts spending a provisional figure that, after 10 years phasing, reached a level of 2 per cent of the global GDP.

But, given the current international political structure, formally multilateral but hardly cooperative, the real problem underlying the management of this volume of funds is, and will be, of a political nature. Indeed, given the global nature of the climate change problem, and the possibility that individual nations behave as "free riders",[33] there is a scant probability that the international community tackles this problem by means of reaching multilateral agreements (MEAs),[34] whose setting up would be difficult, while its by-passing would be easy.

In this regard it is our view that if the world does not progress towards a global democracy (a new UN) with capacity for enforcing matters assigned to it (including environment), the probability of successfully solving the problem of climate change and its derivatives (massive migrations), or other problems related to other global public goods, will remain low. Certainly this is not a desirable perspective.

The Case of the Kyoto Protocol as a Proof of Ineffectiveness

An example of the difficult arrival to efficient solutions by means of international agreements is the case of the Kyoto Protocol signed in 1997. In fact, disregarding the somewhat insufficient efforts deployed by many negotiators along the several decades that the process lasted,[35] this "international agreement" was not signed by the most

32. Recently, the so-called Stern Report announced that the cost of "doing nothing" could be equivalent to 20 per cent of global GDP at the end of 2100.

33. The possibility of different countries to behave as free riders is two folded. Every generation of each country may be interested in passing the charge of the correction to the next one; and every country may be interested in passing the charge of the correction to other countries.

34. MEA means Multilateral Environment Agreement.

35. After the Conference of the UN on Human Environment (1972), in Stockholm, a process of scientific analysis, negotiations among parties, etc., started. In 1990 this process received a serious push forward by the UN: the initiation of the elaboration of a Convention on Climate Change. Regrettably, it had taken 18 years to simply recognise the problem. The Convention was adopted in New York in 1992, and 155 countries adhered and signed it during the Summit of Rio de Janeiro in the same year (1992).

relevant global polluters (US, China, India, etc.). Nevertheless, the Kyoto Protocol finally "came into force" in 2005.

Once the negotiating stage of the Protocol was concluded, its signing in 1997 gave additional-final contents (aims and means) to the Convention, previously agreed in Rio in 1992. As a result a limit for the emissions of CO_2 along the period 2008-2012 was provisionally established, and ways for implementing the reduction of emissions, mainly through specialised markets,[36] were also defined.

Later on, complementary negotiations on implementation of the Protocol also became convoluted. The meetings in Buenos Aires (1998) and The Hague (2000) proved that it was difficult to reach an agreement on the temporal flexibility required by different nations to fulfil their obligations, and on sanctions for countries that do not comply with commitments.

On top of this, the arrival of the Bush Administration to the White House meant a significant blow to the negotiations of those days. The Bush Administration not only put on the desk the idea of the incompatibility of the Protocol with the interests of the US, but also denounced some central aspects of it as "irrational". In particular, the US rejected the "exaggerated cost-benefit relation" of actions stemming from the Protocol; the "lack of equity of some principles of the Convention" (according to which developing countries would not assume significant reduction of emissions); and above all, the "doubtful scientific explanation of climate change".[37]

Of course, this rejection generated deep and widespread dissatisfaction and irritation. Finally, the EU took the lead for rescuing the Protocol and after several political battles in global fora[38] along

36. These mechanisms will be explained in the lines below.

37. Fortunately, many federated states of the US, including California, are already enacting laws for the reduction of emissions of CO_2 in their respective territories. But the US federal government has for long remained insensitive to the issue. Note however that, in his speech on the State of the Nation in 2007, Mr. Bush finally acknowledged the existence of the problem.

38. We here refer to the Transatlantic Summit in Gothenburg (2001), the COP's celebrated in Marrakesh (2001), New Delhi (2002), and Milan (2003), and the world Conference on Climate Change celebrated in Moscow (2003).

the period 2001-2004, the Russian Federation also signed in 2004,[39] and the Protocol started its ruling in 2005.

On the scope and real effects of the Kyoto Protocol on Earth warming and climate change, many comments have been made. Although the Kyoto Protocol shaped an almost generalised conscience on the convenience of fighting against climate change, and created a global market of permits in relation to CO_2 reductions,[40] there is today an almost generalised conviction that the Protocol will not have much impact on emissions, and therefore on the current speed of climate change, which conversely seems to be experiencing a negative acceleration. This is because the established global target was too modest, too inconveniently distributed[41]—not forcing developing countries to significantly cut their emissions—and because the main polluters today (US) or in future (China and India)[42] were not signers of the Protocol.

To improve the present degrading situation of global environment, some economists have presented some alternatives for action: 1) the introduction of a worldwide homogeneous carbon tax,[43] instead of the market of emission permits combined with caps, as foreseen in the Protocol; 2) the implementation of a system of carrots and

---

39. According to the Protocol promoters, the signing of Russia was indispensable for its taking off, given the fact that the previous rejection of others had left the Protocol without significant world consent.
40. This market, masterminded on the principles of the Protocol, started its working in the EU, with the negotiation of an ad hoc European Directive. This EU Emissions-Trading Scheme limits the total emissions of CO_2, and then gives freedom to polluters to negotiate polluting permits among them. On principles and criticism on these negotiable permits, we will come back in the item 5.3.
41. The target was to re-drive emissions of CO_2 by the main polluters to their levels of 1990. This target was seriously criticised by developing countries. They complained "why the developed countries have more right to pollute than the developing ones while the global warming has been induced by them...In this regard no one has convincingly explained why the West (US) has the right to pollute the rest without paying for it." Stiglitz, J. (2006: 245). Book already mentioned.
42. In November 2007 China has established a Clean Development Mechanism (CDM) fund, probable to prepare its embodiment in the second Kyoto Protocol.
43. A single and homogeneous carbon tax—which should globally generate a level of fiscal revenue in consistency with a meaningful reduction of global emissions, and not simply with their maintenance—has the advantage that it enables the non-publication of national targets and calculated revenues. Note additionally that, under this system, the signing countries would have no need of transferring funds to any multilateral institution. Stiglitz, J. (2006: 253). Book already mentioned. Observe, however, that this lack of transfers would not solve the problem of the historical pollution and the non-payment of rich countries for having historically polluted the others (developing ones).

sticks, thus imposing commercial sanctions through WTO[44] to those countries which do not comply or do not sign the Kyoto Protocol; and 3) penalisations for over-logging.

Note that, as far as rainforest deforestation[45] is another source of the accrual of greenhouse gases and Earth Warming, a significant increase of replanted rainforests, encouraged by means of concession of "credits" (for parallel increase of emissions), would help to biologically stock carbon (CO_2) emissions. Observe in this regard that the Kyoto Protocol foresaw mentioned concessions, while, disappointingly, overlooked symmetric penalisations for over-logging.

As a result of the well-acknowledged limited attainments of the Kyoto Protocol, two additional lines of action could be implemented in the mid-long term. 4) One that for the moment is just placed in the sphere of science—trying to stockpile the issued CO_2 "underground"[46]—and 5) and much more important than the rest, to urgently include the administration and provision of a healthy global environment into the agenda of a new democratic UN, as defended by us, by putting in common all available scientific knowledge, adaptation and mitigation policies, and sufficient financing to solve the problems.

Climate Change and Human Resettlements

Letting aside the currently growing illegal migrations, induced by the sharp economic inequality among nations and the restrictive rules for access of foreigners to jobs in rich countries—and all that in a context of access to full and live information by poor in developing countries—we will here focus on the massive human resettlements that will become a priority in some decades, if climate change continues with its current trend and speed.

---

44. *Ad hoc* sanctions were foreseen in the Montreal Protocol. These sanctions enabled the taxation of imports, or the import limitation of products containing CFCs. These commercial sanctions, if introduced in the Kyoto Protocol-2, could be seen as a penalisation introduced by importing countries just to balance the "implicit subsidies" (lack of polluting taxes) introduced by governments of exporting countries that do not comply with the Kyoto Protocol.

45. Note that in the last years, about 20 per cent of the rise of the greenhouses gases concentration in the atmosphere has been induced by over-logging or massive deforestation.

46. Till the moment, no one knows how this stockpiling could be implemented.

Indeed, although the current volume of displaced people[47] in the World, mainly coming from economic-ethnic civil wars (in Africa and Asia) has reached millions, this phenomenon will be considered as an almost irrelevant precedent in comparison to the migration and resettlement problems that the climate change may provoke in the future.

In fact, according to scientists, if the average temperature of the planet rises in the 21st century more than 2° C., the sea will meaningfully raise its level, thus flooding a part of the seaside cities. In big countries this will provoke significant internal migrations. Conversely, in smaller or estuarial countries,[48] displacements will necessarily imply external migrations, in some cases of a massive nature. In certain countries (landlocked or not), external migrations could also be the result of the reduction of water availability induced by the climate change.

In absence of a global authority and in a likely context of non-solidarity, one may imagine what could occur on the planet, if the amount of the internationally displaced people by political causes (wars) or by climate change, reached figures of around 150-200 million (around 2.5-3% of the current global population). We do believe that in this case, the induced problem could be unbearable if such movements of people had to be realised in a compressed period of time, for instance in two or three decades, and if the people should have to be resettled in already inhabited territories.[49] Note that in such circumstances, and for the first time in the history of mankind, a mega movement of people would take place just for surviving.

---

47. The current displaced people (by wars, ethnic cleansing, etc.) amounting at around 20 million—who live in neighbouring countries, normally in tents—use to be subject of several forms of abuse.
48. *Ceteris paribus*, one has to expect that an estuarial country like Bangladesh (today with near 150m. people)—which in monsoon time gets flooded up to one-third of its surface—will along the 21st century remain permanently flooded to that extent of its territory. This implies that the precarious sustainability of this country will worsen in future and that Bangladeshi migrations to other countries will become a necessity.
49. A precedent of massive migration to already inhabited territories is that of the Exodus of Jews to the Palestine territory after the Second World War. Observe that, from a quantitative perspective, 150-200 million people displaced abroad along 3 decades, due to climate change, means an average of 5-7 million per year, a figure similar to the current population of Israel. This means that, in absence of a global democratic governance, the world would have to face in a brief period of time up to 30 cases like that of the Palestinian one: indeed, a non-imaginable situation.

Note that, in absence of a global authority with enforcement capabilities, a factual or attempted massive displacement of people towards neighbouring inhabited countries could be considered as a "casus belli" by the receiving end. This could trigger even preventive military actions for the defence of own territories. Indeed, mentioned massive migrations (or attempts) provoked by climate change could drive, in absence of democratic global governance, to an unprecedented political and humanitarian catastrophe.

Since the initial environmental problem would have been partially ignited by rich countries, western actions to resist sharing negative consequences on global warming—by not accepting migrations forced by climate change—would be an unacceptable political position from the perspective of global democracy.

Consistently, a previously established new and democratic UN, with enforcement capabilities, would probably be the only way out to avert the human and political devastation that could follow a significant climate change.

Uneven Results in Other Environment Protection Treaties (MEA)

In cases in which an environmental problem has technical solutions that do not imply significant costs, adopted environmental policies on a multilateral treaty base could be, and have been, successful.

In this regard, the most successful intervention was reached in relation to the problem of the ozone layer depletion. When in the late 80s it became clear that the existing hole in the ozone layer had been caused by emissions of chlorofluorocarbons (CFCs), nations of the world, in order to protect life on earth from harmful solar radiation, met in Montreal (Canada) and signed in 1997 a treaty that required that the levels of production and consumption of CFCs were cut by half by 1999. Today most of the signing countries have consistently complied with the protocol and, as a result, the ozone layer seems to be recovering.

In relation with the so-called acid rain—this being a case of national or trans-national (but not global) pollution, regional agreements among neighbouring countries (REA) on the control of sulphur dioxide emissions—which gives rise to "acid rain"—have also been successful.

In what touches the cleanness of the urban air (quantity and quality of particulates in it), every country has its own legislation that adjusts more or less to certain internationally agreed standards. Nevertheless, generalised rise in respiratory diseases in almost all cities of the world, in particular in children (asthma) and elderly, is an indicator of the widespread failure of mentioned policies.

In relation to emissions with global repercussions (CO_2), we have to highlight the widespread felt need of reducing the environmental impact of the transport sector (urban, interurban and international, also by air); a sector whose progressive global environmental damages have become more difficult to tackle than those induced by other activities. This is due to the fact that private motorisation has been the conditioning variable for the urban development in the last half a century (mainly in the West), a model that these days is hastily reproduced in the developing world, thus globally speeding up CO_2 emissions.

In our view, and against current trends in private consumption, developed and developing nations of the world should agree on an integrated transport policy, which should place much more emphasis on public transport, thus restricting the use of private vehicles, mainly in cities. Of course, reaching such an agreement would be difficult and, after getting consent, commitments would easily be bypassed. Conversely, if a global democratic body existed, reaching an efficient decision on the issue and its further enforcement would be much easier.

Examples of Mismanagement of Common Renewable Resources: Fishing and Forest

In former overview on the evolution of global environment and common natural resources administration, with particular emphasis on those that have had negative consequences for mankind, we have chiefly considered the growing scarcity of water and the problems of Earth warming and climate change, mainly related with the combustion of carbon fossils (oil, coal, gas, etc.) and overdone logging.

Hereunder we will analyse other fields of the international economy that will also require a global solution for sustainability: the administration of seas and rainforests, and their productions.[50]

---

50. The seas and oceans have a direct role, absolutely essential for life on the planet, consisting of: 1) the provision of fresh water which, under the form of rain, snow, etc., falls on the continents, thus making possible animal and human life, agriculture, and also industrialisation; and 2) the provision of fish for human feeding.

The Problem of Fisheries: Fishing in International Waters

Note that the administration of the seas implies, to some extent, the administration of all waters of the system. Indeed, the pollution of seas is mainly caused by emissions of dirty waters into the rivers that finally flow to the sea, or by emissions of filthy waters or liquids from boats or from factories placed at sea side. As far as the administration of emissions into the rivers and into marine territorial waters is (still) a competency of national states, we will here focus on the correct administration of international waters and their productions (fisheries).

The comparison of features of marine and inland fisheries may give us a clear insight in the complexity of the free sea fishing systems. In inland fisheries, conflict management will be mainly local, and consequently it will hardly require the intervention of global authorities.[51] The case is totally different in marine fisheries out of territorial waters, in which access to fish is open, property rights are not defined (all this compounded with the variable location of migratory fishes),[52] reciprocal cooperation is not guaranteed, and consequently "free riding" will be an almost sure result.

Former characteristics of marine fisheries in international waters—prone to over-fishing, as proven by evidence[53]—make necessary that the management and administration of this global common resource has to be implemented by an international authority, capable of devising sustainable policies and enforcing rules for sustainability.

The complexity of such an administration practically discards the workability of international treaties. Note in this regard that the sovereignty of nations gives them the opportunity of opting out, which hinders consensus building on inclusive treaties, and consequently

51. In this context, eventual conflicts will have to do with the existence of different groups of people that are interested in commercial or recreational fishery, or in the use of the waters with other purposes: irrigation, electricity production, etc. Vide Arlinghaus, R. *et al.* (2002). "Reconciling Traditional Inland Fisheries Management and Sustainability in Industrialised Countries", *Fish and Fisheries*. 3.

52. In territorial seawaters every state has competencies for the administration of its waters, including authorisation of foreign boats for fishing against economic compensation.

53. Worldwide, some 25 per cent to 30 per cent of all exploited fish-populations in marine waters experience some degree of over-fishing; and another 40 per cent ranges from heavily to fully exploited. (Vide *National Research Council*. "Decline of Sea Turtles: Causes and Prevention", Washington DC: National Academic Press.) Indeed, between 1980 and 1990 the number of over-exploited fish populations multiplied by 2.5.

makes difficult enforcement for conservation. Regrettably, till now this is the current and non-delivering system for administration of common marine fisheries.

Entering into technical matters, we have to underline that till now the management of open-sea fisheries, often conducive to failure,[54] has mainly been based on a bio-centric perspective, that is to say on targets "nominally" focused on "sustainability of stocks" and "captures" by species, and not on a more comprehensive and modern approach, based on the analysis of ecosystems.[55]

In brief, current fishery management usually takes into consideration: 1) appraisal of the stock sizes of species; 2) selection of harvesting targets and strategies for captures at short, medium and long term; 3) establishment of rules for implementation; and 4) control and enforcement.

In this traditional context, capture-strategies are defined in a very simple way (referred for instance to constant catches, to sustainability of the stock in function of its previous evaluation, etc.). Development of these strategies implies the definition of norms directed to the regulation of inputs and control of the fishing effort;[56] to the control on permitted catches;[57] and to the control on technical procedures for fishing.[58] Indeed, most fisheries continue using today many of these input-output-technical controls (logbooks, control of landings, checks by sea patrols, etc.) to reach the desired targets for species.[59] Unfortunately, although new satellite systems of control are in use

---

54. One additional proof of these failures is the fact that, despite the increased fishing effort, the global yield of fish—measured in weight—has remain almost constant in the last decades; and this despite the fact that technological advances have made easier the locating and capture of the most valuable species.

55. Charles, A. (2001). *Sustainable Fishery Systems*. Oxford: Blackwell Science. The new perspective includes references to environmental quality, biological integrity, and biodiversity.

56. For instance, it is usual to define per specie, the number of boats, the average vessel capacity, the fishing intensity, and the permissible time fishing area per boat.

57. Among them, we could quote: control on the total captured weight of allowable catches in a specific fishing area; quotas for individual fishers, legal (minimum) limits of the sizes of the captured fishes, etc.

58. These controls refer to where, when and how fishers may fish, thus defining closed areas and closed seasons; what instruments may be used for fishing (mesh or hook size), etc.

59. Vide. Caddy, J.F. (1999). "Fisheries Management in the 21st Century: Will a New Paradigm Apply?", *Reviews in First Biology and Fisheries* 9.

today, illegal (violating fishing rules) or misreported captures[60] continue being common, thus inducing reduction of stocks and captures at long term.

From the perspective of sustainability of stocks, several strategies have been put in use, ranging from the choice of a "maximum sustainable yield" (MSY) and corresponding total (maximum) allowable catches (TAC),[61] to the so-called "optimal sustainable yield" (OSY). Note that the first strategy may contain serious problems such as that of the possible overestimation of the MSY or TAC, due to the simplistic assumptions[62] used for their reckoning.[63] Mentioned concept of MSY is often judged as misguiding because it does not take into consideration the age structure of catches, the problems related with multi-species fisheries and catches, etc.

Bearing in mind these sources of uncertainty, and from the perspective of the temporal stabilisation of captures and profits—relevant for fishers and for the fish-processing industry—the strategy for sustainability has moved in some cases to lower levels of fishing effort. At times, the so-called Optimum Sustainable Yield (OSY) has been adopted as a target. This OSY places the fishing effort between the minimum fishing effort compatible with maximum profit—which would imply a restricted rate of captures, as a monopolist would do—and the maximum effort combined with nil profit.[64]

Mentioned sources of uncertainty, also affecting the accurate definition of the OSY, use to be compounded by others not considered

60. Watson *et al.* (2001). "Systematic Distortions in World Fisheries Catch Trends," *Nature*. 414.

61. As far as catches do not exceed surplus, population of fishes will be in equilibrium. Under the simplest assumptions underlying "logistic growth", the maximum sustainable yield (MSY) will be located at the mid point between zero and the maximum stock of fish. Unfortunately, if MSY were overestimated this strategy would be conducive to catastrophic results.

62. Note that fishing not only alters the abundance of stocks, but also affects the age of maturity, the population structure, the sex ratio and the genetic make up of population. Consequently, models for calculation of MSY and optimum catches should also include all these aspects affecting the composition of stocks.

63. A detailed explanation on how to reckon MSY may be found in Karjalainen, J. *et al.* (2005). *Sustainability in Fisheries Management*. vide the web.

64. Observe that having free access to fishing, total cost—including minimum wages and retribution to capital—will become equal to total revenues, this putting an economic limit to further fishing.

in the traditional calculation of optimum catches.[65] These uncertainties have encouraged the FAO[66] to defend a more precautionary approach based on the needs of future generations, on the avoidance of non-reversible changes, on the initiation without delay of the necessary corrective measures, and on the setting up of an institutional and legal framework for fisheries management; and all this under the principle that, in case of uncertainty, priority should be given to preservation of the resource and consequently to conservative harvesting.[67]

Unfortunately, there is little consensus on how such precautionary approach should be implemented, and on how to turn theory[68] into practice against the backdrop of shot-term economic and political pressures. Note that any protective measure uses to be objected by fishing communities, who always ask environment authorities—national or international—to clearly prove the alleged consequences of freer fishing.

Summarising, we have to underline that uncertainty on stock sizes and on the accuracy of assessment models for defining maximum captures, and absence many a time of an ecosystem based analysis[69] has produced almost everywhere conservation failures and serial

---

65. These additional sources of uncertainty have to do with: the underlying random in the fish population dynamics, the existence of observation errors, the lack of complete information, and the uncertainty in implementation of policies.
66. FAO of UN (1995). *Precautionary Approach to Fisheries. FAO Fisheries Technical Paper 350.1.*; vide also FAO (1996). *Precautionary Approach to Capture Fisheries and Species. Technical Guidelines for Responsible Fisheries.*No.2.
67. The quicker these initiatives are adopted, the more rapid will be—if possible—the recovering of the species; note that some of them, those of short maturity like sardines, anchovies, herring, menhaden, etc. could recover very fast, once reduced the fishing pressure on them. Other species, affected by serious over-fishing and climate change will confront difficult recovery, or even extinction.
68. On the theory of fishing vide. Anderson, L.G. (1986). *The Economics of Fisheries Management.* Ed. John Hopkings University Press. Baltimore.
69. Note that single species management, as that considered in the lines above, is based on the assumption that the dynamic of any specie is not significantly affected by other changes in the fish community or in wider environmental contexts. Nevertheless, one should not forget that catching certain species directly affects other species (due to by-catching), thus reducing the stocks of the latter. Predation of some species by others must be also considered. Consequently, the combined effects of over-fishing, discarded by-catches, habitat degradation, and fishing-induced food-web-changes, alter the composition of the marine ecosystems, thus producing negative results. Note also that overdone catches of big predators—larger and long living species—induce population explosion of other not so desired species; and that exaggerated removal of lower trophic-level species (sardines, anchovies and herring) may induce increased population of their competitors, and decline of their predators.

depletion.[70] Indeed, recommendations to national governments, sometimes in delay—coming from the corresponding UN body (FAO)—have not produced the desired effects in relation to fishing sustainability, thus proving the necessity of a global authority with capacity of enforcement. Perhaps a future World Environment Organisation (WEO), a global body to be created for the protection of the global environment under the aegis of a new democratic UN, should be the agency also to administrate the renewable natural resources, including fisheries.

In relation to the issue here discussed, this authority should introduce a new approach to open-sea fisheries that should minimally include: 1) a higher investment and a full commitment in relation to the supervision of fishing; and 2) implementation of a proactive, precautionary and adaptive management regime, founded on an ecosystem-based planning and on marine zoning. Note that such ecosystem should also include humans in the model.[71]

The Case of Deforestation: Misuse of a Renewable Resource

Letting aside some problems referring to global environment—as that of overusing the available fresh water, or that of wastes issued to the air (mainly CO_2)—we will now refer to another problem also related to Earth warming and climate change: the protection of rainforests and some endangered species living in them.

Starting with the foundations of forest exploitation, we have to clearly state that although from the perspective of owners, trees in a forest should economically be treated like crops in a field, forest production differs from agriculture in two essential aspects: 1) forest are often of public domain, thus posing special problems stemming from open access (communal overexploitation), or from concession to private firms for monopol:stic exploitation;[72] and 2) forest are

70. Serial depletion refers to the fact that when priced species become scant, alike but less valuable ones start being captured. This is a typical trait of the over-fished ecosystems. Murawsky, S.A. (2000). "Definition of Over-fishing from an Ecosystem Perspective", *Journal of Marine Science* 57. ICES.

71. Dayton, P. *et al.* (2001). *Ecological Effects of Fishing*. Pew Oceans Commission. Taken from the Web.

72. Declaration of forests as "public domain" enables the authorities to give open access to everybody for the forest use; or to auction it to private firms or individuals for monopolistic exploitation.

susceptible of deforestation, which may give rise to diverse external costs as soil erosion, climate modification and losses in biological diversity.[73] Note that these two special characteristics of forests are often connected: insecure future rights on access to forests' exploitation, combined with expected political change, normally triggers a "cut and run" strategy in forest management and, as a result, an increase in the severity of the registered negative externalities.[74]

Rapid or overdone deforestation, sometimes officially encouraged to increase exports, has often been the result of the existence of deep inequalities in wealth and power in the involved societies. These inequalities (by action of the most powerful citizens) have paved the way for the diversion (or extinction) of the collective benefits coming from the existence of these public resources,[75] thus imposing to third parties—current poor or future generations—the costs of the negative externalities induced by over-logging.

To exploit the forests rationally, only fully mature trees of around 30-50 years age should be logged; and this without damaging the adjacent ones,[76] and while an equal number as the logged ones is replanted. Unfortunately, up to recently, a minimal part—less than one per cent of tropical forest—has been managed in this way.[77]

By destroying the sponge effect of the rainforest—which retains the rained water in the rainy season—deforestation makes easier the erosion of soil which, besides negatively affecting land productivity, induces obstruction (clogging) of waterways and dams, thus increasing the risk of flooding while reducing water storage capacities.

---

73. Boyce, J.K. (2002: 104). Book already mentioned.
74. The absence of guarantees for continuing exploiting the forest after a certain period of time—because the concession could in future be given to another firm—has many times induced acceleration of exploitation without minimally renewing the logged forest.
75. A common example of this miss-use in poor countries is the provision of logging permits to cronies of politicians. These cronies often sit either in the boards of MNC or in foreign companies with local subsidiaries, precisely established to export natural resources; and this while, in many cases, authorities of importing countries keep forests (in national parks) untouched.
76. In 1987, the Asian Development Bank estimated that the lateral damage in forest exploitation in the Asia-Pacific region was around 60 per cent; and that the net exploitation of the total logging was just 40 per cent. ADB (1987). *A Review of Forestry and Forest Industries in the Asia-Pacific Region*. p.117. Manila.
77. Vide Scott, M. (1989). "The Disappearing Forests", in *Far Eastern Economic Review* 12. January. p.35.

In addition to former effects, tropical deforestation contributes to a worldwide climatic change by altering a part—the carbon fixation by trees—of the natural global cycle (the other is altered by carbon dioxide emissions).

Current deforestation also results in the extinction of many plants and insects each year. Note in this regard that till now only a minority of tropical forests species has been analysed for the future use of mankind.[78] Consequently, since these potential benefits stemming from the rational tropical-rainforests exploitation may also profit all human beings without exclusion, it is clear that we are here again in the domain of an additional positive global externality. Consequently, forest exploitation should be supervised, coordinated and administered by a new democratic UN, through WEO.

Certainly, population growth, unbalanced wealth and power structures and myopic or corrupted politicians (at times financially sustained by foreign corruptors) are variables that contribute to the current situation of non-sustainability of the rainforests of the world. Indeed, a situation that should urgently be overturned.

Externalities and Environment: A Theoretical Consideration

Having described the worrying situation of the environment (water and air) and the growing scarcity of some relevant renewable resources at a global scale, and after recommending some solutions for sustainability and conservation, we will now analyse the economic foundations of our recommendations.

In this regard we have to remember that under certain ideal conditions described by neo-classical economists,[79] markets play a crucial role in the promotion of efficiency, thus rationally allocating the available resources and making capitalist economies more productive than others.

This does not mean that market economies, as well as their public sectors, do not contain significant economic failures that will have to be corrected. In particular, free private markets often induce more

---

78. Cufield (1985). "A Reporter at large: The Rain Forest." *New Yorker*, 14 January, p.59.
79. All handbooks of microeconomics describe these ideal conditions.

production than convenient while in other cases they induce shorter offers than necessary. This is respectively due to the existence of negative or positive externalities. Free private markets also lead to social failures, that is to say, to situations in which some people do not reach decent standards of living or lack minimum social protection.

Market Failures

Taken for granted the necessary existence of an official and stable definition of property rights,[80] and the governmental enforcement of private contracts for the working of capitalist economies, neoclassical economists have long ago accepted the possible existence of five different forms of economic market failures: 1) The lack of competition including the possible existence of the so-called natural monopolies; 2) The existence of the so-called public goods; 3) The existence of externalities; 4) The existence of incomplete markets; and 5) The failures of information.

As a by-product of the market economy, some neoclassical economists have also warned us on the possible appearance of non-desirable distributions of income and wealth, some times defined as a "social" failure that should be corrected by the public sector by means of using fiscal and public expenditure policies.[81]

The normative analysis of the public sector[82] additionally clarifies the convenient use of certain instruments—fiscal and social expenditure policies—to correct the economic and social failures of markets. Note that in principle the use of mentioned instruments should be

---

80. In some societies land is held in common, thus everyone being freely allowed to use it for grazing. As proven by evidence, this system of common property of land drives finally to over-grazing with losses for all. The current situation of fish exhaustion in many areas of the oceans is also the result of the non-precise definition of the property rights of nations. Lack of private property definition in old communist countries also acted as a disincentive for the correct maintenance of some common goods (apartments, etc.)

81. A second argument for public intervention, in this case in absence of economic market failures, consists in the convenience of overturning possible wrong decisions made by individuals, even in the case that they are perfectly informed. We are here referring to the use of alcohol, drugs or cigarettes, that the state should try to avoid; or the non-use of seat-belts or gyms, that the state should promote. We are respectively talking about the so-called "demerit or merit goods".

82. "Normative analysis" is concerned with what should be done to change, in the most efficient way, current non-desirable situations. Conversely, "positive analysis" just explains how the reality works, thus not entering in any additional value judgement.

conditioned to the fact that the costs of information, political process, bureaucracy, etc. involved in the implementation of the new policy, plus the losses of citizens negatively affected by political corrections, do not offset or surpass the expected gains coming from the change.

Externalities: Private Solutions

Air and water pollution are just two examples of a much broader range of induced externalities. In fact, when an individual or firm undertakes an economic action that has a negative or positive[83] effect on another individual or firm for which the latter is respectively not paid or does not pay, we are respectively in front of negative or positive externalities. When this happens, the level of the corresponding production or consumption will be socially incorrect:[84] excessive in the case of existence of negative externalities, because their social costs[85] will not have been included in the costs of production; and defective in the case of existence of positive externalities[86] since part of the total demand will not have been considered.

Observe that under certain and restrictive circumstances, private markets could perfectly deal with the problem of externalities, without resorting to any public intervention. Internalising the externality by forming economic units of sufficient size, as to transform the externality in an internal cost or profit, is the most elemental way of solving the problem.[87]

---

83. In some cases, economic actions of individuals or firms transfer advantages to others without being paid by them, a benefit that is known in Economics as a "positive externality". Most frequent is, however, the opposite case, that of "negative externalities" or disturbances, transferred to others by polluters.
84. Vide on this issue, Stiglitz, J. (2000: 215). Book already mentioned.
85. Social costs are those exceeding the private ones (understanding by private ones the costs of raw materials, energy, use of land, labour, machinery, etc. paid by producers to the providers of mentioned goods and services).
86. If producers could cash in the social profits induced by a positive externality generated by them, they would increase their economic production. But due to the fact that the only "visible" demand is the private one, this will force a shorter production than that reachable if social demand was also perceivable.
87. The formation of communities of owners (neighbours) is a simple way of internalising the externalities (positive or negative) that the individual behaviour of each one could induce to the rest.

At times, externalities can also be dealt with just by the assignment of property rights.[88] Note however that even though property rights for a common resource were not assigned to single individuals or were not well defined, the market could at times find efficient ways for dealing with the externality. We are here referring to what is known as Coase Theorem[89] solutions.

According to this theorem the involved parties will get together and make due arrangements as to internalise the externalities. Nevertheless, the final result of the arrangements will depend basically on the symmetry or asymmetry of the initially defined property rights.[90] Consequently, the determination of who should compensate whom will depend on the defined or non-defined property rights and other parameters.

Note alternatively that legal systems devised to protect private contracts, could also provide *ex-post* protection against undergone negative externalities. In fact, all legal systems make responsible the party who injures other parties, thus forcing it to pay compensation. So, in case of externalities, the courts will be the organs that will have to define explicitly the realised "injure" (externality), and the compensation to be received by the damaged parties.

Once explained some private forms of solving externalities, one could wonder on their real usefulness. Indeed, if their effectiveness were proven, interference of public sector would not be necessary, and vice versa. Nevertheless there are several reasons that, in general, will make government intervention indispensable.

The first reason has to do with the fact that some goods involved in externalities contain traits practically identical to public goods

---

88. This is for instance the case of "common exploitation" of land or seas, which has normally induced problems of over-grazing or over-fishing. In all these cases, if the resource could be divided and assigned in property (sold) to different individuals or nations, everyone would have incentives to make sure the better exploitation of the resource.

89. Coase, R.H. (1960). "The Problem of the Social Cost", *Journal of Law and Economics* No. 3.

90. To understand this dependency, the case of smokers is frequently quoted. In a train, if smokers are in a compartment of non-smokers (in which is clearly defined the right of not breathing the smoke of others), the smokers will have to pay (compensate) the non-smokers for smoking. Nevertheless, if non-smokers want to have a clear atmosphere in a smoking compartment, these non-smokers will have to pay the smokers not to smoke. Finally, when the smoking right is not properly defined, if the loss of non-smokers exceeds the gain of smokers, the non-smokers may get together and compensate the smokers.

(clean air and water), which necessarily implies the intervention of the public sector. The second reason refers to the existence of imperfect information; this is a circumstance that may make impossible the arrival to a private efficient solution.[91] Thirdly, if not all the involved owners become associated—as required to internalise an externality—owners that do not join could behave as "free riders". And fourthly, keeping the group united will require significant costs of transaction and information, in particular if the group is large. These transaction costs will be particularly intensive if the group enters into judicial processes.[92]

Consequently, private systems for addressing externalities have many a time not worked, or have worked in a very poor way. This has forced the public sector to intervene.

Externalities: Public Solutions

Public solutions to externalities could be classified in two broad categories: 1) solutions based on the working of markets; and 2) solutions based on direct regulations. The first category tries to arrive at efficient (market) solutions by means of establishing incentives (subsidies) or disincentive (taxes) to the production of those goods that respectively induce positive or negative externalities.[93] Conversely, the second category will consist of establishing a simple physical limit to emissions.

Solutions Based on the Working of Markets

Even though many neoclassical economists agree that markets do not lead in many cases to efficient allocation of resources, they believe that the infrastructure of markets may be used to restore efficiency.[94] In fact, "acting through markets" solutions, capable of curbing the level of environmental externalities, may adopt three different forms:

---

91. When property rights are not well defined, bargaining may not be necessarily conducive to a position of stable equilibrium.

92. In most of cases, the judicial costs could be greater than the possible gains to be obtained with a favourable verdict.

93. For instance, a carbon-tax per tonne of emissions of CO_2 to the air would induce less polluting processes of production.

94. In the following lines we will focus on the problem of pollution of the environment. Note however that the method of analysis used here is the same as that applicable to any other form of negative externalities.

1) fines or taxes; 2) subsidies for pollution abatement; and 3) introduction of marketable permits of pollution in combination with predefined pollution limits or "caps".

The simplest way of solving the problem of pollution by means of using the existing markets, is the establishment of fines or taxes in proportion to the amount of emissions; and this in order to bridge the existing gap (externality) between the private and the social marginal costs of production, being in general the latter higher than the former. Note that these fines should, in principle, be just corrective taxes—also called Pigouvian taxes[95]—exclusively oriented to reach economic efficiency, and by no means to increase public revenues.

As deducible and proven, if negative externalities (pollution for instance) exist, and firms were not taxed in Pigouvian terms, the volume of production would be comparative larger, the prices lower, and the pollution not addressed. If, conversely, a Pigouvian tax were accurately calculated and levied, the level of production would be reduced, the prices would rise, and the level of pollution would significantly dwindle.

Observe that firms may reduce their total emissions by producing less—as already mentioned—or, alternatively, by changing the methods (or technology) of production. *Ceteris paribus*, these changes will increase costs[96] and, as frequently assumed, marginal costs of the pollution control will rise. Logically, under this strategy, firms will spend in pollution control to the extent that the marginal cost of the pollution-control remains under the Pigouvian tax (to be paid by firms when they do not introduce new methods of production).

But when pollution is not taxed,[97] unless the government subsidises the pollution-abatement expenditures of firms, the latter will not be encouraged to reduce their emissions because the benefits received

---

95. As we will mention in the lines below, A.C. Pigou was the first neoclassical economist who seriously studied the problem of externalities.

96. These changes will include direct expenditures for pollution control devises, alteration of the used mix of inputs (raw materials), etc.

97. Sometimes, Pigouvian taxation is not easy to be reckoned in advance, if the government wants to set a certain (maximum) level of pollution. Alternatively, subsidising the abatement pollution costs could induce serious problems of efficiency, as mentioned in the text. Consequently, choosing between these two options could be a matter of political decision.

by them will be negligible.[98] Observe, additionally, that this system of subsidies will not enable to reach an efficient allocation of resources because the received subsidies will reduce the total marginal "private" costs, thus not making equal social cost and benefits.

Looking to alternatives, polluters will always prefer subsidies for pollution abatement instead of paying Pigouvian taxes for the realised emissions. The reasons are obvious: 1) in case of subsidies for pollution abatement, the production will be higher; 2) the profits will also be higher; and 3) the prices lower. Note that, in this case, subsidies will be paid by general taxpayers (although not for reaching efficiency), while the alternative Pigouvian tax will be paid by those who pollute which will induce a more efficient allocation of resources.

After discussing the relative merits of Pigouvian taxes and subsidies for pollution abatement, we will finally refer to the marketable permits system, currently the most fashionable way for dealing with the pollution problems. According to this system, the amount of pollution authorised by the government to the different firms will be initially fixed.[99] In order to reduce pollution and to encourage the process, the public sector will allow those firms producing emissions under their pollution target, to sell with profit a fraction of their "right to pollute".

Observe that under this system, firms will be willing to sell permits to the extent that the market prices of the permits are larger than their marginal cost of reducing pollution; buying them in the opposite case. Due to the working of the market, an equilibrium price for the permits will be reached, thus ensuring this system—like that of Pigouvian taxes—economic efficiency.

One has to acknowledge that this system of marketable permits has a clear advantage over the tax system: with the system of taxes the public sector will not know in advance the final volume of emissions of the firms. As a result, if the pollution level finally becomes too high, the Pigouvian tax will have to be risen to achieve the desired

98. In this case, and due to the subsidies for "pollution abatement" paid by the government, the main receivers of benefits will be the residents in the neighbourhood.

99. For instance, the allowed emissions in the current year could be authorised for every firm, up to a limit of the 95% of those emitted in the year before.

level of pollution. This lack of accuracy does not happen with the system of tradable permits because the government will initially establish the maximum (allowed) pollution level.

But economists know that the system of marketable permits also contains some relevant dysfunctions. The first is that those firms that had spent a lot in preserving the environment before the distribution of permits, will receive less permits for polluting; and vice versa those firms which were initially very pollutant (note additionally that under this system the new entrants would not receive permits and will be forced to buy them).

Although the latter problem could be solved by means of distributing the permits on a current production bases (instead of according to the past pollution of every polluter), there is a second problem much more subtle than the former one: since the geographical location of pollutants is not considered at all under this scheme (which, to be fair, should have led to a discrimination of the permit prices)[100] the resulting market-price of the permits will be a bad indicator of the desires of the people living in the different locations.

Besides former inconveniences, we have to highlight that mentioned cap and trade schemes could also cause additional economic damage, due to the proven volatility of the permit prices.[101] It is also said that the cap and trade systems provide less incentives to innovation than the introduction of a generalised pollution tax, which clearly establishes a minimum return for any innovation (note that innovations under the cap and trade system would push down the price of the permits, thus reducing the comparative incentives).

Note finally that, whatever the system used for curbing pollution, if the targeted volume of reduction of emissions were low or non-significantly rigorous, or there were free-riders, all the mentioned three strategies would not reach the final pursued end: to stop pollution.

100. The right to pollute in the neighbourhood of a big city should be more expensive than in other faraway, or at seaside, places.

101. Both big Cap and Trade schemes working today—The EU Emissions Trading Scheme for CO_2, and America's market for trading sulphur-dioxide permits (to reduce acid rain) suggest a very acute volatility of the permit prices. *The Economist* (2007: 78) June 16. Note additionally that if the cap is badly defined (being compatible with excessive emissions) and the permit prices fall, the incentives for innovation will result negatively affected.

Other Ways of Addressing Pollution

Although most economists believe that solutions based on the working of markets are the best for curbing externalities and pollution, governments have for long mainly used "direct regulations".[102] Note as well that although these direct systems of pollution control have done their job—though just tackling part of the additional induced pollution—they have not worked efficiently, since they have not introduced incentives to reduce the pollution under established standards.

Observe that these "direct regulations" have usually been based on performance; that is to say on the amount of certain necessary inputs to produce the output. One has to recognise that it is more efficient to focus on performance—either for implementing "direct regulations" or for using any market based mechanism[103]—than on any other variable for control. Besides, we have to highlight that the main reason to focus on inputs instead of outputs is that inputs are easier to control than outputs.[104]

Politics and the Financing of Externalities

Note that former discussion has been centred on the ways to deal with externalities (mainly reduction of emissions). Currently, a part of the debate has shifted towards the financial incidence of the anti-pollution policies, that is to say towards the analysis of who is ultimately paying for pollution-cleaning, and who should pay for it.

Observe that the different ways of dealing with pollution will have different distribution impacts. Remember for instance that firms always will prefer subsidies for equipment to abate pollution, than to pay taxes or buying tradable permits.

In strict economic terms those who pollute should pay. Nevertheless firms always lobby to avoid pollution costs (or taxes), on the pretext that it is always difficult to prove who gains with the environmental policies of governments.

---

102. We are here referring to standards of emissions for cars, emissions of hazardous chemical gasses coming from factories, prohibitions of smoking in certain places (public offices, transport systems, etc.), restrictions on fishing and hunting, etc.
103. Stiglitz, J. (2000: 231). Book already mentioned.
104. For instance it is more difficult to measure the pollution that comes out of a chimney than the number of filters used by a factory to significantly reduce the pollution issued out of the chimney.

In general, taxes on production or purchase of tradable permits will make that the producers and the directly involved consumers lose—due to subsequent smaller productions and profits and higher prices—while the gainers will be the (more dispersed) taxpayers, who will see their tax burden alleviated. However, due to the lack of lobbying capacity of the potential gainers in this case, national environmental administrations have sometimes opted for the less efficient system—subsidies on pollution abatement—that will induce no charges to polluters.

Note that this pollution treatment by governments in favour of national firms is alike to that given by governments to national producers in relation to international trade, thus many a time protecting them in an unjustified way from international competition, in detriment of consumers.

International Externalities: Difficulties for Correction

Up to this moment we have discussed the different ways, private or public, of dealing with the problem of externalities. Note however that the former discussion has been made without quoting the words "transnational or global". However, former discussion would remain incomplete if international-global externalities generated by the economic activity in one country—with spill-over effects for other nations or for the whole world—were not considered.

In relation to pure local and national externalities, we may affirm that the above-mentioned public solutions could be successfully applied in any "democratic" country whose citizens start considering the environment as something to be protected. Note however that the level of exigency of the rules for national environmental protection could be different in every country, and adapted to the feelings of own citizens. This heterogeneity of national legislations—as we will see—induces some problems when productions with polluting processes are exported.

Nevertheless, much more significant problems will appear when a part of the economic activity (production of goods and services) of a country, induces negative spill-over effects on neighbouring countries or on the global environment.

On the first issue—the case of exports reaching the global market from countries with different rules for the protection of national environment—some economists have recommended that every country should be free to establish own legislation on national environment.[105] Indeed, this suggestion could be useful to protect the comparative advantages of poor countries, but at the same time it could give arguments to the rich ones—based on competitiveness—to not address their own pollution.

Alternatively, this pro-individual-freedom of action in relation to national environmental policies could also be useful to support the introduction of new protectionist rules in the West, on goods coming from poor and highly polluting countries. In fact, this manoeuvre has already started to be used, despite the fact that the accumulation of wealth in rich countries was achieved, along many decades, practically without environmental restrictions;[106] restrictions that the West today exert—and without delay—on developing countries.

Letting aside the export problems stemming from the existence of differentiated national rules on national environment, what indeed seems inexcusable is the harmonisation of the national environmental legislations in relation to global environmental issues.[107]

Using standard neoclassical analysis and centred in Pigouvian taxes for solving the problem,[108] Nordhaus explained in 1995 that, for global pollutants, the marginal benefits obtained from the reduction of emissions are likely to be common to all countries while marginal abatement costs are different when legislations are not the same. Consequently, in circumstances of common legislation, that is to say after a process of homogenisation—Nordhaus added—it would be possible to establish a single level of pollution tax that will

105. On this issue we will be back in the item 5.5.

106. Industrialised countries try today to force the setting up of tough national legislations on environment in developing countries, in order to protect their own domestic economic activities (which pay pollution taxes). When these legislations are not in place, rich countries often put claims in WTO, or directly establish anti-dumping rights on exports coming from developing countries.

107. Nordhaus, W. (1995). *Locational Competition and the Environment: Should Countries Harmonise their Environmental Policies?*, in Siebert, H. (ed.) (1995) *Locational Competition in the World Economy*. Tuebingen. In this work Nordhaus pointed out: "policies targeted (in relation to) local environment problems should be left to the discretion of individual countries."

108. Along his line of reasoning, Tobin was thinking on a carbon tax.

equate the marginal benefits and the marginal costs of every nation, thus enabling to reach efficient solutions for global environment issues.[109] Note however that this proposal of Nordhaus, although useful, was incomplete because it did not take into account the historical non-payment of induced externalities by current main polluters.[110] Consequently, we do believe that in parallel to the general establishment of the same taxes for global pollutants, rich countries should also compensate the poor in exchange of realised old pollution with current effects on climate change.

Nevertheless, the reality has not followed (and it is not following) the Tobin-way towards homogenisation of taxes[111] on global pollutants. As far as a multilateral homogenisation of the environmental regulation should avoid the "prisoner's dilemma"—associated with unilateral standard setting—one could wonder why it is so difficult to reach consensus on these issues, conducive to homogeneous legislation on global pollutants (a common carbon tax or an inclusive system of cap and trade).

But the answer is quite simple: homogenisation of taxes (or setting up of a totally inclusive system of cap and trade) has not only to do with problems of efficiency and competitiveness among nations, but also with the indispensable readjusting of the absolute standards of life of all citizens, whose desirability is not shared in the same degree by all political parties in every nation. As a result, easy and rapid homogenisation of national taxes (or legislation) on global pollutants should not be expected in a context of "national democracies"; hence our call, also in this case, for the establishment of a new World Environment Organisation, depending on a democratically restated UN.

---

109. Vide. Cole, M. (2000). *Trade Liberalisation, Economic Growth and Environment*. EE: UK. p.114.
110. The basic principle in environmental protection, "those who pollute must pay", should not be interpreted "from now onwards", precisely when rich countries have decided to start the process. Undeniably, if the environmental degradation stock is positively related with the reached wealth, rich countries should start paying—of course in a phased way—their historical pollution debt to the others.
111. Note that the most relevant western governments are today more inclined to favour a more inclusive "cap and trade" system than to introduce a common tax on carbon (this is a tax on fossil fuels, e.g. oil, with the aim of reducing their use in order to protect the environment).

Besides the already considered national and global externalities, we have also to mention the so-called trans-boundaries externalities,[112] which are neither local (national) nor global ones. According to the view of Nordhaus, former analysis and conclusions for global externalities will not be appropriated for intermediate cases. Indeed, in these cases the most appropriated treatment would be the establishment of regional (bilateral or multilateral) environmental agreements (REA).

Democratisation and Environmental Ownership

One of the different ways in which firms or people may exert power over others is by imposing environmental costs on them. Note that this cost-imposition is not strictly intentional—since dirtying other peoples' air or water is not an end in itself—but simply a side effect stemming from maximisation of production or consumption, in a context of existence of certain external costs; costs that producers and consumers seek to minimise, passing them to others.

Indeed, the capacity of economic actors to impose external costs on others will depend on the relative power of those who generate pollution, *vis-a-vis* those placed at the receiving end of the external costs.

Concentration of Power and Environmental Degradation

Economic activities that engender pollution generally produce winners and losers. Note that losers often do not exist because they belong to future generations; or although existing, they are not aware of the current environmental degradation; or if existing and knowing, they have no power to countervail actions of polluters.

It is a general rule that in polluting actions, those relatively powerful will be the winners and those relatively powerless will be the losers. As a result, the volume of environmental degradation will generally increase the larger is the difference in power among the

112. There are some activities, which induce trans-boundary environment degradation, that have a less widespread geographical impact than those that issue global pollutants. Among the most relevant regional (non-global) pollutants we could mention nitrogen oxides and sulphur dioxide, both the causes of acid rain.

different citizens.[113] This means that pollution will increase the more unevenly the power is distributed in societies.

Observe that the economic power of the different layers of society has mainly to do with their different levels of relative wealth,[114] thus giving advantage to the rich. Nevertheless, effective political power uses to be much more concentrated than wealth; and its concentration will depend on the nature of the ruling political system, democracy or dictatorship.[115]

Mentioned stable relation between concentration of power and environmental degradation, suggests that democracy—which by itself will distribute the power—could promote environmental protection. This does not mean that democracy will necessarily and quickly solve all problems of environmental degradation in all countries.[116] In fact, the causes of the, at times, poor reactions of democracies against environment degradation, are mainly the lack of information on its consequences, and the different valuations of citizens and politicians of polluting actions. Additionally, we should not forget that preferences of citizens could be manipulated by mass media in favour of the present generation (without quoting the following ones) and the powerful.[117]

Note as well that such positive relation between the existence of democracy and the easier correction of environmental problems, should not imply that environmental protection should wait till the consolidation of (national or global) democracy. Dictatorship or other non-representative systems could also start the process of environment

---

113. There are exceptions to this rule of behaviour. Sometimes exceeding power is unduly used to practise excessive environmental protection in benefit of the rich and in detriment of the poor. For instance, demolishing slums, visible from rich quarters, would have little social benefit for the rich and significant costs for the involved poor. Consequently, insufficient or exaggerated protection of environment or non-renewable resources, could generate welfare losses to society.

114. In multiracial or multicultural societies, determinants of the power distribution will be even more complicated.

115. In former Soviet Union, a country with a rather egalitarian income distribution, the existent political power concentration paved the way for higher levels of environmental degradation and resources depletion. Note that these costs were imposed on the society without informing it.

116. Note that, sometimes, environmental degradation has reached a practically irreversible state, for which even (national) democracies cannot find a solution.

117. Becker, G.S. (1983: 392) "A theory of competition among pressure groups for political influence", *Q.J.E.* No. 48(3).

protection by means of introducing countervailing powers among the different social groups involved in the generation or reception of negative externalities.

Finally, we should not forget that the global society is not democratic. This has for long given rich nations the opportunity to pollute other countries and the global environment without paying for it. Of course this circumstance would radically change with the introduction of a new democratic UN, which would empower poorer nations, thus favouring global environment.

Democracy, Property Rights and Instruments for Environmental Protection

We have explained that in issues related to the protection of environment, democracies (although not all) have in the last years started using the so-called "market-based solutions"—as for instance the system of "tradable pollution permits"—while developing countries have (till now) mainly resorted to physical "limits" to the emissions of pollutants.

Note that a system of "tradable permits" may at first sight seem more democratic because it works through the market; but in fact the selection of this instrument (to fight against pollution) would only be democratic if the ways of establishing the pollution targets (the "caps") were democratic and if the "permits to pollute" were also democratically distributed.[118] On the other hand, the establishment of physical limits to pollution—caps without trading permits—could also be perfectly democratic. Indeed, all democratic countries also use these limits to fight against some forms of pollution.

As far as political action on environment will have to act on physical assets, inputs or outputs, this forces us again to discuss "property rights". Note that along the last century, the definition of property rights has not remained static. It has ranged between two main conceptions: one radical—according to which property rights should be perfectly defined and absolutely preserved—and another more functional, according to wnich property rights should be considered as a tool to serve certain economic and social ends as efficiency, growth and justice.

118. Note that a market of "tradable permits" only may start working after the definition of pollution targets and the distribution of permits.

Consequently, the radical version of property rights supports absolute immobility of these rights; while the functional one considers property rights as something variable according to changes in values, technology and institutions.

Surprisingly, after decades of following the more flexible version of property rights in all main western countries, a neo-conservative doctrine, the so-called "free market environmentalism", is today defending the idea that "any right not withheld by prior legislation or legally held by others, should necessarily remain with the current landowner. This would imply for instance that wetlands, if not explicitly protected by previous law, could be used by owners for drying and building. According to "free market environmentalists" forbidding these activities to owners would imply a "public taking" which should entail compensation.

Observe that this extremist approach ignores that property rights on land (nature) all around the world are partially based on previous takings (appropriations).[119] As deducible, such extreme approach puts the rights to pollute on the side of property owners, who in any case should be compensated for not polluting. *Mutatis mutandis,* this irrationality means that society should compensate smokers for abandoning their habit of smoking.

In this regard, we do believe that modern states should conciliate traditional private property rights[120]—necessary for sustainability of capitalism—with a new need, felt by people, of having a more liveable ambience, prone to be deteriorated if an unrestricted industrialisation continued ruling.

Therefore, what we could call "democratisation of the environmental ownership", based on the principle that all the people should have the right to a clean and healthy environment, introduces an additional limitation in the domain of the traditional property rights; although

---

119. Remember again the article of Hirschleifer, J.(1993) "The Dark Side of Strength", in which the different views of Adam Smith and Machiavelli on how to reach wealth, are described.

120. Traditional expropriation (with compensation) of private property by public sector for the realisation of public works, roads, etc. is something admitted by any sort of capitalism all over the world.

this time without any compensation.[121] But property rights will always have to exist if we want to keep alive a moderate sort of capitalism capable of sustaining democracy, a political system (national or global) indispensable for solving the current pending problems of mankind.

Economic Growth and Environment Degradation

Mainly as a consequence of the production and consumption growth, since the beginning of the Industrial Revolution "industrialising" countries started experiencing environmental degradation and resources depletion. Note that such degradation and depletion was for long rather proportional to the GDP growth rate. Nevertheless, from a moment onwards,[122] such (national) environmental degradation started tending to be less than proportional to economic progress.

In fact, as a consequence of economic development and the shift of the domestic production from industry to the services sector (which is significantly less pollutant), both combined with the implementation of policies to protect national-domestic environment, the trajectory of the domestic per capita pollution has recently experienced a turning point in many developed countries.

This means for developing countries that, in future, from a certain per capita income level onwards, their per capita emissions with exclusive incidence on their national environment will also tend to decrease.

Nevertheless, other forms of pollution—those of global consequences—have hardly stopped growing. This has occurred because in this case, as expectable in absence of a formal authority at a world scale capable of defining and enforcing agreed global rules, "free riding behaviour" has worked, thus averting the appearance of favourable turning points.

---

121. Observe that property-rights have historically undergone reallocations and redefinitions. Reallocations may drive to a more equitable distribution or to a greater concentration of wealth. Redefinitions may drive to an improvement or to a greater degradation of the environment. Consequently, both changes will have to be decided democratically and in a sustainable way.

122. This turning point in (national) environmental degradation may appear at a different time in every country, according to its economic and political progress (national democratisation uses to play a significant role on the relative reduction of national pollution). This phenomenon will be hereafter analysed, when we explain the so-called "environmental Kuznets curve".

Considerations on the Environment in the 19th Century and First Half of the 20th

Letting aside the notable although incomplete and, to some extent, misguiding[123] contributions of Malthus,[124] Marx[125] and other authors along the 19th century in relation to the determinants of economic growth, we have here to pay special attention to John Stuart Mill. Particularly in relation to his concern on the social and environmental problems induced by the then observed unrestrained economic progress.

In the wake of the unprecedented economic growth registered in Britain as a consequence of the Industrial Revolution, Stuart Mill expressed in his writings a clear discomfort on two of the contemporary major problems he observed: 1) that of the negative evolution of the income distribution; and 2) that of the visible destruction of nature, caused by the ongoing rapid industrialisation.[126]

Despite this intellectual precedent, with the appearance of neoclassical economics in the last third of the 19th century, the connection between nature and economy for long remained neglected. Only in 1920, A.C. Pigou started pioneering in this field, thus becoming the first economist who seriously studied the impact of externalities and pollution on economy and society.

---

123. Indeed, the initial contributions of the classical authors to the theory of growth were fragmental, thus not containing a complete explanation of the causes of the steady growth. Only after the relevant contributions of J.M.Keynes in its General Theory, first complete theories on the economic growth phenomenon were formulated. In particular we could here mention the Harrod-Domar model, the neoclassical approach of Solow, and the endogenous model of growth original by Rommer. In all these contributions, the role of the saving and investment rates and the evolution of technology were as important as, or even more, than the evolution of population.

124. Malthus, T.R. (1798). *Essay on the Principle of Population*. Reprinted in 1970 by Penguin. London. According to this author, the fundamental cause of poverty was the pressure that the population growth exerted on resources. In his view, as far as initially there was no resources restriction, population increased geometrically while agricultural production only increased arithmetically. In the long term, this dissociation of growth rates would provoke poverty, famines, diseases and a population adjustment.

125. Marx, in disagreement with Malthus, pointed out (in his magnum work *The Capital*), that poverty was not so much caused by the relative scarcity of natural resources but by the social injustice stemming from the private owning of property of the means of production.

126. Indeed, Mill, J.S. (1871) in his *Principles of Political Economy*, underlined that: "Nor is there much satisfaction in contemplating the world with nothing left to the spontaneous activity of the nature; with every rood of land brought into cultivation; with every flowery wasted or natural pasture ploughed in; with all quadrupeds or birds not domesticated by men exterminated as their rivals for food."

Following him, microeconomics started distinguishing between the private cost of production and the social costs of it, the later including not only wages, raw materials, etc., but also the externalities, as analysed in lines above.

Hotelling,[127] who in 1931 provided a rigorous analysis on the optimal use of non-renewable resources,[128] was another exception to the almost general neoclassical disregard of nature.

To the extent that since mid-20th century, scarcity of raw materials and environmental disasters became more perceivable than before, the interest of academicians for the relation between economy and nature increased considerably; mainly during the 60s, with the contributions of Carlson and Boulding.[129] In particular, Boulding strongly warned on the defective and miss-guiding use of the GDP as a measure of the speed of progress of national economies. Note that this warning was mainly due to the fact that the GDP did (and does) not take into account either the involved use in production of non-renewable resources, or the waste and emissions induced by production or consumption activities.

Report of the Club of Rome and Further Assessments

With all these new problems and concerns on the desk, D.& D. Meadows (and their team) drafted in 1972 a famous report for the Club of Rome[130] that, for the first time, induced a global debate on environment and exhaustible resources. As suggested in the report, with an assumedly fixed quantity of food and non-renewable resources, plus forecasted continuous growth of population and industrial capital, the model of Meadows predicted a mid-long term collapse (initially

127. Hotelling, H. (1931). "The Economics of Exhaustible Resources", *JPE* 39. Hotelling proved that, under certain circumstances, the price of the resource (once deduced the extraction costs)—should increase over time at a percentage rate equal to the interest rate. Vide also Pindyck, R. and D. Rubinfeld (2003). *Microeconomics*. Fifth Edition, Prentice-Hall India. p.553.

128. Cole, M.A. (2000). *Trade Liberalisation, Economic Growth and Environment*. EE. UK.

129. Carson, R. (1962). analysed in his *Silent Spring* the catastrophic impact of the indiscriminate use of chemicals (pesticides and insecticides) in the long term. Boulding, K. (1966) in his *Economics of the Coming Spaceship Earth*, rigorously considered the relations among production, growth, resources depletion and environmental degradation, thus recommending a fast setting up of growth limitations to end current reckless "economic growth", based on the absurd assumption of the limitless availability of natural resources.

130. Vide. Meadows, D. *et al.* (1972). *The Limits to Growth: A Report of the Club of Rome's Projection on the Predicament of Mankind*. New York: Universe Books.

forecasted for 2010), mainly due to the progressive depletion of non-renewable resources.

A major critique of the said report came from Cole *et al.*[131] who introduced a possible temporal lengthening in the availability of non-renewable resources, due to the likely discoveries of unknown deposits, and the possible recycling of natural resources formerly used. In their analysis, Cole *et al.* also introduced technical change, future shift of the internal composition of output favourable to the services sector, and possible substitution of factors in the production process, as variables that could additionally lengthen the projected period of depletion of non-renewable resources.

On the wake of the restatement by Cole *et al.*, two currents of opinion appeared: 1) an optimistic one[132] which, based on economic and engineering history, wrongly proclaimed the limitlessness of the human inventiveness to solve the problems of pollution and depletion; and 2) a pessimistic one,[133] which not only questioned the success of past growth as badly measured, but also transmitted fears on the future intractability of the natural resources problem.[134]

In those days (1973), a very different argument on the growth debate came from the so-called Second Law of Thermodynamics, also known as the Entropy Law. In particular, Georgescu *et al.*[135] emphasised the physical limits of the economic growth, a position additionally clarified by Rees in 1990.[136] As mentioned, mankind

---

131. Cole, H.S. *et al.* (1973). "Thinking about the Future; a Critique to the Limits to Growth". Sussex University Press.

132. Vide, among others, Beckerman, W. (1974). *In Defence of Economic Growth.* London: Jonathan Cape.

133. Vide Le Monde (2006). 30 juillet. "L'obscure lubie des objecteurs de croissance". In this article it was said; "There are today some economists—whom we could call "growth objectors"—who preach for the convenience of initiating a process of "economic decrease" to save the planet. Indeed, a difficult manoeuvre full of risks, based on a full mistrust on the capacities of humans for improving their existence." p.2.

134. Lecomber, R. (1975). *Economic Growth versus Environment.* London: Macmillan.

135. Georgescu *et al.* (1973). "The Entropy Law and the Economic Problem", in Daly (1973) *Towards a Steady-state Economy.* New York: Freeman.

136. Vide Rees, W. (1990). "The Ecology of Sustainable Development", *The Ecologist* 20. In this article, Rees paid attention to the fact that in an isolated system, available energy and matter are continuously and irrevocable degrading towards an unavailable state. Since entropy is a measure of the amount of energy that is unavailable for doing work in a thermodynamic system, a piece of coal will contain available energy and therefore it will have low entropy. However, once the coal is burned the energy will not be longer available but dissipated under the form of heat, smoke and ashes, thus having high entropy.

has access to two sources of free energy (with low entropy): 1) the terrestrial stock of mineral deposits; and 2) the flow of solar energy, which enables the production of renewable resources. As both of them are fixed, growth and physical production not based on solar energy will increase entropy and make environmental problems worse, thus implying an eventual limit to growth.[137]

Based on former limits to growth imposed by the Entropy Law and on some ethical considerations,[138] Daly *et al.* (1993), making an additional step started supporting the convenience of a change in the economic aims of nations. In their view, the main new aim should consist of abandoning our generalised "growth-mania" and, instead of it, defining a certain stationary state[139] for the planet, in which a constant physical (natural and man-made) capital and a constant stock of population should be the intermediate targets to be achieved by the international community.

Once arrived at a new equilibrium, this would imply a global population birth rate equal to the death rate, and a gross investment equal to the physical capital depreciation. As a derivative, physical capital will be more durable and, following the First Law of Thermodynamics[140]—according to which, a part of the inputs used in the production process would go to the environment under the form of wastes and emissions—additional pollution and resources depletion would be minimised.

---

137. Ekins, P. (1993). "Limits to Growth and Sustainable Development. Grappling with Ecological Realities", *Ecological Economics*. No.8. p.272.

138. Daly, H. *et al.* (1993) in their *Valuing the Earth: Economics, Ecology, and Ethics*. MIT Press, underlined the incomplete view of traditional Growth Theory as lacking of a complete means–ends spectrum. As he suggested, "although our perception on reasonable ends is vague, a non-consideration of them would make the establishing of priorities impossible." p.20.

139. The term "stationary state" is borrowed from classical economists, mainly from Adam Smith and David Ricardo. Note however that the stationary state imagined by Daly contains profiles in relation to per capita income, consumption, etc., superior to those of the equilibrium at low level (consistent with subsistence wages) imagined by Smith and Ricardo. In fact the characteristics of Daly´s stationary state are more in line with the conclusions and corollaries of the neoclassical model of growth, once included in it growing technology and knowledge, changes in the distribution of income, and evolving allocation of resources. All this would imply the sustainability of a qualitative change in the economy without increasing its physical size.

140. According to this Law, energy cannot be created or destroyed.

On the Concept of "Sustainable Development"

Irrespective of the acceptability of mentioned contributions, in the 80s, former debate on the "limits to growth" shifted towards a new basic concept, which would enable to know where the world was and where it was going to: we are here referring to the concept of "sustainable development".

After preliminary discussions, in particular after the publication of the Brundtland Report,[141] this concept reached the top agenda of the UN and the World Bank. Its importance was not felt only in practical macroeconomics and in the theory of growth, but even in the preamble at the act of creation of the WTO (in 1995), the intention of promoting trade was clearly related with "sustainable development".

Regrettably, decades after its first enunciation, the concept of "sustainable development" has not been sufficiently outlined, while the political support for its materialisation has been minimal. The alleged reason is that any proposal on this concept depends on previous ideas of proponents. This has led some authors to reject this concept due to its vagueness and purported uselessness. However, we do believe that resorting to these arguments has just been a pretext to delay the required huge socio-economic adjustments that the practise of "sustainable development" will finally require.

Despite former pretexts of vagueness and uselessness, and bearing in mind—as Pearce[142] clearly emphasised—that the common characteristic of any version of "sustainable development" should contain a commitment to the principle of equity, be this intra-generational or inter-generational, we could define sustainable development[143] as the only approach capable of meeting our needs today, without compromising the capacity of future generations to meet theirs.

Although there is a certain accord on the convenience that every future generation should have access to a capital stock at least as large

141. World Commission on Environment and Development, 1987.

142. Pearce, D.W. (1993). *Blueprint Three: Measuring Sustainable Development*. London: Earthscan.

143. The definition has been taken from the Brundtland Report.

as the current one, a main source of disagreement has come from the interpretation of the nature of the stock (man-made or natural)[144] of capital to be maintained. According to Pearce, this consideration divided the concept of sustainable development in two versions, the weak one and strong one.

Accordingly, the weak version of sustainable development, would only require the maintenance of the "aggregate" capital stock bequeathed to following generation. Logically, the proponents of this form of sustainability assume that the two forms of bequeathed capital (man-made and natural) are substitutes, an assumption that is not accepted by supporters of the strong version, who only accept to preserve for future generations the current natural capital.

Former concepts of sustainability as described by Pearce—weak and strong—are similar to those explained by Batie,[145] who in 1989 defined the weak form of sustainable development as a conditioned form of economic growth, subject to certain environmental constrains.

In fact, this weak form of sustainable development is the only approach that has successfully permeated social conscience[146] in the West; although, to say the truth, mainly in relation to what we have defined as national environment degradation, but not so much in relation to the global environment preservation. Growing awareness of the national environmental problems in industrialised countries has induced a reaction for limiting emissions to (national) air or waters, the result of which has been the appearance of a turning point in the per capita (national) pollution of these countries. Note that, according to some authors,[147] mentioned change of trend in the West could compensate at a global scale, the current national environment degradation in many developing countries.

---

144. Man-made capital is composed by direct or indirect means of production produced by humans, such as machinery, industrial installations, infrastructures, etc. And natural capital is formed by arable land, fossil fuels, rainforests, habitat, clean water, etc.
145. Batie, S. (1993). "Sustainable Development: Challenges to the Profession of Agricultural Economics", *American Journal of Agricultural Economics*.
146. This new social conscience has, at times, mobilised western entrepreneurs that have willingly collaborated with their governments on developing policies to curve national environmental degradation.
147. Bernstam, M. (1991). *The Wealth of Nations and the Environment*. London: Institute of Economic Affairs.

In opposition to such socially "successful" weak and geographically limited forms of sustainability, partisans of stronger forms of it have pointed out that the assumed high substitutability of natural and man-made capital is non realistic.[148] Consequently, the intergenerational equity, defended by all schools of sustainable development, could only be attained by means of the strict maintenance of the stock of natural capital, while man-made capital should also be kept at its current level in order to avoid additional depletion of natural resources.

A logical derivative of the former (strong) understanding of sustainable economic growth is that, historically economic growth should have been conditioned to the maintenance of the natural stock of resources. Consequently, a significant part of the wealth apparently "created" in the developed world since the Industrial Revolution, would have been a simple statistical mirage,[149] combined with a substantial geographical-international shift of natural resources[150] in times of colonialism.

This would have occurred because mankind has used natural resources to "transform" them in man-made capital, without taking into account the cost of the used natural resources and the environmental degrading.

New Indicators of Production and Welfare

Despite former criticism, the levels of the real GDP and its growth rates continue being common indicators of the degree of success of economies. Surprisingly, even assumedly updated multilateral institutions as the WB and the IMF continue supporting (pro-balanced) economic policies, based on "GDP growth", small rates of

148. In this regard, Daly (1990: 3)—in his article "Towards some operational principles of sustainable development" *Ecological Economics*. No. 2—wrote: "Do extra sawmills substitute for diminishing forest? Do more refineries substitute for depleted oil wells? Do larger nets and fleets substitute declining fish populations? On the contrary, the value and productivity of sawmills, refineries, and fishing nets and fleets (man-made capital) will decline with the decline in forest, oil deposits and fish. Natural capital, as provider of food, water, raw materials and energy, is complementary (not substitute) to man-made capital. At times, natural capital, as absorber of emissions (case of the rainforests), is also complementary to the man-made capital that generates mentioned emissions."

149. Rees, W. (1990). "The Ecology of Sustainable Development." *The Ecologist* 20: 20.

150. Note that a significant part of these geographical shifts of resources (natural and made-man) was realised in times of Colonialism; and this letting aside the trade of slaves, then considered as cargo.

inflation, etc. It is about time to acknowledge that the defective way of measurement of the GDP makes this indicator inaccurate and, occasionally, misguiding.

In fact, quite a number of economists oppose today the use of the GDP as a measure of economic success. And they do it for two different reasons: 1) because of its deficiencies as an indicator of the economic production; and 2) due to its incapacity to represent the current level of welfare of a society. In order to correct mentioned failures, critics have made two suggestions: a) the convenience of an urgent correction of the way of measuring the GDP, by subtracting from it any used or destroyed natural resource (including environmental degrading); an adjustment that would doubtless reduce historically "registered" growth rates; and b) the replacement, at mid-term, of GDP by another more appropriate indicator of welfare.

The main deficiency of the GDP as a measure of the annual production of a country stems from its failure to treat natural capital in the same way as it does with man-made capital. In fact, instead of deducing amortisations to move from the GDP to NDP[151]—as made in relation to man-made capital embodied in the new production—the use or destruction of natural capital is simply not considered, resulting in a distorted and magnified picture of the net added value of the economic activity of a country.[152] From another perspective, we should underline that to include as gross production (GDP), mining or logging of raw materials and forests at their market prices, which not only include the annual added value of these activities but also the price of assets not produced in the exercise (mineral deposits or capital-rainforest), is a clear mistake that inflates the value of the GDP.

151. Cole, M. (2000: 58). Book already mentioned. In the systems of national accounts, Gross Domestic Product (GDP) does not take care of the amortisation of man-made capital, but Net Domestic Product (NDP) does it, by means of deducing from GDP the man-made capital amortisation to measure the net added value within the country.

152. For instance, Repetto *et al.* (1989)—in *Wasting Assets: Natural Resources in the National Income Accounts*. World Resources Institute—suggested that if depreciation of oil, timber and topsoil were taken into consideration when analysing the Malaysian economy, average annual economic growth between 1971 and 1984 had only been 4 per cent as opposed to the official 7 per cent.

Another significant deficiency of GDP reckoning refers to the accountancy treatment of the expenditures in defence and police; in fact they are treated as final goods and not as intermediate ones. Observe that these expenses made to protect society, against healthy accountancy criteria are treated as final goods, which suppose to count real costs (of protection) as benefits.[153] To this respect, we share the view of many authors who consider that these costs should mainly be excluded from the positive components of the GDP.[154]

Note that with the introduction of the above-suggested corrections, many debates on growth would automatically disappear, because any nation that would have based "its growth" on the depletion of own resources (by means of exporting raw materials) or on rearmament, could not have registered any growth when using these two more appropriate measurements.

A more suitable indicator of production sustainability and economic progress of an economy would be the evolution of its so-called net-net saving. Indeed, "if an economy counts with a gross saving (internal or external) at least as large as the sum of the depreciation of man-made capital, plus the depreciation of natural capital (non-renewable resources depletion plus environmental damage), plus military expenditures, then this economy could be registering some sustainable growth" (positive net-net saving). Conversely, if its net-net saving were negative, all registered growth would have been just apparent and not real.

Although this net-net saving could be considered as a better indicator of the economic progress than the currently used GDP growth rate, it also contains some problems, as pointed out time ago by Nordhaus and Tobin;[155] authors who created an alternative indicator of social welfare, called Measure of Economic Welfare

---

153. *Strictu sensu*, no one should be extremely happy for having a strong defence system. A strong defence system, as any other intermediate good, is necessary; but it will only enable the peaceful consumption of the rest of produced final goods, something that perhaps could not occur in absence of defence expenditures. Consequently the accountancy treatment of the defence expenditures should be equivalent to that of raw materials (necessary but just intermediate goods to obtain the final ones).

154. Pearce, D.W. (1993). *Blue Print Three: Measuring Sustainable Development*. London: Earthscan.

155. Nohaus, W. and J. Tobin, (1972). "Is Growth Obsolete?", in *Economic Growth*. NBER, No.96 E. Columbia University Press.

(MEW). Indeed, this indicator should in due time replace—or at least complement—the old GDP.

According to the ideas of Nordhaus and Tobin, the value of the personal consumption and the value of leisure and non-marketable work, should be the major components of the MEW index, which should not include some expenditures as defence, costs of commuting to work, etc., considered as intermediate goods. Some years later, Zelotas (1982)[156] proposed another index, similar to the former one but also considering environmental factors (private pollution and resource depletion) whose costs should be deduced from mentioned MEW.

It is relevant to note that, although the GDP of the US grew from 1950 up to 1965 at an annual rate of 2.2 per cent, the corresponding growth rate of the MEW over this period—when applying the approaches of Nordhaus and Tobin (and Zelotas), would have been less than 1 per cent; a small growth rate that—according to Zelotas—continued ruling between 1965 and 1975.

Although these indexes and others alike,[157] are difficult to be constructed, and even more difficult to be calculated on a monthly or quarterly basis as governmental economists need for their economic analysis and reconsideration of the applied policies, we have to emphasise that all this research has at least proven that the GDP is a bad indicator of economic success from the perspective of sustainable development.

Now that "development sustainability" and concerns on climate change has today become the core of the international economic debate, we consider that it is high time for the establishment of a new method of calculating the level and growth rate of a reliable indicator of welfare, at least on an annual basis. This would enable to scrap at mid-term the obsolete, although currently used, GDP, inherited from the times of Stone, Kuznets and others.

The So-called Kuznets Environment Curve (KEC)

As described in the lines above, there is a moment in the economic

156. Zelotas, X. (1982). *Economic Growth and Declining Social Welfare*. New York University Press: New York.

157. Cole, M. (2000: 62). Book already mentioned.

development of countries, in which (national) environmental problems (emissions), measured in per capita terms, may start a process of dwindling. In this regard, we will now refer to some economic studies directed to prove mentioned possibility.

It is known that the KEC assumes the existence of an inverted U-shaped relationship between the per capita income and the per capita environmental degradation. Indeed, as per capita income rises, factors such as shifts in the sector composition of production— progressively more tilted towards services (hardly polluting)—introduction of more efficient and cleaner processes for the production and use of energy, and higher demand of environmental regulation, will lead to a declining and eventually negative marginal change in the per capita (national) pollution.

Although the pioneer study on the issue was realised by Grossman and Kruger[158] (1991), many others followed it.[159] Many of them tried to adjust KECs mainly for local air pollutants, either in the form of per capita emissions or in relation to urban polluted-air concentrations. After abundant analysis at this level, and although several critiques emerged—some of them even doubting the existence of KECs—the reality is that today there is a growing academic consensus on its existence, at least at national level.[160]

Construction of KECs has been realised for several forms of emissions at a national-local level,[161] mainly in developed countries, and, in general, the obtained results point out a clear direction: pollutants with a local short-term impact on environment have registered turning points at lower levels of per capita income[162] than those of long term local effects; or than those with a more international or global incidence.

---

158. Grossman, G. and A. Krueger, (1991). "Environment Impact of a North American Free Trade Agreement." *Working Paper* No. 3914. NBER. Mass.

159. The KEC, is just a reduced form of some mathematical relations, thus matching correlations but not necessarily expressing causality.

160. Cole, M.A. (2000: 65) Book already mentioned.

161. In particular, KECs have been estimated for carbon dioxide (CO_2), CFCs, methane, nitrogen oxides, sulphur dioxide, suspended particulate matter, carbon monoxide, nitrates, municipal waste, energy consumption and traffic volumes.

162. In the Western World, per capita emissions of local air pollutants—with the exception of transport emissions—are falling in general, this resulting for the time being in a reduction of total emissions with national repercussions.

Indeed, as Grossman suggested in 1994,[163] this may have happened due to the fact that local-national democratic governments have a far greater incentive at mid term to remove or tame local-national pollutants. This is due to the perceivable impact on elections of anti-polluting actions by communities who in future will have to confirm politicians in their current political postings.

As far as the impact of the international-global pollutants on local communities is less clear, local-national democratic governments will have little incentive to unilaterally remove or reduce the national emission of global pollutants.[164] If they did that, they would be financing free riders of other states that would profit, without paying, from mentioned undertaken (national) actions on global pollutants.

Clearly, as in other cases of global public goods, only an international authority for designing, financing and enforcing rules to protect the global environment would be capable of addressing the problem. Otherwise, global pollutants could *sine die* continue growing in parallel with the per capita income, thus driving the planet to a global catastrophe.

Environment and International Trade

The GDP growth rate experienced by any outward oriented economy uses to be significantly influenced by its exports-imports growth rates, that is to say, by the growth rate (positive or negative) of its net external demand.

Connected with the degree of trade aperture of an economy, we have to additionally note that the ratios Export/GDP or Imports/GDP are in general large when the per capita income of the nation is high (and vice-versa). However, it occurs that in rich, geographically extended and very populated nations or economic units, as for instance the US or the EU, the relation between exports and imports and their GDP is small. Consequently, any development associated with

163. Vide, Grossman, G. (1994). "Pollution and Growth. What do we Know?", in Holding *et al.* (eds.). *The Economics of Sustainable Development*. Cambridge University Press.

164. There are exceptions. If the costs of reduction of emissions with global impact were not high, it would not be difficult to reach and fulfil an international agreement on the issue, as it has been the case with the CFCs (Montreal Protocol) for correcting the problem of the ozone hole.

international trade will affect large and very populated countries (or economic unions) relatively less than the others.

Since environment degradation is a phenomenon mainly related to productive activities, when a growing part of the domestic production is exported, the commercial activity will contribute to increase domestic pollution. To the extent that manufacturers of exports do not locally pay environmental taxes to offset induced externalities or depletion of resources,[165] this non-payment could induce claims by importing countries, based on an alleged unfair competition.[166]

As a result of the different environment legislations and the mutual international trade relations, several developments may emerge (or have historically emerged): 1) In the last two centuries those exporting countries specialised in dirtier (industrial) productions automatically increased their per capita pollution levels (case of the West, then specialised in heavy industry, machinery, etc.); and vice-versa in the case of countries specialised in cleaner (agriculture) activities (case of the developing world) where pollution levels hardly grew; 2) Observe however that, from one moment onwards,[167] things changed when the West started dislocating also its dirtier productions to developing countries, precisely to get rid of the heavy pollution problems induced by former specialisation. Among other variables, this dislocation process was encouraged by the existence of highly permissive environment legislations at the receiving end, while increasing employment was an urgent need in poor countries, which welcomed FDI also for dirty industrial activities; and 3) Almost simultaneously, and paradoxically, it also occurred that rich countries started putting barriers to some imports coming from developing countries, on the pretext of environmental dumping,[168] or due to the

---

165. Due to the non-existence of ad hoc legislations, lack of payment of environmental taxes is frequent in developing countries.

166. The European Commission could in future set stringent targets for energy efficiency in items such as electrical appliances, cars, and many other industrial products. Consequently, these new global standards could be applied to all imports flowing into the EU markets, including US manufactures. Vide *Financial Times* (2006: 1) October 17.

167. Late 70s onwards, western governments started the definition and enforcement of (national) environmental standards, which helped to promote industrial dislocation towards countries with less exigent standards.

168. Environmental dumping refers to the non-consideration by an exporting country of some, many, or all environmental costs of production, thus assumedly offering its products which do not comply with the standards at lower prices than those produced in the West.

fact that productive practices realised in developing countries were seen as detrimental for the global environment or biodiversity.

In front of such geographical shifts and, at times, over-consideration of environmental trade-dumping-problems posed by the West, reactions of individual states and the multilateral institution in charge, (WTO),[169] have been disappointing. Lack of harmonisation of national environmental legislations (on industrial processes), caused by the particular interest of every one, have scarcely helped to solve, on a more rational basis, the special problems stemming from environmental issues when products are exported.

Besides this, lack of cooperation and coherence among different involved UN agencies (UNCED, ILO, etc.) and WTO has significantly contributed to the current chaos in relation to the protection of the environment.

Indeed, one should not expect too much from the environmental correction attempts coming from national administrations of foreign trade, or from WTO, because the volume of the international trade has always been a small part of the total volume of goods traded in the world (intermediate and final goods traded at national and international level).

We have to additionally clarify that, in relation to traded "polluting" productions, the role of the WTO has been modest and self-restrictive, and mainly consisting of commercially penalising those countries that have remained far away from the environmental norms and taxes ruling in rich countries. Even more, in general, the WTO has driven its control and sanctions just on the contents of imported goods as subjects of consumption, and barely in relation to their production processes,[170] thus mainly ignoring the environmental degradation in exporting countries.[171] Even more, reactions of the WTO, allegedly to protect the environment, are usually initiated only on the basis of claims posed by importing parties.

169. Note that the WTO uses the unanimity rule for reaching breakthroughs, a rule that is non-operative because it gives a real veto-right to any country.

170. The so-called Singapore issues, repeatedly rejected by developing countries, included new trade-linked issues such as Investment and Trade, Competition Policy, Transparency in government procurement, and Trade facilitation.

171. Esty, D. (1994). *Greening the GATT: Trade, Environment and the Future*. Washington D.C.: Institute for International Economics. p.51.

Historical Evolution of International Trade Rules and Environment

To start with, we have to state that the environment did not receive significant attention when in 1948 the GATT was created. This lack of attention reflected the almost nil importance conceded in those days by founding-countries to ecological issues. Despite of it, article XX of the Agreement provided numerous exceptions to the principle of the "most-favoured nation", also including exceptions related to national environmental regulation.[172]

In particular we could here quote article XX(b) (ruling even today, although re-defined) that enables exceptions to the WTO principles, when member-states implement measures 'necessary to protect human, animal, or plant life or health; and article XX(g), that opens a door for special treatment related to the conservation of exhaustible natural resources, provided that members do not make exceptions among imports coming from different countries.

In relation to the evolution of trade rules, we have to say that in the early GATT rounds of negotiations (in the 40s and first 50s) the liberalising concessions were significant in number, but to some extent redundant with other protective instruments. Observe in addition that throughout the period 1948-1979 the agricultural sector received a different treatment than the industrial one, the latter being the basic ground for commercial negotiations in that time span.

Things started changing in the Tokyo Round (1973-1979). With much more countries involved, and a more ambitious agenda, non-tariff barriers (quotas and subsidies) on agricultural products[173] started being discussed although with meagre results. A real achievement of the Tokyo Round was the creation of a code of standards,[174] directed to minimise the use of standards as a non-tariff barrier. Despite

---

172. Note that Art. XX provides exceptions for some considered "illegal actions". These "illegal actions" were defined at the inception of GATT to mainly protect public morals or to preserve national heritage. Although not mentioning the word "environment", sections XX(b) and XX(g) enable a certain flexibility in interpretation, thus providing importing countries with an element for environmental protection, when WTO rules on trade. Vide Cole, M. (2000: 10). Book already mentioned.

173. In relation to discussions on quotas and subsidies, we should here mention the case of the Common Agricultural Policy of the then CE, and the significant subsidies to national agriculture products granted by the US and Canada governments.

174. This code is only applicable to its signatories, which are bound to follow the established guidelines for applied standards, with prior notification to other signatories.

this agreement, nations continued at convenience imposing stricter standards in order to protect "human, animal or plant life and the environment", as today underlined in the re-defined Art. XX(b).

Finally, in the Uruguay Round (1995), the focus was on: 1) addressing the different treatment of the agricultural sector[175] with respect to the industrial one; 2) projecting reductions of non-tariff barriers in the mentioned two sectors; 3) inclusion of more countries, in particular developing ones; and 4) extension of the coverage of GATT to: trade of services, intellectual property, and trade related investments.

Indeed, the most significant area of purported advance in the Uruguay Round was that of the "markets accessibility". In fact, after this Round, trade in agricultural goods resulted progressively aligned with that of the industrial ones, while all forms of protection other than tariffs became illegal.[176] Another relevant area of reform was that related to export subsidies; in particular, Art. XVI of the Agreement declared illegal the use of such subsidies, with the exception of those referred to agricultural products.

Limited Relevance of WTO Trade rules for the Protection of Environment

Turning again to environment, we have to say that the Uruguay Round extended the scope of the "technical barriers" to trade—formerly accepted and signed in the Tokyo Round—to processes and methods of production, thus advancing[177] in relation to the Tokyo achievements.

The Uruguay Round also affected other aspects related to environment. First of all, direct payments by governments to Agriculture (subsidies) were allowed, provided that they were used for the improvement of the environment (reforestation, etc.). Secondly, the Uruguay Round also agreed to a rule on the Application of

175. Breakthroughs were made in all areas used for supporting domestic agriculture: market access; export subsidies; etc. Regrettably, implementation has not followed committed agreements.

176. Mentioned Agreement stated that no new non-tariff barrier would be created, while all existing non-tariff barriers should in future be converted into tariffs.

177. We have to underline that these process and production methods are officially considered just when they leave a trace in the final product. If for example, the production of a good leaves a trace of the use of a banned chemical intermediate good, national authorities of the importing country could legitimately prevent the import of the final product.

Sanitary and Phytosanitary measures; a rule that was signed to prevent interested and exaggerated use by importing countries of certain ad hoc norms to defend their own productions.

Finally, in the context of the most important achievement of the Uruguay Round—the setting up of the WTO—a new organism was created in 1995: the Committee on Trade and Environment (CTE). This committee drafted a Report that, presented at the Ministerial Conference in Singapore, posed a series of possible legal restrictions to trade, on the bases of the use of certain undesirable production processes.[178] As expectable from the then political climate, this proposal was rejected.

Note that the CTE suggested in its report the convenience of reaching multilateral environmental agreements (MEA) in order to tackle global environment problems, thus discarding—as basically useless—individual ad hoc actions to solve mentioned problems. A further issue addressed by the CTE was that related to the export of domestically prohibited goods. This was done on the wake of complaints addressed by developing countries to the GATT on the fact that hazardous substances were being exported to them.[179] As a result, the so-called Basel Convention established a deal in relation to trade of hazardous substances.

Summarising,[180] we could say that the GATT-WTO provisions for the protection of the environment are still minimal. In fact, most of the undertaken incipient actions have been realised in the aftermath of the Uruguay Round Agreement. On the other hand, we have to underline that the creation of the CTE within WTO represents just a step in a direction that, due to the WTO organisational defects, does not seem to be the best.

---

178. In this conference, issues related to the so-called social dumping (f.i. when using children as workers), environmental dumping (when producing goods with less restrictive environmental rules), accessibility to public sector procurement, etc., were rejected by developing countries. These countries have till today kept their rejecting positions on these so-called Singapore issues.

179. We could here refer to the recent (attempted) export to India (for scrapping) of the French old carrier "Clemenceau". Finally, this boat returned to France because it contained a big amount of amianthus that—banned in France—could also be lethal for Indian workers. Surprisingly, recently Indian authorities have agreed that the old cruise-ship France, also containing amianthus, will be dismantled in India.

180. Cole, M.A, (2000: 18). Book already mentioned.

Towards a More Integral and Rational Environmental Policy

Taking into account: 1) the current hazardous trends of environmental degradation in many of its aspects, particularly at global level; 2) the trade off between national corrections on global emissions and national competitiveness, at times in a context of poverty; 3) the difficulties to reach multilateral agreements on future corrections of global or regional emissions among different countries with different levels of per capita income; 4) the historical and current structure of responsibilities for global environment degradation, in which rich countries regrettably keep the leadership; 5) the present growing pressure on raw materials and non-renewable resources, particularly after the recent embodiment of emerging Asia (China and India) into the process of growth; and 6) the current trend towards democratisation in the world, we do believe that a new multilateral organisation on environment with capacity of enforcement will have to be created.

We have already mentioned in Chapter 4 that the provision of global public goods—as for instance the protection of the global environment as discussed here—will require the promotion of a new and democratic UN, this being the sole way for significantly improving global governance in the field of the global public goods and externalities.

In this regard, we should not forget that for democratic decision-making, UN bodies would have to be supported by a majority of popular votes.[181] Logically, this will force the current rich western countries (in minority of population) to cede power to majorities (Asians). If this cession does not become a fact, current negative trends in the provision of global public goods—including environment—would continue; and consequently mankind would be doomed to also fail in the protection of the environment.

Contrary to our proposal—based on the consideration that public goods of different levels should be administrated by democratic bodies positioned at each level, including a multilateral one charged

181. Decision-making based on non-weighted votes of member-countries in a new UN would not be a democratic procedure. Indeed, to attribute the same weighting vote to Malta than to China would be nonsense from a democratic perspective.

with the administration of global public goods (also environment)—some authors, perhaps purporting being "more realistic", have just recommended in relation to environment protection the creation of a World Environmental Organisation (WEO*)[182] depending on the current non-democratic UN.

According to them, this organisation—to be created to overcome dysfunctions of the ruling Multilateral Environment Agreements (MEA)[183]—would raise the level of international environment policy-making to a similar status as that of trade policy-making (WTO), thus (allegedly) better protecting the environment. Mentioned WEO*, which could operate in a similar way and with a similar organisation as the WTO, could embody current existing institutions such as the United Nations Environment Programme (UNEP)[184] and the United Nations Fund for Climate Change Control (UNFCCC).

It is our view however that, concerning global environment, suggested WEO* will not be able of bringing democratic and workable solutions for four main reasons: 1) Due to the likely inefficiency of this WEO* in relation to decision-making (consensus)[185] in a field in which future national competitiveness will be the key variable determining the member-states preferences; 2) because at the end of the day, emerging conflicts with other multilateral institutions (f.i., with WTO) would have to be solved either by an arbiter or by an Economic Security Council (as suggested) commanded by the current veto owners in the UN Security Council, which would not provide a

---

182. WEO* is the one proposed by mentioned authors. Note that WEO as proposed by us, will be an offspring of our proposed democratic UN.

183. Leaving aside the Kyoto Protocol, the most important MEA ruling today is the so-called Montreal Protocol, (also) signed in 1997, in relation with the use of CFCs, a substance that allegedly damages the ozone layer. Note that these agreements (MEA) contain, in general, "trade based enforced mechanisms" to prevent free riders undermine them. For instance, the Montreal Protocol forbids its signatories from trading with non-signatories in products containing CFCs.

    Leaving aside increased claims against mentioned agreements (MEA)—presented at times as contrary to the WTO rules—these MEA contain an additional problem of consensus in relation to agreement-building. As a result, agreed standards have been, or could be in future, of a very low restricting level, thus not sufficiently encouraging nations for enforcing better standards in domestic production, or for averting imported goods that could potentially harm the global environment.

184. Cole, M. (2000: 19). Book already mentioned.

185. In the current non-democratic global context, an organisation for dealing with specific problems, as that of mentioned WEO—always of voluntary embodiment—would also have to work on the base of unanimity (consensus).

democratic solution; 3) because the funding of (suggested) WEO* by members would be problematic, given the fact that this institution would lack democratic legitimacy to define global environmental taxes (on new pollutions); and 4) above all, because without previous democratisation of the institution for levying progressive per capita taxes on accumulated global environment degradation—related with the degree of development of the different countries—acceptation by developing countries of restricting rules on current and future industrial production would be practically impossible.

Additionally, if this institution—as deducible from current conservative ambience in rich countries—was created with a small budget, was not democratically organised as it currently happens with many other multilateral institutions stemming from the current UN, and was mainly devised for the realisation of studies and as a forum for discussion and decision (like WTO), current hazardous trends in environmental issues and resources depletion would continue in detriment of the sustainability of the Earth environment.

In such a defective institutional context, uncertainty on the long run supply of raw materials and basic resources (including oil and drinking water), likely conducive to political instability, will *sine die* remain, thus prompting deceleration of the real GDP growth rate and eventual reduction of middle classes in many countries, which could additionally undermine democracies.

As the reader may imagine, the setting up of an international (multilateral) democratic organisation[186]—a new democratic UN with the assignment of providing global public goods and correcting global externalities, as well as with capacity for the enforcement of own resolutions—will not be easy; but in the long term it will have to be created because it would be the sole institution capable of solving the current pending common problems.

Summary of the Chapter

We have started the Chapter with the description of the current

186. Note that, although having in some cases rendered significant services to the cause of peace and equality, the current UN is just a poor caricature of democracy, and as a consequence a useless political machinery to guaranty a healthy global environment, and the sustainability of capitalism and democracy.

situation and trends of environment and natural resources availability. After paying attention to some geographical aspects (urban or rural; and local, national, or global) of the environmental problem, we have made a clear reference to the most prominent losers (at mid-long term) of the current deterioration of the environment: the poor of the world, who mainly live in countryside (around 50% of global population live in rural areas, and 75% of total poor live in countryside), and many of them in South Asia and Sub Sahara Africa.

In relation to water availability, we have underlined the dramatic situation of Sub Sahara; but we have also mentioned that, in 2020, 2/3rd of the total population of the world will likely be submitted to a situation of growing scarcity of water. We have also referred to the underlying problem of water quality—which negatively affects life expectancy and labour productivity of workers—a problem that is today mainly touching Africans and Latin Americans.

In relation to climate change—provoked by the growing consumption of fossil fuels—and associated responsibilities, we have stated that, as an average, the high-income countries consume nowadays five times more energy in per-capita terms than the mid-low income countries. This means that with a 16 per cent of the total population, rich countries consume around 50 per cent of all consumed energy.

We have additionally mentioned that, of all energy consumed in the world today (2003) only a small part of it (13%) is clean energy, with only 4.5 per cent coming from new energy sources (3.1% in 1970). This means that the latter, conversely to what is desired, has not grown especially fast.

Deepening into climate change, we have reviewed the antecedents, commitments and capabilities of the Kyoto Protocol (signed in 1997) in order to significantly reduce in future the emissions of CO_2 (responsible for climate change). After conceding that the Kyoto Protocol introduced a significant innovation, the marketable "pollution permits"—a system of pollution-control non-exempted of problems—we have underlined that, as expectable, this Multilateral Environment Agreement (MEA) as others, has not resulted totally inclusive (many of the main polluters are not committed), its targets have been clearly insufficient to tackle the problem, and the definition and distribution of responsibilities in relation to CO_2 emissions, in the past or in the future, has really been ill formulated.

Continuing with climate change, we have depicted the overwhelming problems of human resettlements (massive cross-border migrations of 150-200 million people towards already inhabited territories) that a continuation of the Earth warming would induce in next decades. Note that these problems could only be solved peacefully in the context of a new democratic UN.

Without overlooking the success of the Montreal Protocol (signed in 1997)—a special MEA that practically solved the problem of the growing hole in the ozone layer induced by the use of CFC—and after commenting other MEA and failing interventions in the transport sector (CO_2 emissions), we have entered into the description of two economic activities that create significant global externalities: fisheries (in international waters) and the over-exploitation of rainforest.

After describing the characteristics of the traditional analysis and management of fisheries (mainly focused on species and referring to stocks sizes, captures, etc.), and after recommending an analytical shift towards ecosystems, we have entered into the discussion on the sustainability of stocks, finally suggesting moderation in captures as the FAO has recently done. This recommendation by FAO has been neglected by many of the involved stakeholders (governments, fishers, etc.) which, behaving as free riders, have induced non-sustainability of most main species. Once again, we have expressed that on this issue—as on others connected with the existence of global public goods and externalities—creation of a multilateral body backed by a new democratic UN will be essential.

Absence of (internal) democracy or malfunctions of it, particularly in developing countries, has been particularly relevant in the explanation of the failed (national) tropical rainforest administration. Note that, apart from Earth warming, excessive deforestation also induces erosion, clogging of watercourses, reduction of the storage capacity of dams, etc.; effects that should be avoided.

Due to the link of deforestation with global warming, we have also recommended the creation of a global rainforest administration that should also depend, through WEO, on a new democratic UN.

For facilitating the understanding of the current and future environmental policy, we have also entered in Chapter 5 into a theoretical consideration of externalities and environment. In this regard, we have described the so-called market failures, in particular those referring to public goods and externalities.

Concerning externalities, we have first of all analysed some private solutions (in particular those stemming from the theorem of Coase). Nevertheless, private approaches have been discarded as a general solution when there are many parties involved; when some or many of the involved parties lack interest in co-operation, which necessarily will induce "free riding"; or when high transaction and information costs appears as to keep all parties united.

Then after, we have entered into the analysis of public solutions to externalities. In relation to those based on the "working of markets", we have described the effects on environment of setting up ad hoc taxes (for instance a carbon tax) for those who pollute (this according to the principle that "those who pollute have to pay"). We have also described the advantages and inconveniencies generated by public subsidies to pollution abatement; and also the advantages and inconveniences of the so-called "cap and trade" schemes, currently the most fashionable system, consisting of setting up ceilings to emissions followed by the distribution of permits to pollute, which may be traded. We have finally described other ways of addressing pollution, as for instance direct controls, via outputs or inputs.

Certain peculiarities of the political treatment of externalities (national or global) have also been considered: 1) homogenisation or not of the fiscal treatment of national externalities and its consequences for the external trade; 2) appearance of trans-boundaries externalities, required for their correction of Regional Environment Agreements (REA); and 3) the case of existence of global externalities in which the problems of building agreements and enforcement rules, are in general unsolvable, even with resort to the so-called Multilateral Environment Agreements (MEA). It is our view that in that case, an integral treatment of the problem by a multilateral institution in charge (WEO), embodied into a new democratic UN, will be essential.

The analysis of the externalities has ended with comments on the influence of democratisation processes on environmental policies. Empirical evidence proves that factual concentration of power is often conducive to environmental degradation.

In general, in non-democratic societies—let us remember that the global society is not democratic—the winners of the political process, the rich, use to shift the environmental costs to the poor (or to future generations), because the transfer of pollution to them will be "legal" and cheap. As a consequence, democratisation (national or global), which in general will empower the poor, will change the society into one prone to protect the rights of the weaker.

This means that if we talk about global emissions or externalities—emissions of CO_2, administration of fisheries in international waters, control of exploitation of rainforests with global effects, etc.—a global policy on these matters should have to be decided and enforced in a new body (WEO) depending on a new democratic UN.

Looking for the global causes of climate change, we have subsequently entered into a description of the incidence of economic growth on environment. Following a brief historical consideration on the scant interest of economists of the 19th century and first decades of the 20th on the relations between economics and nature (till the pioneering works of Pigou and Hotelling), we have reviewed the first environmental warnings of Boulding and, above all, those contained in the Report of the Club of Rome.

Following criticism on the exaggerated (pessimistic) conclusions of the Club of Rome, we have entered into the analysis of the so-called "sustainable development", a concept that, in its different versions—weak and strong—took shape in the 1980s. Indeed, only a weak version of sustainability, just "committed" to transfer to following generations a volume of total capital (natural and man-made) equivalent to that currently existent, has today permeated the conscience of the global society. Nevertheless, given the fact that natural and man-made capital forms are not substitutes, some economists have defended the idea that a great part of the past growth rates has just been a pure fiction, because corresponding environment degradation and natural resources depletion have not been subtracted from the calculated GDP series.

Looking deep into this problem of incorrect growth measurement, we have considered two modern indicators of production and welfare such as the "net-net saving", or the so-called "Measure of Economic Welfare", as being capable of substituting with advantage, or at least complementing the inaccurate and often misguiding concept of GDP.

Chapter 5 has also entered into the description of the so-called Kuznets Environmental Curve (KEC). This is a U-invested curve that—relating per capita emissions with per capita GDP—proves that, in relation with some specific emissions of a local or national scope of easy correction at short-mid term, there is a turning point after which per capita GDP growth will induce reduction of per-capita emissions. Unfortunately, this KEC hypothesis has not worked in relation to global emissions, which in our view will only be tamed in the long run by the setting up of a new democratic global UN, today inexistent.

We have analysed as well the incidence of the different growth stages of nations on national (heterogeneous) environmental legislations, industrial dislocation, and international trade. Particularly, a brief analysis of the official treatment given by GATT and WTO to the environmental issue along the different processes of negotiations (Trade Rounds) has been made, and we have concluded that indirect penalisations in customs of goods whose prices do not include environmental costs, will by no means be sufficient as to protect global environment.

Chapter 5 has ended with a comment on the possible policies earmarked to improve the global environment and to protect renewable and non-renewable common resources. Given the traits of the exploitation of mentioned resources, prone to gather free-riding behaviour, thus inducing progressive worsening of global environment and resources depletion, our recommendation is the creation of a WEO depending on a democratic UN, charged with the administration and enforcement of adopted rules.

In front of our proposal, other authors, trying to preserve national sovereignty, only have dared to suggest the building up of new MEA (or REA for regional environmental problems) or the improvement of the old ones; or at most, the creation—as suggested—of a World Environment Organisation (WEO*), with a similar political structure (based on paralysing consensus) as that of current WTO.

However, difficulties in the construction of consensus for decision making (rule of unanimity instead of majority), likely emergence of coordination problems with WTO, assumed lack of capabilities for homogenisation of taxation (connected with global environmental issues), and a likely small budget for the institution given the current neo-liberal economic trends on the planet, are traits that do not enable to expect a sufficient delivery from such a "new" multilateral (WEO*) institution depending on current non-democratic UN.

6

Capitalism and Democracy in the 21st Century

Democratic Global Governance for Sustainability

Current State of the Democracy-Capitalism Combination

It is well known that new ideas in the domain of social sciences (economics and politics) do not use to dislodge the old ones till the moment in which the latter are almost unanimously judged as unworkable.[1]

The extent at which the world today is moving forward in a fast but chaotic way, with a significant number of variables that no one controls[2] but that are seriously affecting all human beings, we do believe that the moment for the initiation of a radical change in the conception of how to provide global public goods and how to administer global externalities has finally arrived. Of course, such change of conception will necessarily have to take place in consistency with the values of democracy, values to which the world is progressively committed.

It is surprising that worldwide only a handful of professional economists have seriously criticised the current and wrong approach to globalisation, while political scientists have hardly promoted democratisation of the UN for the legitimate funding and provision of global public goods (peace, security, global environment, space and sea exploration, global economic regulation, etc.) and for the correction of global externalities (administration of renewable and non-renewable common natural resources).

---

1. In this regard, vide. among other methodological approaches, that of Kuhn, T. (1971). *The Structure of the Scientific Revolutions*. Website.
2. We are here referring to certain global public goods and externalities.

Fear to disagree with the mainstream and subsequent consequences on the professional careers of critics—as explained by Feyerabend[3]—has caused the absence of significant and founded criticism in relation to the current deficiencies of globalisation and the detrimental absence of a global democracy. Instead of introducing new original ideas, the main contribution of international leaders and scholars has been just to streamline the already non-delivering political machineries.[4]

However, the major pending issues that mankind will have to confront in next decades will necessarily force the dislodging of obsolete economic and political ideas; and also the abandonment of non-democratic international practices carried out nowadays by a self-selected number of privileged rich countries, which many a times speak and act on behalf of the "international community"[5] without having been invited to do so.

Criticism on the current "going back to basics" in the micro-economic field (pure neo-classicism) as initiated in the Reagan-Thatcher time, should have started or intensified in the very 80s when the theoretical and practical economic pendulum started moving in favour of exaggerated privatisation and purported short-term efficiency. Note that this "going back to basics" laid the foundations for a renewed wealth concentration and worsening of the personal income distribution, this time at a global scale.

As far as sustainability of (national) democracies requires well-extended middle classes, and the construction of global democracy will encourage widespread national democratisation, it is absolutely necessary that current capitalism urgently repairs the distributive leaks (nationally and globally) that the said going-back-to-basics has produced; and this in order to guarantee the future floatability of the democratic system.

---

3. Feyerabend (1975). *Against the Method.* New Left Books.

4. It is well known that the recently attempted UN-reforms have not entered either in the issue of the decision-making concerning common affaires in the UN and its agencies, or in the necessary taking over of certain global functions or activities, till the moment inefficiently, and at times illegitimately, provided by some privileged states.

5. Many times, when referring to the interests of the "international community", they mainly allude to those of the West, which only counts with 16.6 per cent of the total population of the World. This implies the neglect of the interests of the majority (83.4%), the developing world.

Note that the current risk of democratic failure in individual nations, stemming from the recent supremacy assigned to short-term "efficiency" in detriment of "equity" and "social protection", may today be similar or higher than that observed one hundred years ago—in times of "traditional capitalism"—when problems of global warming and climate change did not exist, and when the global concentration of income and wealth were less acute.

After having explained in previous chapters many new phenomena observed in the economic and political spheres, and before drawing some conclusions and recommendations, we will summarise in the lines below the main data and findings of our book.

Profile of the World at the Beginning of the 21st Century

Although for a while it was thought that with the end of the Cold War (in 1991) the international political tensions would disappear, thus giving way to a long period of political stability under the assumed US hegemony, the reality of the 90s and the first half of 2000s has paradoxically confirmed the opposite.

Among the variables and factors that in the last 15 years have induced rising international tensions among nations we could quote: 1) The progressive poisoning of the Israel-Palestine conflict, in which the continuation of a biased "mediation" of the West has increased the degree of tension between the Arab-Muslim world and the West; and this while Arab-Muslim countries continue producing a significant part of the oil needed by Western countries; 2) The war against international terrorism as declared by the US, a war impossible to be won by means of conventional military attacks on formal states (Afghanistan or Iraq); 3) The unconcealed manoeuvres of the US by means of increasing the number of its military bases in several Euro-Asian countries and islands, in order to consolidate its international political advantage, thus upsetting Russia which, being even today a political superpower and UN veto-owner, may also use its "energy weapon" (mainly gas) against those disturbing it; 4) The trend of certain "peculiar" states to endow themselves with nuclear weaponry in order to guarantee their own survival; something rejected by Western nuclear powers through the UN Non Proliferation Treaty; 5) The appearance on the economic global scene of two new mega-powers, China and India, that in some decades may drive the historical and present relevance of some individual EU countries to unimportance; and 6) The continuation or accentuation, in a context of full and live information, of the mistreatment of developing countries by the rich ones, materialised in: a) a registered reduction of the Official Development Assistance (ODA) in real terms and in terms of the donors-GDP during a great part of the period, mainly in the 90s; b) the FDI coming from the West, which only attends to the more relevant developing countries, including exporters of expensive raw materials, and not to the poorest LDC; c) a very limited access of the poorest developing countries to relevant markets (agriculture and services) in the industrialised world; d) a growing western pressure for opening internal markets of developing nations to industrial imports and FDI coming from the West; and e) a biased and very limited possibility of human migration from South to North.

Besides international political and economic tensions, generalised worsening of the internal income distribution has in the last 15 years been consistent with a new move towards short-term "consumerism" in many industrialised and developing countries. In the last years, reckless provision by western central banks (mainly those of US and EU) of exceeding liquidity to fight against cyclical downturns, has developed—via low interest rates and wealth effects on assets—a general trend towards progressive borrowing of families to consume more and more industrial goods in a physically non-sustainable way and in detriment of the global environment.

In connection with these undesirable economic changes towards consumerism, one should not forget other problems stemming from the current western philosophy of life, also tilted towards radical individualism. A philosophy that: 1) has exaggeratedly returned towards short term efficiency in detriment of equity, thus forgetting the destitute (nationals or foreigners) as if they could not react against injustice, and 2) forced people in many countries to work more and more hours in detriment of their necessary leisure, and 3) encouraged irrational consumerism instead of environmental protection, and 4) promoted the homogenisation of culture and habits of different peoples, at times even in detriment of enriching diversity.

Note that this "modern" way of life is today scantly disputed; and this as if consumerism, significant downgrading of national and international equity, quasi-absence of leisure for a relevant part of mankind, and progressive environment deterioration could be sustainable.

On the Global Economic Situation After Three Decades (1973-2007) of Liberalisation

We have analysed in Chapters 2 and 5 the current economic situation of the world, its recent history and its expected evolution. This has been done because some of its trends—growth with unfair distribution and environmental degradation—are introducing elements of economic and political non-tenability that, in our view, could only be corrected by means of introducing democratic global governance.

Economic trends have been deduced from the credited figures of Professor Maddison, completed with available economic information up to 2007. After considering the evolution of GDP, population growth, and per capita GDP, in relation to the different regions of the world, it has become patent that the period 1973-2007 has been the period of Asia; a period of comparative rapid growth in this continent that will likely last several decades more in the first half of the 21st century.

Additional characteristics of this period 1973-2007 have been: the reduction of the global population growth rate; the problem of ageing of many national populations, particularly in Europe and Japan, and the multifaceted African drama, intensified by the extraordinary; population growth rate (near 3 per cent) in a period (1973-1998) in which the "golden age of capitalism" was already over.

The main cause of the registered economic shift towards Asia in the past 25 years has been the entrance of China, and later India, in the international division of labour. Note that the huge comparative advantage in industry and some services of these two countries—stemming from low wages and long working hours of labourers, combined with the use of modern technology imported from the West—may induce another three or four decades of rapid growth. This expected long period of rapid growth is mainly related to the existence of a huge amount of active population (around 400 and 350 million in China and India respectively) currently attached to rural activities, that will be transferred to other sectors at a speed that will depend on the limited capacity of annual absorption of employment by non-agricultural sectors.

In the West, artificial accumulation up to the 90s of industrial jobs with high wages had necessarily to result—after the liberalisation of capital movements in the first 90s—in a process of industrial dislocation and outsourcing, mainly towards Asia. On the other hand, the continuation of segmentation of national labour markets, in a context of full information, had to induce growing illegal migration to the West, mainly stemming from the huge wage gap and the lack of decent job opportunities in LDC.

Indeed, while engineering a self-interested, slow and partial economic liberalisation in the period 1945-1990 (mainly focused on international trade of industrial goods and raw materials, while forgetting other sectors and labour markets), the West introduced a severe dysfunction, which artificially enlarged the wage-gap between developed and developing nations while hindering the growth of employment in poorer countries.

In this context of artificially enlarged wage-gap, additional steps towards globalisation undertaken from 1990 onwards, although favouring a mild reduction of the absolute number of the poor in the world (people under the poverty line) they have been negative for many in terms of national income distribution. Indeed, over the past 16 years the personal income distribution has worsened in most countries in all continents: 1) in the developed countries mainly due to the industrial dislocation towards Asia and the competition of imports induced by low Asian wages in combination with rocketing profits in Western MNC; and 2) in Asia due to the temporary semi-stagnant salaries (agriculture and other sectors), a typical result of the first stages of the development process, as explained by Lewis, and reflected in the well-known Kuznets curve on economic progress and personal income distribution.

Some partial observers, exclusively focusing on the relative reduction of the number of poor in the world, have constantly proclaimed the success of the recent steps towards globalisation. However, mentioned reduction of the number of poor has not deactivated the increasing social malaise in many developing countries and LDCs since, due to the existing full and live information across the planet, only unconditional economic convergence—if it had moved at significant speed—and improved personal income distribution, could have created strong expectations and hope among the poor.

In relation to such "unconditional convergence", we have deduced from macroeconomic figures and analysis of Maddison, Stiglitz, UNDP, etc., and against less credible conclusions of others—mainly Sala-i-Martin—that far from converging, the world today is more uneven than ever.

Observe additionally that despite unfair commercial rules and biased globalisation, developing countries—particularly Asians—have in the last 10-15 years rapidly gained share in the total world trade, reaching today a figure of 29.6 per cent of total exports. Note also that, in the last 10 years (1995-2005), the annual average of intra-regional growth rates of exports of goods has been higher in all developing regions than the total world average; and this while corresponding figures in the West have been inferior to the said average.

In particular, in last 10 years (1995-2005) the two Asian macro-regions commanded by China and India, have increased their mutual exports at annual rates of 16-17 per cent, around the double of the average growth rate of trade (7.8 per cent) of the world; a circumstance that combined with the rapid GDP growth rates of China and India confirms the unavoidable shift of the economic gravity centre of the world towards Asia.

On the Non-tenable International Political Institutions

From our analysis one may clearly deduce that the current political situation and most of the current international political institutions in the world are not tenable in the long run due to diverse political and economic reasons: 1) Existence of global public goods (peace, security, global environment, space and sea exploration, etc.) and global externalities, whose desirable and democratic provision and correction do not match with the current non-democratic political institutions of the world: UN, Security Council, NATO, US Army and allies, Kyoto Protocol and other MEAs, UN Programmes, G-8, G-20, Quartets, etc. In fact, most of these formal or informal institutions or organs were not designed either for the democratic provision of mentioned public goods or for the correction of global externalities, but with other purposes; 2) As a result of the current international political structure, the setting up of priorities and provision of global public goods and correction (or disregard) of global externalities affecting all mankind, is defined by a self-selected group of countries—the West, commanded by the US—which, counting only with 1/6th of the world population, tries, but with progressively less success, to impose its will on the rest (5/6th of the total population); and 3) Current multilateral institutions, based on treaties "among equals", and mostly not totally inclusive, are clearly obsolete to many of their purported ends, and do not serve any longer to solve relevant common problems of mankind.

Although some successful interventions (cease-fires, food-aid, etc.) have partially put the important failures of the current UN (failures in conflict resolution, global environment protection, etc.) in disguise, the reality is that significant political problems have remained with us since the very birth (1945) of the UN.

Cases as the Israel-Palestine one or that of Kashmir, both alive since 1947-48, generating several wars in each case, and constant tensions, with relevant spill-over effects on the international community—particularly in the first one in which a community of 1.5 billion people (Muslims) has felt humiliated by the West—prove that the UN has only worked to solve problems in which the main players were not directly affected. Note that this is a logical derivative of the political (non-democratic) power structure of the UN as designed at its inception. Observe as well that in the past 60 years and in major international political crisis (Cuban missiles crisis, fall of the Soviet Union, India-Pakistan mutual nuclear threat, etc.) the UN hardly played a role.

To the former political tragedies, we should add the scant practical attention of the current international political structure to certain aspects of the economic growth of the planet: 1) the growing internal and external inequality of the personal income distribution; 2) the progressive destruction of the global environment; and 3) the progressive depletion of natural resources; issues in which the West has—by action or omission—a major responsibility.

In consistency with mentioned lack of delivery of the UN in relation to global public goods and externalities, often provoked by veto-owners, western states have for long focused their "multilateral" activities (in the UN or in other institutions) on issues that could give them advantage in political and economic domination: the "selective" enforcement of the Non Proliferation Treaty (NPT), and the attainment of successful (for the West) trade and energy negotiations. When convenient, democracy has been selectively promoted by the West as an instrument for changing adverse regimes, and not at all to encourage indispensable "global democracy", in which they would be in minority.

Socio-economic Micro-changes and Sustainability

Leaving aside the main current trends and problems in global economics and international politics, we will now refer to other significant micro-changes, some of them negative, which may progressively undermine capitalism and democracy.

Indeed, to the dramatic reduction of private cost of transports (excluding the social ones) and to the manifold applications of the ICT revolution, both of them positive phenomena that have significantly increased labour productivity and reduced unitary costs of production, we should add some negative sociological changes—towards irrational individualism and destructive consumerism—nowadays occurring in the West and in many developing countries.

Mentioned trend towards individualism re-blossomed in the past 80s when public micro-interventionism started ebbing in the West, and the alternative doctrine that encouraged collective but inefficient solutions (radical socialism and communism) bankrupted.

In absence of visible alternatives, western economies (and many others) turned towards a sort of capitalism, not concerned with equity, that preached as valid for all countries and circumstances, the absolute pre-eminence of the private sector in production and trade, the indispensable freedom in internal and external markets, the necessary discipline and balance in public and external accounts as well as in monetary affairs, etc.

The purported economic expectations from this approach were a continuous growth—based on the rapidly growing productivity of labour—and absence of cyclical fluctuations induced by a better knowledge in relation to the administration of the economies. Indeed, a naïve expectation that vanished with the bursting of the IT bubble at the beginning of 2000; and again in 2007 when the global community was shaken by another episode of bubble bursting, this time starting in the (sub-prime) mortgages market in the US.

Mentioned trend towards economic privatisation and liberalisation without social concern—which meant a revival of traditional capitalism—materialised in the degradation of the social protection systems (mainly in Europe), and in the non-development of these systems in many developing countries. Note that this non-development has made the creation of broad middle classes in developing countries difficult, thus hindering in these countries the promotion of sustainable democracies.

In this regard, one should not forget that an overdone trend towards individualism and totally free markets often ignores the efficiency of some forms of collective consumption (for instance urban public transport), and the long-term effectiveness of public environmental protection and correct administration of natural resources.

Even more, in a context of informed societies, the induction of sub-optimal (personal) income distribution by the recent approach to neoclassical-capitalism has tended (and will *ceteris paribus* tend) to create internal unrest as well as international political problems. In relation to the latter, one should not underestimate the negative influence of the West on the developing world. Note in this regard that Western governments—instead of facilitating unconditional economic convergence for promoting stability—have for long induced divergence, either willingly (by means of establishing biased trade rules, providing scant ODA, or limiting migration) or somewhat unwillingly (providing many developing countries with scant FDI, etc.).

Current capitalism also hides other negative socio-economic and political trends that we have detected: 1) A polarised pursuance of "short-term" micro-efficiency with an overdone derivative concerning working time as a strategic variable for increasing competitiveness; and 2) A propensity to hastily homogenise culture and political organisation.

In relation to short-term efficiency, the issue of working schedules has recently gained plenty of attention, particularly in Western Europe, where political leaders constantly recommend that working time of labourers should not be reduced but increased, since—in their view—this would enable to improve the competitiveness of Western Europe in front of Asia (and some Eastern European countries). However, as we have explained, competitiveness may be restored or offset by other procedures, as for instance a depreciation of the national currency (the Euro in the EU case) in combination with other supportive policies, when a collective decision for cutting down the weekly working schedule is made.

We have to emphasise that working time and leisure form one of the most important "trade offs" in human life. In this regard we do believe that leisure time, or time for socialisation, should not be minimised because its reduction has negative consequences on the psychological health of individuals and on family life. As a consequence, we do believe that in the 21st century leisure time should be considered as a merit to be protected by the governments, and not as a useless time for the economic game, as some neo-liberals use to proclaim.

Exaggeration on the convenience of working more hours per week, enables firms to force their labourers "to live to work", while "more moderately working to live" would not only be in the interest of workers—who therefore would have more leisure time—but also in favour of the environmental protection by means of reducing over-consumption.

Fast and forced homogenisation in cultural and political life across the world neither does make any sense nor is globally democratic. In fact, to put pressure on local communities to hastily force homogenisation (westernisation) in some cultural behaviours and alleged human rights (for instance forcing free multi-party elections in poor and multi-ethnic or multi-religious communities), and even in the way of organising the economy (forcing hasty introduction of recommendations of the Washington Consensus, etc.) has many a time been counterproductive and resulted, occasionally, in civil wars.

As history has repeatedly proven, cultural, economic and political peculiarities of countries use to automatically change along the economic development, and along their progress in education and knowledge. Consequently, relevant homogenisation is rather a matter of time and sufficient economic development support. But contrary to inertial trends along economic development, we opine that essential (when non-irrational) cultural peculiarities should be preserved.

A Global Contradiction: Purported Competition in Economics and Hegemony (Monopoly) in Politics

After describing global economic and political data, their implicit trends, and some microeconomic contradictions or irrationalities in the world today, we have devoted special attention to a nuclear contradiction of the current capitalism-democracy combination. Observe in this regard that the so-called unique competitive economic system, as defined and defended in the 90s by the Washington Consensus, is not at all consistent with the current absence of democratic global governance, or, alternatively, with the promotion of a (non-competitive) political uni-polar world as it came into fashion after September 2001.

To understand such inconsistency, one should note that, within western democratic countries, the market economy (capitalism) and other aspects of common interest of citizens, including defence, justice, police, etc., are ruled by a governing system that establishes regulations and priorities. But observe that mentioned monopolistic power of the state is democratically shared by all franchised citizens, who through political parties and balloting competition, are represented in parliament and government, thus securing a coherent competitive socio-economic and political system, for the prevention of abuse and the promotion of prosperity.

Nevertheless, mentioned (competitive) distribution of socio-economic and political power does not work today at a global level. In fact, after the last steps of economic globalisation (1990-2007), the international distribution of economic power has changed at a world scale, apparently becoming more concentrated than before (and this against the purported target of increased economic competitiveness).

At the same time there has been a factual attempt to monopolise the international political power. And this has occurred against the convenience of averting international abuse, and against the convenience of promoting a global democratisation for the legitimate definition of global priorities and implementation of actions in relation to global public goods or externalities.

In this respect, we believe that to gain consistency and to prevent economic abuse by MNC, a new global democratic governance should be established in the field of international economic affairs, to settle sustainable global economic regulation. But the problems of mankind are not exclusively related to international economic transactions and global economic regulation. There are many other global public goods (peace, security, global environment, etc.) and global externalities which also require—and more urgently than the global economic affairs—global democratic governance to reach fairness and functionality. Indeed, economic globalisation plus the existence of relevant global public goods and externalities have time ago created the need for a new democratic global governance under the authority of a new democratic UN.

Till the moment of arrival to this desirable new democratic global governance for common global issues—under which economic and political competitiveness among actors would be guaranteed, thus preventing abuse and promoting efficiency and equity—we do believe that, following a second best criterion, economic globalisation plus existence of relevant global public goods and externalities requires, as a minimum, the existence of international countervailing powers.

It is paradoxical that in a historical period prone to the extension of (national) democracy (1990-2007) and, consequently, prone to the additional redistribution of (national) power, a political uni-polar world was promoted. Observe that such political uni-polar doctrine defended the twisted idea that the US—to which the rest of western democratic allies should adjust or submit—could easily and for long dominate the world, in "benefit of mankind".

Note that this idea of a uni-polar world tried to re-introduce in history the concept of "benefactor empire", a concept that contains a deep contradiction in terms because it ignores basic or instinctive human tendencies towards self-interested actions, including the appropriation of wealth of others (through different approaches, as wars, political pressure, monopoly prices, biased economic negotiations, seduction, etc.) as explained by Machiavelli. Remember that democracy was reintroduced two centuries ago to oust the tyrant malefactors from power or to oust the illustrated benefactors not interested in counting with the opinion of people for the setting up of political priorities (indeed, the main priority of most politicians, parties, and empires, has historically been to remain in power).

Consistently, the attempted re-introduction of a "benefactor empire" should be considered as a regressive move, if the world wants to shift towards global democratisation for solving the global pending problems. As a proof of such regressive manners, one should note that, even the only multilateral (non-democratic) governing body that the world had in first 2000s, the UN, was placed in a secondary layer by the main global player, following the UNs "political inefficiency" to withhold a "rapid action" (Iraq war), allegedly undertaken in interest of an "international community" that had not authorised the operation.

We do believe that, from a global democratic perspective, this purported Empire, although supported by an internally democratic metropolis, the US—which counts with less than 5 per cent of the population of the planet—cannot arrogate itself the roles of "moral arbiter and neutral mediator". This is because it has many a time acted against the explicit interest of a majority of the world population the developing world—whose representatives were often not consulted or simply ignored.

Additionally, we have the experience on the ground that without counting with the rest of the international community, the US, or minority western coalitions led by it, cannot solve any pending global problem today, such as the correction of global externalities, improvement of the global environment, or upgrading the global security.

Even more, we have to underline that, from the perspective of our concept of "global democracy", indispensable for the fair governance of a sustainable world, the behaviour of the US in global issues has in the last six years been rather undemocratic and paralysing.

Prerequisites for Sustainable Democracy and Capitalism

In Chapter 4 we have also described the mutual interactions between capitalism and democracy not only from a national perspective but also from a global one. Indeed, indispensable reorganisation of the multilateral institutions to provide with democratic legitimacy "global public goods" (peace, human security, global environment, global economic regulation, etc.) and to correct "global externalities", is something that in our view will occur before the end of the first half of the 21st Century. Otherwise environmental sustainability of the planet will not be guaranteed, while conditions for tenability of democracy in some industrialised countries will become progressively degraded, due to growing inequality in income distribution and shrinking middle classes.

From another perspective, we have underlined: a) that, willy-nilly, global capitalism needs at mid-long term global democracy for survival (to rule it); otherwise the current globalisation process would likely reverse due to growing discontent among or within many nations; and b) that democracy needs for its survival mild forms of capitalism, that is to say mixed economies of market. Raw forms of capitalism as recently devised by neo-liberals (alike to "traditional capitalism", as described in Chapter 3) are normally conducive to progressive worsening of the personal income distribution, which may eventually provoke personal insecurity, undermining of democracy, and even failure of the state.

Note that (secular) democracy—although working at any time and in any place on the base of an unpleasant "self-interest axiom" applicable to voters, politicians and bureaucrats—is a political system with moral superiority with respect to any other alternative. Observe as well that democracy is much more than the mere realisation of timely general elections and that national democracy will have to fulfil some conditions to be considered as such. Indeed, extreme economic and social differences among individuals or other heterogeneities (ethnic, religious and regional differences) will make it more convoluted to reach national democracy, or to sustain it.

As a derivative of our analysis of history, we have discarded the wrong (*non-sequitur*) ideas that multiparty elections will necessarily (in any place) bring sustainable democracy; and that democracy will necessarily drive (in any case) to economic development and prosperity.

In order to understand the working of democracy and its sustainability, we have analysed the limits of the democratic debate, stressing the importance of concepts such as the "re-assignation of income vs. its marginal redistribution" and/or the acceptable "equity system" of capitalism. Subsequently, different sorts of majority decisions have been analysed—those of "general interest", the so-called "singled peaked" and those known as "fractional"—being the latter risky for the tenability of democracy. Significant endowments with "windfall" resources—oil or diamonds—that may also avert, or make difficult, reaching democracy or weaken it (in certain countries or situations) have also been considered.

We have found that "re-assignment" of income—that is to say successive and massive political substitution of groups of citizens, rich by poor or vice-versa (or one ethnic group by another), in postings, income, and wealth—results incompatible with durable democracy. We have also observed that socialist systems or capitalistic ones with big public sectors, which implies windfalls for many citizens, are also prone to hinder the development of democracy or to undermine it. We have deduced as well that "pure free market system"—as that desired today by neo-liberals—will likely generate progressive concentration of income and wealth (monopolies, concentrated property, etc.) that will likely tend to deteriorate middle classes and "the degree of acceptance" of capitalism.

With reference to private property or wealth, we have found that sustainability of democracy does not require a "sacred" respect to private property. Indeed, to the extent that some (marginal) income may be re-assigned in democracy without undermining it, re-assignment of some property (or wealth) far from being negative will also be positive for sustainability of democracy. For instance, inheritance taxation, public rights on water and subsoil, limitations on labour contracts, etc., are instruments that, being apparently against private property or freedom of contracting, ultimately play in favour of democracy because they, by introducing more "equity", make capitalism more acceptable. Nevertheless, these considerations should not make us forget that private property is consubstantial to capitalism because it is the materialisation of economic success; a materialisation absolutely necessary for stimulating risky efforts and investments.

We have also confirmed that the existence of a high-extended number of civil servants, particularly when they belong to the political party in power, will not play in favour of democracy either, because re-assignment of income will be relevant in this case. Existence of "social fractions" in a nation, based on ethnicity, religion, geography, etc. will also be counterproductive for sustainability of national democracy, because these parties may participate (for central governance) in coalitions-contra-natura, voting "fractional" and against general interests in order to obtain own economic or political advantage.

In addition, the existence of different levels of public goods makes that the provision of the global ones (peace and human security, global environmental protection, etc.) has also to be democratically carried out for gaining legitimacy. Correspondingly, the history of building democracy will not finish when all countries of the world become (national) democracies—as notionally defended by neo-cons—but when the World as a whole becomes globally democratic.

Situation of the Global Environment

We have found that the most prominent losers in relation to current deterioration of global environment and availability of common resources are the poor of the world; poor, who mainly live in countryside, mostly in South Asia and Sub Sahara Africa (note that around 50 per cent of global population still live in rural areas, and that 75 per cent of the total poor live in countryside).

In relation to water availability, we have underlined the dramatic situation of the Sub-Sahara region; but we have also pointed out that, in 2020, 2/3rd of the total population of the world will be submitted to a growing scarcity of water. Additionally, problems of water quality—which negatively affects life expectancy and labour productivity of workers—will continue being well extended in the developing world.

Concerning responsibilities in relation to climate change, provoked by the growing consumption of fossil fuels, we have stated that the high-income countries consume nowadays, as an average, five times more energy in per-capita terms than the mid-low income countries. This means that with around 16 per cent of the total population of the world, rich countries consume around 50 per cent of all consumed energy.

Note that from all energy consumed in the world (2003) only a small part of it (13 per cent) was clean energy, with only 4.5 per cent points coming from new energy sources (3.1 per cent points in 1970). This means that contrary to desirable, and taking into account the rapid growth of the global consumption of energy, the relative production of clean energy coming from new energy sources has hardly advanced.

In connection with climate change, we have reviewed the antecedents, commitments and capabilities of the Kyoto Protocol (signed in 1997), devised to significantly reduce the emissions of CO_2 (causing earth warming). After conceding that the market of "pollution permits" has been a positive innovation (although not exempt of inconveniences), we have certified that—as expectable—this Multilateral Environment Agreement (MEA) has not been inclusive (many of the main polluters did not commit themselves), its targets have been insufficient to address the problem of climate change, and the distribution of responsibilities in relation to CO_2 emissions has been ill devised, leaving most developing countries aside.

Without overlooking the success of the Montreal Protocol (also signed in 1997)—indeed an exceptional MEA that seriously initiated the correction of the growing hole in the ozone layer induced by the use of CFC—we have also focused on two global externalities with severe incidence in the future availability of collective renewable resources: 1) overdone activity in fisheries (in international waters); and 2) exaggerated exploitation of rainforests.

We have also found that the absence of (internal) democracy often explains the lack of treatment of negative (national) externalities, particularly in developing countries. Empirical evidence proves that concentration of power often results in environmental degradation. In general, in non-democratic societies—let us here remember that the global society is not a democratic one—some individuals or groups in power usually shift the environmental costs to the poor or to future generations, since in non-democratic contexts this transfer of costs will be "legal", easier and cheap (at times at nil cost). Consequently, democratisation, which should empower the poor, will often change the society into more protective of the rights of the weaker.

Making a simple exercise of extrapolation, this means that if we talk about global emissions or global externalities, the global policies to be implemented on these issues should be democratically decided and enforced by a global agency depending on a new democratic UN. Indeed, this change of orientation would empower the poor of the world (developing countries), thus ultimately endowing them with better environment and extended resources availability at mid-long term.

After some theoretical considerations, we have also highlighted the direct incidence of economic growth on environment. Recognising the scant interest of the economists in 19th century and first decades of the 20th for the relations between economics and nature—which for long diverted the endeavours of economists towards an unbalanced analysis of the reality—we have firstly paid attention to the ultra pessimistic warnings on environmental degradation contained in the Report of the Club of Rome.

Following criticism on the exaggerated conclusions of the Club of Rome, we have entered into the analysis of the so-called "sustainable development", a concept that, in its different versions—weak and strong—took shape in the 1980s. Certainly, only a weak version of sustainability—solely "committed" with the transfer to following generations of a volume of total capital (natural and man-made) equivalent to what the former generation received—is today defended by mainstream economists and multilateral institutions. Nevertheless, given the fact that natural and man-made forms of capital are not substitutes, some economists have underlined the existence in the last two centuries of monotonous trends towards progressive deterioration of environment and depletion of natural resources. As a result, they have pointed out that a substantial part of the "registered" GDP growth has been fictitious, since the involved (social) costs of environmental degradation and natural resources depletion have systematically been excluded from the reckoning of GDP.

Looking deep into this problem of the correct growth measurement, we have referred to some modern although insufficiently developed indicators of production and welfare, such as the "net-net saving" or the "Measure of Economic Welfare", both capable of complementing the misguiding GDP as an economic indicator of production and collective welfare.

In relation to the so-called Kuznets Environmental Curve (KEC)—which suggests that there is a turning point after which per capita GDP growth will induce reduction of per-capita emissions—we have insisted on the idea that this KEC hypothesis has not worked, and *ceteris paribus* will not work, in relation to global emissions. The reasons for this failure lie: 1) in the impossibility of correction of global emissions by individual nations at short-mid term; indeed, not being politically rewarding in next elections for any (national) party in power, one should not expect serious national initiatives for the correction of global emissions; and 2) in the practical impossibility of reaching a totally inclusive MEA and of enforcing it for avoiding free riding at a global scale.

Conclusions and Recommendations

Once overviewed the main economic data and trends, and the political findings of our book, we have observed that the mutual interaction between capitalism and democracy are at the core of them.

Although in the world today it is often taken for granted that steady economic prosperity requires underlying capitalism, and that capitalism needs democracy to survive, we have clarified that these statements are only valid if implemented capitalism and democracy adjust to the concept of sustainability.

Indeed, a lack of adjustment to sustainability is the reason why, historically, some forms of democratisation have not guaranteed either sustainability of democracy or economic prosperity. Mentioned non-adjustment to sustainability also explains why some forms of non-equitable capitalism have ultimately undermined prosperity and democracy.

Observe that prosperity and capitalism may "temporarily" flourish without underlying democracy; but it is our view that the absence of democracy, in a context of informed societies, will in the long run provoke serious socio-economic problems that will likely halt further economic prosperity, as could occur in China if democratisation were *sine die* delayed. Observe also that formal democracies in a context of non-informed societies, that is to say, with strong rates of illiterate population, may not bring economic prosperity, as it happened in the period 1974-1980 in India.

Although former considerations are generally referring to national democracies, we could easily extrapolate them to the world as a whole. In this regard, we should not forget that we live today in a world in which a global and prosperous non-equitable capitalism coexists with a non-democratic global political system. Insofar our deductions are correct, current global situation will not be sustainable unless the sole political institution we have for the solution of global issues, the UN, becomes democratic; and unless it makes resolution on violent conflicts, global environment protection, fairer personal income distribution and reduction of national income disparities its top priorities.

Roads for Reaching Sustainable Democracy in Nations

As repeatedly mentioned in the text, recent attempts by western powers for selectively imposing democracy by force—among others in Afghanistan and Iraq—have not been precisely successful. Attempts in the past of forcing multiparty elections under the threat of economic or political sanctions (Palestine) also failed, as historically most attempts to force political modernisation from outside countries and by outside powers failed.

Even more, numerous enforced multi-party elections in new states (after independence from colonisers or from the dismantling of the

Soviet empire) have resulted either in one-time-multi-party elections to select the "leader for life", or civil war as a consequence of break-off parties based on religion, ethnicity or regional exclusivity. This is why we have focused on roads for reaching sustainable democracy.

Consequently, we do believe that to put pressure to celebrate multiparty elections under the assumption that they will bring sustainable democracy, and automatic economic prosperity is a serious mistake. Indeed, history has proven that these sequencing "free elections—sustainable democracy—economic prosperity" requires the fulfilment of several conditions concerning the maturity of the nation building process in the involved society, conditions that in many cases have not been met.

Analysing history of democracy building, political scientists have deduced several traits that a society has to gather to become a sustainable democracy. A first characteristic that the society has to meet to be a serious candidate for reaching the stage of sustainable democracy is to develop an extended middle class, built up on the mixed economy of market in which private sector arranges most of economic activities while public sector administrates the public goods, the correction of externalities and the social failures (income distribution).

In connection with extended middle classes, the level of education of the masses has always played a relevant role in the maturity of societies. In fact, it is possible to organise free elections in the frame of an illiterate society, but it is very difficult to sustain the democratic process in this context. One should not forget that there is a significant positive relation between the level of education, position of women in society and other aspects of a well-woven social fabric, and the feasibility of sustainable democracy. A first derivative of the former argument is that national governments and multilateral institutions should in future make easier the access to education of a majority of people, in particular women. Similarly, rights of women should have a sound base in the juridical system, as this issue could cause significant delay in the development process, as experienced in the Arab-Muslim world.

In third place, and also in consistency with the first condition—existence of an extended middle class—the economic activities of the involved society should rather be diversified in order to guarantee sustainable democracy; this means that the economic activity should not mainly be based on windfalls (oil, diamonds, etc.) but on diversified private productions. In fact if these windfalls were significant—amounting for instance up to 40-50 per cent of the GDP—reaching democracy or sustaining it would be more difficult due to the unavoidable political temptation to assign income to certain ethnic or geographic groups or even clans or families, thus at times creating magnum problems in relation to income distribution or respect to minorities.

As a fourth characteristic, we do believe that the more homogeneous a society is in terms of religion, ethnicity or geography, the easier will be the construction of a sustainable democracy, because the less probable will be the application of sectarian policies. Consequently, in the nation building process of new states, since societies are often non-homogeneous in terms of religion, ethnicity or geography, the process of democratisation should be developed in several stages. This means that first electoral processes should exclude the participation of parties based for instance on religion, ethnicity or geography. Note that participation from the very beginning of such parties in the democratisation process could drive governments to sectarian behaviour and eventually to uprisings and civil wars, as it has been the case in almost all the countries of Africa.

Besides such conditions for reaching sustainable democracy, we do believe that the creation of a global democracy—as we recommend in the text—could encourage and enhance the internal democratisation process for small sized non-democratic countries, that had received membership in the new democratic UN. Note that big sized nations formerly non-democratic only would be acceptable as members of the new UN if they internally have reached a serious level of sustained democratisation.

In function of the necessary traits that must gather a society to reach sustainable democracy, we have to clearly reject any form of imposition of democracy from outside by bilateral army intervention or by means of establishing bilateral economic and political sanctions. Note that this bilateral external imposition of national democracy would be intrinsically an undemocratic manoeuvre from the perspective of global democracy. In fact, it would be a blatant contradiction to impose national democracy by force, when those supporting imposition do not want to create a global democracy—a new democratic UN—an institution that would be the sole body with legitimacy for democratically imposing, in certain restrictive situations, economic or political sanctions for enhancing democracy.

Consequently, the only thing that the West should bilaterally do for speeding up democratisation processes in certain countries is to work for progressively inducing the underlying societal traits as outlined above, by means of investing in developing cooperation (basically: education, health and infrastructures). Indeed, investment in these sectors was the key in the democratisation process followed by the West, a process that took around a century.

Global Democracy as a Prerequisite for Global Sustainability

As described, the existence of different levels of public goods and services within a country makes it convenient that the provision of them must be realised by governments at every level (local, regional or national). This provision, to have democratic legitimacy, will have to be decided and supported by democratic representation (parliaments) at every level. Rising the level of governance, we may automatically deduce that a legitimate provision of global public goods (peace and human security, global environment protection, space and oceans exploration, global economic regulation, etc.) will have to be decided, and supported by a democratic representation at global level, and executed by a global government with competences on these issues.

Observe that pre-emptive unilateral (or grouped) actions, as recently undertaken by some countries (as for instance the invasion of Iraq) to "purportedly" defend themselves and the "international community", may have severe negative spill-over effects (for instance oil price hikes) on the entire global community, whose opinion and consent should not have been bypassed.

Consequently, given the current unbalance between the received negative spillover effects and the lack of consultation in relation to undertaken actions, we do believe that any political interpretation

according to which one or a group of aristocratic countries may take initiatives for delivering global public goods (peace and security) to the international community, in absence of a global democratic representation—that they themselves refuse to promote—is essentially non-democratic.

Of course, when describing this "breaching of global democracy" by the so-called "aristocratic countries", we are just referring to principles that the West proclaims to promote and defend at national level, while rejecting them at a global one. Indeed, this is a remarkable double standard of the West in relation to the way of understanding a very simple political concept: democracy.

In our view, to the extent that global public goods exist, and that they will have to be democratically provided, the history of building democracy will not finish when all countries of the world become (national) democracies, but when the World as a whole becomes democratic; that is to say, when a global democratic body (a new democratic UN) decides, supports and enforces collective actions on peace, security, global environment, global externalities, etc.

Needless to say, that in future all matters affecting global society (global public goods and externalities) will have to be at the agenda of this body, which necessarily will have to have supremacy on national parliaments in relation to global issues. Consequently, besides such peace and security provision, issues stemming from population growth, climate change (reduction of emissions of CO_2), massive human resettlements, administration of natural resources of common interest, be these renewable (fisheries, forest, etc.) or not (water, oil, minerals, etc.), space and sea exploration, common economic regulation for ruling international economic transactions, etc., will have to be on the agenda of this body (and on those of its specialised agencies).

To put a couple of examples on the inefficiency of the current administration of global public goods, we will firstly refer to the problems related to global environment. Note that, similarly to the national experience in many non-democratic countries concerning failed management in the fields of national rainforest and fisheries, the so-called multinational environmental agreements (MEA) are perceptibly insufficient to solve current problems of global environment. This is due to the fact that these MEA are respectful with the preservation of national sovereignty of the non-signing states which, being at times the main polluters, clearly behave as free riders. At the same time, these MEA cannot cope with the practised free riding within the signing ones. Consequently, only a global body with democratic legitimacy and enforcement capacities will be able to fairly and efficiently deal with this problem.

The same argument could be applied to a second example: the current global dysfunction created by the existence of multinational corporations (MNC) capable of bypassing national rules of economic policy, without any global democratic control, thus often acting against national interests of nations. Observe that, in principle, this mismatch could only be solved by the unification/homogenisation of rules for doing business at a global scale; global economic regulation that, being a global public good, should also be defined by a global democratic body with capacity of enforcement. And this against the mere economic orientations on homogenisation realised by current non-binding "gentlemen agreements" in international forums (G-8, IMF, etc.).

Although the formation of global democratic bodies with enforcement capacities (a new democratic UN and its agencies) could today be considered by current short-sighted politicians as a mere childish dream, we do believe that current failing global developments in the political, economic, and environmental spheres will force its formation already in the first half of the 21st century.

Globalisation and Economic Consequences

Although the so-called "process of globalisation" only became fashionable in the early 90s as a result of the liberalisation of movements of capital in those days, the reality is that already from the mid 70s the process of external liberalisation of national economies received a serious impulse, although mainly focused on the interchange of industrial goods. Note that from the 70s onwards, the long practised import-substitution policies in many developing countries started ebbing, while public interventionism at micro-economic level started fading away all over the world.

Observe in addition that, while the 90s witnessed a new form of international economic liberalisation, this time focused on capital movements, the international mobility of the human factor did not receive any additional liberalising impulse. As a result of the long sustained asymmetries in the liberalisation of movements of goods, service, and factors at a world scale, an additional and huge wage gap between rich and poor countries was built up from mid 70s to the early 90s, while significant creation of employment in developing countries resulted repressed.

Against this background, the embodiment of China, India and South-East Asian countries into the international division of labour initiated a colossal change in the direction of the global trade. The flows of FDI directed to these countries also passed a landmark, favouring these nations *vis-à-vis* the rest of the developing countries. Industrial dislocation of Western firms towards the Asian countries, in combination with a rapid internal shift of labour in booming Asia towards industry and services, accelerated their growth rates, and initiated a shift of the economic gravity centre of the world. And this while western Trade Unions, which up to the 90s had fought for economic protection, entered into a process towards irrelevance as a consequence of the dislocation of Western factories towards Asia. Such irrelevance will only be reverse if Trade Unions become multinational.

Theoretically one cannot expect that the West will automatically profit from this economic shift towards Asia—as some have suggested—since many western countries will likely lose international market shares and internal jobs in agriculture and industry. Even more, a blind faith in the possibility of a rapid and long-lasting creation of (productive) jobs in the service sector in the West seems to us mere wishful thinking since the West is already losing its monopoly in research and development in modern technology. The mere fact of the overwhelming numbers of annual graduates in mathematics, science, engineering and medicine in China and India will make Western competitiveness in services difficult.

Aligned with these rational expectations, Western initiatives to raise significant barriers against penetration of Asian exports will be a temptation. Although these protectionist manoeuvres could be "justified" or disguised under the coverage of countervailing taxes to those "non-exacted" in origin—in relation to environment protection and/or phyto-sanitary security, or on the alleged misuse of the labour force, or as a penalty for not having within Western countries sufficient maintenance and service on imported manufactures—external and counterproductive feedback effects of these defensive manoeuvres should not be overlooked.

As a first feedback effect, the West should not forget that their protectionist measures could accelerate the already autonomous trend towards rapid increase of the regional trade in the developing world, particularly in Asia. Consequently, mentioned short-term defensive manoeuvres would work in due time against the interest of the West.

Observe additionally that such protectionist movements of the West would also be against the economic philosophy of the proposed (by us) new democratic WTO. This institution would have to democratically re-define the global trade rules and the domain of ruling, and to penalise undemocratic actions, as those mentioned above, eventually undertaken by a minority group of members (remember that the West only counts with 16% of the total world population).

A Forgotten Issue of Globalisation: Labour Migration

As described in Chapter 2, migration of labour has not been part of the process of globalisation in the second half of the 20th century. This means that in the past 55 years ongoing protectionism of labour in the West has been the last national bastion against globalisation. But observe that this defensive movement has not come from some "weird" NGOs (supporters of the anti-globalisation movement) but from the most prominent and "wise governments on earth", the Western ones.

Indeed, this sustained position against free movements of labour across the world, lacks any theoretical support in the context of neo-classical economics. Note in this regard that, while the free-market doctrine is at the core of the current globalisation move, Western governments who, paradoxically, do encourage geographical reallocation

of labour at national scale, ban receptions of foreign labourers. The political reasons underlying such banning are clear: admitting free international labour migration, although conducive to a more efficient economy at a world scale, would almost guarantee a government defeat in next (national) elections, due to the created expectations among nationals of job losses and real wage reductions.

Letting aside mentioned political inconveniencies, but also likely advantages for the receiving countries induced by the new inflows of workers (increase of GDP, labour costs reductions, increase of public revenues, eventual improving of the population pyramid, etc.), one has to deduce that restrictive rules on migration in a context of full information, low costs of transport, and impossibility of sealing frontiers, will result (as it has already occurred) in growing illegal migration.

In order to reduce the problems stemming from illegal migration, we do recommend several political actions. The main one would consist of lowering push factors in migrants-sending countries by means of significant increase in the western cooperation (ODA) in the fields of education, health and infrastructures in these countries. As proven in Chapter 2, to the extent that these investments in LDC are not provided by foreign private sector (FDI), funding for these investments will have to come from multiplied public foreign funds (ODA) administrated by a specialised agency (UNICO) of the new democratic UN, as explained in the text.

Given the fact that these investments will only have a significant impact at long term in the reduction of migration-push factors, complementary measures should have to be taken at short-mid term to positively channel some of the current migration flows. Among them we could mention facilitation of short-term labour contracts with strict organisation of return.

In relation to the absorption of qualified migrants, as Western countries prefer, receiving governments should take into account the eventual harm inflicted to those LDCs with scant internal supply of professionals, and at least compensate them for the investment in human capital—usually paid by the local poor (via indirect taxes)—realised on these qualified migrants.

Current Capitalism and Necessary Reforms

At the beginning of this chapter we have described some economic and political variables whose trends have introduced serious dysfunctions in current global capitalism. We do believe that to correct mentioned dysfunctions it will be indispensable—among other things—to reformulate some of the existing economic rules, while the non-existence of others will have to be dealt with. Let us not forget that defined (or re-defined) global economic rules, compulsory for all global players, should also be considered as global public goods.

We think that "total deregulation to encourage competition", as some defend in relation to internal or global economic transactions, is a mix of demagogy and ignorance, because competition may also blossom in a regulated context for the sake of the game and players, as it happens in the world of sports (e.g. in football). Note, conversely, that total deregulation would not be in the interest of society, since it would finally undermine the quality of the provided goods and services; would facilitate the monopolisation of markets in detriment of consumers; and would deteriorate the personal income distribution of citizens, thus slimming middle classes and, possibly, jeopardising democracy.

For instance, in certain contexts, total deregulation of labour markets may induce precariousness, forced geographical mobility, long working schedules, dominance of the interests of the firms over those of labourers, and eventual plummeting of real wages to adjust to foreign competition. Observe that, as explained in the text, these are just short-term movements towards economic efficiency with likely counterproductive economic, social and political effects at mid-long term.

In this regard we have learned from history that, as a result of the worsening of the personal income distribution during a long period of time—a phenomenon to which "free capitalism" is clearly prone—democratic systems will tend to become non-tenable, due to growing internal unrest and violence. Consequently, the total-final sum of the deregulation of labour markets and others, or the

non-regulation of them, could be negative, and not positive as neo-liberals use to proclaim. Truly, as the economy must serve men and not the opposite, governments should treat leisure time or time for socialisation as a merit good, thus protecting it.

In relation to recommendations made by the Washington Consensus in favour of hasty deregulation of certain markets, which for long had remained regulated, we do believe that this is a theoretical mistake that should not be repeated in future. Note that hasty deregulations could only be implemented without significant economic and political costs in an ideal world in which all factors would be instantaneously mobile. Nevertheless, as human life is always attached to a certain culture (language, habits), geography (nationality), and family life (marriage, children, etc.), to think that labour should be as flexible and mobile as financial capital is nonsense. As it would also be nonsense to think that physical capital may be instantaneously used for any alternative production.

Consequently, given the fact that economic production will always be submitted to significant inflexibility or inertia, economic reshuffling will require time for adjusting. Therefore, we consider as economically irrational any hasty application of policies that try to introduce long scope economic reforms.

We do also believe that, concerning privatisation of public firms and public services accumulating losses, the rapid selling out of the available physical assets of privatised firms that were bought for almost nothing, and dismissal (without compensation) of contracted labour by the new owners, should be forbidden. Otherwise, this would mean the end of the economic activity of the firm, while the new owners would have obtained a lot of money in economic detriment of the state. Consequently, privatisation of public firms in countries in transition—and therefore with weak institutional structures—should be realised with caution. In our view, fast privatisation in this context, as often recommended by the IMF, could be politically counterproductive (because it could induce serious "political re-assignment" of wealth) and negative for the development of democracy.

Returning to markets, and given for granted the convenience of existence of certain rules in some of them, we will now refer to the introduction of certain rules applicable to international economic relations.

In particular, we do believe that current heterogeneity of rules and institutions in relation to production (standards and environment), taxation, and economic interchange among the different countries participating in the international division of labour tends to falsify the terms of competition. Note that these heterogeneities use to finally imply complicated and, at times, biased adjustments at frontier to preserve the profitability of national firms.

Consequently we do believe that, if we want to keep globalisation alive and in progress, the world willy-nilly will have to enter into a process of economic homogenisation or harmonisation; and not only in relation with rules on international transactions—trade, movements of capital, etc.—but also in relation to the provision of some national public goods and the correction of some national externalities, whose differentiated treatment could significantly affect the national terms of trade.

In this respect, there are two ways for reaching economic homogenisation or progressive harmonisation: 1) just a unilateral downwards process in the West towards homogenisation, by and by converging to the scant levels (in GDP terms) of public expenditure and social protection in the current developing world, as it has been suggested by multilateral institutions for allegedly gaining competitiveness; or better, 2) reaching a negotiated convergence towards a position in the middle of the way, with both types of countries—developed and developing—moving towards "desirable" targets for main public activities and services, as to be defined in future by a new democratic UN.

Urgent Need for Bridging the Economic Gap and Improving Personal Income Distribution

Letting aside other complementary micro-reforms quoted in the text (referring to working schedules, etc.), and entering now into indispensable global economic corrections for sustainability, we will underline the priority of overturning the current distributive trends of capitalism.

Capitalism has registered in the last two centuries an almost constant growing economic gap measured by the growing disparity of the per capita GDP of nations (Maddison, 2001); and this while in the last 15 years additional steps towards globalisation have consolidated the trend (initiated in the early 80s) towards worsening of the personal income distribution within many rich and developing countries, which could result at mid-long term in severe political problems.

In order to start a manoeuvre for progressively bridging the economic gap to avert future internal and external political problems and violence, and to promote democracy; and given the fact that private foreign financing (FDI, etc.) have remained practically absent in almost all LDCs in the last decades, we do believe that it will be necessary not only to significantly increase the volume of ODA up to a 100 billion US dollars, as some "compassionate" Western leaders have suggested, but to multiply it.

We have figured out that an amount of around US$ 400-450 billion—equivalent in comparative terms to around two per cent of the joint GDP of traditional donors—should be the minimum annual ODA to significantly bridge the economic gap of LDC and other low-middle income countries over one generation. Taking into account its current bilateralism and fragmentation, scant volume, geo-political distribution, irrational conditionality, and even recent fictitious rising, we do believe that the current official system of public transfers (ODA) to poor countries, should not only significantly increase its annual amount—as mentioned—but should also be administrated by a global, neutral and efficient economic body for co-operation, under the aegis of a new democratic UN.

This body, a UN Institution for Co-operation (UNICO) as proposed by us, should establish a budget whose funding would come from a worldwide additional taxation on inheritance, thus mainly affecting the richest citizens in both rich and poor countries. Note that this source of revenues is the most neutral and easiest way of gathering the needed figure, without any detriment of the markets efficiency. Contrary to the current trend in the West towards minimisation of the inheritance tax, allegedly to protect heirs for their continuation in business, we do believe that mentioned protection could easily be facilitated (by fractioning its payment). Observe that the revenue increase coming from this additional taxation would endow global capitalism with "more acceptability" by poor countries, and would provide them with compensation from past colonial mistreatment. We think that other recent suggestions for rising development financing such as the Tobin Tax on capital movements, or the recharge on plane tickets, are non-neutral (because they only affect to specific activities) and insufficient sources of funds.

In relation to the current trend towards worsening of the personal income distribution, it is our view that the today's fading trade unions in the West will have to join forces with trade unions of developing countries to become multinational or global, following the wake of MNC. We think that when, as a result of the increased globalisation, the process of convergence of real wages became more patent—perhaps in two or three decades—trade unions will also be able of becoming multinational or global, as MNC, thus recovering their old role as economic countervailing powers for eventually increasing real wages and employment and, above all, for strengthening sustainable democracy.

Rationale for Undertaking "Anti-Climate-Change" Action

Although some stubborn scientists and conservative politicians continue rejecting the case of Earth Warming as a problem caused by the industrialisation process in connection with reckless and massive logging along the last two centuries, and others believe that "future" technological advances will enable the global cooling of the environment—the so-called solution B—the majority of scientists believe that while in the last 10,000 years the Earth climate remained stable, recent man-made greenhouse gases seem to threaten former stability.

Projections on future developments concerning climate change are a complicated and uncertain task. Nevertheless, initial—although revisable—analysis of mainstream scientists suggest that *ceteris paribus* the temperature on Earth will increase along the 21st century by between 1.4°C and 5.8°C. Note that increases over 2°C could lead to catastrophic rises in sea levels, rapid increase of the number of

extreme weather events such as hurricanes, flooding and droughts, falling agriculture production, and famine and mass population movements.

Due to the fact that global warming has innumerable indirect effects on the climate system, no one can be sure of their sequencing and total costs. However, former uncertainty should not drive us to inaction. Indeed, similar to the fact that most advanced countries spend between 1.5-2.5 per cent of their GDP in defence, although the probability of being attacked is almost nil; and in the same way that most western individuals take insurance policies to protect their assets against an unlikely fire, nations and individuals should do the same in relation to climate change to avoid "perhaps not very likely" catastrophic results.

Although—in a context of uncertainty—alternative economic evaluations on the costs of doing nothing to reduce emissions of CO_2 range from 5-20 per cent of the total GDP by the end of the 21st Century, it would be wise that the world starts spending a provisional figure that, after 10 years phasing, should reach a level of two per cent of global GDP. To the extent that in next decades current environmental threat fades, such figure could be reduced; or increased in the opposite case.

Now then, given the strongly nationalistic and scantly multilateral international political structure, the main problems underlying the management of such a volume of expenditure—two per cent of global GDP—would be its fragmentation and lack of coordination.

Even more, given the global nature of the problem of climate change, and the high probability that individuals or firms of some nations behave as consented "free riders", there is a scant likelihood that the international community tackles this problem by means of reaching a new Multilateral Environmental Agreement (MEA) on the issue, whose setting up could be difficult (not all countries would sign), while its by-passing would be easy and cheap.

In this regard it is our view that if the world does not progress towards a global democracy (a new UN) with capacity for enforcing matters assigned to it—including the administration of global environment and externalities—the probability of successfully solving the problem of climate change and derivatives, or others related to additional global public goods or externalities, will remain low.

Rational Approach for Solving International Terrorism

As we have insisted along this book, there is no military solution for international terrorism. Attacking a formal state even though it shelters terrorists (or finance it) by means of conventional military actions (Iraq, Afghanistan) produces so intense lateral damages (human and assets) that far from solving the problem, it increases its dimension by multiplying resistance and hatred towards occupiers.

Observe that terrorism with a supporting ideology is a self-reproductive enemy that could only be military defeated by means of a total extermination of the societies that allegedly shelter them. As far as this would represent genocide, this barbaric "solution" historically practised by totalitarian and brutal regimes should be fully discarded. These are reasons why we favour the use of dialogue, intelligence, police, and political and economic means to solve the problem; and we are not alone in this.

Although neo-conservatives use to affirm that international terrorism has nothing to do with poverty and political exclusion, pointing out that the attackers of the Twin Towers in 2001 were well educated people of middle class families, the reality is that the attackers did not act alone but as part of an organisation whose main objective was the punishment of those western societies they considered responsible for political, religious, economic, or social mistreatment of the Muslim (Arab) communities in the world. To achieve their objective, these organisations undertook (and undertake) actions that do not discriminate between military and civilian targets.

As the influence of neo-cons and their false simplifications are today ebbing, more and more voices (even in the West) have started supporting the idea that the development of Muslim-Arab terrorism has also been induced and promoted by the long trajectory of the Palestine-Israel conflict, which from its very beginning was treated by the West on terms of double standards. From one moment onwards, these double standards were compounded by the deployment of US military bases in Saudi Arabia; an action that additionally harmed intimate religious feelings of many Muslims, who consider these bases placed in holy land as humiliating.

If we add to the above essential causes, the political exclusion domestically experienced by many Arab communities—who often do not feel represented by their governments—the personal experience of discrimination and exclusion of Muslim communities living in (or relating to) the West, and the abject poverty accumulated in some parts of the Muslim world (Gaza, Afghanistan, Bangladesh, Pakistan, etc.), growing of anti-western sentiments, hatred, and even call for jihad, are socio-political phenomena that should have been foreseen.

As mentioned, regimes either oligarchic or without western democratic homologation govern many Arab countries. These non-democratic governments often excuse their limitations in political representation as a mean to defend their societies against eventual theocratic governance that could arrive from the application of the rule of majority; a final result also rejected by the West.

Note in addition that current western political positioning, accepting oligarchic Gulf regimes, while in other places rejecting on the one hand the limited democracy, and on the other not accepting democratic results when inconvenient (Palestine and Algerian cases), is just an impossibility-game not consistent with their "democratic" preaching. No wonder that Muslim-Arab communities, simplifying the issue, believe that the West is in the region only for the oil and neither to encourage democracy nor to support human rights.

Against this background, any durable solution should deal with the core problems. First of all, the international community should urgently bring into working a "two states" solution as foreseen by the international community (UN) in 1947, including fielding international peacekeepers.

Secondly, as far as arrival to democracy is a process from within, clearly related to economic development and investment in human resources, the "western community" should resist temptations of military interventions to dislodge (or to disarm) current "inconvenient" non-democratic regimes. Instead of that, the West, discarding as useless political and cultural pre-conditionings, should significantly increase—through a neutral institution as UNICO—the current aid to the poorest communities. This aid should be mainly directed to the development of capital and human resources, under the consideration that after a while, economic development and progress in education and knowledge would necessarily reduce religious radicalism and promote democracy.

Last but not least, the West should abandon arrogant behaviour based on the alleged superiority of its culture and religion, because one thing is to feel superior—practically all nations know these feelings—and other is to provoke and insult on the basis of these feelings, thus misusing "freedom of expression". Note that "freedom of expression" was something brought to politics to protect the highest principles of democracy and not at all as a cover up for insult, despise and discrimination of others.

Main Traits of a New Democratic UN to be Set-up

Arguments for the Creation of a New Democratic Body for Global Governance

As we have insisted along the text, the creation of a global democratic governing body will be indispensable for at least five main reasons. The first relates to the global provision of peace and security with democratic legitimacy, which will also imply the affectation of the main global economic levers to peace and security efforts (significant increase of ODA, trade facilitation, migration restructuring, etc.). We should not forget Gandhi's remark that "induced or consented poverty is the most abject form of violence."

The second has to do with the existence of other international public goods (healthy global environment, space and oceans explorations, basic research, global economic regulation, etc.) and global externalities—the latter affecting the use of renewable and non-renewable global resources—issues that will have to be administrated and enforced globally and with democratic legitimacy.

The third relates to the solution of future global socio-economic conflicts, subsequent to current climate change. It is likely that earth warming and climate change (by the rise of the level of the seas and/ or by desertification) will induce massive migrations in next decades, and a need for resettling abroad 150-200 million people in already inhabited countries. Observe that the reallocation of such a mass of human beings in non-vacant territories, and in absence of a global authority, would be traumatic, and perhaps highly violent.

As a fourth reason, we have to mention the need for an international democratic approach in population (indirect) control and human security in the world. Note that the growth of global population—with its parallel growing needs for food, shelter and transport—should in future be considered itself as a global externality, which will condition environmental sustainability and climate change.

Finally, as a fifth reason, we consider global democratic governance as indispensable to protect and promote national democracies. This could be done by means of introducing global economic regulation and actions that enable convergence of per capita income, and as a result growth and consolidation across the world of extended middle classes.

In our view, global democratic governance (a new democratic UN) will be indispensable for improving the current hazardous trends of the personal income distribution within many countries. Note that—in principle—this negative trend could be democratically reversed towards a sustainable position if, after winning election, former political opposition behaves in this field differently to former incumbent. Nevertheless, as far as in the world today most governments (of right and left) economically behave the same way—allegedly to protect commercial competitiveness—democratic alternation of national governments will not guarantee a healthy personal income distribution and, consequently, the subsistence of a widespread middle class and sustainable democracy.

Although the above mentioned reasons should be more than enough to convince all well-intended and co-operative UN players for supporting a democratic reform of the UN, we have no doubt that, given the chaotic political situation of the world today and the vested interests of current aristocratic nations, a serious positioning, perhaps initially in block—for maintaining the current status quo—will face up to any movement for democratising the UN.

Nevertheless, with the arrival to maturity of relevant emerging countries (China, India, Russia, Brazil, etc.), and after the accumulation by them of sufficient economic weight and decisive political clout, the initial opponent block—mainly formed by western UN-permanent members and followers—will progressively lose steam; and if this block remain attached to their somewhat unfair historical roles, the possibility of political (and economic) isolation of some of the erstwhile dominant aristocratic members will quickly grow. Even more, if this stubborn position of current aristocratic countries and followers continued for long, a bifurcation of the current UN would in due time become a logical derivative.

Notwithstanding the likely initial opposition of current privileged countries to any change towards global democracy, we do believe that taking into consideration the existence of global public goods and global externalities, some of them already in a very critical situation, and given the fact that the last reference of democracy is the "majority rule", the creation of a new and democratic UN will at most be a matter of one or two decades.

Profile of a New Democratic UN

As defended by us, a new democratic UN, whose competencies would be limited to the five above mentioned functions and their intermediate targets—indispensable for sustainability of capitalism and national democracies—should be more united and less divided than the current UN, with sufficient (multiplied) funding, and endowed with power for enforcement in all assigned activities.

Its profile could be defined by the following characteristics: 1) The most important and supreme ruling organism of the new UN would be the General Assembly, whose decisions would be taken by democratic majority, that is to say, taking into account, although non-linearly, the size of population of all member states (weighted votes); 2) The General Assembly of the new UN would mainly deal with the approval of the annual budgets for its functions, the provision of global public goods and the correction of global externalities, the programming and co-ordination of actions of the UN agencies, the top appointments or substitutions of civil servants in them, etc; 3) All issues related to peace, security, and emergency would be delegated to a new Security Council; 4) The new Security

Council would be formed by a geographically balanced representation consisting of 24 members—eight with long-term (10 years) tenure and 16 with short-term (two years) tenure, all of them elected by the General Assembly; 5) Decisions in the new Security Council would be made by simple or sufficient majority, thus removing the so-called veto-rights and veto-owners; 6) Enforcement of Security Council decisions would be realised by the UN armed-forces, permanently deployed at different bases in all continents for rapid action; 7) Any UN member-country which disobeys resolutions of the Security Council, including the use of its own army against the general will, would be—as a minimum—expelled from the UN and all its agencies; 8) The remaining activities of the new UN, described and recommended in the text (and others), would be executed by additional UN Agencies.

Referring now to certain UN agencies—which in future would have a similar democratic structure—we will now focus on those whose activities have (and will have) special effects on the global economic development. Concerning the renewal of IMF, we suggest a serious change in its way of decision-making and doing business, in order to avert non-neutral (political) behaviour in global financial matters. Dominance of the US in this institution, as well as in the WB, has often turned both institutions into tools for framing the US foreign policy and for spreading underlying neo-conservative economic philosophy. No wonder that this dominance and neo-conservative ideology has finally undermined the credibility of these institutions, particularly that of the IMF, which has today reached a practically meaningless role.

In relation to a new WTO, to be brought under the aegis of the UN, we do believe that its decision-making should also change towards democracy (majority rule) in order to overcome current paralysing consensus. We are also convinced that WTO is not the correct institution to solve problems or disputes related to global environment, due to the fact that international trade for largest countries is a small share of their total (polluting) production of final and intermediate goods. We also think that WTO is not the correct institution to settle problems on migration, labour conditions, etc.

The institution that should deal with labour and migration issues is the International Labour Organisation (ILO). This institution, after its democratic reform, would establish new rules for labour migration, which should not only bear in mind the interests of the receiving nations, but also the needs of sending countries in a context of solidarity. Note however that, due to its paramount relevance, the administration of the likely massive human resettlements induced by climate change would have to be dealt with in the UN General Assembly.

Besides former reshufflings, the creation of two new UN Agencies, the WEO and UNICO, would be decisive. The World Environmental Organisation (WEO), devoted to the preservation of the global environment and to the administration of the natural common resources (renewable or not), would include current UN agencies for environment and would have to count with financial sufficiency and capacity for enforcing own resolutions, including fining and (provisionally) closing of factories across the world which do not comply.

Finally, the United Nations Institution for Co-operation (UNICO) to which, among others, current WB and UNDP should embody, would be the UN Agency charged with the task of rapidly (in one generation) and significantly reducing the economic gap between rich and poor nations of the world, as an intermediate target for the promotion of global peace and security. Rapid and sufficient assistance in case of natural catastrophes would also be a main job of UNICO.

We do believe that if UNICO was endowed with sufficient funding—coming from an additional taxation (up to 20%) on the inherited wealth by individuals all over the world, that would produce annual revenues up to around US$ 400-450 bn—this institution would be the best instrument for improving the relations among individuals and peoples across the world. Consequently, as a result of the UNICO activities, devoted to the promotion of solidarity for equitable development, poverty in the world would significantly be alleviated in one generation.

On top of this, a democratic reorganisation of the UN should count with financial autonomy and capacity for enforcing resolutions. This capacity should include the setting up of a permanently deployed UN army in all continents, commanded by a new Security Council.

In the present world in which democracy is of a paramount value, it makes no sense to be democratic at a domestic level to solve common national problems, as it is today the case in all the developed countries, while at the same time most of them—following the US (and being altogether a minority group of around 16 per cent of the global population)—try to impose their will to the majority (around 84%) in relation to common global issues, such as peace and human security, global environment, correction of global externalities etc.

These double standards of the minority West means, to describe it in plain words, that while internally behaving democratically, it externally performs autocratically and against solidarity, thus ignoring many a times the rights and interests of 86 per cent of the population of the world.

Profiles of Sustainable Capitalism and Democracy at Mid 21st Century

Bearing in mind all the data and conclusions drawn in former items, we may now outline the possible profiles of global capitalism and democracy after the three or four coming decades: 1) As global capitalism will ultimately need global democracy for survival, and global democracy, as always, will be in need of mild-acceptable forms of capitalism for sustainability, a system of mixed economies of market combined with factual social-democracies will be dominant in the majority of nations in the world; note that we have introduced the predicate "factual" because social-democracy will be the pattern of the economic behaviour of most governments, regardless of their alleged political positioning among the rest of national parties; 2) As global capitalism will require for its sustainability an efficient and legitimate provision of global public goods (peace, security, global environment protection, global economic regulation, etc.) and an appropriated correction of global externalities, a new and democratic UN will be dealing with the main common problems of mankind, based on democratic decision-making and recognised enforcement capabilities; 3) Relevant UN agencies will have been renewed or created ex-novo, being the WTO, WEO and UNICO the most outstanding ones; 4) Many developing countries—including the emerging ones, the mid-income countries and current LDCs—will witness fiscal systems more prone to direct taxation and widespread social protection, thus converging with those of the West, whose current trends to relatively reduce direct taxes and to severely degrade social protection of workers, will have been arrested; 5) After significant convergence of real wages at global scale, trade unions will finally have recovered their former countervailing capacities lost in (current) times of mismatching between global actions of MNCs and national scope of traditional trade unions; 6) The role of markets in relation with transactions of private goods and services will be essential at national and global scale for reaching economic efficiency, although rules for economic competition will have been reshaped in order to gain environmental and political sustainability; 7) As a consequence of the co-ordinated efforts of WEO and the quasi-arrest, arrest or inflexion of the global population growth, earth warming and climate change processes will have significantly reduced their current dramatic outlook, while modern technology will have become central in the catering for energy security and safe drinking water; and 8) After decades of economic development action by UNICO on poorest countries—facilitating catching up and economic diversification in them—and after the global democratic deactivation of persistent problems resulting from the WW2 and the decolonisation process, the risk of international terrorist actions will have decreased significantly, if not passed to the files of history.

Observe finally that this new panorama—foreseen for 2030-2050—will be totally permeated with the concept of democracy (national and global). In particular, global democracy—mainly though UNICO and WTO—will have made possible a significant bridging of the initially existing economic gap between rich and poorest nations; will have deactivated growing malaise provoked by current trends in personal income distribution; and will have rationalised the applied policies for environment protection and natural resources preservation.

In this context, and for the first time in history, and just by a peaceful resorting to representative democracy at a global scale, supported by the UN intervention armed forces, the international community—this time totally and democratically represented in the UN—will have been capable of achieving a fairer and sustainable global society.

End of Hegemonic Powers in the World

Along the different chapters of the book, while discussing the urgency of building up a global democracy for sustaining global capitalism, we have suggested that after 15 years of arrival to a purported global hegemony, the US has today entered into a trend of political and economic degradation, resulting in urgent need of "coalitions of the willing" for its interventions, for which even colourless small states in remote areas are welcomed.

Mentioned degradation of the US as a leading power has taken place against the background of a global society in which the power play is changing quickly and a number of prickly conflicts and sentiments have emerged, including: 1) An explosive Middle East (conflict Israel-Palestine, chaos in Lebanon and Iraq, Kurds-Turkey skirmishes, etc.) with growing influence of Iran in the region; 2) No clear solution for the occupation of Afghanistan and Iraq amidst growing withdrawal of military support by allies; 3) US ally Pakistan, in possession of WMD, shifting towards a failed state and progressively running out of control of the US; 4) Emerging China, hastily gaining economic and political supremacy in Asia, while Russia is recovering its influence, and US ally Japan is becoming more and more isolated in the region; 5) Growing influence in Latin America of populist leftist regimes, which increasingly express anti-American sentiments; 6) Growing anti-Western feelings in the Islamic world—nothing less than 1/5th of the world population—while neo-conservatives in the West fuel Islam phobic fears, both developments gearing to violent escalation; and 7) and more important, a US economy in decline with clear signs of losing leadership (huge commercial deficit, significant public deficit due to war against terrorism and tax reductions, falling dollar, growth based on consumption combined with worsening income distribution, etc.).

Above-mentioned facts and feelings support our view that we are currently witnessing the end of the purported global hegemonic rule of the US. But, irrespective of the meaning and implications of the word "hegemony"—which may refer either to regional or to global supremacy enjoyed by a country on others—we do opine that current political and economic circumstances, induced by developments in the last decades of the 20th Century, will make in future any global hegemonic rule impossible.

Indeed, huge military advantage sustained by a booming economy, non-definition or irrelevance of human rights in connection with lack of means for rapid information sharing on committed atrocities, and classical demography in backward countries whose population could easily be decimated violently without significant costs, made it possible in the past that hegemonic powers could in their own sphere of influence (mainly regional) practise large scale killings in occupation wars or when ruling submitted nations. Let us not forget that these practices would today be defined as genocide.

However, former list of enabling circumstances for exerting hegemony (regional or global), or for practising dictatorship within countries, have practically disappeared. First, the progressively wider definition of human rights in the last half of the 20th century followed by an intensive surveillance on their fulfilment, and by progressive and generalised disapproval of violent solutions, in particular when they imply lateral killings of civilians, has made difficult both gaining wars for further economic exploitation or solving security problems in occupied territories. And this despite the eventual huge "investments" in weaponry and human assets devoted to these military actions. Note additionally that due to the ICT revolution (photographs and films made with small cameras or cell phones, in some few minutes sent abroad by satellite) the scrutiny of human rights violations is today realised on line and in broad public, which leaves no time for cosmetic reaction on committed mistakes, thus rapidly undermining the prestige of the aggressors (regional or global hegemonic powers).

In last decades, knowledge and democracy has also favoured significant steps forward in dismantling hegemonic power. Note that in other times the existing knowledge-gap in weaponry and navigation enabled corresponding hegemonic powers to exert overseas strong domination on others without any "responsibility" in front of the then non-existing "international community". However, all this has today dramatically changed since the knowledge-gap on weaponry—including progressive facility for the production of WMD—and transports has narrowed, information sharing and networking have boomed and democratic feelings are today reaching a (global) level prone to rapidly stigmatise those who act violently without democratic legitimacy (consent of the international community).

On the other hand, purporting to be the sole intelligent and good guy—while alleging to enjoy the most advanced civilisation and at the same time showing disrespect for others (countries and civilisations) as some Western countries do—is something completely out of reality in a democratising world in which the alleged "under-civilised" are in majority (84% of the global population live in developing countries) and whose elites are very well educated (many times in the West).

With all mentioned data on the desk—progression of human rights and democracy, narrowing technological-weaponry-gap, and arrival to a world of full and live information—one has to accept that demography has acquired a new and predominant dimension in relation to global issues. But note that the structure of the world population has dramatically changed in the last 50 years, favouring developing countries, thus making political domination on them even more difficult.

In fact, from a global population of 2,500 million people in 1950 the world has moved to a figure well over 6,500 million in the year 2005, of which 2,400 million were the joint population of China and India. And this while in 2005 the US population counted with less than 300 million (4.5% of global population) and that of the West only reached altogether 16 per cent of the total inhabitants of our planet. As a consequence, purported or dreamt hegemonic behaviour by any western country with its population in minority and in relative decline is practically impossible in the current pro-democratic political framework.

Note also that *ceteris paribus* lack of parallelism in growing defence expenditures—realised to gain or keep hegemony—combined with insufficient or relatively low economic growth has always forced the economic bankruptcy of hegemonic powers (remember the recent cases of Britain and the Soviet Union). Indeed, to try gaining or keeping hegemony is ultimately a strong bet in terms of the involved economic resources that has a unique political justification: the use of the armed forces as an economic asset for further appropriation (in its multiple facets, even those non-violent) or for the defence of former geographical or economic takings. Nevertheless, we do believe that these Machiavellian strategies for appropriation in a world nearing global democracy, is not longer acceptable.

Summarising, the world today is a world in which power is much more balanced and shared than in the past, reason why western fears for the appearance of a following global hegemonic power that could substitute the US—with disadvantage for the West—lacks any logic.

We understand concerns of the West in relation to current and future loss of political and economic privileges it enjoyed in other historical circumstances, when democracy was not a so generalised value. But what should really concern the West and its citizens is the eventual incapacity of the West for peacefully adjusting to the new times of necessary income and power redistribution, in fact first derivatives of the recent process of economic globalisation. Non-acceptance of democracy and its economic consequences has always been a temptation for the rich. However, a strategy of non-acceptation of global democracy will not work in future because then the rich will be totally dependent on the collaboration of the majority (developing countries) to solve the huge pending problems of mankind (administration of peace, security, environment, etc. and correction of global externalities).

Therefore, to try reaching or purportedly keeping hegemonies to bypass political negotiations with the majority of mankind in a global parliament—that is to say, in a new democratic UN as proposed by us—will not only be a non-updated and non-winning action, but also a suicidal economic strategy.

We do firmly believe that the time of hegemonies (regional or global) is over and that the time of global democracy is arriving. Of course, the earlier arrival of global democracy will be the better for all, including the West.

References

Abel, A. and B. Bernake, (2001). *Macroeconomics*. Pearson Education.

Ahluwalia, M. (2000). "Inequality, Poverty and Development", in G. Meier (ed.), *Leading Issues in Economic Development*. 7th Ed. Oxford University Press.

Anderson, L.G. (1986). *The Economics of Fisheries Management*. Baltimore: John Hopkins University Press.

Arlinghaus, R. *et al.* (2002). "Reconciling Traditional Inland Fisheries Management and Sustainability in Industrialised Countries", *Fish and Fisheries*. 3.

Arrow, K. (1951). *Social Choice and Individual Values*. NY: John Wiley and Sons.

Arrow, K. *et al.* (1995). "Economic Growth, Carrying Capacity and the Environment", *Ecological Economics* 15(2).

Ajayi, S.I. (2006). *L'IDE et le developement economic en Afrique. Congrés International sur l'acceleration du developement de l'Afrique le 5 premieres annees du 21-iéme siecle*. Tunis. 22-24 November.

Batie, S. (1993). "Sustainable Development: Challenges to the Profession of Agricultural Economic", *American Journal of Agricultural Economics*.

Barro, R. (1990). "Government Spending in a Simple Model of Endogenous Growth", *QJE* 106.

Becker, G. (1983) "A Theory of Competition Among Pressure Groups for Political Influence", *QJE* No. 48(3).

Becker, G. *et al.* (1990). "Human Capital, Fertility and Economic Growth", *JPE*, 98.

Beckerman, W. (1974). *In Defence of Economic Growth*. London: Jonathan Cape.

Bernstam, M. (1991). *The Wealth of Nations and the Environment*. London: Institute of Economic Affairs.

Bhagwati, J. (1995). "Democracy and Development: New Thinking on an Old Question". Rajiv Gandhi Memorial Lecture. Rajiv Gandhi Foundation.

Barro, R. (1999). "The Determinants of Democracy", *Journal of Political Economy* 107.

Boyce, J.K. (2002). *The Political Economy of the Environment*. UK: EE Publishing.

Brams, G. (1975). *Games Theory and Politics*. Free Press.

Brauer, J. (Ed.) (2000). *A Millennial View on Defence and Peace Economics*.

Buchanan, J. (1949) "The Pure Theory of Government Finance. A Suggested Approach", *JPE*. Dec.

Buchanan, J. and G. Tullock, (1962). *The calculus on consent*. University of Michigan Press.

Caddy, J.F. (1999). "Fisheries Management in the 21st Century: Will a New Paradigm Apply?", *Reviews in First Biology and Fisheries* 9.

Charles, A. (2001). *Sustainable Fishery Systems*. Oxford: Blackwell Science.

Coase, R.H. (1960). "The Problem of the Social Cost", *Journal of Law and Economics* 3.

Cole, H.S. *et al.* (1973). *Thinking about the Future; a Critique to the Limits to Growth*. Sussex University Press.

Cole, M. (2000). *Trade Liberalisation, Economic Growth and Environment*. UK: EE.

Coulomb, F. *et al.* (2000). "Disarmament: A Century of Economic Thought", in J. Brauer, (Ed.) *A Millennial View on Defence and Peace Economics*. Web.

Cufield (1985). "A Reporter at Large: The Rain Forest", *New Yorker*, 14 January.

Daly, H. *et al.* (1993). "Valuing the Earth: Economics, Ecology, and Ethics", MIT Press.

Datt, R. and K. Sundharam (2004). Indian Economy. 49th Edition. New Delhi: S. Chand & Company. p.29.

Dayton, P. *et al.* (1995). "Ecological Effects of Fishing". Pew Oceans Commission. Taken from the Web.

Debray, R. (2005). "Malaise dans la civilisation, suite", *Le Monde* 26th November p.27.

Downs, A. (1957). *An Economic Theory of the Democracy*. New York: Harper.

Eaglesman, J. (2006). "Blair Admits the West is Losing the War on Terror". *Financial Times*. August 2nd.

Ekins, P. (1993). "Limits to Growth and Sustainable Development. Grappling with Ecological Realities", *Ecological Economics*. No.8.

Elson, D. (1998). "The Trade-off between Equity and Efficiency". Comment to the report "Gender and Economic Development". Netherlands Economic Institute.

Enderwick, P. (2007). *Understanding Emerging Markets. China and India*. New York: Routledge.

Esty, D. (1994). *Greening the GATT: Trade, Environment and the Future*. Washington D.C.: Institute for International Economics.

FAO (1995). "Precautionary Approach to Fisheries", *FAO Fisheries Technical Paper* 350.1.

FAO (1996). "Precautionary Approach to Capture Fisheries and Species Introductions", *Technical Guidelines for Responsible Fisheries*. No.2.

Faujas, A. (2006). *"Record d'investissements pour les pays en developpément en 2006"*, *Le Monde*. 31 May.

Feyerabend, P.C. (1975). *Against Method: An Outline of an Anarchistic Theory of Knowledge*. London: New Left Books.

Financial Times (2006). "Summers and Rubin to Highlight Lagging Wages". July 25.

Findlay, R. (1990). "The New Political Economy: Its Explanatory Power for the LDC", *Economics and Politics* 2.

Friedman, M. (1956). *Introduction to Positive Economics*. Chicago University Press.

Fukuyama, F. (2004). *State-building, Governance and World Order in the 21st Century*. French version: La Table Ronde, Paris.

Georgescu *et al.* (1973). *The Entropy Law and the Economic Problem*, in Daly (1973) *Towards a Steady-State Economy*. New York: Freeman.

Gordon, R. (2003). "Two Centuries of Economic Growth: Europe Chasing the American Frontier", quoted in *The Economist*, February 8.

Grossman, G. and A. Krueger, (1991). "Environment Impact of a North American Free Trade Agreement", *Working Paper* No. 3914. NBER. Mass.

Grossman, G. (1994). *Pollution and Growth: What do we know?*, in Holding *et al.* (ed.), *The Economics of Sustainable Development*. Cambridge University Press.

Halliday, F. (2005). *The Middle East in International Relations. Power, Politics and Ideology*. Cambridge University Press.

Hirschleifer, J. (1993). "The Dark Side of Strength". *www.eumed.net*

Hotelling, H. (1931). "The Economics of Exhaustible Resources", JPE. No.39.

IMF (2006). *International Financial Statistics, Year Book*.

Judt, T. (2006). "Why Israel cannot always rely on America's helping hand", *Financial Times*. May 23.

Karjalainen, J. *et al.* (2005). *Sustainability in Fisheries Management*. Vide the web.

Kapur, D. and J. McHale, (2005). "Give us your Best and Brightest", quoted in *The Economist*, November 5. p.86.

Krugman, P. (2007). "Seduced by the Wealth?" *The New York Times-Le Monde*. November 10. p.2.

Lal, D. (1994). "Participation, Markets and Democracy", *Working Paper* 20, Human Resources Development and Operation Policy. World Bank.

Lane, F. (1979). *Profits from Power*. State University of New York Press.

Lecomber, R. (1975). *Economic Growth vs. Environment*. London: Macmillan.

Legrain, P. (2006). *Immigrants. Your Country Needs Them*. Little, Brown.

Le Monde (2006). "L'autre échéc en Irak: l'économie," 19-20 February. p. 2

———. (2006). "Bilan contrasté en Europe pour la reduction de gaz á effet de serre", 23rd June.

———. (2006). 22 July. "La CNUCED denonce une croissance 'sans employ' dans le pays le plus pauvre", p.9.

———. (2006). "L'obscure lubie des objecteurs de croissance", July 30. p.2

Linn, B. (2006). "Globalisation must be Saved from Global Utopians". *Financial Times*. May 30. p.13.

Lucas, R. (1988). "On the Mechanics of Economic Development", *JME* 22.

Maddison, A. (2001). *The World Economy. A Millennium Perspective*. Paris: OECD.

Malthus, T.R. (1798). *Essay on the Principle of Population*. Reprinted in 1970 by London: Penguin.

Meadows, D. *et al.* (1972). *The Limits to Growth: A Report to the Club of Rome's Projection on the Predicament of Mankind*. New York: Universe Books.

Meredith, M. (2005). *The State of Africa. A History of Fifty Years of Independence*. UK: Simon and Schuster. Free Press.

Musgrave, R. and P. Musgrave, (1984). *Public Finance in Theory and Practice*. Mac Graw-Hill.

Murawsky, S.A.(2000). "Definition of Over-fishing from an Ecosystem Perspective", *ICES Journal of Marine Science* 57.

Nash, J.F. (1950), "The Bargaining problem", *Econometrica*.

Norhaus, W. and J. Tobin, (1972). "Is Growth Obsolete?", in *Economic Growth*, NBER. No.96 E. Columbia University Press.

Nordhaus, W. (1995). "Locational Competition and the Environment: Should Countries Harmonise their Environmental Policies?", in Siebert, H. (ed.) (1995). *Locational Competition in the World Economy*. Tuebingen.

Nurkse, R. (1953). *Problems of Capital Formation in Underdeveloped Countries*. Oxford University Press.

Ozbudun, E. (1992). "Constitution Making in Democratic Transition", *East-South Systems Transformations*. University of Chicago. *Working Paper*, No. 20.

Parker, R. (2006). *John Kenneth Galbraith. His Life, his Politics, and his Economics*. Canada: Harper.

Pappe I. (2006). *The Ethnic Cleansing in Palestine*. Oneworld.

Pearce, D.W. (1993). *Blueprint Three: Measuring Sustainable Development*. London: Earthscan.

Perkins, D. *et al.* (2001). *Economics of Development*. 5th Edition. Norton.

Piketty, T. (2006). "The Evolution of Top Incomes" *NBER WP* 11955. January.

Pindyck, R. and D. Rubinfeld, (2003). *Microeconomics*. 5th Edition. India: Prentice-Hall.

Prestowitz, C. (2006). "Three Billion New Capitalists: the Great Shift of Wealth and Power to the East", *The Economist* July 29, p.73.

Przeworski, A. *et al.* (1994). "Democracy and Development". Paper presented at the *Nobel Symposium*, Upsala. August.

Przeworski, A. (1995). *Sustainable Democracy*. Cambridge University Press.

Rahman, R. and JM. Andreu, (2002). Financing Economic Development and Human Security. New Delhi: Rashtriya Printers.

———. (2004). *Responsible Global Governance*. New Delhi: Academic Foundation.

———. (2006). *China and India: Towards Global Economic Supremacy?* New Delhi: Academic Foundation.

Rees, W. (1990). "The Ecology of Sustainable Development", *The Ecologist*, No.20.

Repetto *et al.* (1989). *Wasting Assets: Natural Resources in the National Income Accounts*. World Resources Institute.

Romer, P. (1990). "Endogenous Technical Change", *JPE* 98.

Rawls, J. (1999). *Collected Papers*. Harvard University Press.

Rosenstein-Rodan, P. (1943). Problems of Industrialisation of Eastern and South-Eastern Europe. *Economic Journal*.

Rotte, R. *et al.* (2000) "On the Production of Victory: Empirical Determinants of Battlefield Success in Modern War", in J. Brauer, (ed.). *A Millennial View on Defence and Peace Economics*.

Rousseau, J.J. (1994). *Du contrat social*. Cèrés Editions.

Samuelson, P. (1954). "The Pure Theory of the Public Goods", *RES*

Saboul, A.(1972). *Precis d'histoire de la Revolution Francaise*. Editions Sociales. Paris.

Sala-i-Martin, X. (2002). The World Distribution of Income. NBER *Working Paper* No.8933.

———. (2006). "The World Distribution of Income: Falling Poverty and Convergence... period" *QJE* 2.

Samuelson, P. and W. Nordhaus, (1999). *Economics*. 16th Ed. Mac Graw-hill.

Schumpeter, J. (1950). *Capitalism, Socialism and Democracy*. Norton.

Scitovsky, T. (1951). "The State of the Welfare Economics", *AER*. P. 303-315.

Scott, M. (1989). "The Disappearing Forests", *Far Eastern Economic Review* 12. January.

Sen, Amartya (2003). *Democracy and its Global Roots*. For a French version vide. *Les racines globales de la démocracie. Pourquoi la liberté n´est pas un invention de l´ Occident* (2005). Editions Payot and Rivages.

Sen, A. (2006). "Mondialisation et Justice Social", *Le Monde*. 20 May 2006.

Srinivasan, T.N. (1995). *Democracy, Markets and Development*. Ámsterdam. Homage to Prof. Tims.

Stark, O. *et al.* (2005). "Again with a Drain? Evidence from Rural Mexico on the New Economics of the Brain Drain", quoted by *The Economist*. November 5. p.86.

Stern, N. (2006). "Report on the Economics of Climate Change", quoted by *The Economist* November 4. p.14.

Stiglitz, J. (2000). *Economics of the Public Sector*. 3rd Ed. Norton.

———. (2006). *Un autre monde. Contre le fanatism de marché*. Fayard.

Summers, R. and Heston, A. (1991). "The Penn World table (Mark4): An Extended Set of International Comparisons, 1950-88", *QJE* 106.

The Economist (2005). "Chose your Poison", 1st October. p. 32.

———. (2006). "Inequality and the American Dream", June 17.

———. (2006). Statistical Section, July 29. p. 92

———. (2006). "The Heat is On", September 9. p. 9

———. (2006). "Bangladesh. The Hole in the Middle", November 4. p.16.

———. (2007). "Smaller Shares, Bigger Slices", April. 7. p.72

Todaro, M. and S. Smith, (2003). *Economic Development*. 8 Ed. Pearson Education.

UN Development Programme (2002). *Human Development Report 2002*. New York.

———. (2004). *Arab-Human Development Report*. New York.

Usher, D. (1981). *The Economic Prerequisite to Democracy*. Basil Blackwell.

Von Mises, L. (1951). *Socialism*. Yale University Press.

Watson, L. *et al.* (2001). "Systematic Distortions in World Fisheries Catch Trends", *Nature*. 414.

Wilentz, S. (2005). *The Rise of American Democracy*. Norton.

Wilson, D. and Purushothaman, R. (2003). "Dreaming with BRICs. The Path to 2050", Goldman Sachs Global Economic website. *Global Economics Paper* No. 99. October.

World Bank (2004, 2005, 2006). *World Development Indicators*.

Zelotas, X. (1982). *Economic Growth and Declining Social Welfare*. New York: New York University Press.

Index

M

N

P

R

S

T

U

V

W